Tree of Liberty

# Tree of Liberty

## CULTURAL LEGACIES OF THE HAITIAN
## REVOLUTION IN THE ATLANTIC WORLD

Edited by Doris L. Garraway

New World Studies

*A. James Arnold, editor*

University of Virginia Press

Charlottesville and London

University of Virginia Press
© 2008 by the Rector and Visitors of the University of Virginia
All rights reserved
Printed in the United States of America on acid-free paper

*First published 2008*

9 8 7 6 5 4 3 2 1

Library of Congress Cataloging-in-Publication Data

Tree of liberty : cultural legacies of the Haitian Revolution in the Atlantic world /
edited by Doris L. Garraway.
 p.   cm. — (New world studies)
Includes bibliographical references and index.
ISBN 978-0-8139-2685-8 (cloth : alk. paper) — ISBN 978-0-8139-2686-5
(pbk. : alk. paper)
 1. Haiti—History—Revolution, 1791–1804—Influence. 2. Haiti—History—
Revolution, 1791–1804—Historiography. I. Garraway, Doris Lorraine, 1972–
 F1923.T975 2008
 972.94'03—dc22

2007035059

# Contents

### III. Literary Representations of the Haitian Revolution

# Acknowledgments

THE IDEA FOR this volume originated at the symposium entitled "The Haitian Revolution: History, Memory, Representation," held at Northwestern University on October 22–23, 2004, at which earlier versions of five essays included herein were presented. I wish to express my gratitude to the many programs and departments at Northwestern that co-sponsored the event, and to the staff of the Department of French and Italian for their help in organizing it. I would also like to thank the contributors to this volume for the groundbreaking scholarship they have offered here, and for their patience and responsiveness throughout the various stages of the project's development. Finally, I wish to acknowledge the individuals who helped make the publication of this volume possible: the anonymous readers of the manuscript for their enthusiasm and productive feedback, Kathryn Krug for her expert copyediting of the manuscript, and Cathie Brettschneider of the University of Virginia Press for her stellar support of the project from the beginning and for her wisdom and good humor throughout the editorial process.

# Introduction

*Doris L. Garraway*

ON JANUARY 1, 1804, Jean-Jacques Dessalines declared the independence of Haiti, thus bringing to an end the only successful slave revolution in history, and transforming the colony of Saint-Domingue into the second independent state in the Western Hemisphere. While for Haitians at home and in the diaspora, the bicentennial year 2004 might have been an occasion to celebrate the moment when Haiti arose as a symbol of the humanity, liberty, and dignity of peoples of African descent and changed the course of world history, it was instead marked by yet another tragic deferral of Haiti's revolutionary dream. By an unfortunate, though presumably not unintended, historical coincidence, in January of the bicentennial year rebels mounted an armed insurgence against the fledgling and much-maligned government of Haiti's first democratically elected president, Jean-Bertrand Aristide, thus leading to his highly controversial deposition, facilitated by French, Canadian, and U.S. forces, on February 28. Upheld by foreign supporters as a "humanitarian intervention" and decried by critics as one more example of the triumph of neocolonialism over the local political aspirations of the poor majority, this event plunged the country into a period of renewed political violence and instability.[1] What is more, in the summer of 2004 the most devastating hurricane in decades ravaged the region of Gonaïves, Haiti's third-largest city and the birthplace of the nation's independence movement, as well as of the bloody revolt against Aristide.

Given the unspeakable strife brought by such political and natural disasters, it may seem a luxury to engage in an act of remembrance of a glorious, phantasied past, as though to screen out the horrors of the present. When viewed, however, in light of the long battle fought by Haitians since the time of independence for their history to be recognized by the rest of the world, this act takes on a greater significance. As Michel-Rolph

Trouillot has so eloquently argued, the momentousness of the revolution was matched only by the speed and efficacy with which it was "forgotten" by the Western world. In describing the Haitian Revolution as "unthinkable" for contemporary observers and subsequent historians on both sides of the Atlantic, Trouillot reminds us of the exceptional nature of its claims in a slaveholding world, as well as the interest the colonial powers of Europe and the Americas had in suppressing the memory of it.[2] The revolution that has historically been silenced in accounts of the "Age of Revolutions" is the one that exposed the ideological limitations of the French and American revolutions, in which vindications of individual liberties rested on a tacit assumption of the right to human property. As the only successful slave revolt in world history and the second anticolonial independence movement in the modern world, after that of the United States, the Haitian Revolution was distinct for being the only one led by the subalterns and the "property" rather than the owners. Hence the unusual degree of mass mobilization that it required compared to other American independence struggles, and the radical assault it launched against colonialism, slavery, and the ideology of white racial supremacy.[3]

Among the most striking aspects of the Haitian Revolution are the variety and magnitude of the interests involved at the outset, and the very different ideas of freedom espoused by members of each of the three main socioethnic groupings in Saint-Domingue: whites, free people of color, and slaves. The outbreak of the French Revolution initially led landowning whites to elect colonial assemblies and intensify their existing demands for greater political autonomy for the colony. Protesting against the "ministerial depotism" of the colonial administration, they clamored for freedom from monopolistic trade policies that restricted the economic and commercial opportunities of local planters. For the property-owning free people of color, on the other hand, the French Revolution presented an opportunity to claim the Rights of Man and Citizen, thus gaining political equality with whites and liberation from the malicious segregationism and legalized racial prejudice that had over time confined them to an ambiguous status between freedom and slavery. Yet it was the entry of the slaves into the debate that forced the Parisian assemblies to concede the humanity of nonwhites, both free and enslaved, and inexorably changed the course of the colonial revolution. In the summer of 1791, a group of slaves from the northern plain of Saint-Domingue began an organized insurrection that quickly spread throughout the colony, destroying hundreds of plantations and auguring the twilight of the colonial social order. The repercussions of the slaves' action extended well beyond the shores of Saint-Domingue. Shocked by the news of this massive revolt and convinced that mulatto rights were the only means by which to preserve the colonial social order, the French National Assembly on April 4, 1792, granted political rights to free people of color. When progressive incursions of Spanish and English forces posed a radical threat to French control of the island, the French commissioner Sonthonax went one step further and decreed the general abolition of slavery on August 29, 1793, which was ratified by the National Convention on February 4, 1794. Soon, however, Sonthonax's power and influence in the colony was surpassed by that of a former slave. Within months of the first uprising, the half-literate former slave and coachman Toussaint Louverture rose to the head of the black movement. In the spring of 1794, Toussaint joined the Republican army and over the next several years galvanized thousands of ex-slaves to fight for Republican France against foreign invasion, acceding to the rank of governor-general and finally to that of commander-in-chief of Saint-Domingue on May 15, 1797.

Although various factions of colonial whites and free people of color continued their battle against the formerly enslaved freedom fighters, and bloody divisions raged even among those black leaders in favor of general abolition, the most significant challenge to the slave revolution came from France itself. Determined to strip those he derisively called "gilded Africans" of their French uniforms and restore French metropolitan authority in Saint-Domingue—an authority that was increasingly flouted by Toussaint as he called for greater autonomy and the adoption of a colonial constitution—Napoléon in 1801 sent to Saint-Domingue the largest expeditionary force ever to sail from France, under the command of his brother-in-law, General Charles Leclerc. Whatever Napoléon's intentions at the outset, as resistance in the colony mounted it became clear that Leclerc's orders were not merely to reimpose French control and "discipline" among the black population, but to reestablish fully the "old regime" of slavery in Saint-Domingue. After several months of fighting, Toussaint surrendered and retired to one of his plantations, only to be denounced to the French by Dessalines and Christophe on suspicion of plotting a rebellion. Although Toussaint's own generals facilitated his arrest by Leclerc and his eventual exile and imprisonment in the Jura mountains of France, they would soon change sides yet again, returning to the leadership of the most massive show of resistance in the history of the conflict in Saint-Domingue. This stage of the Haitian Revolution, frequently referred to as the War of Independence, began in October 1802 and represents the transition within the revolution from the fight against slavery to one against French colonial authority, the ultimate guarantor of both slavery and white supremacy in the colony. Facing off against Leclerc's and later Rochambeau's war of extermination, and joined by the former free people of color commanded by Alexandre Pétion, Jean-Jacques Dessalines led a civil and military force of ex-slaves to victory over the French, thus declaring the independence of the colony and the permanent abolition of slavery.[4]

Although the historical study of the Haitian Revolution has flourished in recent decades, particularly in the wake of the 1991 bicentennial of the first slave insurrections (witness the substantial studies by David P. Geggus, Carolyn Fick, Laurent Dubois, and Pierre Pluchon),[5] scholarly understandings of the cultural, literary, and philosophical legacies of the Haitian Revolution in the Atlantic world have lagged considerably behind. What is particularly striking is the dearth of references to Haiti in recent scholarly debates about "Black Atlantic" modernity, transnational and diasporic movements, and even postcolonialism, a phenomenon that may be attributed to the lack of paradigms for understanding a revolution that does not conform to dominant theoretical models of anticolonial nationalism and Black Atlantic cultural hybridity.[6] Indeed, the Haitian Revolution differs greatly from the "nativist" paradigm of later anticolonialisms, for in the discourses produced during and after the Revolution, the affirmation of racial equality was coupled with an explicit and spirited embrace of universalist political rhetorics and cultural values prevalent in Europe. This is most famously apparent in Toussaint's appropriation of the universalist slogans of the French Revolution, his devotion to France as the defender of liberty and equality, and his apparent sense of pride in French citizenship and military service.

Yet the numerous colloquia and lectures organized around the world to commemorate the bicentennial of Haitian independence attest to an unprecedented rise in scholarly interest in the Haitian Revolution across disciplines, thus necessitating a serious reappraisal of its cultural legacies, as well as a consideration of its importance for debates in postcolonial, Black Atlantic, Caribbean, and New World studies.[7] This is the goal of the present collection of essays. Bringing together the latest research on the Haitian Revolution by scholars of French and francophone studies, English, comparative literature, history, Latin American and Caribbean studies, and African American studies, this collection is wholly dedicated to interrogating the literary, historical, and political discourses that the Revolution has produced and inspired throughout the Atlantic world.

Historical studies of the effects of the Haitian Revolution in the wider world have focused mainly on the immediate economic, political, and social consequences of the Revolution. The most exhaustive book on the subject to date is *The Impact of the Haitian Revolution in the Atlantic World*, edited by David Geggus.[8] For a perspective on the cultural reception of the Haitian Revolution in the "West," humanists and social scientists in the anglophone world have generally turned to Michel-Rolph Trouillot's powerful 1995 book *Silencing the Past: Power and the Production of History*. In this work, Trouillot argues that the Haitian Revolution was unthinkable within the philosophical milieu of late-eighteenth-century slaveholding world and has since been systematically suppressed in Western historiography and humanistic scholarship. Trouillot's argument about the silencing of the Revolution draws on and extends important work done in France by Yves Benot in his two studies of the role of "the colonial question" and colonial events in the French Revolution, *La Révolution française et la fin des colonies 1789–1794* and *La démence coloniale sous Napoléon,* work that has been continued and broadened by historians Marcel Dorigny and Pascal Blanchard.[9]

Yet Susan Buck-Morss's widely influential, if controversial, article on the impact of the Haitian Revolution on Hegelian philosophy has forced many scholars to consider the extent to which events in Saint-Domingue and Haiti may well have inaugurated radical new ways of thinking about subjectivity, freedom, and consciousness in Europe. In "Hegel and Haiti," Buck-Morss argues that the dialectic of lordship and bondage in Hegel's model of the struggle for recognition leading to self-consciousness in the slave was profoundly influenced by news of the Haitian Revolution, thus positing the fundamental role of Haiti in the development of Western philosophy. Since Trouillot's and Buck-Morss's key contributions, the most influential intervention into the debate about the Revolution's cultural impact has been Sibylle Fischer's seminal 2004 book, *Modernity Disavowed: Haiti and the Cultures of Slavery in the Age of Revolution*. In it, Fischer calls attention to the tremendous shock waves of fear that reverberated in the neighboring slaveholding colonies of Cuba and the Dominican Republic in the aftermath of the revolution, thus leading to conscious and unconscious ideological filtering and modes of suppressing the news in literature and art. Fischer argues that the West's disavowal of the Haitian Revolution was essential to the construction of a hegemonic notion of modernity that excluded the political goals of racial equality and racial liberation.

Trouillot's, Buck-Morss's, and Fischer's scholarship has proven ground-breaking for thinking through the significance of the most radical revolution of the Age of Enlightenment for the philosophical foundations and preoccupations of Western modernity. Yet more research and critical reflection is needed in order to draw out the political meanings inherent in the Revolution and its discourses, and the ways in which it not only influenced, but also transformed and radicalized, European Enlightenment philosophy. In addition, as Joan Dayan's pathbreaking 1995 book *Haiti, History, and the Gods* has shown, literary scholarship has much to contribute to interpretations of the published texts and early histories of the Haitian Revolution—including those signed by its most legendary figures, Toussaint Louverture and Jean-Jacques Dessalines—with an aim toward assessing the significance and particularity of the Haitian Revolution as a cultural movement, as an anticolonial struggle, as an early assertion of Black Atlantic subjectivity, and as an ambiguous claim on modernity. Moreover, Trouillot's, Buck-Morss's, and Fischer's analyses have left largely unexplored the varied and profound literary and historiographic treatments of the Haitian Revolution that proliferated in Haiti and on both sides of the Atlantic in its immediate aftermath and in the two following centuries, as sympathizers, critics, and putative inheritors of the Revolution reinterpreted the significance of its political demands and reassessed the heroism and failures of its leaders.

Indeed, if the Haitian Revolution has been "silenced" in dominant historical and cultural traditions of Europe and North America, this was after having been the object of vociferous debate, impassioned rhetoric, and often sensationalist writing throughout the Atlantic world in the decades following Haitian independence. With the continuous flow of refugees of all colors to North America from the 1790s into the early nineteenth century, and the fear engendered in whites by a black revolution so close to its shores, the Haitian Revolution would be remembered for generations in the United States, particularly in the Antebellum South where it was held up as evidence that "race war would be the only result of the universal emancipation of slaves."[10] Yet for France in particular, the Haitian Revolution was far from easy to forget, since to do so would have meant forgoing all hopes of reconquering the island. In the immediate aftermath of the Revolution, sensationalist first-person survival narratives provided the French reading public with scenes of black savagery and white victimhood that vindicated assertions of the rights of France and its exiled colonists to the ownership of the island and its inhabitants, and of the inherent legitimacy of slavery.[11] For years, recolonization schemes abounded among planters and their political allies, including openly genocidal plans to eliminate the entire black population so as to eradicate any memory of freedom in Saint-Domingue.[12] More balanced or romantic representations of the Revolution and its black heroes, such as those by Antoine Métral and Victor Hugo, found a favorable reception among the French public only after two decades of Haitian independence, and contemporary with Charles X's formal recognition of Haitian independence through a treaty obliging Haiti to pay a massive indemnity and to grant favorable terms of trade with France.[13]

Yet much more time would be required for the Haitian Revolution to be so entirely suppressed in French historical memory that a French president could deny that Haiti had ever belonged to France. In March 2000, the French president Jacques Chirac made a public statement affirming in all apparent candor that "Haiti was not, properly speaking, a French colony," adding that "we have in fact had amical relations with Haiti, notably insofar as we share the same language."[14] Such an extreme example may very well suggest the importance of historicizing the "silencing" of the Haitian Revolution so as to take into account the strategies necessary to eradicate from official discourse and collective memory not only the revolutionary events in Saint-Domingue, but, as importantly, Napoléon's failed mission to retake the colony and reestablish human bondage there. Marcel Dorigny has uncovered one significant instance in the official suppression of the war in Saint-Domingue in the choreography of General Leclerc's funeral, which scrupulously avoided Paris and suppressed references to the mission that occasioned his death. For Dorigny, this kind of occultation continues to this day, given the lack of any reference to Saint-Domingue or Haiti in the Musée de la Marine's recent commemorative exhibition on Napoléon's overseas ventures and dream of empire, held in the very year of the Haitian bicentennial.[15] Clearly, over time the elision of the Haitian Revolution and the Leclerc expedition in French memory has become imbricated with the broader evasion of the history of colonial slavery in the French Caribbean in French historiography and cultural memory, for what is denied is not only that Haiti was lost, but that it was ever a part of France.[16]

It is perhaps only in consideration of the enormous volume of written and oral accounts and stories of the Haitian Revolution that proliferated on both sides of the Atlantic from the 1790s through the first several decades following the establishment of Haiti that the hegemonic power and accumulated effects of such instances of silencing may be fully apprehended. At the same time, the itinerary of the suppression of the Haitian

Revolution in the West renders all the more remarkable and worthy of study the undeniable resilience of the memory of the Revolution in the work of some of the most accomplished creative writers of the past two centuries throughout the Atlantic world, from Hugo and Alphonse de Lamartine in France; to Alejo Carpentier, Derek Walcott, Aimé Césaire, Édouard Glissant, and Marie Chauvet in the Caribbean; to W. E. B. Du Bois, Langston Hughes, and Frederick Douglass in the United States; to Bernard Dadié and Léopold Senghor in Africa. While many of these writers' works on Haiti have been studied in isolation, more scholarship is needed to assess the enduring cultural afterlife of the Haitian Revolution, both in terms of the evolution of literary and artistic representations of events in Saint-Domingue and in terms of the Revolution's effects on the formation of racial and political ideologies in the Atlantic world at specific moments in time.[17] The role of Black writers and other cultural producers writing and thinking against slavery, European colonial hegemony, and white supremacy demands special attention here, given the signal importance of the revolution in Haiti as a radical affirmation of black humanity and subjectivity in a slaveholding world. In her book-length exploration of selected works from the nineteenth century, *Black Cosmopolitanism: Racial Consciousness and Transnational Identity in the Nineteenth-Century Americas,* Ifeoma Nwankwo argues persuasively that the Haitian Revolution had a fundamental impact on the racial and political identifications of people of African descent insofar as it forced them to define themselves and their struggle for emancipation and racial uplift in relation to a transnational black world that included Haiti.

With Nwankwo's pathbreaking contribution, we may begin to perceive the significance of the Haitian Revolution for figures such as Frederick Douglass, Martin Delany, Mary Prince, and the Cuban Plácido. However, many questions remain about the impact of events in Haiti on politics and literary production in this and other periods and cultural contexts; about the ways in which representations of the Haitian Revolution by writers of diverse racial and geographic origin have shaped understandings of Atlantic modernity, the Enlightenment, Western imperialism, postcoloniality, and race as an ethnic and political signifier; and about the ideological importance of the myths and legends that have emerged through the process of rewriting, retelling, and reinterpreting the Haitian independence struggle in different times and places.

Looking at the Haitian Revolution as a product of memory and cultural interpretation, the contributors to this volume interrogate the literary, historical, and political representations that the revolution has produced and inspired across time and space, and across national and linguistic boundaries. They critically explore not only the powerful claims, rhetorical strategies, and political philosophies professed by the revolutionaries themselves in their manuscript and published documents, but also the place of the Haitian Revolution in the literature and thought of writers from nineteenth- and twentieth-century Haiti, the Caribbean, France, and North America. Essays examine the stories, myths, and heroes that have been revived in different times and places, while considering the implications of such memories for claims of belonging in imagined communities on the basis of race, nation, and class. In addition, the volume explores the ramifications of the Haitian Revolution for theoretical understandings of modern anticolonial movements, postcolonialism, nationalisms, black transnationalism and diasporic identifications, and the Enlightenment and its associated discourses of freedom, human rights, and universalism.

The organization of the volume emphasizes the historical range and analytical focus of the contributions. In the first section of essays, entitled "Reading the Revolution: Contemporary Discourse and Ideology," Ada Ferrer, Deborah Jenson, and Doris Garraway analyze the discourses and political ideologies of the Haitian Revolution through critical interpretations of many of the most fascinating and influential texts that it produced. These include the correspondence of Toussaint Louverture and other ex-slave insurgents, Spanish archival letters, reports, and newspapers, informal oral discourse, the early Haitian constitutions, and the Declarations of Jean-Jacques Dessalines.

As Ada Ferrer argues in her essay "Talk about Haiti: The Archive and the Atlantic's Haitian Revolution," the meanings of the Revolution and its political claims looked and sounded different in different communities and at various locations in the Atlantic world, depending on who was "talking." In her analysis of the words, images, ideas, and narratives that circulated around the hispanophone Atlantic, as well as the channels of communication—official and unofficial, written and oral—through which individuals from various social classes and ethnic groups produced "talk" about Haiti from the inception of the Revolution until well after the declaration of independence, Ferrer challenges Michel-Rolph Trouillot's assertion of the silencing of the Haitian Revolution. As she argues, such silencing was possible only in a clamorous discursive field. While much was said about Haiti, certain claims and narratives won out over others, thus suppressing other possibilities for naming and interpreting the Revolution. Ferrer's research thus demonstrates that rather than merely pointing up a silence around the Revolution, the historical archive contains traces of the conflicts in language, conceptual categories, and stories, as well as the power relations that determined what was told and remembered about the revolution and its primary actors.

In "Toussaint Louverture, Spin Doctor? Launching the Haitian Revolution in the French Media," Deborah Jenson further documents the competition among contemporary actors to shape the meanings and reception of the Revolution by turning to the textual production occurring within revolutionary Saint-Domingue, and in particular, to Toussaint Louverture's construction of a mediatic persona through his eloquent correspondence and strategic interventions in the French press. By casting Toussaint and other ex-slaves as the masters of "spin," Jenson focuses on what was arguably the most radical aspect of the Revolution; the seizure by slaves of the French language and their written enunciation of their demands so as to infiltrate the French media, win over the French reading public, and expose the hypocrisy of the right-leaning Assembly. Looking in particular at Toussaint's contributions to the French newspapers *L'Ancien moniteur* and *La Gazette de France* between 1797 and 1802, Jenson argues that writing and "spin" were essential to revolutionary strategy as the means by which Haitian revolutionary leaders gained control over their public representation, which was severely compromised by negative French coverage of the general slave insurrection as an act of barbarism and proof of blacks' incapacity for civilization. Only by taking control of their mediatic image could black revolutionaries negotiate succesfully with the French government and reshape public perceptions of the revolution.

In "'Légitime Défense': Universalism and Nationalism in the Discourse of the Haitian Revolution," I examine the uniqueness of the Haitian Revolution both as a modern revolution and as a specifically anticolonial revolution, by analyzing the role of universalism in Haitian revolutionary discourse by figures such as Léger-Félicité Sonthonax, Toussaint Louverture, and Jean-Jacques Dessalines. Locating postcolonial theory's elision of the Haitian Revolution in its assumptions about the role of cultural nationalism in anticolonial movements, I propose the concept of "universalist nationalism" through which to understand a flexible political discourse that drew upon French Republican universalism and Enlightenment rhetoric and that also founded a movement of national independence. After first tracing the emergence and gradual hegemony of universalist republican discourse as a means of articulating the political goals of black insurgents, notably Toussaint Louverture, I examine the transformation of Toussaint's assimilationist nationalism into a separatist one. I argue that although Haitian Revolutionary nationalism was largely rooted in the claim that Haiti was the only true defender of the universal human right to liberty, the universalism of the Revolution remained a paradox insofar as it continued to express itself through the particular rhetoric of French Revolutionary republicanism and relied on the rule of exclusion as the basis for Haitian identity.

The second section of essays, "After the Revolution: Rethinking Emancipation, Postcolonialism, and Transnationalism," builds on the concerns of the first by pointing out the ways in which the Revolution forced a reappraisal of the theoretical foundations of radical antislavery and anticolonialism, as well as the role of black racial consciousness and transnational identifications in such projects.

Ifeoma Nwankwo's contribution, "'Charged with Sympathy for Haiti': Harnessing the Power of Blackness and Cosmopolitanism in the Wake of the Haitian Revolution," highlights the ways in which the Revolution provoked a profound reorientation of Black Atlantic identities in the nineteenth-century Americas, as writers and public figures reacted to the paranoia that Haiti instilled in the Atlantic world's white power structure. Looking in particular at the representation of the Cuban revolutionary and writer, Plácido, in Atlantic proslavery discourse and in the antislavery novel *Blake* written by the African American writer Martin Delany, Nwankwo argues that whites' fear of the revolution was expressed through fantasies of racial solidarity and alliance among nonwhites who in some cases shared little in common on the ground, but whom whites feared would unite in a transnational assault against the slaveholding elite. This paranoia, as exhibited in legal documents, published literary works, and political discourse, in turn contributed, Nwankwo argues, to the conditions of possibility for black racial imaginings across boundaries of geography, language, and color. This essay thus points up the irony that although the Haitian Revolution could not openly profess its own messianism on the world stage because of apprehensions about a massive military retaliation by the colonial powers, white fears of a transnational racial movement stimulated black writers and activists elsewhere to take up just that goal, which in turn led to new understandings of the possibilities and limits of black racial consciousness in the Atlantic world.

The following essay by E. Anthony Hurley turns to the memory of the Haitian Revolution in the French Caribbean department of Martinique, where the Revolution has stood as a model both of black liberation and of the perilous ambiguities and disillusionments of post/colonialism. In

"Is He, Am I, a Hero?": Self-Referentiality and the Colonial Legacy in Aimé Césaire's *Toussaint Louverture*," Hurley places this text, published in 1962, in relation to the political and ideological struggles of the author, both as a visionary negritude writer and as a political leader of the colonized. He argues that Césaire's study of Toussaint Louverture offered the poet a means by which to critically reexamine his own roles as anticolonial leader and advocate of assimilation as a way out of colonialism. In his extended discussion of Césaire's treatment of the various social and political conflicts that constituted the Haitian Revolution, Hurley explores Césaire's often conflicted attitudes toward the divergent modes of liberation practiced by Toussaint, such as military revolt and assimilationism. Hurley's analysis thus recasts Césaire's historical essay as an inquiry into the relationship among revolution, decolonization, and political independence in postslavery Caribbean societies.

In her essay "Irrational Revolutions: Colonial Intersubjectivity and Dialectics in Marie Chauvet's *Amour*," Valerie Kaussen examines the importance of the Haitian Revolution for black political imaginings and anticolonial theories in Haiti itself through the work of one of the most powerful twentieth-century Caribbean writers. Kaussen focuses in particular on the literary inscription of desire, terror, and political oppression in the first book of Marie Chauvet's trilogy, *Amour, colère, folie* (1968). By placing Chauvet's writing in relation to contemporary philosophical reflections on the master-slave dialectic in the writings of Alexandre Kojève and Frantz Fanon, as well as the memory of the Haitian Revolution, Kaussen argues that Chauvet herself produces a theory of decolonization that rewrites the Hegelian dialectic and rethinks the possibilities of revolution in post- and neocolonial Haiti. In particular, Kaussen views the protagonist Claire Clamont as engaged in a "quest for recognition" expressed through sadomasochistic fantasies as well as violent acts and attempts at political protest. By linking this quest and its contrary expressions to Haiti's material history of racial and political oppression, Kaussen argues that Claire's sadomasochistic fantasies represent the ultimate means by which she identifies and engages with the suffering community and performs a revolutionary act.

Chris Bongie's essay "*Chroniques de la francophonie triomphante:* Haiti, France, and the Debray Report (2004)" reorients the discussion of the transnational frame in which the Haitian Revolution has been reinterpreted by examining language-based claims of transnational solidarity initiated in the former colonial power on the occasion of the Haitian bicentennial. In particular, Bongie explores the published report of the French government commission charged with evaluating the state of Franco-Haitian relations in the wake of erstwhile Haitian president Aristide's calls for the French state to pay reparations to Haiti to compensate for the enormous indemnity France required as a condition of its recognition of Haitian independence in 1825, which it deemed a necessary compensation for "property" lost in the Revolution. Bongie identifies this report, entitled *Haïti et la France* and authored by the eminent French sociologist Régis Debray, as the most important book on Haiti published in France during the bicentenary year. By rigorously analyzing the exoticist imagery and ideological connotations of its vision of *francophonie,* Bongie reads the Debray report as an attempt by France to substitute symbolic gestures and rhetorical performances of the *"devoir de mémoire"* for the kinds of justice, retribution, and repentence called for by postcolonial criticism and by Aristide himself. The debt to Haiti will never be repaid, he suggests, only denied through forms of assistance inscribed under the sign of the gift: foreign aid, cultural missions and institutes, symbolic forms of "cooperation," and the rehabilitation of the French language in Haiti.

The third and final section of the volume, "Literary Representations of the Haitian Revolution," examines cultural memories of the Haitian Revolution as expressed in fictional portrayals of the Revolution and the literature that it inspired throughout the Atlantic world.

A. James Arnold's far-reaching critical survey of literature on the Haitian Revolution, entitled "Recuperating the Haitian Revolution in Literature: From Victor Hugo to Derek Walcott," examines the aesthetic, geopolitical, and ideological determinants and implications of the major literary treatments of the Haitian Revolution produced in the past two centuries in Europe, the United States, and the Caribbean. Through his readings, Arnold shows that whereas the major nineteenth-century European literary representations by Wordsworth, Lamartine, Hugo, and others have tended to celebrate the Romantic ideal of the black noble savage (often an incarnation of Toussaint Louverture), Caribbean writers such as Carpentier, Césaire, Glissant, and Walcott have adapted forms of modernism so as to counter the discourse and practices of Western colonialism, all the while making the Revolution conform to the ideological demands of negritude, magic realism, Marxism, or creolization. What is fascinating is that, as Arnold demonstrates, such representations are often at cross purposes with the political ideologies of the Revolutionary heroes themselves, particularly in the case of Carpentier. On the other hand, Arnold contends that Césaire's theatrical representation of

the Revolution risks reifying the kinds of binary logics derivative of colonialism that have contributed to the internecine strife characteristic of
postcolonial Haiti.

Returning to the Haitian context, Jean Jonassaint provocatively asks
to what extent the Haitian Revolution has been both the origin and the
primary impetus of nineteenth-century Haitian literature in his essay "Toward New Paradigms in Caribbean Studies: The Impact of the Haitian
Revolution on Our Literatures." Through close textual analysis of the
Haitian declaration of independence and other works, he argues that, far
from being absent from Haitian literature as is sometimes assumed, the
texts and discourses from the revolutionary period provided the basis for
literary production in all genres in the nineteenth century, and the influence of the Revolution continues to be felt in twentieth-century Haitian
theater. By highlighting in particular the features of the first written text
by a Haitian, the Gonaïves Declaration by Dessalines/Boisrond-Tonnerre,
which he contends had a marked impact on nineteenth-century Haitian
literature, Jonassaint shows the centrality of both the Haitian and French
Revolutions to the early Haitian literary imagination.

Paul Breslin completes the volume by interrogating the Haitian Revolution as a literary trope in the work of francophone and anglophone
Caribbean writers in his essay "The First Epic of the New World: But
How Shall It Be Written?" Yet in contrast to Arnold and Jonassaint,
Breslin probes the ways in which the Haitian Revolution has been oddly
*resistant* to representation in literature. He does so through a trenchant
analysis of consonant and divergent themes, narrative patterns, ideologies, characterizations, structures, and aesthetic practices found in the
corpus of plays and novels by Derek Walcott, Aimé Césaire, Édouard
Glissant, C. L. R. James, Alejo Carpentier, and Marie Chauvet. Breslin
argues that as an object of representation, the Haitian Revolution forced
Caribbean writers to stretch the conventions of epic, romance, tragedy,
and farce in order to render its successes as well as its all-too-apparent
failures and ideological ambiguities for contemporary readers. Breslin
thus charts both the unavoidable allure and the daunting elusiveness of
the Haitian Revolution—what he aptly calls "the iconic event in the West
Indian quest for freedom"—for twentieth-century Caribbean writers.

What all of the essays in this volume share is a commitment to opening
up an interdisciplinary dialogue about the cultural and political significance of an event still often viewed through the lens of repetition and
mimicry, if considered at all in the history of Enlightenment, anticolonialism, and Western modernity. Only by restoring a sense of the range

and complexity of contemporary discourses and cultural legacies of the struggle for slave emancipation and independence in Haiti can scholars effectively reverse the silence deplored by Trouillot, thus reestablishing the Haitian Revolution as an event of world-historical proportions. Always available for reinterpretation and inexhaustible in their significations, the textual inscriptions of this revolution thus constitute so many figural roots of the tree of liberty, the symbol eloquently deployed by Toussaint Louverture when on June 7, 1802, he was forcibly embarked on the ship "Le Héros" bound for France: "By overthrowing me [*me renversant*] you have only cut down the trunk of the tree of liberty of the blacks; it will grow back by the roots, which are deep and numerous."[18]

## Notes

1. The circumstances of the removal of President Aristide from power, and the degree of U.S. involvement in his deposition, have become the object of much scholarship and polemical commentary. For a political and historical analysis, see Noam Chomsky, Paul Farmer, and Amy Goodman, *Getting Haiti Right This Time*; and Peter Hallward, "Option Zero in Haiti," For a cultural interpretation, see Deborah Jenson, "From the Kidnapping(s) of the Louvertures to the Alleged Kidnapping of Aristide"; and Chris Bongie, "*Chroniques de la francophonie triomphante:* Haiti, France, and the Debray Report," this volume.

2. Michel-Rolph Trouillot, *Silencing the Past.*

3. On the significance and scope of the Haitian Revolution as compared to other slave revolts in world history, see Robin Blackburn, *The Overthrow of Colonial Slavery, 1776–1848,* 33–67, 161–265; David Patrick Geggus, *Haitian Revolutionary Studies,* vii–ix, 55–69; Eugene D. Genovese, *From Rebellion to Revolution.*

4. The preceding historical summary draws on the following historical works on the Haitian Revolution: David Geggus, "The Haitian Revolution," *Haitian Revolutionary Studies,* 5–32; Laurent Dubois, *Avengers of the New World;* C. L. R. James, *The Black Jacobins;* Horace Pauléus-Sannon, *Histoire de Toussaint-Louverture;* and Pierre Pluchon, *Toussaint Louverture: Un révolutionnaire noir d'Ancien Régime.*

5. Geggus, *Haitian Revolutionary Studies;* Carolyn Fick, *The Making of Haiti;* Dubois, *Avengers of the New World;* Pierre Pluchon, *Toussaint Louverture: Un révolutionnaire noir d'Ancien Régime,* the follow-up to his earlier *Toussaint Louverture: De l'esclavage au pouvoir.* See also Laurent Dubois and John D. Garrigus, *Slave Revolution in the Caribbean 1789–1804: A Brief History with Documents.*

6. On the "Black Atlantic" as a theoretical construct for understanding the relation of African diasporic cultural production and political thought to "the intellectual heritage of the West since the Enlightenment," see Paul Gilroy, *The*

*Black Atlantic: Modernity and Double Consciousness.* For instructive critiques of Gilroy's work with respect to studies of slavery and the Haitian Revolution, see Joan Dayan, "Paul Gilroy's Slaves, Ships, and Routes"; Sibylle Fischer, *Modernity Disavowed,* 33–38. For a major intervention into debates about black diasporic identity that identifies the Haitian Revolution as a signal event in the formation of black transnationalism, see Ifeoma Kiddoe Nwankwo, *Black Cosmopolitanism,* discussed below. On the usefulness of models of anticolonial nationalism in postcolonial theory for understanding the Haitian Revolution, see Doris L. Garraway, "*'Légitime Défense'*: Universalism and Nationalism in the Discourse of the Haitian Revolution," this volume.

7. In addition to the Northwestern University symposium "The Haitian Revolution: History, Memory, Representation," held October 22–23, 2004, major academic conferences on the Revolution and its effects were organized at several U.S. colleges, universities, and institutions. These included "*Pays revé, pays réel:* Legacies of the 1804 Haitian Revolution," held October 22–23 at the University of California, Los Angeles; "Haiti and the Hemisphere: 1804–2004," held October 3, 2004, at New York University; and "The Haitian Revolution: Viewed Two Hundred Years After," which took place at the John Carter Brown Library from June 18 to June 20. In the Caribbean, a major conference was held at the University of the West Indies, St. Augustine, Trinidad, and Tobago, in June 2004 entitled "Reinterpreting the Haitian Revolution and Its Cultural Aftershocks." On commemorations of the Haitian Revolution and of the death of Toussaint Louverture in France, see Jacques de Cauna, ed., *Toussaint Louverture et l'indépendance d'Haïti,* especially 39–56.

8. David P. Geggus, *The Impact of the Haitian Revolution in the Atlantic World.* An earlier source on the impact of the Haitian Revolution on the U.S. South is Alfred Hunt, *Haiti's Influence on Antebellum America.*

9. Marcel Dorigny, "Aux origines: l'indépendance d'Haïti et son occultation"; Nicolas Bancel, Pascal Blanchard, Françoise Vergès, *La République coloniale.*

10. Hunt, *Haiti's Influence on Antebellum America,* 2.

11. See, for example, Gros, *Isle St.-Domingue, province du Nord. Précis historique,* 3 vols. (1809). For a fictionalized narrative of white victimhood and escape see, for example, the anonymous *Histoire de Mesdemoiselles de Saint-Janvier* (1812). Jeremy Popkin reminds us, however, that insofar as they represented educated white male prisoners as captives subordinated to the interests and strategic designs of black revolutionaries, survival narratives from Saint-Domingue often demonstrated that "people of color could not only destroy a white society, but create functioning armies and social systems," thus implicitly undermining the ideology of white supremacy. Jeremy Popkin, "Facing Racial Revolution." On images of blacks in French accounts of the Haitian Revolution and in its aftermath, see also Léon-François Hoffmann, *Le Nègre romantique,* especially 134–41, 168–72; William B. Cohen, *The French Encounter with Africans: White Responses to Blacks, 1530–1880.*

12. See, for example, Antoine François Claude Ferrand, *Sur les moyens de reconquérir Saint-Domingue* (1808), cited in Yves Benot, *La démence coloniale*, 124; and Claude-Pierre-Joseph Leborgne de Boigne, *Nouveau système de colonisation pour Saint-Domingue*. The latter text was the object of a point-by-point rebuttal by the early Haitian publicist Baron de Vastey in his *Réflexions politiques*.

13. Antoine Métral, *Histoire de l'expédition des français à Saint-Domingue;* Victor Hugo, *Bug-Jargal*. On the recovery of abolitionist sentiment and favorable portrayals of blacks in the 1820s, see Hoffmann, *Le Nègre romantique*, 150–72. On the history of the official recognition of Haiti by France, see David Nicholls, *From Dessalines to Duvalier*, 62–66.

14. Statement made during a joint press conference in Pointe-à-Pitre, Guadeloupe, with Percival J. Patterson, prime minister of Jamaica and president of Cariforum, on March 10, 2000, quoted in Dorigny, "Aux Origines," 47.

15. The exhibition "Napoléon et la mer: Un rêve d'empire," took place from March to August 2004. See Dorigny, "Aux origines," 48–49.

16. On the suppression of French colonialism and slavery from French historiography and official memory, see Trouillot, *Silencing the Past,* and Louis Sala-Molins, *Le Code noir ou le calvaire de Canaan* and *Les Misères des Lumières*.

17. See especially "Haiti, 1804–2004: Literature, Culture, Art," special issue of *Research in African Literatures;* "The Haiti Issue" of *Yale French Studies,* edited by Deborah Jenson; "Profondes et nombreuses: Haiti, History, Culture, 1804–2004," special issue of *Small Axe,* edited by Martin Munro and Elizabeth Walcott-Hackshaw; "Haiti et l'Afrique," special issue of *Présence Africaine;* and the collection *Reinterpreting the Haitian Revolution and Its Cultural Aftershocks,* edited by Martin Munro and Elizabeth Walcott-Hackshaw. Unfortunately the latter two journals and book were released too recently for their findings to be taken into account by the contributors to this volume. For earlier, pioneering work on the topic, see also Daniel-Henri Pageaux, *Images et mythes d'Haïti;* and Vèvè A. Clark, "Haiti's Tragic Overture: (Mis)Representations of the Haitian Revolution in World Drama (1796–1975)."

18. Quoted in Pauléus-Sannon, *Histoire de Toussaint-Louverture,* 3:107.

# Talk about Haiti

## The Archive and the Atlantic's Haitian Revolution

*Ada Ferrer*

IN THINKING about the legacies of the Haitian Revolution in the Atlantic World it is tempting to think in binaries. The revolution produced fear and terror among whites, hope and inspiration among slaves and free people of color. The revolution resulted in the radical end of slavery in Saint-Domingue; elsewhere (for instance, in Cuba, southeastern Brazil, and parts of the southern United States) it served as a catalyst to further enslavement. And in postcolonial Haiti itself the promise of radical revolution went unfulfilled as the despotism and mass poverty of colonial servitude were reconfigured in the postcolonial period.

The same kind of double structure is present when we think of another legacy of the Haitian Revolution, namely the construction of a powerful silence around the Haitian Revolution. Among the most important and persuasive expressions of this critique are Michel-Rolph Trouillot's 1995 essays "An Unthinkable History" and "The Three Faces of Sans Souci."[1] In these works, Trouillot argued that contemporaries were incapable of apprehending a revolution made by enslaved men and women. Limited by that incapacity, they reverted to explanations about the decisive role of outside agitators, the pernicious effects of French Revolutionary ideology, and the miscalculations of slaveowners and statesmen. Rarely if ever did they consider the power or consciousness of slaves themselves. According to Trouillot, this contemporary inability to understand the Revolution helps explain the relative absence of the Haitian Revolution in the production of historical knowledge. Unprecedented and unmatched in its challenge to slavery and colonialism, radical in its outcome, it remains little known compared to other world revolutions. Though more studied in the last decade than ever before, it still easily earns the label penned by Trouillot in 1995: "the revolution the world forgot."[2]

But if Trouillot has provided a much-needed and powerful condemnation of the relative silence that has surrounded the Haitian Revolution to the present, other authors have shown that at the time, as news of the slaves' actions erupted onto the world stage, everyone seemed to be talking and thinking about events in Saint-Domingue. As Julius Scott has amply demonstrated, from South America to New England news of the Revolution spread across linguistic, geographic, and imperial boundaries. And even in Europe, according to Susan Buck-Morss, the events were known to "every European who was part of the bourgeois reading public," who apprehended the Revolution as "the crucible, the trial by fire for the ideals of the French Enlightenment."[3] If this was silence, it was a thunderous one indeed.

My purpose in this essay is not to refute the idea—now so powerful in the literature—of a silencing of the Haitian Revolution, but rather to get inside and move beyond that claim. I contend that before we can understand the meanings of Haiti, we must first explore the ways in which Haiti was talked about as it was created. What news circulated? Through what specific points of contact? Among whom? With what language and images? And with what kinds of resonance? As these kinds of questions suggest, our focus is not only on the content of Haitian news, but also on the social and physical networks that helped produce, circulate, and transform rumor and observation into news and eventually into historical narrative and explanation.

To engage in this kind of exploration, I ground this study in Cuba, a neighboring island where consciousness of Haiti and its revolution was particularly strong. The easternmost point of the island was only about fifty miles away from Haiti. Early in the Revolution, slaveowners from the French colony arrived by the thousands, carting slaves, seeking refuge, and telling stories of black vengeance and physical desolation. Throughout the decades following Haitian independence, there were continuous scares and rumors about imminent Haitian invasions into scarcely populated eastern territory. So, in many ways, in Cuba the Haitian Revolution felt immediate and urgent. That urgency, however, derived not only from physical proximity or patterns of migration, but also from the fact that Cuba was in a sense beginning to supplant Haiti. In terms of sugar production, it was coming to occupy the place formerly held by French Saint-Domingue. Cuban planters, merchants, and bureaucrats were highly conscious of this; and, in fact, they explicitly saw themselves as following in the footsteps of, and eventually surpassing, their once-prosperous French counterparts in Saint-Domingue.[4] One of the immediate effects of the

Revolution on this neighboring island was thus the importation of an ever-growing number of enslaved Africans, to work the sugar that was finally making Cuba the most profitable of colonies. Here, then, the Revolution produced a potentially powerful contradiction: at the same time that it created a heightened consciousness of slave rebellion and power, it also produced a massive rise in the actual number of slaves. It is in this setting that I explore the material and quotidian links between a revolution that was dramatically dismantling slavery in Saint-Domingue and a colonial society that was at the same moment erecting a profitable and growing slave system in Cuba.

In what follows I will focus on two distinct streams of information entering Cuba from revolutionary Saint-Domingue. I chose these two in particular for several reasons. First, because they are in many ways unexpected and suprising. Second, because they highlight on the one hand how rich and detailed was the information arriving and on the other hand the diversity of the social actors it reached. And, third, because an examination of both routes encourages one to reconsider some of the broad categories that scholars have used in talking about the Revolution's impact in the Atlantic World and to reflect more generally on the way historical knowledge is produced.

### Witnessing Revolution

In Cuba, word of the slaves' uprising in Saint-Domingue arrived just days after it started. A stream of almost continuous information would follow over the next thirteen years. Letters of private French citizens, addressed to French and non-French residents of Cuban cities, circulated from hand to hand, sometimes reaching local Spanish authorities. Copies of printed proclamations, reports, and newspapers arrived with letters or smuggled aboard ships. Official pleas from authorities in Saint-Domingue reached Spanish officials in Cuba and elsewhere. Subsequent ones arrived, under very different circumstances, from other officers of France, for instance from the mulatto general André Rigaud, as he did battle against the forces of Toussaint Louverture, the principle black leader on the island. But Louverture, as well, was in communication with the Spanish governor of Santiago de Cuba, in at least one instance even offering his aid to the embattled provincial governor whose city was lacking in basic foodstuffs and receiving little sustenance from the capital.[5] In Cuba, then, communications arrived regularly from central players of the Revolution.

Indeed, sometimes the very players arrived, relaying news and opinions in person. French officers and troops leaving Saint-Domingue for France often did so by way of Cuban cities such as Santiago and Havana. When Vézien Desombrage, French commander of Jérémie, evacuated the colony in 1793, he stopped in Santiago, providing the governor there with extensive information on the state of the French colony. Several years later, in 1800, when the officers, soldiers, and families of the forces of André Rigaud evacuated Saint-Domingue after their defeat by the forces of Toussaint Louverture, they chose the same route. Their presence in Santiago de Cuba, said the governor of that city, had become widely known among the local population.[6] At the end of the war, defeated French troops, now in greater number, also evacuated by way of Santiago. Informed of the massive arrival of French soldiers, the captain general in Havana ordered the provincial governor in Santiago to confine these troops to their ships so as to avoid all contact with Spanish subjects. But these measures did not prevent local residents from seeing and learning of the evacuating soldiers, leaving their once prosperous colony in the hands of men of color, many of them formerly enslaved.

If one source of news was French soldiers passing through Cuba en route from Saint-Domingue to France, another—more important for our purposes—was the Spanish and Cuban soldiers and officers who experienced firsthand the revolution in Saint-Domingue. Recall that during the war between France and Spain from 1793 to 1795, the theater of war and revolution was not limited to the French side of the island. Spanish forces claimed French territory, and Spanish commanders mobilized and collaborated with the leaders of former French slaves, such as George Biassou, Jean François, and, most famously, Toussaint Louverture. Spanish forces thus had regular contact with the slave revolution that would make Haiti. And, as it turns out, many of these Spanish forces were composed of men who had come directly from Cuba and who then returned to Cuba with that experience and those stories in mind.

The Cuban regiments began arriving in Spanish Santo Domingo during the summer of 1793, approximately two months after Spanish governor Joaquín García pacted for the services of armed French slaves, who came to be known as the black auxiliaries. The soldiers arrived under the command of Matías de Armona, who from exhaustion and utter frustration at having to embody and make material the alliance between the Spanish monarchy and the slave forces of Saint-Domingue, grew ill and was replaced by another Cuban, Juan Lleonart. Upon arriving, both officers seemed perplexed and disturbed by this alliance, which they understood as one between a legitimate army and bands of runaway slaves. Their discomfort deepened as they gradually came to see Spain's complete reliance on these forces. By April 1794, Spain held a large swath of territory formerly belonging to France, controlling such cities as Gonaïves, Marmelade, Petite Rivière, Fort Dauphin, and Mirebalais. But the commanders of the Cuban regiments insisted repeatedly that this control was illusory. To hold these towns, they were completely reliant on the black auxiliary forces, the allegiance of whom was, at best, painful and, at worst, transitory.

The tables seemed to have been turned. The Spanish depended on former slaves for military victories and relied on their magnanimity for their continual survival. Armona complained that the black forces saw the Spanish ones as tributaries who were obligated to supply them with food, drink, money, and other resources in order to preserve any sense of security. He complained that the auxiliaries gave themselves military ranks and titles, that they wore imposing military and royal insignia, that they tried to act like men, acting "with a certain air of superiority, as if *we* needed them and *we* have to please them."[7] The correspondence between the auxiliary forces and these Spanish-Cuban commanders gives a sense of this inversion. White officers wrote to former slaves addressing them as friends and exuding deference even as they called for obedience. New black officers wrote with demands, their documents stamped with images of trees of liberty topped with crowns sustained by naked black men.[8]

In military ritual and ceremony, the inversion was given material form and official sanction. Toussaint and Biassou were regaled in San Rafael in early 1794, each receiving a gold medal from the king of Spain in honor of their services as his loyal vassals. At the ceremony, it was the officers of two Cuban infantry units who awarded the medals. It was men from the Cuban regiments who gathered to witness the concession of this highest honor, who played the military music, who paraded with the medal recipients, and who joined the two black officers in a lavish two-hour meal prepared in their honor.[9]

In an examination of the contact between Haitian leaders and these men from Cuba, one thing that emerges powerfully is the attempt of the latter to apprehend and in a sense classify the political, military, and social landscape that lay before them. To do this, the Cuban officers engaged in a two-pronged interpretation of their new allies. On the one hand, they observed them closely and tried to read into their behavior larger designs. They watched carefully and imputed significance to the way black commanders approached their camps, the way they announced their arrival, the composition of their guards, and many other things, all to make predictions about black loyalty or treachery. But if circumstances required this kind of close reading of allies' behavior, in practice the Cuban commanders just as often engaged in what might be called a kind of "intuitive sociology," where the form and protagonists of events were thought be knowable almost intuitively, with little reference to events and facts on the ground.[10] So, when the commanders began predicting black auxiliary attacks on the Spanish and Cuban forces, they did so principally with reference to what they saw as the inherent character of the rebels. These white Cuban and Spanish observers could close their eyes and not refer to anything specific, and still feel confident predicting what they saw as the inevitable outcome of a military and political alliance with former slaves.

On an even more basic level, we see how these officers, confronted with a large army of rebel slaves only nominally under their command, struggled to apprehend and classify the situation before them. How, for example, were they to approach the black commanders on which they now depended? They knew the black rebels were officially auxiliaries, but they often noted that really they were "runaway slaves." The officers' reports sometimes seemed to acknowledge that their own system of classification did not correspond with that of the slave rebels. Armona, for example, routinely recorded such discrepancies. "They," he said, referred to their positions as encampments, but he called them *"palenques."* He mentioned that they refered to themselves as generals, brigadiers, and lieutenants. He seemed about to record a difference in the way the Spanish named these same leaders, but then added, sheepishly almost, that they called them that, too. His discomfort suggests that the situation—that is the power of the forces led by black rebels—was making old labels (such as maroons) inappropriate, and new ones (such as general for a former slave) plausible, but still not so natural as to go unmarked.[11]

The alliance between the two groups ended in 1795, when Spain lost the war to France and ceded Santo Domingo. At that point, these Cuban and Spanish officers returned to Havana with physical artifacts from the war, many with slaves purchased or taken from the scenes of upheaval in Hispaniola, and all with firsthand accounts of revolutionary turmoil. On separate ships, roughly at the same time, Spanish authorities in Santo Domingo also embarked the black auxiliaries for Cuba. The Marqués de Casa Calvo, another Cuban-born officer from a very prominent Havana family who was then commander of Bayajá, where Jean François had staged a massacre of approximately seven hundred white French residents then living under Spanish rule, witnessed this embarkation. Faced with the certainty of seeing the perpetrators of this massacre headed for his native Havana (where his family was making a fortune on sugar worked by slaves), he decided to intervene. He wrote the governor of Havana a letter that was pained and urgent. It was pained because he confessed how agonizing he had found it to have to establish "a perfect equality" with a "Black man who though he called himself a General, did not escape from that sphere to which his birth and his origins in slavery had relegated him." The letter was also urgent, because he was imploring the Cuban governor to turn away the black forces and to forbid their entry in Havana. He begged him

> not [to] lodge or settle in the bosom of the flourishing island of Cuba, loyal and faithful to her King, nor within the boundaries [*recinto*] of Havana, these venemous vipers. . . . I am almost an eyewitness to the disgraceful day of the 7th [of July], I am as well of the desolation of this whole Colony, and I have stepped on the vestiges of their fury. These are, even if painted with different colors, the same ones who assassinated their Masters, raped their Mistresses, and destoyed all who had property on this soil at the beginning of the insurrection. Why more reflections, if with these alone the human heart is horrified.[12]

In truth, Calvo had nothing to worry about, since Las Casas, without having been an eyewitness to the massacre, had already voiced strong objections to his superiors in Madrid. He prevented Jean François and Biassou, or any of the seven hundred members of their entourage, from disembarking in Havana, though the ships were moored in the harbor some time. In opposing the settlement of black leaders Jean François and Biassou, Las Casas argued that they were dangerous and that they horrified a white population that counted so many slaves and free people of color in their midst. He even stated that the very names of Jean François and Biassou already resounded in Cuba like the names of great conquerers. He may not have been exaggerating. In several Cuban slave conspiracies uncovered in the period and aftermath of the Haitian Revolution, slave witnesses spoke to the significance and appeal of the figure of Jean François. In 1812, for example, during the Aponte Rebellion, one of the largest and most interesting rebellions in the history of the island, numerous enslaved and free witnesses made ample references to the 1795 visit of the two black generals, despite Las Casas's refusal of permission to disembark.[13]

The claim, and indeed the scattered evidence, that the reputations of these two black generals were already well known on the island is of course important. It suggests that all kinds of news—not just official news—was circulating. Moreover, it suggests that this news circulated not just among colonial authorities or soldiers or a well-connected elite, but rather that the population as a whole was coming into contact with news of black rebellion against enslavement and eventually against colonialism.

## Reading the Revolution

If the historical record seems to portray a Cuban world in which Haitian news reached a wide cast of characters, it also strongly suggests that this cast included people of color, slave and free—people who were sure to give such news very different spins than, say, a planter turned commander. Surviving records give us precisely this sense, as they allow us to explore some of the routes by which people of color learned of Haiti and the ways they thought about it.

The very first news of the Saint-Domingue slave insurrection appears to have arrived in Cuba on August 27, when a French officer appeared in Baracoa, Cuba's easternmost city and the one closest to the French colony. He arrived with a clear description of events and an urgent plea for aid.[14] The first indication that the news had reached the population of color comes almost as early, but—unfortunately—is significantly less clear. Here I am referring to a very brief, very vague entry in the meeting minutes of the Havana city council, an entry moreover the main subject of which is ostensibly a city butcher shop and not enslaved or free black people. In the entry, dated September 9, 1791, city council members tried to explain a sudden shortage of pigs at the city butcher shop for pork. The only explanation they proferred—and one they did not like—seemed to be that the shop was short of pork because people of color in Havana had begun sacrificing pigs in honor of insurgents in foreign colonies. A council member then went on to lament the potential influence of foreign blacks on their own slaves.[15] So just over two weeks after the start of the slave revolution in Saint-Domingue, people of color in Havana appeared to know of their acts. The entry further suggests that local blacks sought to honor the rebels and that they may have done so by sacrificing pigs. Here, of course, we cannot help but think of the Bois Caïman ceremony in which Haitian revolutionaries probably took blood oaths and sacrificed a black pig in preparation for the war they were about to commence.[16]

The question of how to interpret this brief mention of Haiti in the documentary record is of course a challenging one. The white official's confidence in alluding to the existence of pig sacrifices among Havana blacks made to honor or benefit foreign insurgents combined with the knowledge that pig sacrifices occurred in preparation for slave rebellion in Saint-Domingue tempts us to take the official at his word. It encourages us to conclude, or at the very least to suggest, that blacks in Havana (whether slave or free we cannot know) had certain knowledge of the Haitian Revolution days after it began and organized ceremonies which resembled the very ceremonies of their slave counterparts in the Northern Plain of Saint-Domingue. That suggestion, of course, leads us to further ones: the possibility that the pig sacrificers in Havana—those descendents of Ethiopia as they are described in the record—felt a powerful affinity, a shared sense of belonging, and a common purpose, with enslaved men and women engaged in the process of making themselves free in what would become Haiti.

But the record itself is highly ambiguous. In the official minutes of the Havana City Council meetings, the pig sacrifice and the Haitian Revolution are explicitly linked—though of course the latter cannot yet be named in that way. But the link is asserted only here and only on the basis of unspecified rumor and speculation. Reading backwards and forwards from that particular meeting, we see that the question of meat and pig shortages in the city was a fairly routine matter of business. The fact of a shortage in August or September 1791 is far from exceptional. The claim that the cause of that shortage was linked to local black solidarity with the revolution was. What is interesting, however, is that another version of that same meeting is available in the documentary record. When in 1794, colonial officials wrote to Madrid to plead that black prisoners from Saint-Domingue not be brought to Cuba to be sold as slaves, they referred to and reproduced the partial minutes from that original September 9, 1791, meeting. But in this later transcription, there was no mention of pig sacrifice. Here, the same colonial official shares instead the news of the arrival of a French ship from Saint-Domingue carrying 292 slaves and fresh information of a massive slave insurrection. News of the arrival of the ship is immediately followed by the same lament that appears earlier about the likelihood that foreign insurgents will corrupt and incite Cuban slaves to rebellion. Thus one written version of the meeting begins with speculation of pig sacrifice, the other with the news of rebellion arriving aboard a French slave ship.[17]

It is impossible to say with any degree of certainty what accounts for the significant discrepancy in the two versions of the meeting. We cannot even say if the difference was one of design or of error in transcription. The records remind us again—in a very tangible way—just how fragmentary and inscrutable can be the traces of slaves' political vision that have survived in the documentary record. Yet for all that inscrutability, both versions of the event suggest that white elites were perceiving and fearing the possibility of precisely that vision. They imagined that slaves in one locale would act in support of fellow slaves elsewhere for a goal that was shared across lines geographical and imperial.

Other records suggest that whether or not actual bonds of practical support ever came to exist, people of color in Cuba clearly had the desire to imagine them. In casual street encounters between free urban blacks and local whites, in confrontations between masters and slaves, in heated exchanges between black suspects and white interrogators, Cuban people of color regularly referred to the Haitian Revolution as something they respected and hoped to emulate. They referred by name to men such as Toussaint Louverture, Dessalines, Christophe, and Jean François. They even said among themselves that they wanted to be captains or leaders precisely like these men. Their testimony, on numerous occasions, explicitly refers to the "feats" of slaves in Guarico, the Spanish colonial name for Cap Français—slaves they now refered to as their *"compañeros."* Slaves recruited others to conspiracy by urging them to do as their counterparts had done in Saint-Domingue, where blacks were now "absolute masters of the land."[18]

While the regular invocations of Haiti by slaves and free people of color leave no doubt that they learned and used knowledge of revolutionary events, on their own these references do not tell us how and from what sources they acquired that knowledge.[19] In what follows, I focus on one source, which according to the captain general of Cuba, the Márques de Soneruelos, was of notable importance in informing Cuba's people of color about the unprecedented events of the Haitian Revolution. The source is a surprising one: an official Spanish newspaper—the *Gaceta de Madrid,* a biweekly publication of the Spanish government in Madrid.[20] What is perhaps surprising in examining this newspaper is that, for all the government efforts to curtail the flow of information, the source with most information on events in Saint-Domingue circulating in Cuba was not a foreign newspaper, but the official newspaper of its own metropole. According to the captain general, the problem this posed was significant. He lamented that the newspaper was so readily available: "It is sold to the public, and everyone buys it, and it circulates well among the blacks," who, he added, read it, discuss it, and analyze its contents "with considerable liveliness."[21] What worried the governor so profoundly was that in the pages of this gazette, Cubans of color encountered substantial and animated news of black rebellion in what had been an orderly and prosperous sugar colony just miles away. Here were stories of the revolutionary terror in Paris, of abolitionist debates in Britain, of war in

Europe. And in regular installments, often reprinted from French, British, and U.S. newspapers, stories of the Haitian Revolution unfolded.

The *Gaceta*'s coverage of the Revolution began in November 1791, with the first reference to the rebellion of the slaves in the North.[22] Coverage continued, with articles on other attacks and massacres, on the abolition of slavery in Paris in 1794, and on Spanish and English attacks on French territory in Saint-Domingue. In 1796, readers first encounter the figure of Toussaint Louverture (though he is not explicitly identified as black until 1800).[23] Although coverage of Haitian events is regular and fairly frequent, we see, not surprisingly, that at certain moments of the Revolution, the coverage intensified. This was clearly the case with the Leclerc expedition which began leaving France in the final months of 1801. The expedition was devised by Napoléon, commanded by his brother-in-law Leclerc, and meant to contain what authorities in Paris saw as the evils and excesses that had taken root in their once-prized colony. The *Gaceta* covered this event in exceptional detail. In almost every number, news appeared of the expedition: readers learned of so many ships gathering for the journey from Brest to Saint-Domingue, of the number of troops and arms to be transported by each. The impression given by the regular dispatches was of an imminent and massive invasion of the colony by metropolitan forces.

Coverage intensified still more with the arrival of the expedition on the coasts of Saint-Domingue in February 1802. Then, readers of the gazette began learning of the reactions of former slaves and their leaders. Arriving at the Couleuvre ravine near Gonaïves, the expedition encountered resistance, cannon shots and hand-to-hand combat from Toussaint's men. When fresh forces arrived at Le Cap, the black leader Christophe refused to grant them entry without the previous authorization of Toussaint. In Port-au-Prince, the rebels set fire to the town before French troops could disembark. Alongside the detailed descriptions of such encounters were reprinted extracts from official reports by Leclerc and Rochambeau (governor of Saint-Domingue) to the Overseas Minister. All this was published in the pages of the newspaper and read, as we know from Someruelos, with much interest in Cuba.[24]

The frequency and nature of the reports turned the news into something like a serialized novel. Little by little, the number of ships leaving Brest grew and grew; little by little the reactions of rebel slaves became clearer and clearer. And as in a novel, sometimes the details of the unfolding events were quite intimate. So for example, the gazette published a quite detailed description of the reunion between Toussaint's wife and her two sons (both of whom had been sent to France to study and who now accompanied the expedition on Napoléon's request). We learned of her embrace, her tears, and the maternal love she displayed. Longer still was the gazette's description of Toussaint's own meeting with his sons shortly thereafter.[25]

In fact, as news of the expedition unfolded, the key questions soon came to center around Toussaint himself—how would he receive the expedition, what would his attitude be, what would his destiny be? The ultimate answer came, of course, with news of his deportation to France in June 1802.[26] Even with Toussaint out of the picture, however, the gazette's readers may have soon begun to surmise that his plans were perhaps bearing fruit. Gradually, more and more articles began appearing about the mounting deaths of French soldiers. They learned of Leclerc's death, and the death of many other officers who only a few weeks earlier had appeared in the gazette's pages as the dogged persecutors of Toussaint and his allies. By the end of the year, almost every number of the gazette seemed to provide evidence of the weakness of the French and the growing power of black leaders such as Dessalines and Christophe.[27]

But the gazette spoke not only of black military victories, it also published articles that gave some insight into the desires and the ideas of Haitian rebels. It published the words of black leaders. The issue of the gazette that had prompted the complaint by Cuban Captain General Someruelos, in fact, contained two translated proclamations by black Haitian leaders. One signed by Dessalines and another by Dessalines, Christophe, and Clerveaux. In both documents, the black leaders invited refugees who had fled the colony to return and live peacefully under the new system being erected. But their invitation also entailed a clear and explicit threat. Speaking of the refugees, the three leaders declared:

> The God who protects us, the God of free men, commands us to extend toward them our victorious arms. But those who, intoxicated with a foolish pride, . . . [those who] think still that they alone form the essence of human nature, and who pretend to think that they are destined by heaven to be our owners and our tyrants, [we tell them] never to come near the island of Santo Domingo, because if they come, they will find only chains and deportation.[28]

This was the proclamation that had so worried Someruelos—a proclamation in which were manifest the power of new black leaders, who forbade the return of Saint-Domingue to its colonial ruler and who were willing to admit only those refugees who deigned to live under a government of former slaves and in a society without slavery.

Just one week after Someruelos penned his attack on the publication and circulation of this document, a new proclamation appeared in the pages of the gazette. This time it was the Haitian declaration of independence, signed by Dessalines on January 1, 1804, and published in the gazette six months later on June 1. We know that other copies of the Haitian declaration of independence had already arrived in Cuba, aboard French ships, for example, and that authorities on the island had done their best to have them confiscated, translated, and sent to Madrid.[29] But in spite of their attempts to limit its circulation, in June we see the declaration now translated, published, and circulating, even among black Cubans, who Someruelos argued were able to acquire the gazette with little difficulty. So, we know that people of color in Cuba were able to read the Haitian declaration of independence, a proclamation of former slaves who had vanquished their masters by force of arms.

Now we can understand more profoundly the discomfort of Someruelos upon recognizing that these words and ideas, that these examples of a new kind of presence and power in Haiti, of a new liberty by and for black people, were circulating in his own colony. It was not only that people of color learned of Haitian news, for according to the gazette itself there was not one black person who did not already know these stories by memory.[30] It was also that with repetition and circulation, the example acquired more and more substance.

## Archives, History, and the Haitian Revolution

Through the pages of the *Gaceta de Madrid,* through contact with soldiers formerly stationed in the theater of war and revolution, and through other multiple routes not traced here, people in Cuba received interesting, detailed, and sometimes intimate news of the world's first black revolution. We know now that whatever sense of fear or hope may have been sparked in Cuba by the example set by Haitian events did not have to be imagined out of whole cloth, but would have likely drawn on ample raw material, on detailed narratives, and suggestive stories available to residents of Cuba regarding those events. So, for example, when alleged slave conspirators in Bayamo relayed the name of Jean François to Spanish authorities, or when during the Aponte conspiracy in Havana in 1812, slaves and free people invoked the names of Jean François, Christophe, and others, both the tellers of and the audiences for those stories would have had ample opportunity to learn of the real Jean François and his exploits. The oft-repeated assertion that Cuban Creole elites feared that any attempt at political liberation would stir the population of color, perhaps makes more sense when we know that members of that elite had firsthand experience in Santo Domingo with unsuccessful attempts to mobilize and contain armed former slaves in support of elite political goals. Cuban men had been defeated by some of those slave forces in 1794–95. Cuban residents had opportunities to witness defeated whites evacuate the French colony and then to read the proclamations of their black victors. The fears or hopes allegedly inspired by the Haitian Revolution would have been shaped by these very concrete contacts and experiences.

The proliferation of substantial, detailed, even intimate talk of the Haitian Revolution does not, however, require that we abandon the important notion of "silence" discussed at the outset of this paper. Rather, it compels us to try to understand more deeply the ways in which such silences (and mentions) were constructed, sustained, and challenged, and the ways particular kinds of historical knowledge and narratives became ascendant.

In 1995, Michel-Rolph Trouillot brilliantly and persuasively argued that the silence that has tended to surround the Haitian Revolution is explained in part by the inability of contemporary observers to understand or narrate the events of the Revolution—and particularly the aspirations and actions of slave rebels—with the language and categories available at the time, or even now. For Trouillot this is a silence in which the archive itself is implicated, as an institution of power that selects, gathers, organizes, and legitimates certain kinds of documents and facts in ways that reinscribe the power already at play in the historical act itself.[31]

I would suggest, however, that a grounded analysis of the ways in which people regularly spoke, heard, learned, and wrote about the Revolution as it unfolded, encourages us to approach the archive in a different way: not as transparent depository of transparent documents, but neither simply as obstacle for historian and accomplice to state power. A more fruitful approach, rather, invites us to see the archive as also containing the traces of the operation of its own power. There, we can trace the processes by which certain silences and narratives are created, reformulated, sustained, and broken. And in the archive, Haiti emerges simultaneously in multiple forms: as a place about which detailed, complex, dense, and unruly stories circulated, and as a name that served as loaded key word, black-and-white image, a brief cautionary (or inspirational) invocation. Indeed, if we focus on the sources themselves, we see these dual uses competing even in the same documents. We see at work, in other words, the very process of silencing, the process of what Trouillot calls archival power itself. It is as if we could see the tug of war, the efforts of narrators to contain events in categories that will not allow them to fit.

We see this, for example, even in the archival use or absence of the very term *Haiti*. Haiti, of course, was the name given to colonial Saint-Domingue immediately after independence. It was the Arawak-Taino name for the island; it signified mountainous or high lands; and supposedly it was the name "on everyone's lips" and the name "enthusiastically welcome[d]" when it came time to name the new country.[32] But though the state became Haiti in name, colonial and metropolitan authorities seemed loathe to use that title; to use it, they must have surmised, would be to recognize the victory of slaves and former slaves and the defeat of European rule. Thus, for example, in Cuba and in the Spanish-speaking world in general, the name Haiti makes only scattered archival appearances in the decades after it was created. Spanish authorities continued using the name Santo Domingo for newly independent Haiti, even when this was the source of great confusion. When officials forbade (yet again) the entry of people from Haiti shortly after independence, they did so without naming Haiti, referring simply to Santo Domingo. The move, of course, caused predictable confusion when local authorities confronted refugees from the formerly Spanish part of the island still called Santo Domingo and were unsure if they also were included in the prohibition.[33] It is revealing irony that those Haitians who helped Simón Bolívar win his anticolonial bid against Spain are identified in the historical record as *"franceses"* rather than Haitians.[34]

The same disconnect between the categories and names deployed by narrators and the complex and unprecedented realities on the ground are evident as well in the ways in which colonial and metropolitan authorities struggled to deal with black heads of state, a category of person unknown to them just years or months earlier. So Captain General Someruelos facing letters from black authorities, opts to seek advice from the metropole. He seems at a loss not only about what political strategies to follow, but even about what language to use, what titles, what tone, and with what consequences.[35] Here the Captain General seemed to echo the Cuban officers discussed earlier in the paper, who arrived in Spanish Santo Domingo, and knew not what to name the troops of former slaves who served as their "auxiliaries," calling them "maroons" and "skirmishers," even as they admitted that they were "the all" of the war.[36]

But the writings of Spanish officials also explicitly acknowledge this struggle to name and narrate the scenes before them with words that could not be made to correspond. In doing so, they left for our archives intriguing traces of the struggle between competing ways of naming the history represented by Haiti. In one revealing exchange between Santiago governor Sebastián Kindelán and the Haitian leader Alexandre Petión, we see in fact two discordant regimes of classification. The Haitian letter refers to the "time of the French" and to the Haitians; meanwhile the letter of the colonial official cannot admit such a reality. Here Haiti even in the postindependence year of 1809 continues to be named as "a foreign colony."[37] In these day-to-day documents of empire, and in exchanges such as these, are revealed the conflicts between different visions of Haiti—Haiti as newly independent nation, and Saint-Domingue as permanent turbulent colony. Such examples—and there are many in the historical record—encourage us to move beyond seeing the archive as an institution that only works to silence particular narratives and legitimate those associated with the victors of history. It is more interesting, challenging, and productive to imagine the archive as a place that may also contain—if we choose to read it that way—traces of the conflicts between competing histories and their would-be tellers.

Take, for instance, the following exchange dating from the final months of the revolution in 1803. By midyear, with the conflict in Saint-Domingue now clearly a war of independence, French troops and white residents began (again) fleeing from the colony and arriving by the boatloads in eastern Cuba. The local governor wrote almost daily letters to his superiors informing them of the number of ships and people arriving constantly to his territory. He had each captain of each ship formally interviewed, and each solicited "hospitality" from the Spanish. In one such request for hospitality, the French officers stressed the fact that England and France were now again at war and that their town was under threat of British invasion. The governor hearing this request showed little compassion and was inclined to deny refuge. If the threat was merely from the attack of a British enemy, then why not flee to another point in the colony? It was not, he added, as if they were threatened by black troops or black rule. Having expressed this doubt and having voiced a familiar—if at the moment alternative—narrative, he overdetermined the nature of the narrative that would ultimately be produced. Formally requesting hospitality days later, that is, stating the official reason for their flight, the refugees' petition now requested hospitality in a more urgent and conformist language. "We left of absolute necessity," they wrote, "because we were about to be killed by black rebels."[38] Here we see clearly how the power and authority of the governor, and perhaps the very exigencies of producing routinized documents of empire, shaped the record of the archive and turned several possible narratives—for example, of imperial war between Britain and France, or of anticolonial struggle between black rebels and their metropole—into a much simpler, starker story of blacks violently sacrificing whites.

In such sources we can see the multiple disjunctures in the way contemporaries wrote and heard about Haiti—the gap between the proliferation of detailed information and the simultaneous emergence of vulgarized, key-word type references to Haiti, as well as the incompatibility between the terms and categories available to narrators and the unprecedented realities and outcomes on the ground. Such inconsistencies serve to illuminate the processes by which a particular kind of historical narrative and a particular kind of historical knowledge becomes ascendant. In these disjunctures we are able to observe colonial power trying to convert the Haitian Revolution, among the most radical and significant of the modern world, into a mere warning, a cautionary tale in black and white, a caricature with only suppressed traces of the will and thought of the black and mulatto men and women who made the Revolution. But if the historical record shows anything at all, it is that that suppression was far from total.

## Notes

I thank Doris Garraway for the opportunity to be part of this volume and of the lively conference at Northwestern University from which it emerged. In addition to the Northwestern audience, I thank audiences at the John Carter Brown Library, the Rutgers Black Atlantic Seminar, the University of Pittsburgh Atlantic History Seminar, the University of Michigan–University of Windsor joint conference on Slavery and Freedom in the Atlantic World, and the graduate students in my Haitian Revolution colloquium at NYU in spring 2004. For comments on earlier versions, I'd like to thank Laurent Dubois, Sibylle Fischer, Mimi Sheller, Herman Bennett, Rebecca Scott, Jean Hébrard, Fernando Martínez, Michael Zeuske, Julius Scott, Gloria García, Reinaldo Funes, Consuelo Naranjo, Manuel Barcia, Walter Johnson, and Doris Garraway. A shorter and earlier version of some of this material appeared in Spanish as "Noticias de Haití en Cuba," *Revista de Indias* 63 (2003): 675–93.

1. Michel-Rolph Trouillot, *Silencing the Past.*

2. Ibid., 71. For important recent work on the Revolution, see especially, Laurent Dubois, *Avengers of the New World;* Carolyn Fick, *The Making of Haiti;* and David Geggus, *Haitian Revolutionary Studies.*

3. Julius Scott, "The Common Wind"; and Susan Buck-Morss, "Hegel and Haiti," 837.

4. On the Cuban sugar boom in this period, see especially Manuel Moreno Fraginals, *El ingenio;* Rolando Ely, *Cuando reinaba su majestad el azúcar.* For an important conceptual discussion of this boom and the emergence of a "second slavery" in the aftermath of the Haitian Revolution and British abolitionism, see Dale Tomich, "Spaces of Slavery, Times of Freedom" and "The 'Second Slavery,'" both in his *Through the Prism of Slavery.*

5. In a letter to Someruelos, Sebastián Kindelán translates and transcribes Toussaint's communication. Governor of Havana Sebastián Kindelán to the Marqués de Someruelos, Captain General of Cuba, 29 April 1800, in Archivo General de Indias, Seville (hereafter AGI), Cuba, legajo 1534.

6. Kindelán to Someruelos, 31 August 1800, in AGI, Cuba, legajo 1534.

7. Matías de Armona to Joaquín García, Captain General of Santo Domingo, San Rafael, 12 August 1793, in Archivo General de Simancas, Simancas, Spain (hereafter AGS), Sección Guerra Moderna (GM), legajo 6855. Emphasis added. Unless otherwise noted, all translations are mine.

8. The reference to the stamp of the tree of liberty appears in Armona to García, San Rafael, 14 August 1793, in AGS, GM, legajo 6855. For a discussion of slave royalism and the on-the-ground compatibility of royalist and republican motifs, see Laurent Dubois, *Avengers of the New World*, 106–8.

9. "Continuación de la noticias de la Ysla de Sto Domingo asta 25 de Marxo de 94" in file "Relación de lo ocurrido en la Ysla de Santo Domingo con motivo de la guerra con los franceses, 1795. D. Antonio Barba," Servicio Histórico Militar, Madrid (hereafter SHM), Colección General de Documentos, Rollo 65, doc. no. 5-4-11-1. The document mentions that General Jean François had received the same honor earlier.

10. The term "intuitive sociology" is borrowed from Arlette Farge and Jacques Revel, *The Vanishing Children of Paris,* 53.

11. Armona to García, San Rafael, 12 and 14 August 1793. In folder "Correspondencia del Brigadier Dn. Mathías de Armona desde 19 de Junio hasta 10 de Septiembre de 1793" in AGS, GM, legajo 6855.

12. Marqués de Casa Calvo to Luis de las Casas, Captain General of Cuba, 31 December 1795, in AGI, Cuba, legajo 1474.

13. "Testimonio de la criminalidad seguida de oficio contra el negro Miguel, Juan Bautista y José Antonio sobre la conjuración que intentaban contra el Pueblo y sus moradores [Bayamo]," 25 August 1805, in AGI, Cuba, legajo 1649. On Aponte, see Matt Childs, "'A Black French General Arrived to Conquer the Island': Images of the Haitian Revolution in Cuba's 1812 Aponte Rebellion," in David Geggus, ed., *The Impact of the Haitian Revolution in the Atlantic World,* 135–56; and José Luciano Franco, "La conspiración de Aponte," and *Las conspiraciones de 1810 y 1812.*

14. See Ignacio Leyte Vidal, Tte. Gob. de Baracoa, to Luis de las Casas, 27 August 1791, in AGI, Cuba, legajo 1435; and 28 August 1791, in Archivo Nacional de Cuba, Havana (hereafter ANC), Asuntos Políticos, legajo 4, exp. 33.

15.  Archivo del Museo de la Ciudad de la Habana, (hereafter AMCH), Actas Capitulares del Ayuntamiento de la Habana Trasuntadas, Enero 1791 a Diciembre 1791, folio 247, 9 September 1791.

16.  For an interesting and persuasive discussion of the Bois Caïman ceremony and the controversy that has surrounded it in the literature, see David Geggus, "The Bois Caiman Ceremony," in *Haitian Revolutionary Studies,* 81–92.

17.  Cabildo extraordinario 12 February 1794, appended to Las Casas to Pedro de Acuña, 19 February 1794, in AGI, Estado, legajo 14, no. 73.

18.  See Ada Ferrer, "La société esclavagiste cubaine et la révolution haïtienne," especially 346–56.

19.  Julius Scott's pathbreaking work first raised this question and offered a brilliant analysis of the currents of communication among people of color, in which sailors figure very prominently. See Scott, "Common Wind."

20.  Larry R. Jensen, *Children of Colonial Despotism,* 6. The gazette was, in fact, one of only two newspapers allowed to operate in the metropole after censorship legislation in February 1791 clamped down on the peninsular press in an effort to prevent the spread of French revolutionary currents.

21.  Someruelos to Sec. de Estado, 25 May 1804, in Archivo Histórico Nacional, Madrid (hereafter AHN), Estado, legajo 6366, exp. 78. A transcription of the letter also appears in Someruelos to Sec. de Estado, 13 August 1809, in AGI, Estado, legajo 12, exp. 50.

22.  *Gaceta de Madrid* (hereafter GM), 25 November 1791, 856.

23.  On the emancipation decree, see GM, 8 April 1794, 394; on the Spanish victory in Bayajá, GM, 1 April 1794, 363–71; on British victories, GM, 24 January 1794, 103–4, and 26 August 1794, 1006–7. The first mention of Louverture that I have found in the periodical is from 2 December 1796 (1024), though he does not appear to be identified as black in the journal until 18 January 1800 (50). Coverage of the conflict between Louverture and Rigaud begins 15 October 1799 (894). For his appointment as prefect, 4 August 1801 (816).

24.  GM, 1801: 1 December, 1214; 8 December, 1230; 18 December, 1236; 22 December, 1278; GM, 1802: 5 January, 12; 23 March, 270; 26 March, 283; 2 April, 313–16; 6 April, 326–29; 9 April, 338–41; 20 April, 376–77; 23 April, 385–86; 18 May, 477–79. Someruelos's letter is the one cited above (AGI, Estado, legajo 12, exp. 50).

25.  Both appear in GM, 21 May 1802, 489–91.

26.  See GM, 1802: 23 March 270; 2 April, 312; 6 April, 328–9; 13 April, 348–50; 20 April, 376–77; 18 May, 477–79; 21 May, 389–91; 1 June, 528; 22 June, 606–8; 6 July, 650–52; 9 July, 664–5; 27 July, 736; 6 August, 780; 10 August, 789; 28 September, 971.

27.  On disease and death among French troops, see GM in 1802: 17 August, 817–8; 20 August, 831–2; 19 October, 1054–55; 14 December, 1241–2; 24 December, 1269; and in 1803: 25 January, 67–8.

28.  GM, 23 March 1804, 267–8.

29. Marqués de Someruelos to D. Pedro Cevallo, 14 March 1804, in AHN, Estado, legajo 6366, exp. 70.

30. *GM*, 18 May 1804.

31. Trouillot, *Silencing the Past,* passim, but especially 48–53. For other important and generative work on thinking about the archive, see especially Arlette Farge, *Le goût de l'archive.*

32. Thomas Madiou, *Histoire d'Haïti,* quoted in Geggus, *Haitian Revolutionary Studies,* 207.

33. AGI, Cuba, legajo 1549.

34. See Robin Blackburn, *The Overthrow of Colonial Slavery,* 345.

35. Someruelos to Junta Suprema, 26 December 26, 1808, in AGI, Estado, legajo 12, exp. 57.

36. Armona to García, San Rafael, 10 September 1793. In folder "Correspondencia del Brigadier Dn. Mathías de Armona desde 19 de Junio hasta 10 de Septiembre de 1793" in AGS, GM, legajo 6855.

37. AGI, Estado, legajo 12, exp. 54.

38. Kindelán to Someruelos, 15 August 1803, with enclosed "Testimonio de los autos obrados sobre la arribada que han hecho a este Pto. de Stgo. de Cuba 5 Goletas y una balandra francesas . . . con varias familias de la misma nación pidiendo hospitalidad," in AGI, Cuba, legajo 1537A. See also J. A. Caballer, Consejo de Indias, 21 February 1804, in Archivo del Ministerio de Asuntos Exteriores, Madrid, Politica, República Dominicana, legajo 2372.

# Toussaint Louverture, Spin Doctor?

## Launching the Haitian Revolution in the French Media

*Deborah Jenson*

HEGEL'S DIALECTIC of master and slave, and his related model of unhappy consciousness, was deeply informed, according to Susan Buck-Morss in "Hegel and Haiti," by the philosopher's reading of news stories about the upheavals in Saint-Domingue during his time in Jena. To make this case, Buck-Morss examined the unusually extensive media coverage of Saint-Domingue in *Minerva,* a newspaper important to Hegel's world outlook, which published between 1804 and 1805 "a continuing series, totaling more than a hundred pages, including source documents, news summaries, and eyewitness accounts."[1] With the hindsight provided by Buck-Morss's research, it seems inevitable that Hegel's profoundly influential paradigm would have emerged in dialogue with the representation of the slave revolution in Saint-Domingue. Buck-Morss's compelling analysis of the diffusion and reception of information about Haiti in the German media raises fascinating questions as to the intellectual reception of the Haitian Revolution in other countries, notably France. Yet the significance of the reception of news of the Revolution cannot be properly understood without considering the more fundamental question of how news was produced within, and exported from, Saint-Domingue during the Revolution, and what role the ex-slaves played in disseminating their political demands and interpretations of events. If, as Buck-Morss argues, "the Haitian Revolution was the crucible, the trial by fire for the ideals of the French Enlightenment," and "Every European who was part of the bourgeois reading public knew it" (837), then the Haitian Revolution as a media phenomenon begs to be explored: not only for its philosophical influence, but for the political significance of the mediatic *prise de la parole* by former slaves.

Buck-Morss sidestepped the interest of the Haitian Revolution in the French media with the observation that "there was censorship in the French press after 1803" (839). Napoléon Bonaparte's increasingly tight control of the French media in the year leading up to the inauguration of the French Empire did indeed limit representation of Saint-Domingue as it approached the 1804 independence, but there was widespread mediatic representation of the Haitian Revolution in France prior to 1803. And even after 1803, despite the undeniably sudden straitjacketing of the news (including the cessation of direct communication between Haitian Revolutionary leaders and the French media), newspapers such as the *Journal des débats* continued to reprint major Haitian stories that ran elsewhere in the world. It was in New York on June 18, 1804, that Dessalines' manifesto of April 28, composed with Juste Chanlatte, was first published, with its visceral language of colonial slavery as cannibalism: "We have paid back the real cannibals in full, war for war, crime for crime, outrage for outrage. I have saved my country; indeed, I have avenged America."[2]

It is not surprising to find, on the date of the republication on August 7 in the *Journal des débats* of this manifesto, that Dessalines' proclamation had unsettled a leading political theorist in France, Benjamin Constant. In his journal, Constant interrupted his reflections on the hypocrisy of morality (he was working on his opus on religion) to ponder his own discomfort with the "savage" style of Dessalines: "I just read Dessalines' proclamation. There is something savage in this negro style that grips those of us who are accustomed to the forms and hypocrisy of the social world with a particular kind of terror. What horror lies in both extremes!"[3] The hypocrisy that Constant was busy critiquing in the "social world" translates for him into a lack, a frightening absence, in Dessaline's manifesto, productively destabilizing Constant's role as a social critic.

Still more immediate than the question of the impact on French thought of media representations of the Haitian Revolution is the problem of how those representations were constructed. In this essay I will argue that the media role of Toussaint Louverture, as traced primarily in texts in the *Ancien moniteur* and the *Gazette de France* between 1797 and 1802 (considered in relation to handwritten letters by Toussaint), was an active and essential component of Haitian Revolutionary strategy.

As we know from current political campaigns, media coverage doesn't just happen, nor is it a neutral forum. "Spin" is a discourse that essentially limits the range of possible descriptions through the repetition of carefully chosen parameters in order to prime public consciousness to receive a political message. In contrast to propaganda, used to instill and implement doctrine, any programmatic content "spin" contains is subordinate to "hype," to popularization of a discourse. "Spin" is often a strategy deployed to counter negative popular perception or media campaigns. Since the insurrection in Haiti had initially brought disastrous press coverage in France—as represented by Claire de Duras in the black heroine Ourika's dashed hopes for a renewed social identity in the wake of popular perceptions of atrocities by the blacks in Saint-Domingue[4]—it was important for Haitian Revolutionary leaders to gain some control of their public representation if they were going to work successfully with the French government. Toussaint was particularly gifted in this area. According to one 1796 account, he was literally (re)named for his ability to open conciliatory dialogue: the Revolutionary activist and chronicler Jean-Philippe Garran wrote, "People say that the name *Bréda* was that of the plantation where Toussaint had been a slave, and that he got the name *the Opening* from his facility in creating conciliatory openings."[5]

The time period of the handwritten letters by Toussaint and of his texts in the *Ancien moniteur* and *Gazette de France* involved a particular need for damage control, as it is the era of Toussaint's difficulties with agents sent by the governments of the Directory and the Consulate. (The handwritten texts in effect show the damage, and the dictated media texts, the damage control.) The agents sent by France had to walk the fine line of working with local leaders while also trying to moderate or undermine their political power, because of the obvious potential of this power to blossom into independence from the metropole. Toussaint's communications with the French public give a positive spin to his political and military triumphs over French agents including Léger-Félicité Sonthonax (expelled from Saint-Domingue in August 1797), Gabriel Marie Théodore Joseph d'Hédouville (expelled in October 1798), and Philippe-Rose Roume (imprisoned in Saint-Domingue in November 1800). I will argue that Toussaint counterbalanced the subversive aspects of his pursuit of political autonomy in a colony teetering on the edge of postcoloniality by "spinning" the Haitian Revolution for an Enlightenment audience.

Yet self-representation in the world media by the leaders of a revolution by slaves can appear paradoxical from a pragmatic standpoint. Experience as a consumer of the media would seem to be a prerequisite to being able to "spin" a revolution, and it would also seem plausible that Revolutionary leaders who had been slaves, including Toussaint Louverture, Jean-Jacques Dessalines, and Henri Christophe, unlike such French-educated men of mixed race as Vincent Ogé and Julien Raimond, had no firsthand acquaintance with the French media. But the latter assumption rests on a presumed impermeability of the boundaries between the worlds of black and white, literate and illiterate, uninformed and informed, that the Haitian Revolution contradicts from its earliest moments. Jean Fouchard has made a case that there were literate slaves in Saint-Domingue, who had gained their skills either through earlier Islamization in Africa or through education by clergy, sympathetic members of white households, or other educated slaves.[6] On a related axis, Catherine Reinhardt has argued that just as the "givers" and "recipients" of freedom in emancipatory conflicts cannot be decisively identified, discourses of freedom in the Haitian Revolutionary era are marked by disjunctive and interstitial forms of representation involving a kaleidoscopic array of participants.[7]

Contemporaneous observers also wrestled with the issue of the discursive mechanisms for Haitian Revolutionary events. The legislator Charles Tarbé speculated on the causes and mechanisms of the "révolte des nègres" in his report to the National Assembly of February 29, 1792: "How can we explain this insurrection by fifty thousand negroes, on the same day, at the same moment?"[8] It was triggered and structured not just by "this imperious and innate need to be free," he suggests, but also by local "festivals . . . celebrated in honor of liberty" combined with "the abundance of writings" about the French Revolution that had been circulating for two years in the colony.

This assertion of the combined influence of Revolutionary festivals and media in Saint-Domingue on revolutionary consciousness among slaves is startling. Certainly in France, as Mona Ozouf and others have shown, Revolutionary festivals were choreographed to provide publicly accessible allegories of Revolutionary values, bolstering the elite print culture version of the Revolution with a larger public spectacle. Colonial Revolutionary festivals of whatever scale would have broadened the colonial audience for print messages beyond the demographics of literacy in Saint-Domingue into the "readable spaces" of public life.[9] Tarbé's contentions deserve more historical exploration than I can provide here. There were Revolutionary festivals in Saint-Domingue later in the 1790s, such as the celebration of the anniversary of the French abolition of slavery around a large tree, "l'Arbre de la Liberté."[10] It is also well known that in Saint-Domingue as in France, colonists adopted symbolic costumes to indicate their political allegiances—not only the *pompons rouges* and *pompons blancs* but also, for members of the *"Assemblée generale,"* a scarf of black crepe to serve as "a distinctive sign . . . to remind everyone of the Assembly members' heartfelt pain," and for the competing *"Assemblée du Nord,"* a scarf with red in addition to black, "the image of the blood saturating their territory" (Garran 2:228–29).

The widespread distribution of French Revolutionary propaganda in the colony was noted by numerous observers besides Tarbé. A 1792 report on *L'état actuel de la marine et des colonies* notes that in the months leading up to the August 1791 slave revolt, "There arrived in the Colony a letter by a Constitutional Bishop [the abbé Grégoire], the goal of which was to incite the slaves to rebel, to conquer their liberty. With it came many other incendiary brochures that announced only too clearly what the *habitants* [colonial property owners] had to fear."[11] The gesture by Bonaparte and Leclerc in 1802 of issuing Creole translations of some of their proclamations, despite the fact that anyone who could read would be a speaker of French even if he or she was a speaker of Creole as well, reflects French awareness that that the content of print texts was reaching nonreader audiences. Both Laurent Dubois and Nick Nesbitt have been struck by the resonance of the discovery of pamphlets of the "Declaration of the Rights of Man" in the pocket of an executed Haitian Revolutionary insurgent.[12]

Haitian Revolutionary discourse arguably emerged in intimate dialogue with Revolutionary documents from France. There are intriguing parallels between the symbolic discursive act that accompanied the beginning of the slave insurrection, the "Serment du Bois Caïman" (Oath of the Cayman Woods),[13] and the "Serment du Jeu de paume" in France. Grégoire's June 1791 "Lettre aux Citoyens de couleur et nègres libres de Saint-Domingue" (Letter to citizens of color and free negroes of Saint-Domingue) dramatically asserted that deputies of color from the colonies had taken an oath at the Jeu de Paume to continue their work until a Revolutionary constitution was finished, but were expelled from the Assembly in May of 1791 because of their race. This expulsion represented "an abandonment of principles and a breach of the religion of the oath" on the part of the French, Grégoire argued.[14] Grégoire returned to the terminology of sacred oaths repeatedly in the letter, as in his exhortation for the slaves to "swear with us to live and die by our laws. One day, the sun will illuminate among you free men only" (24).

Colonists were convinced that this text had been highly influential in the slave milieu. The colonist Joseph-Pierre Du Morier wrote, "There are very few Negroes who know how to read; but it is by those few that the texts that stirred rebellion in the workshops of the plains of the Cap were read in the nocturnal assemblies."[15] Dubois concurs that many participants in assemblies leading up to the revolt were effectively delegates, "privileged slaves" (97) such as drivers and *commandeurs* or workshop overseers. These delegates were not only capable of mobilizing large numbers of subordinates, they were at times familiar with the Revolutionary debates raging in colonists' social gatherings.[16] Although it has been well established that the ceremony of the Bois Caïman contains elements similar to some found in West African blood pacts,[17] assessment of the reception of French Revolutionary media suggests that the "Oath's" influences may have well been more syncretic. One overlooked detail which again suggests the importance of Revolutionary models on the slave insurgency is an anonymous memoir by the procurer of the Clément plantation, "Révolution de St. Domingue." This firsthand witness claims that Boukman made a plantation manager from whom he took a cache of weapons on the night of August 22 sign a "déclaration."[18]

Sometimes the dissemination of French Revolutionary media among nonwhite or mixed-race populations of Saint-Domingue was even more direct than letters and articles destined indirectly to a public of slaves: Toussaint himself reportedly subscribed to the French newspapers. In an interview with an anonymous "citizen newly returned from Saint-Domingue" that was published in January 1799 in the *Moniteur,* we learn that "In order to keep abreast of current events, he [Toussaint] contacted a European philanthropist to whom he sent the necessary funds for a subscription to the French newspapers." In addition to his journalistic subscriptions, Toussaint had been coached by a sort of mixed-race political mentor prior to his own definitive engagement with the cause of the slaves: "At that time a man of color, known for his zeal in defending the cause of his brothers, helped Toussaint likewise to conceptualize the project of being a champion of his own."[19]

Certainly a "Toussaint" figures *in* the French media very early on, as a signatory of a lucid and compelling address to the National Assembly dated December 6, 1791, only three and a half months after the beginning of the slave revolt. Tarbé's *Rapport* to the National Assembly presents this document, which closed with the notation "Signé Jean François, *général,* Biassou, *maréchal-de-camp;* Desprez, Mauzeau, Toussaint, et Aubert, *commissaires ad hoc.* Au Camp général de la Grande-Rivière, le 6 décembre 1791" (11). Although there was more than one "Toussaint" active in this historical context, there are several reasons to believe that the Toussaint in question was the one who would become the *ouverture* or opening between demographic factions in the Revolutionary conflict. I will contextualize the operations of political dialogue in the Camp de la Grande-Rivière before returning to the question of Toussaint's role in this document.

General François Kerverseau was one of the contemporary observers (Garran was another) who claimed that Toussaint had initially served as the *secretary* of Georges Biassou in the Revolutionary camp of the Grande-Rivière. In this main insurgent camp, where the imprisoned local colonial official and future chronicler M. Gros was serving as the secretary of Jean-François, Biassou and Jean-François had become the primary leaders after the decapitation of Boukman in mid-November. Like most other colonial historians, Kerverseau was hardly a sympathetic observer, and yet his descriptions allow, as Dubois puts it, insurgent voices to "bleed through" the hegemony of colonial discourse. Kerverseau viewed Toussaint as a "puppet master," pulling the strings of negotiations from behind the "curtain" of his meager role as secretary:

> Toussaint, influenced by his long enslavement and the veritable education it had provided in the areas of flattery and dissimulation, knew how to mask his feelings and conceal his intentions, and was thus an even more terrible instrument *in the hands of the disorganizers.* He was the one who presided over the assembly at which Jean-François, Biassou, and others were chosen as leaders, because their size, strength, and other physical advantages seemed to suit them to a military command role. As for himself, puny and sickly, known to his comrades as *Skinny Stick,* he said he was only too honored by the position of secretary to Biassou. It was from this obscure post to which he had relegated himself that, hidden behind a curtain, he served as puppet master for the whole plot. . . . He knew how to read and write, and he was the only one who did.[20]

Kerverseau fails to contextualize Toussaint's puppet mastery in relation to the many people of color and white prisoners in the camps who did know how to read and write, such as the hostage secretary Gros. At best, Toussaint may have been the only one *among the blacks* in this particular camp who knew how to read and write. But since the blacks were at this point the main force of the insurgency, his position to translate from the inside may indeed have given Toussaint unusual communicative power. Gros himself would claim, "Without the negro Toussaint at Bréda, . . . the conference would have ended in a stalemate."[21] If Toussaint as *"commissaire ad hoc"* was effectively a master of discourse, a spin doctor, in the meetings of the insurgents with the civil commissioners, this would have given him a significant additional layer of training in the language of colonial and Revolutionary politics.

Tarbé contextualizes the address as a response to two important points of legislation passed by the National Assembly in September, news of which had only reached the camp of the slaves via the *commissaires civils* who had arrived from France in the final days of November. The insurgent camps were deeply disappointed by the news that although the king would continue to control the *"exterior regime"* of colonial policies, notably in the area of trade, "laws concerning the state of unfree persons and the political status of men of color and free blacks" (Dubois 125) would be passed within the colonies. On the positive side, the National Assembly had passed an amnesty for those involved in "acts of revolution" (ibid.) both in France and in the colonies. The insurgent document responds to these two points in detail.

With regard to the amnesty, the representatives of the slave camp state that although in the previous months they had been "caught up" in the "great misfortunes" afflicting the colony, they now wished to "cooperate in the future." As concerned the thorny problem of local control of race-based policies, the insurgents proposed that the king's recent acceptance of key revolutionary documents should have jurisdiction in the colonies as well. The document praises the formalized ideals of the French Revolution concerning race (the decree had after all proclaimed that "All men in France, of whatever color, hold full rights of citizenship"[22]) and expresses the slaves' anticipation that these ideals would be applied to the colonies in the near future. It notes that the king's acceptance of the Constitution was officially "for the mother country, which necessitates a regime that is absolutely distinct from that of the Colonies" (Tarbé 7). Yet in the spirit of the king's "paternal solicitude" if not yet in the letter of the law, the spirit of his "feelings of clemency and goodness, which are not laws but heart-felt affection," the speakers in the address believe that the spirit of the Constitution "must cross the sea." They go on to suggest to the Assembly that "it would even be useful for you to declare, . . . that it is your intention to attend to the fate of the slaves" and to make this declaration known promptly to the slaves' "leaders" (10).

The problem with representations of Toussaint as not only a signatory but also an important contributor to this early printed Haitian Revolutionary treaty is that his level of literacy has always been controversial. His status as a hero of the Haitian Revolutionary patrimony no doubt has served as an obstacle to assessment of his linguistic capacities (and furthermore to the establishment of a reliable corpus of the texts he generated), since from the standpoint of a certain Haitian francophilic nationalism, semiliterate writings by Toussaint could be seen as a stain on the honor of his legacy. From other standpoints, the political coming to writing of a former slave is a remarkable phenomenon, the complexities of which should be unveiled. To what degree did Toussaint really have command of spoken and written French?

Documents issued by Toussaint range from those not only transcribed but signed by secretaries, to those transcribed by secretaries but signed by Toussaint personally, to occasional letters written entirely in his own hand. I know of two of the latter kind that date from 1798, along with a handful of letters and letter-like documents that overlap with Toussaint's memoirs, written during his captivity in France in 1802. Given the abundance of Toussaint's dictated communications and his apparent ease in composing the two 1798 and the 1802 documents, it seems likely that other handwritten texts are either scattered in diverse archives, lost or destroyed, or in the hands of private collectors. Even the two handwritten letters I will examine here are not widely known; Dubois notes the importance of Toussaint's correspondence, but qualifies flatly that his "letters were not written by his own hand" (173).

The handwritten letters answer the question of Toussaint's particular French abilities in direct self-expression (although not the separate question of his French abilities in the dialogic process of dictating and editing the formulations of secretaries, which I will address later). However, because of their nonpublic nature, they are not entirely typical of Toussaint's public relations statements. After the address line of the first letter in question, Toussaint writes *"nallant et venant"* (while coming and going), which presumably meant that he was on the road (where perhaps he lacked a secretary), although the sensitive nature of the correspondence itself might also have justified not using a secretary.

This letter is an epistle of invective dated simply from year six of the revolution, on Toussaint's official stationery, addressed to the "general and agent of the Directory in Saint-Domingue," who, although unnamed, is most likely Hédouville. The unusual quality of the language in the letter is only rarely inspired by Creole structures. The most strikingly "foreign" quality of Toussaint's writing, which is not at a first glance comprehensible to a francophone reader, in fact derives from nothing more "foreign" than his phonetic orthography, relatively arbitrary punctuation, and unconventional syllabic separations of words. Toussaint had in effect learned enough French, and enough writing, to create his own linguistic system for transcribing the complex political and military discourses of his environment.

The letter, marked by a strong reliance on repeated figures of speech, expresses righteous outrage and personalized conflict. As noted above, Hédouville was one of several agents sent by France with whom Toussaint entered into conflict over issues of political influence and jurisdiction. The Directory, briefly under the power of the former colonist Viennot de Vaublanc, had essentially sent Hédouville to limit Toussaint's power. Not only Hédouville but his subordinates, whom Toussaint mentions in the letter, were openly careless in their dealings with Toussaint despite his preeminence in the colony.

Dubois summarizes the dynamics of Toussaint's resentment: "He [Toussaint] had reason to be angry with the French Government, which had sent a man with no colonial experience, surrounded by a racist entourage, to give him orders" (219). In the letter, Toussaint depicts the Citizen Agent as an enemy of the republic and of men, but this general man, ambitious and concerned for his own interests, yet honorable, also seems to represent Toussaint himself. According to Toussaint, the Citizen Agent is a master of "passing" in the sense of making a thing pass for its opposite, and this pattern of misrepresentation causes Toussaint pain. Here is a transcription and a translation of figure 1 (in the translation of which I have tried to avoid both the historical trend of editing Toussaint's utterances beyond recognition, and such literalism that the meaning remains obscure):

> Enmi de la chose publique, Enmi de lordre et la tranquilité, de homme pour leur in te ré par ticulier, de homme, an biseiux. veut fer pa cé lé mal pour le bien, et le bien pour le mal, on faite, pa cé les tenebre pour la lu mier, et la lu mier, pour les tenebre. Il veut que ce qui et dous soi amer, et que ceu qui et a mer soi dous, il et dous leureux pour de homme don neur, trété de la sorte, conte Citoyen a gent, sur Toussaint louverture et sa pa rolle.[23]

> [The enemy of the public thing [the republic], enemy of order and tranquility, of men for their particular interest, of ambitious men, wants to make evil pass for good, and good pass for evil, in fact he passes darkness for light, and light for darkness; he wants what is sweet to be bitter, and what is bitter to be sweet. It is painful for men of honor to be treated in this way. You may count, Citizen Agent, on Toussaint Louverture and his word.]

Toussaint's metaphor of political pain and his use of a quasi-medical spiritual discourse is characteristic of a broad array of his communications. Through figures of pain and healing, he conveys a vivid psychological and physical political subject, even though here he is not just the pained subject, but also the doctor threatening to excise the pathology at its source:

> Les remed pallia tife né fon que fla té le mal. et il fau la lé a la source, pour le guérire, comme vous ne conné ce pa la colonni. je crin con vous de tourne de

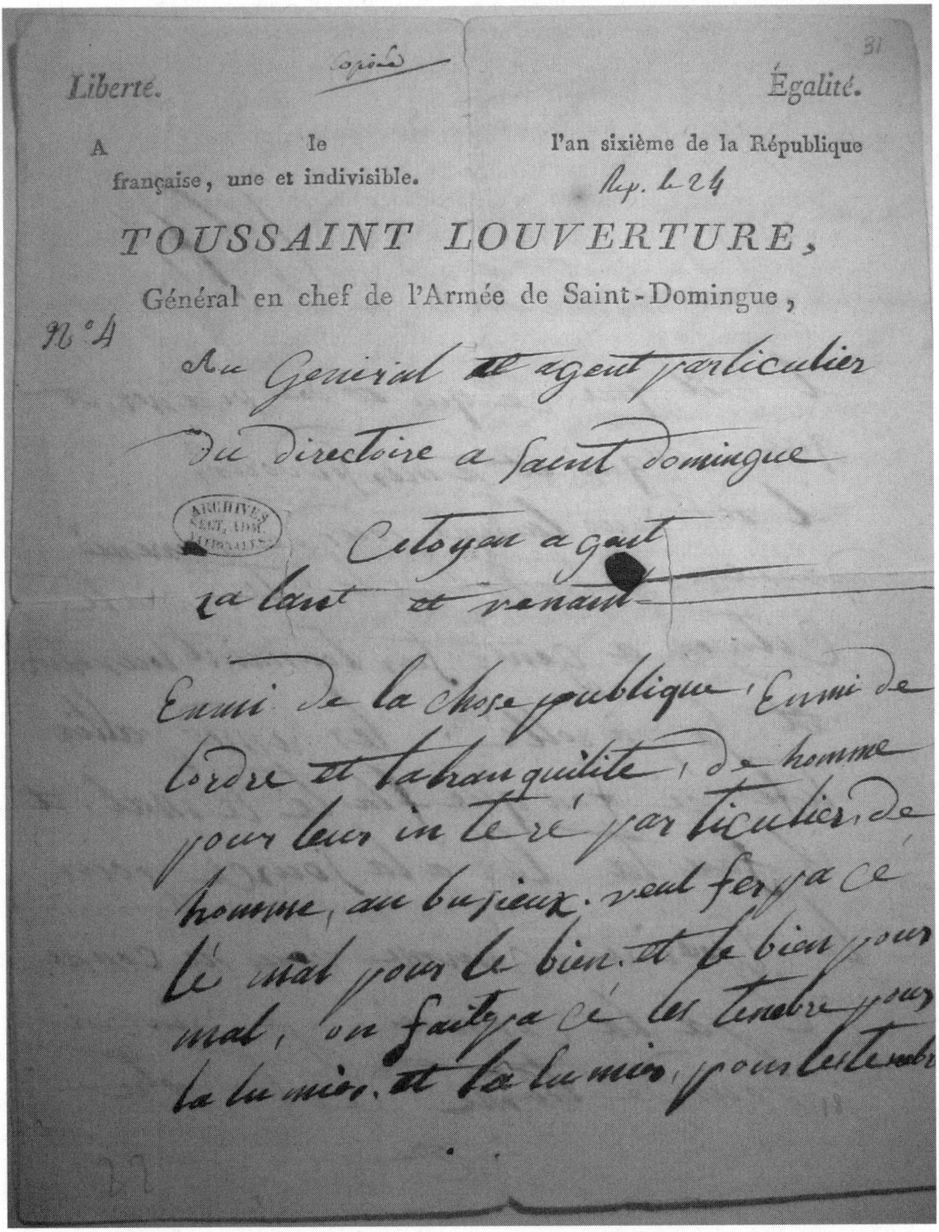

Fig. 1. Letter from Toussaint Louverture to the general and agent of the Directory in Saint-Domingue, Year Six. (Document preserved at the Centre historique des Archives nationales, Paris, AF III 209)

tou votre Bonne in tan tion pour le bien de la republique, et an coura gé vos
subordonné qui périron mille foi pour les salut de la colonni, et les xecution
de zordre du directoire quil nou ce ra trans metre par vous,

> Salut et respec,
> Toussaint Louverture

[Palliative remedies only flatter the pathology, and one must get to the source
to heal it. As you do not know the colony, I fear that you are being diverted
from all your good intentions with regards to the well being of the republic,
and are encouraging your subordinates who will perish a thousand times for
the colony and the execution of the orders of the Directory that will be trans-
mitted to us by you,

> Salutations and respect,
> Toussaint Louverture]

This discourse of wounding and healing would reappear in one of the
final texts handwritten by Toussaint during his imprisonment in the Fort
de Joux, in which he describes Napoléon, ironically enough, as the doctor capable of healing the wounds of Toussaint's rupture with France:
"Gairice mes plai illé tre profound, vous seul pouvé porter les remède
saluter et lanpéché de ne jamai ouvrir, vous sète médecin."[24] (Heal my
wounds it is very deep, you alone can apply healthful remedies and prevent it from ever opening, you are a doctor.)

Another handwritten letter (see fig. 2) dates from this same period
and conflict. It is addressed to the black general Dessalines, who in
1804 would become the leader of independent Haiti. This letter has a
telegraphic military urgency: it makes no attempt to persuade or dramatize. It is surprising that in a personal letter to a close associate on
military matters, Toussaint chose to communicate in his nonstandard
French—presumably at the risk of being misunderstood—rather than in
Creole. Since his instructions were followed and the Haitian generals pre-
vailed, however, we can assume that Dessalines was in fact familiar with
Toussaint's particular discourse and had no trouble understanding it.

In the letter, written in October of 1798, Toussaint addresses Dessalines
as "Commandant an chef de la vile de St mar et de pandance" (Commander in chief of the city of Saint Marc and its dependencies), a reference to their triumph over the British in Saint Marc earlier in 1798.
The elimination of the French/British conflict brought tensions between
the French and the local army to a head. The letter concerns Toussaint's
adoptive nephew, the general Moyse, who was in charge of Fort-Liberté

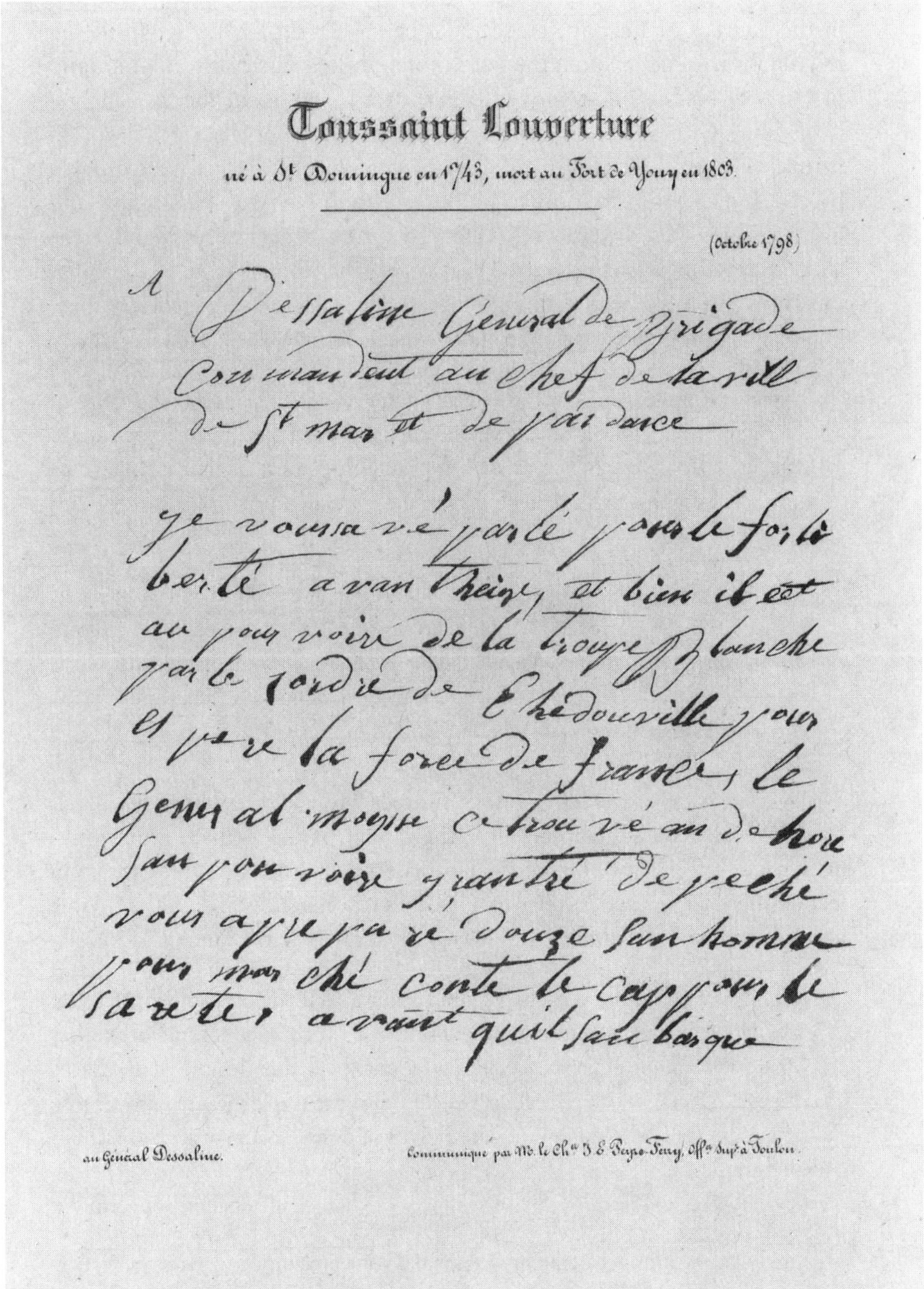

# Toussaint Louverture

né à St Domingue en 1743, mort au Fort de Youy en 1803.

(Octobre 1798)

A Dessaline Général de Brigade
Commandant au Chef de la ville
de St mar et de yacdance

je vousa vé parlé pour le fort le
berté avan theiry et bien il est
au pour voir de la troupe blanche
par le (ordu de Chédouville pour
et vé la force de france, le
Genral moyise ce trouvé au dehou
san pouvoir y rantré de peché
vous a yu pa vé douze sun homme
pour mon ché conte le cap pour le
sareté, avant quil san barque

au Général Dessaline.          Communiqué par Mr le Chr J E Payso-Ferry, offr sup à Toulon.

Fig. 2. Letter from Toussaint Louverture to General Dessalines, October 1798.
(Autograph File, T. Houghton Library, Harvard College Library)

in the vicinity of Le Cap. Hédouville believed that Moyse was rallying the blacks to rebel against the conditions of their agricultural labor, and in October Hédouville removed Moyse from his post at the fort and replaced him with a local black official. Moyse called on Toussaint, who in turn summoned Dessalines and Christophe, and the French were quickly routed. On October 23, only five months after his arrival, Hédouville and his associates were forcibly re-embarked for France. (Interestingly, in the letter Toussaint seems intent on preventing the French from embarking, but this may have been a preliminary strategy to first seize their papers and garner intelligence prior to their expulsion.)

> Je voussa vé parlé pour le for liberté a van theiye, et bien il est au pour voire de la troupe Blanche par le zordre de Hedouville pour li pere la force de france, le general Moyse ce trou vé an de hore san pou voire y rantre de peché vous a pre pa ré douze san homme pour mar ché conte le cap pour le sa rete, avant quil san barque.[25]

> [I had spoken to you concerning the Fort Liberty the day before yesterday. Well, it is in the power of the white troops, on the orders of Hédouville to liberate the French forces. General Moyse found himself outside [the fort] without being able to get in. Hurry up and prepare twelve hundred men to march against Le Cap to stop them, before they embark.]

The second page of the letter refers indirectly to the fact that many black soldiers had been sent home after the defeat of the British, and would now need to be remobilized. It also orders Dessalines to treat the new leadership of the fort in terms that eerily foreshadow Toussaint's later handwritten complaints about his own kidnapping to France in 1802.[26]

> Au ci tau re su ma letre prene vo pré cotion a re te le commandement de la place fete le metre an suite san pouvoire par le avec qui ce soi prendre tou ce papier quel conque et fer me sa me son fer metre cet fami de hore, fete pase les ce lé par le conmiser de pourvoire Executif prandre tou le mesure nese ser a ce suget requi tous le solda qui on te te ranvoyer, donné meme ordre a Chalb[27]
> Salut amities
>
>                                        Toussaint Louverture

> [Immediately upon receiving my letter take your precautions, arrest the leadership of the place, have him then put without being able to talk to anyone at all, take all his papers of whatever kind, and close his house, have this family put out. Send the sealed documents to the Commissioner of Executive Powers,

take all the necessary measures on this point, summon all the soldiers who were sent away, give these same orders to Chalb.

Salutations, friendship,

Toussaint Louverture]

The closing, *"amitiés"* (friendship), is a unique departure from Toussaint's usual formalities, and gives a glimpse of the register of personal relationships among the black revolutionary leadership.

When Toussaint dictated his letters to secretaries, he apparently gained considerable expressive benefits from the processes of dialogue and revision that were involved. The most satisfying account of the mechanisms of Toussaint's transcribed correspondence is in M. E. Descourtilz's 1809 *Voyages d'un naturaliste,* which describes the Revolutionary leader's genius in dictating and editing messages via his secretaries. Descourtilz, who had been taken prisoner by the Haitian army, recounts the scene of writing:

> I saw him in few words verbally lay out the summary of his addresses, rework the poorly conceived, poorly executed sentences; confront several secretaries presenting their work by turns; redo the ineffective sections; transpose parts to place them to better effect; making himself worthy, all in all, of the natural genius foretold by Raynal.[28]

Descourtilz's description of Toussaint's redactive talents is especially interesting because it documents a composite writing process based on Toussaint's mastery not only of dictation, but also of the transcription and production of texts by numerous secretaries. Descourtilz also claims that Toussaint was committed to the use of French rather than Creole: "I was very poorly received one day when I tried to speak the patois of the country with him, because he only used it to harangue the workshops or his soldiers" (3:251). This contrasts with Dessalines' ideas of the politics of language, a contrast that reflects the individual dynamism of linguistic and rhetorical strategies among Haitian Revolutionary leaders. Descourtilz recounts that Dessalines foreswore the use of French after Napoléon's armies had landed in 1802, in a conscious appropriation of the local discourse and a rejection of colonial semiotics:

> Dessalines, when he began openly to articulate his opposition to the expeditionary army, avoided and detested their very idiom; this is why he chided very severely the son of a landowner from Gonaïves, who, even though he was a Creole from Saint-Domingue, got it into his head to speak French: "You have

a language of your own," he said with a scathing look, "why seek to have others instead?" (3:281)

Toussaint's "writing" method on a certain level parallels that of Napoléon, who was also known for his skill in issuing statements through secretaries, yet it also points to a singularity of media representations in the Haitian Revolutionary context. In both their production and their reception, Haitian media representations are partly verbal and partly "print," partly individual and partly collective. Written texts in the Haitian Revolutionary context, from the address from the Camp de la Grande-Rivière to Napoléon's Creole proclamations to Toussaint's letters, bridge gaps of language, literacy, nation, and social status.

These obliquely generated letters, proclamations, and addresses *were* the stuff of media reporting in that era. Rather than a journalist's byline, articles on international matters were often preceded by oblique notations such as "Le gouvernement a reçu officiellement, sur la situation des Colonies, des nouvelles intéressantes" (The government has officially received interesting news concerning the situation in the colonies). An individual, like Toussaint writing to the Directory, or a group, such as the Camp de la Grande-Rivière writing to the Assemblée, would issue statements, and these statements were, at the will of the government and the media, disseminated as news. This chain of media communication is so indeterminate in terms of author, audience, and writing technology, that it resembles Freud's description of the unconscious as a "mystic writing pad," except that here the "unconscious" is the oblique, conflictual space between Revolutionary slaves, Revolutionary masters, and the secretaries that connected them.

The journalistic element of political correspondence in this time period reveals its unusual communicative power: letters and proclamations published in the press had the power to mold public opinion. They should, as such, be categorized in the company of political writings normally seen as more "public" and "permanent" by the print audiences of modernity, notably political essays, or political letters in anthologized form.

Yet the mediation bridging Toussaint's speech acts and the polished French texts that represent him to us of course leaves open the possibility that his secretaries were responsible for some of the content as well as the form of his formal communications. This is precisely the claim made by Jules Michelet's young wife, Athenaïs Mialaret, whose father allegedly had served as Toussaint's secretary during the Revolution. She asserted in her autobiographical preface to Michelet's combined naturalist and biographical meditation *L'Oiseau* that during the Revolution her father had helped to articulate Toussaint's thought. As yet, no basis has been found to either prove or disprove her contention, but it indicates the vulnerability of Toussaint's verbal legacy to appropriation. It furthermore suggests that Romantic writers may have seen Toussaint as a Romantic character written by history, speaking lines that they would like to have articulated for him.

> [My father] found himself in the great crisis of Toussaint Louverture's reign. This extraordinary man, who had been a slave until the age of fifty, who felt and divined everything, did not know how to write or formulate his thoughts. His was the domain of great acts rather than words. He needed a hand, a pen, and more: a young and bold heart to provide the heroic language for the hero, the words for the situation. At his age, did Toussaint come up with the noble formula *The first of the blacks to the first of the whites* on his own? I would doubt it. Or at least if he did come up with it, it was my father who wrote it.[29]

Yet even in speech acts divided between speaker and writer, Toussaint had a very distinctive style that counters such a suggestion that there were colonial "puppet masters" (to return to Kerverseau's trope) speaking for Toussaint. Even the ambiguities and ironies of his statements and alliances recur sufficiently throughout the years of his generation of texts to be encodable as "authentic." The singularity of his voice calls into question strict associations of authorship with the individual print genesis of texts, since he is arguably very much the author of his dictated writings.

In the years between the defeat of the Spanish in Santo Domingo in 1795 and the beginning of the Napoleonic military expedition of 1802, Toussaint engaged very actively in representing his cause. He consistently invested a simultaneously emotional and philosophical tone in his official communications. An issue of the *Moniteur* from January 1797 notes that the government had received "Une première lettre du général Toussaint Louverture, . . . [qui] annonce que la France peut compter sur l'armée de Saint-Domingue qu'il commande" (111). (A first letter from general Toussaint Louverture . . . [which] announces that France can count on the army of Saint-Domingue under his command.) In the letter itself, Toussaint praises the French for their benevolent emancipatory acts and implies that the slaves who have been glorified as men rather than objects will behave only to the credit of France: "Jamais la France ne se repentira d'avoir rendu libres des hommes qui se glorifient d'un titre qui les honore, et qui fait leur bonheur" (112). (France will never repent of having freed the men who justifiably revel in a title that honors them and constitutes all their happiness.) Toussaint clearly knew how to flatter his audience; freedom in Saint-Domingue is presented as an abolitionist gift, rather than a self-emancipation wrenched from tyranny. In a second letter, Toussaint claims that the courage born of the slaves' new liberty will inevitably overcome the English enemies of France: "Nous ne tarderons pas à faire sentir aux Anglais ce que peut le courage né de la liberté." (We will not delay in making the English feel the brunt of a courage born of liberty.) The French emancipation of the slaves is presented as an affective investment that will be rewarded with fidelity, just as the slaves' freedom is such an edifying, transformational experience that all their actions will be cast in the image of its glory. As is evident in the above quotes, Toussaint's speech style is emotional, welding, as he noted in an address to the people of Saint-Domingue, "les principes et les sentiments"[30] (principles and feelings).

In January of 1798, the *Moniteur* published a long letter from Toussaint in which he forcefully rebuts an injurious report by the former colonist Vaublanc on the trustworthiness of the black army:

> Rendez auprès du Directoire combien est grande l'affliction que m'a causée le rapport de Vaublanc, relativement aux noirs; . . . quelle injustice! quelle fausseté! . . . quel coup de foudre pour un coeur sensible comme le mien, qui aime ses frères et met tout en usage pour les rendre dignes des bienfaits que la France leur a accordés par son immuable decret! (134)

> [Convey to the Directory the great affliction that Vaublanc's report concerning the blacks has caused me; . . . what injustice! What falsity! . . . What a thunderbolt for a sensitive heart like mine, for one who loves his brothers and does everything possible to make them worthy of the benefits that France has granted them through her immutable decree!]

Toussaint is careful to include all of France as the addressee of his message: "Déclarez de ma part à la France entière, que si elle se montra protectrice de l'humanité souffrante et abandonée, elle n'aura jamais lieu de se repentir de ses bienfaits." (Declare to all of France on my behalf that if she will show herself to be the protector of suffering and abandoned humanity, she will never have reason to repent of her good deeds.) Although he uses metaphors of fraternity to refer to the blacks, his tone casts the French nation and its representatives almost as a parent-saviour, and the inhabitants of Haiti as children. The slaves were "suffering humanity," now "restored to themselves." Toussaint makes himself the personal guarantor of the blacks' future virtuous behavior: "Dites-leur que je me rends leur caution." (Tell them that I will be their guarantee.) Toussaint's "spin" on the Haitian Revolution is ideologically oblique. It foreshadows what Françoise Vergès calls the "colonial family romance" created through French Republican colonial rhetoric,[31] and yet Toussaint is not only participating in the construction of this discourse, he is also using it to camouflage his own political autonomy in relation to the agents sent by France.

In effect, whereas Lamartine would be criticized for his 1850 play *Toussaint Louverture* for seeming to put a Lamartinian discourse into the mouths of the former slaves,[32] Toussaint himself spoke like Lamartine *avant la lettre*. (Following the troping of Toussaint as the *"Napoléon noir,"* perhaps we should actually call him the *Lamartine noir;* or perhaps we should call Lamartine the *Toussaint blanc*.) Toussaint arguably figures in the ranks of the French or francophone pre-Romantics, including Bernardin de Saint-Pierre and Rousseau, who graft subjectivity and *citoyenneté* together. This Enlightenment discourse provided preconditioning for Romantic conceptions of the political self.

French readers were apparently attracted to this passionate and sensitive voice wooing their sense of justice, compassion, or fidelity. Toussaint's letters in the press were quoted at length or in their entirety, as news stories. Sonthonax's own access to the press after he was compelled to return to France provides a telling contrast. In February of 1798, the register of the *"Conseil des cinq cents"* in the *"corps legislative"* notes in the *Moniteur* that when Sonthonax requested the chance to defend himself verbally against Toussaint's accusations, his plea was initially turned down. Only after two members had pointed out that "Sonthonax being a representative of the people, the Council cannot very well refuse him the opportunity to defend himself against the grave claims that have been made" (146), was he allowed to proceed. This triumph over his apparently hostile audience gained him little media attention, however, as the remainder of the article reads, in its entirety: "Sonthonax has the floor; he enters into all the details relative to his mission."

In April of 1799, the *Moniteur* printed a letter from Toussaint in which he referred to his difficulties with the agents sent by France with metaphors of stormy horizons and clear dawns: "Enfin, après les orages qui ont obscurci notre horizon politique dans les derniers jours . . . , l'aurore a relui pour le peuple de Saint-Domingue" (638). (At last, after the storms that have darkened our political horizon in recent days . . .

light has dawned again for the people of Saint-Domingue.) He says that once he has ensured the happiness of the inhabitants of the colony and the triumph of France, he will be able to die happy, "et mon dernier soupir sera une expression de reconnaissance pour la République, comme mes derniers regards se tourneront vers elle." (And my last breath will be an expression of gratitude for the Republic, just as my last look will be to her.)

Toussaint "spun" the Haitian Revolution with great rhetorical and strategic power, counterbalancing and at times overwhelming the narratives of French leaders stationed in Saint-Domingue, such as Sonthonax. This capacity for self-representation on the part of "suffering humanity" was in itself a revolutionary discovery for the bourgeois European reading public. What remains to be integrated into our cultural understanding is how, in the midst of our cult of the *droits d'auteur*, of originality in print culture, a distinctive and revolutionary voice can make itself heard in a hybrid, collaborative, even collaborationist, medium—as "news." Produced by authors characterized by linguistic difference and partial literacy, through transcription and cross-cultural negotiation, it was received by readers characterized by deficits in reading problems of human equality. Toussaint's engagement in trans-Atlantic political dialogue would decisively exceed the limitations on discursive self-representation by nonwhites in colonialism as enforced by slavery and racialist social hierarchy, creating a discursive "opening" parallel to the historical "opening" of the Haitian Independence.

## Notes

Because this essay analyzes Toussaint Louverture's literacy and writing style in public and private correspondence, quotations from Louverture are given in the original French as well as in English translation. All translations are mine unless otherwise noted.

1. Susan Buck-Morss, "Hegel and Haiti," 838. Further references to this and all other works cited more than once will be made parenthetically in the text.

2. *Journal des débats et loix [sic] du pouvoir legislative et des actes du gouvernement*, 7 August 1804.

3. Benjamin Constant, *Journaux intimes*, 123.

4. See Claire de Duras, *Ourika* (MLA edition, 1994), 20.

5. J.-Ph. Garran, *Rapport sur les troubles de Saint-Domingue*, 2:313.

6. See Jean Fouchard, *Les Marrons du syllabaire*.

7. Catherine Reinhardt, "French Caribbean Slaves Forge Their Own Ideal of Liberty in 1789."

8. Charles Tarbé, "Rapport sur les troubles de Saint-Domingue," 25.

9. See Roger Chartier, *Lectures et lecteurs dans la France d'Ancien régime.*

10. Agent Roume, "Discours," 16 Pluviôse An 7 [February 5, 1798] (Port-Républicain: Gauchet et Co., 1798), 1.

11. J. A. Le Brasseur, *De l'etat actuel,*31.

12. See Laurent Dubois, *Avengers of the New World,* 105; and Nick Nesbitt, "The Idea of 1804," 29.

13. See David Geggus for an assessment of current historical research on the Oath, *Haitian Revolutionary Studies,* 81–92.

14. The text I consulted for Grégoire's letter is a colonial denunciation of it, providing a colonist's vituperative gloss and the original text in side-by-side columns. Anonymous, *Dénonciation de M. l'Abbé Grégoire et de sa LETTRE du 8 Juin 1791, adressé aux Citoyens de couleur et nègres libres de Saint-Domingue, et des autres Isles Françaises de l'Amérique, etc.* (Paris: Au Bureau de la feuille du jour, 1791) 18–19.

15. Joseph-Pierre Du Morier, *Sur les Troubles des colonies,* 37.

16. H. Pauleus-Sannon's three-volume classic, *Histoire de Toussaint Louverture,* 1:203.

17. See Robin Law, "La Cérémonie du Bois Caïman et le 'pacte de sang' dahoméen," 131–47.

18. Anonymous manuscript, "Révolution de St. Domingue, Contenant tout ce qui s'est passé dans la colonie française depuis le commencement de la revolution jusques au depart de l'auteur pour France," October 1792, contained in the *Notes historiques de Moreau de Saint-Méry,* Archives d'Outre-mer, F3 141, 203: "Le 22 aout à onze heures du soir, le nègre Bougman cocher de l'habitation Clement dont j'étais procureur, a la tête de quelques nègres venus du Limbé et d'autres du quartier de l'Acul va sur l'habitation . . . s'empare des armes du citoyen Tutheil, charpentier et gérant de cette habitation et après s'être contenté de lui faire signer une Déclaration à sa guise, il l'emmène avec lui." (On August 22 at eleven o'clock at night, the negro Bougman, the coachman on the Clément property where I worked as the steward, arrived at the head of a group of perhaps twenty negroes from Limbé and other parts of the Acul region . . . seized the weapons of Citizen Tutheil, who worked as the carpenter and manager of the property, and after asking him only to sign a Declaration of sorts, brought him along with him.) There is unfortunately no further mention of this mysterious declaration brought by Boukman on the opening night of the slave insurgency.

19. *Réimpression de l'Ancien moniteur, seule histoire authentique et inaltérée de la Révolution française depuis la réunion des Etats-généraux jusqu'au Consulat* (Paris: Plon, 1854) nivose an VII [January 1799], 585 bis.

20. Kerverseau's statement is cited in Beaubrun Ardouin, *Études sur l'histoire d'Haïti,* 51.

21. Cited in Pierre Pluchon, *Toussaint Louverture,* 73.

22. *Loi portant que tout homme est libre en France, et que, quelleque soit*

*sa couleur, il y jouit de tous les droits de Citoyen, s'il a les qualités préscrites par la Constitution, donnée à Paris, le 16 Octobre 1791,* based on the "Décret de l'Assemblée nationale, du 28 septembre 1791" (Paris: De l'imprimerie royale, 1791), 2.

23. *"La chose publique"* (the public thing) may be a learned echo of *"res publica"* (republic). Toussaint Louverture, Letter to the "general and agent of the Directory in Saint-Domingue," Year Six, Archives nationales de Paris, AF III 209, 31.

24. Toussaint Louverture, handwritten postscriptum to his memoirs, Archives nationales de Paris AF IV 1213, 28.

25. Pierre Dominique Louverture to General Dessaline [*sic*] [in facsimile], October 1798. Autograph File, T. Houghton Library, Harvard College Library.

26. See the discussion of Toussaint's handwritten 1802 texts in my article "From the Kidnapping(s) of the Louvertures to the Alleged Kidnapping of Aristide."

27. "Chalb" most likely should be read as "Charles B," the Haitian general Charles Belair.

28. M. E. Descourtilz, *Voyages d'un naturaliste à Saint-Domingue,* 3:245–46.

29. Jules Michelet, *L'Oiseau,* xx.

30. Toussaint Louverture, letter to the inhabitants of Saint-Domingue concerning the execution of Moyse, le 5 frimaire, an X [16 November 1801], *Journal du soir, Courrier de la République française,* feuille du 30 pluviose an X [30 February 1802], n. 717, no pagination.

31. See Françoise Vergès, *Monsters and Revolutionaries.*

32. Léon-François Hoffmann cites the anonymous critique of the play in the *Bibliothèque universelle de Genève:* "L'auteur paraît ne pas s'être le moins du monde inquiété de la couleur de ses personnages, il l'a complètement abandonnée au teinturier du théâtre. Ses personnages, en effet, ont beau avoir la peau noire, ils parlent tous le langage de *Jocelyn* et des *Méditations.*" (The author seems not to have concerned himself in the slightest with his characters' color, delegating this question entirely to the costume designer. His charactres may have had black skin, but they all spoke the language of *Jocelyn* and the *Meditations.*) See Hoffmann, "Introduction," *Toussaint Louverture,* xix.

# "Légitime Défense"

## Universalism and Nationalism in the Discourse of the Haitian Revolution

### Doris L. Garraway

IT IS NOW commonplace for scholars to lament, after Michel-Rolph Trouillot, the profound silence that has surrounded the Haitian Revolution in Western humanities discourse over the past two centuries, a silence Trouillot attributes in large part to the persistence in French and American historiography of formulas of denial, erasure, and banalization that relegated the Haitian Revolution to the realm of the "unthinkable" in late eighteenth-century Europe. Trouillot contends that, unable or unwilling to imagine that slaves had the capacity to mount an organized insurrection, let alone that such an uprising could lead to the creation of an independent state, whites in Europe and the Americas forced events in Saint-Domingue to conform to their colonialist worldview, thus denying their revolutionary significance.[1] Although important scholarship in historical and literary studies has begun to reverse this trend, what is remarkable is the relative obscurity of the Haitian Revolution in the field of inquiry that has emerged in the recent decades precisely to revoke the silence in humanities scholarship around the impact of colonial power relations and discourse on European knowledge and cultural production, postcolonial theory. A close examination of many of the most influential theoretical texts and reference books in the field reveals few mentions of Haiti, or its revolution.[2] In the rare instances where we do find references to Haiti or to the best-known Haitian revolutionary hero, Toussaint Louverture, a pattern emerges that is uncannily similar to the strategies of denial documented by Trouillot; notably, the Haitian Revolution is inscribed under the figure of repetition and subordinated to the French Revolution, seen as the original signifier of the modern political values of human liberty, equality, and natural right.

In his essay "Race, Time, and the Revision of Modernity," Homi Bhabha evokes the Haitian Revolution in order to challenge Michel Foucault's conception of the spatial dimension of the "sign of modernity," or the French Revolution, the decipherment of which, Bhaba suggests, introduces a "time-lag" into the contemporaneity of modernity itself. For Bhabha, Foucault's formulation ignores the extent to which spatialization may profoundly affect the ways in which modernity is experienced in various locations, thus creating the conditions in which the reception of the event is also the site of the event's undoing, or of its resignification. Turning to C. L. R. James's *The Black Jacobins*, Bhabha asks, "what do we make of the figure of Toussaint . . . at the moment when he grasps the tragic lesson that the moral, modern disposition of mankind, enshrined in the sign of the Revolution, only fuels the archaic racial factor in the society of slavery?"[3] While drawing attention to the ways in which the putatively universalist values of the French Revolution were initially subordinated to the interests of colonial capital, Bhabha's reading of James presents Toussaint as a mere spectator in the tragic unfolding of a modernity that begins elsewhere and whose colonial iteration necessarily bespeaks continued racial oppression, rather than as an actor in the drama of modernity who, more than any of his French contemporaries, contributed to defining and defending the ideal of universal freedom. Even when explicitly raising the question of "subaltern agency" in "the translation of modernity," Bhabha evokes Saint-Domingue as illustrative of a "contra-modernity," in which "progress is only heard (of) and not 'seen,'" a formula that ignores the slaves' profound response to the partial iteration of modernity on the colonial margins. There may be theoretical reasons for Bhabha's insistence that the spatialized reception of modernity on the margins enables the reinforcement of archaic forms of racial and aristocratic privilege. But by eliding the agency of Toussaint and the slaves of Saint-Domingue, Bhabha misrecognizes the potential of spatialization to result in a more radical modernity insofar as the resistance of the enslaved exposes the hypocrisy of European Enlightenment and forces a new understanding of its ideals of freedom and citizenship.

A similar occlusion occurs in Robert Young's magisterial *Postcolonialism: An Historical Introduction*, which surveys the major instances of European colonialism and imperialism, and the liberation movements that opposed them throughout the world. Whereas the author devotes almost half of the book to a historical and ideological analysis of the "theoretical practices" of anticolonial freedom struggles in Africa, Algeria, Ireland, India, China, and Latin America, the only mention of the movement in Saint-Domingue, arguably the first of these, appears in a chapter on *European* anticolonialism. There, events in Saint-Domingue are presented as "a slave revolt" that compelled the French National Assembly to "liberate its colonies," thus realizing what Young considers to be the assimilationist "anti-colonialism" of political radicals such as Brissot and Condorcet.[4] Errors of fact aside (critics such as the late Michèle Duchet would eagerly contest the claim that any of the Enlightenment philosophers were uncompromisingly opposed to colonialism), this depiction empties the struggle in Saint-Domingue of any significance as an anticolonial revolution. The effect is to silence the revolutionary birth of Haiti and to attribute anticolonial agency there exclusively to the French Revolution and to the European Enlightenment establishment.[5] That these forms of unconscious erasure persist in postcolonial theory is especially ironic given that it was Aimé Césaire, one of the most influential critics of colonialism of the twentieth century who, in his historical essay on Toussaint Louverture, condemned what he considered to be the "absurd" error of treating the revolution in Saint-Domingue merely as a chapter of the French Revolution, arguing instead for its significance as a revolution in itself: "It is absolutely necessary that we understand that there is no 'French Revolution' in the French colonies. There is in each colony a specific revolution, born on the occasion of the French Revolution, connected to it, but unfolding according to its own laws and with its own objectives."[6]

Critics of postcolonial theory have long noted its selective attention to modern British and French imperialism in Africa and South Asia, and its frequent elision of the early modern phase of Spanish and European colonialism in the Americas from its purview.[7] A further reason for the erasure of the Haitian Revolution by postcolonial theory may be found in its poststructuralist orientation, which accounts for the field's critical view of Western humanism, Enlightenment universalism, and the anti-imperialist thought that drew from these traditions, such as is apparent in much Haitian Revolutionary discourse.[8] Yet I would like to suggest that one of the most compelling reasons why postcolonial studies has not dealt fully with the Haitian Revolution has to do with the limitations of categories of nationalism through which scholars typically characterize modern anticolonial movements, categories that cannot fully account for the Haitian case. Especially influential here has been the work of Benedict Anderson, notably his contention that far from being an original European product, nationalism was an invention of the colonial world in its move to break away from the colonial powers.[9] Whereas one might expect the second postcolonial nation-state in the Western hemisphere to be referenced in Anderson's historical typology of nationalisms, it is not, and neither is it assimilable to any of the models he studies at length. While on one hand, Haiti does not fit the paradigm of the Creole nationalisms in the United States and Latin America, where mostly white minorities gained independence from the colonial powers while exhibiting a kind of frontier nativism, even as they retained European cultural values and a white supremacist social order, neither does the Haitian Revolution display the kinds of cultural nationalisms that characterized anti-imperialist struggles in India and Africa, where colonized peoples infused their claims to sovereignty with nostalgic professions of their cultural, linguistic, and historical origins and difference from Europe. Although scholars differ on the extent to which anticolonial nationalisms were mimetic or derivative with respect to European models,[10] the prevailing assumption in postcolonial studies has been that nationalism is the sine qua non of anticolonial revolution. This assumption goes along with some equally prevalent ideas in classical theories of nationalism, which tend to favor its European manifestation; notably, the idea that nationalism is essentially "modern," and accompanied the attempt to actualize politically the modern ideals of liberty and progress through the creation of nation-states.[11] As Étienne Balibar puts it, "everywhere that nations exist nationalism reigns."[12]

There are obvious reasons why the case of Haiti defies these assumptions about the putatively nationalist basis of anticolonial resistance. On one hand, the fact that in 1791 more than two-thirds of the slaves in Saint-Domingue were African born, and of various national and ethnic origins, would seem to preclude the possibility of any specifically cultural nationalist claim being at the root of the independence movement, even a local Creole one. Moreover, since in the latter phase of the Revolution the ex-slaves were fighting for independence as the only way to secure their freedom, their demands were largely rooted in abstract principles of human liberty and natural right. Yet, to dismiss entirely the question of nationalism from consideration of Haitian Revolutionary discourse would be to ignore one of the most fascinating conundrums of the Revolution. Whereas in Europe, nationalism has arguably been the ironic condition for the dissemination of "universal" rights through the creation of nation-states which ensure for their citizens the defense and guarantee of those rights, the Haitian Revolution raises the question as to the extent to which universalism itself—notably, the demand for universal liberty—can become a nationalist discourse, or can form the theoretical basis of an independence movement.

In some sense, this question had already been raised by the French Revolution, in which for the first time in French history, the idea of the "nation" rose to near sacred levels of adoration and respect, arguably replacing divinity and the absolute sovereign in the collective imagination, yet where the feeling of nation-ness was demonstrably anti-nativist, rooted rather in the universalistic claims of the Rights of Man and Citizen and the goal of popular sovereignty.[13] In this case, the very ideals of "free" and "equal" citizenship became the particular cultural feature of French nationalism; universalism was itself a particularism.[14] In the case of Saint-Domingue, however, a broader set of questions emerges having to do with the adoption or not of French citizenship and nationality by ex-slaves once their de facto emancipation was formally ratified by the National Assembly, as well as their eventual repudiation of Frenchness in favor of an unmarked claim to the right of universal freedom once the French abandoned the goal of general liberty. Is the Haitian Revolution therefore the limit case of a modern revolution without nationalism? On the other hand, if Haitian nationalism was a universalism, was it a derivative one, that is, discursively based upon the principles of the French universalism it repudiated as false? In this case, the question arises as to the extent to which the universalism of Haitian Revolutionary discourse challenged the particularist, imperialist presumptions of the French variety without reproducing its own forms of exclusion, or remaining trapped within a new particularism. In our postmodern era in which universalism is deemed both paradoxical—always already a particularism—and itself a colonizing, totalitarian discourse, in what sense, we might ask, can universalism found an anticolonial politics?

## "Free and French"

In a provocative formulation, Étienne Balibar conceives the "paradox of universalism" to be that it is invariably haunted by the violence, real or symbolic, required to deny the internal other.[15] In the classical Marxian reading of the Enlightenment and the French Revolution, the paradox of the claim of universal freedom derives from its constitutive particularism, due to the fact that only part of civil society emancipates itself and undertakes the general emancipation of society by equating its own aims with the emancipatory aims of the whole community. This community is produced, in turn, through the exclusion of the sector deemed oppressive by the dominant group, the nobility.[16] What is striking is that in the case of Haiti, this process was in some sense reversed; that is, the paradoxes of the emancipatory project were due not merely to the fact that freedom from slavery represented the aspirations of a particular sector projected onto the whole, but also to the fact that when this struggle was defined in universal terms, it became indissociable from a claim to belonging within the French Republican social body. From the inception of the August 1791 slave uprisings in the northern plain of Saint-Domingue, different social and political actors struggled to shape the meaning and definition of freedom for the slaves. Although for some, freedom meant the destruction of the whites and the overturning of the entire colonial system, for others freedom signified the ability to form one's own political and social communities, to work for pay, or to abandon the plantation system entirely in favor of subsistence farming.[17] Over time, however, insurgent leaders and French Republican commissioners defined freedom from slavery almost exclusively as a universal, natural right in accordance with the 1789 Declaration of the Rights of Man and Citizen. Ironically, therefore, it is precisely when the demand for liberty was spoken in universal terms that freedom was seen as indissociable from membership in a particular community, that of citizens, "free and French."

Although not all demands of general liberty were couched in the language of Republican universalism (insurgent leaders also spoke in the name of kings African and European), for many ex-slaves and free people of color claiming the Rights of Man as declared by the French National Assembly was an especially powerful means of contesting slavery and racial prejudice and denouncing the hypocrisy of Revolutionary leaders. In some cases, revolutionaries of color claimed not only the right to speak and represent the abstract universal "Man," they also demanded inclusion in the French nation, that is, the right to be recognized as French. This assimilationist strategy is clear from the text of a petition signed by a local assembly of "citizens of all colors" in the north of Saint-Domingue and dated August 25, 1793, just four days before the French civil commissioner Sonthonax declared the general abolition of the slaves in the north: "We demand the rights that nature itself has conceded to us, the rights of man, liberty, safety, property, resistance to oppression. France has guaranteed them to all men. Are we not men? . . . What barbarous law has given to Europeans the right to carry us to a foreign land and to give us over to eternal torture? You expatriated us; well! Let your fatherland [*patrie*] become ours; but we want to be recognized free and French."[18] The political significance of this demand for French citizenship becomes clear when we consider the paradox of the Declaration of the Rights of Man and Citizen. For while this document conferred a set of rights on all people on the basis of their humanity alone, the legislative power whereby such rights were proclaimed and defended identified itself as representative of the "French people," who were, according to the logic of national sovereignty, the unique beneficiaries and ultimate source of the laws protecting the putatively universal rights. The implication is that, as Balibar puts it, "foreigners have no defense as humans unless represented by a sovereign state."[19] By both speaking on behalf of universal man and identifying themselves with French particularism, the petitioners thus proposed a radically pluralized view of the French nation and obliged all French citizens to fight for and defend their rights.

Yet, as the right to liberty was simultaneously avowed as universal and coupled with a demand for French nationality, both insurgent and Republican leaders privileged the political aims and economic interests of the larger French nation in ways that often limited or denied the agency of former slaves and free nonwhites and excluded other forms of political association from the condition of freedom. The conflation of natural rights claims and demands for general liberty with French economic interests is apparent from a letter issued in July 1792 by the insurgent leaders Jean-François, Biassou, and Charles Belair to the Colonial Assembly and the French commissioners in Saint-Domingue. This letter is notably the first instance in which the insurgent leaders are known to have advocated general liberty.[20] In it, they declared their humanity and justified the slave insurrection as a legitimate fight against oppression and as a defense of their natural rights as enumerated in the Declaration of the Rights of Man and Citizen. However, in return for general liberty for slaves and a general amnesty for insurgents, the leaders offered to stop fighting and lead the insurgents back to the plantation, where they would work as paid laborers.[21] Thus in order to enlist French support, the insurgents vitiated the concept of "general liberty" by compensating the French through the maintenance of a disciplined labor regime.

Although Biassou, Jean-François, and Belair grounded their demands for general liberty in a notion of their common humanity rather than in the idea of French citizenship, the connection between natural rights claims, calls for French nationality, and limits on the rights of putatively free "citizens" was clearly articulated in the general abolition decree promulgated by the civil commissioner Leger-Félicité Sonthonax on August 29, 1793. Faced with the invasion of Saint-Domingue by English and French forces as well as the rising slave insurgency, and convinced that the only way for the French to save the colony was to gain new recruits among the slave population, Sonthonax took the apparently radical step of extending the Rights of Man to all the slaves in the colony. Yet what is fascinating is the nationalism with which he justified an abolition that was clearly opportunistic and in some sense redundant, given that the insurrection involving tens of thousands of ex-slaves had been raging for almost two years and had left much of the colony's northern plain in ruins. After proclaiming that "men are born and remain free and equal in rights," Sonthonax rationalizes the timing of his decision to recognize slaves' humanity, coming as it did two years after the Rights of Man had been declared in France and almost one year after his arrival in Saint-Domingue.[22] Addressing his audience as "citizens," Sonthonax claims that he had been sent to Saint-Domingue to "prepare gradually . . . the general manumission of slaves," and blames the entrenched resistance of proslavery whites and the savagery of the blacks for the delay in doing so. So strained were relations between the two groups, he argues, that had he abolished slavery immediately, the newly freed slaves would have thrown themselves on their former enemies, killing the innocent with the guilty. This peculiar explanation may be read both as a tacit reproof of black violence against whites, and as a means of denying the continuing insurrection against which he was fighting, for Sonthonax suggests that it is not slavery itself but a sudden liberation that would have caused blacks to rise up against their former masters. Now that the worst of the whites, whom he derisively calls "tyrants," "slave traders," and "cannibals," have fled or died (although not at the hands of slaves; rather, as "victims of their powerless rage"), he feels safe in issuing the general abolition.

Sonthonax offers two further explanations for the abolition, both of which suppress the oppositional agency of insurgent forces and frame black freedom in terms of French Republican ideals. He first insists that blacks "owe" their freedom to the free people of color for having shown them an example of how to "defend the rights of nature and humanity": "Never forget, citizens, that you got from them the arms that have conquered your freedom; Never forget that it is for the French Republic that you have fought, that, of all the whites in the universe, the only ones who are your friends are the French."[23] The word "arms," used in its metaphorical sense, has the effect of effacing the militarized violence through which thousands of ex-slaves pressed their demands for freedom against Republican forces. Here, "arms" refers instead to the rights claims of the free people of color, who, slaveholders themselves, had fought for equal rights with whites in the language of Republican universalism, by claiming the Rights of Man. In this way, Sonthonax frames the black freedom struggle as a plea for those natural rights conferred only by the French Republic (as opposed to the English or Spanish monarchies, which were also competing for insurgent black allegiance), and hence as a bid to join the community of French citizens. Sonthonax thus contains the meaning of slaves' struggle for freedom within the nationalist ideology of the Republic itself; despite the fact that blacks were fighting against a Republic that had thus far refused to grant them freedom, Sonthonax defines the fight for freedom as always already a fight *for* the Republic, hence for the right to be French.

Having effectively occulted the oppositional agency of the ex-slave forces, Sonthonax depicts the abolition decree as an act of benevolence by the French government in distinctly familial terms: "The Republic adopts you among its children."[24] But this act of generosity required unlimited returns, for, as Françoise Vergès has pointed out in her trenchant analysis of French Republican colonial discourse, "in the colonial family romance, the colonial *don* (gift) transformed the colonized into children permanently indebted to La Mère-Patrie."[25] Sonthonax continues: "Having become citizens by the will of the French nation, you must also be zealous defenders of its decrees; you will defend without a doubt the interests of the Republic against kings, less out of a feeling of independence than out of gratitude for the benefits that she has given you. Freedom has brought you from a state of nothingness to one of existence. Show yourselves worthy of it." Sonthonax's proclamation here echoes the nationalist ideology put forth by pro-Republican theorists such as the Abbé Sieyès and even the mulatto Julien Raimond. As Laurent Dubois has shown, Raimond used the language of national responsibility to counter the appropriation of Republican discourse by the slave insurgents and the expansion of citizenship that they advocated.[26] For Sonthonax, liberty conferred by the Republic obliged the formerly enslaved to enrich . France through their labor: "Prove to France, through your activity, that by associating you to her interests, she has truly increased her resources and her means."[27] Thus despite the declaration that enslaved blacks and "mixed-bloods" are now "free to benefit from all the rights attached to the quality of French citizens," article 2 of the accompanying ordinance proclaims that they will be subjected to a "regime" that includes forced labor and constraints on freedom of movement. In all, Sonthonax's abolition decree sought to deny the scale and ideological complexity of the slave revolution and redefine freedom as perpetual service to the metropole.

It would be a while longer, however, before this idea of freedom became hegemonic in Saint-Domingue, for the most powerful ex-slave leader, Toussaint Louverture, still refused to join the French Republican army. What is fascinating, however, is that perhaps the earliest recorded instance of Louverture's embrace of general emancipation was arguably a direct response to the public demands for general liberty and French citizenship that gave Sonthonax the confidence to follow through with his emancipation decree.[28] In an August 25 letter addressing a group of Republican-allied free people of color in Le Cap who had emancipationist leanings, Toussaint Louverture presents himself and his allies as the "first authors" of the cause of general liberty. Summarizing the rhetoric of the Rights of Man claimed by his mulatto rival, Chanlatte, Louverture argued that only he had the right to lead the fight for those rights: "It is up to me to work for them, and this right is accorded to me as the first one given to a cause that I have always supported. . . . Having begun, I will finish. Join me and you will enjoy your rights sooner."[29] Claiming the French Republic to have been defeated in Europe, Louverture attested that his inspiration came neither from whites nor free people of color, but from God, and signed his letter as "General of the armies of the king." Toussaint's reactive deployment of Republican rights discourse suggests his awareness of its power to galvanize slaves and free people of color. A few days later, he issued what is perhaps his most famous proclamation: "I am Toussaint Louverture, my name has perhaps become known to you. You must be aware [*vous n'ignorez pas*], brother, that I have undertaken vengeance, and that I want Liberty and Equality to reign in Saint-Domingue. I have been working from the beginning to bring them into existence. . . . Unite with us . . . and fight with us for the same cause."[30]

Toussaint's royalism leaves open the question of whether his use of universal rights discourse could have founded an emancipation project independent from French interests. Within months, however, Toussaint had changed sides and joined the Republic, thus becoming its most valued military leader. Just as important, Toussaint became the greatest proponent of French nationalism in Saint-Domingue. By nationalism, I mean a form of sacrificial and at times militaristic devotion that supersedes all other political commitments and identifications, as in Eric Hobsbawm's definition.[31] Toussaint's nationalism consisted of select elements of Republican nationalism, notably its suspicion of any culturalist claims to common roots, blood, language, or tradition, in favor of a view of the nation as a collectivity bound by a common commitment to putatively universal human rights and united against a common enemy, royalism. Downplaying equality in favor of liberty, Toussaint's nationalism was expressed through the rhetorical task of making freedom French, notably through the idea that the French Republic was both the author and sole provider of liberty, which could be protected only through assimilation with the French nation. Essential here was the concept of slavery long used in French Enlightenment discourse to characterize domination by monarchical absolutism. As Susan Buck-Morss has most recently argued, slavery was the root metaphor used by Western political philosophers to protest not against the actual enslavement of millions in the New World, but rather against forms of royal "despotism," aristocratic privilege, and taxation that suppressed bourgeois ambition at home.[32] Likewise, Republicans portrayed the French Revolution as the liberation of the slaves of the absolutist king into a state of self-governance.[33] Once the Republic actually abolished real slavery in the colonies, this rhetoric was instrumental in the humiliation and pacification of the other rebel leaders who were supported by England or Spain. In his June 13, 1795, letter to Jean-François and Biassou, who were officially in the service of the Spanish crown, Toussaint defended the sincerity of the French abolition by equating the Spanish monarchy with real colonial slavery: "We intend to prove to you that anyone who is a subject or vassal of kings is but a vile slave, and that only a republican is truly a man . . . We are republicans, and consequently free by natural right."[34] Here, Toussaint draws on a century of Enlightenment rhetoric to demoralize his opponents for choosing to remain slaves by virtue of their political association with monarchs. Excluding royalists from the human, Toussaint attributes both humanity and natural rights to the political condition of republicanism itself.

Whether or not Toussaint believed his own rhetoric, he relied on such nationalist demagoguery to sway independent rebels, unify blacks and free people of color, suppress internal dissent, and secure his hold on power. Essential to these aims was the discourse of family romance first evinced in Sonthonax's abolition decree. In a letter to independent black insurgent leader Dieudonné who was rumored to have ties with the English, dated February 11, 1796, Toussaint identifies himself as "black like you" and argues that blacks can only be happy, free, and equal "by serving the French Republic," which he describes as *"ma patrie."* In an effort to win Dieudonné's trust, Toussaint invokes the trope of the Republican family: "Is it possible, my dear friend, that at the moment at which France triumphs over all the royalists and recognizes us as her children by her beneficent decree of 9 Thermidor, that she accords to us all of the rights for which we are fighting, that you would allow yourself to be fooled by our old tyrants, who only use some of our unfortunate brethren to charge the others with chains?"[35] In Toussaint's model of filiation, freedom is inseparable from French nationality. France's maternity of blacks and mulattoes is a function of her having extended to them the freedom and legal protections of Republican citizenship. Likewise, the French Republican governor Étienne Lavaux is their father owing to the trust and authority France has placed in him. In a proclamation to African rebels at Saint-Louis du Nord dated April 25, 1796, Toussaint exclaims, "What will the French say when . . . they learn that after the gift they have just given you you have been so ungrateful as to dip your hands in the blood of her children?"[36] As in Sonthonax's abolition decree, Toussaint's narrative of family romance places the ex-slaves in a passive, subordinate, and dependent position, constantly owing gratitude, devotion and service to France for the gift of freedom. In his correspondence with the governor, Toussaint himself overflows with expressions of filial attachment, repeatedly addressing Lavaux as *"mon bon papa,"* "my father," and my "benefactor," and signing his letters with phrases such as "your affectionate and submissive son."[37]

By representing France as the benevolent donor of the freedom and equality that blacks and free people of color were fighting for in Saint-Domingue, Toussaint particularized those ideals as French and at the same time demanded that the ex-slaves satisfy certain requirements in order to be deserving of them. In this respect, the dissemination of ostensibly universal values through a nationalist rhetoric served particular interests, notably those of the landowning elite, which now included increasing numbers of free people of color and ex-slaves, and Toussaint himself.[38] In addition to military service Toussaint required absolute subservience to what he called "French law," a euphemism for the code of coerced labor he instituted during his increasingly autocratic reign. Toussaint attempted to lure rebels to the French cause by proclaiming that only those citizens who allied themselves with the French standard would be placed "under the safeguard and protection of the law."[39] But the law proved illusory, for by redefining liberty as "a liberty without license, a liberty founded on reason, good morals, and religion," Toussaint used the military and the law to force cultivators back onto the plantations on which they had labored as slaves, arresting anyone who resisted this imposed state of "public tranquillity."[40] Speaking in the name of the French Republic, he swiftly eliminated the basic freedoms of the slaves, using the moralist exhortation of virtue and religion to justify his repression of other understandings of freedom.

More than any other Revolutionary figure, therefore, Toussaint Louverture epitomized the nationalist universalism of Haitian Revolutionary discourse; that is, the joining of universal claims to French nationalist rhetoric in ways that tied the fortunes of black freedom fighters to French national interests. Especially compelling is Toussaint's confidence in his ability to represent the French universal, as evidenced in his alleged advocacy, sometime around the time of the drafting of the constitution, of an imperialist project in West Africa to be undertaken by him under the banner of France. Several historical sources refer to Toussaint's plan to conquer, with the help of a thousand soldiers and a handful of his best officers, vast territories in coastal West Africa so as to abolish the slave trade, establish "civilization," and make Africans "free and French."[41] The question thus arises as to the relation between Toussaint's nationalism and his imperialism. Étienne Balibar has argued that cultural imperialism enacts the universalist project of nationalism by imagining the imperialist nation as "the specific instrument of a more essential mission and destiny which other peoples cannot but recognize." In this respect, imperialism is transformed from "a mere enterprise of conquest into an enterprise of universal domination, the founding of a civilization."[42] Yet while Balibar dates the French instance of this transformation to the nineteenth century, the French Revolution arguably offered the first emergence of an imperialist nationalism when the Girondins trumpeted the universal ideals of freedom and equality as the basis for the "liberation" and incorporation of foreign populations into "La grande nation," or greater France. French Revolutionary imperialism, which began after the deposition of Louis XVI and continued with the rise of the Thermidorians in 1794, raised the possibility of a universal French nation in which foreign peoples might join as "universal patriots" in "sister" republics ultimately subordinated to French interests.[43] It is within this context that Toussaint Louverture's designs for Africa must be situated. Erecting himself into a putative "liberator" of African peoples in the name of France, freedom, and "civilization," Toussaint's plan exhibits the fundamental paradox of a universalism whose limits are tested in the political and whose rights can only be guaranteed by a nation state. Although his apparent solution to the effective exclusion of Africans in Africa from the Revolutionary cause of universal liberty was to expand the French nation so as to include them, this imperialist scheme would have deeply vitiated the twin pretensions of universal equality and freedom, thus further exposing the antinomies of universalist politics. Likewise, the fact that Toussaint imagined this project as a black man from the colonial periphery signifies both his particular investment in French imperial expansion as the only means by which to eliminate slavery and racial prejudice around the world, and his acceptance of imperialism's no less invidious cultural racism and nationalist implications.

Toussaint's transformation of French Revolutionary universalism into an imperialist civilizing mission, his self-representation as both a citizen and a national of France, and his equation of Frenchness with an ideal of universal liberty, should not, however, be taken at face value as signs of his blind respect of French sovereignty and authority and his desire to "be" French. Toussaint's rhetorical nationalism is equally if not more significant as an indication of his subversion of the exclusionary tendency in French nationalism, which was increasingly apparent in the late 1790s as the more conservative Directory assumed power and the planter lobby clamored for the reinstitution of slavery in the Caribbean colonies. In this sense, we can view Toussaint as attempting to head off the transformation of blacks into "false nationals" to be denied or expelled in order for the French nation to reconstitute itself after the Revolution.[44] Just as important, however, Toussaint's nationalism must be seen as performative, meant to mask his increasingly independentist politics, undertaken arguably to protect against an eventual attempt by Napoleonic France to reimpose slavery. Although pursued in the name of France, Toussaint's seizure in 1801 of the Spanish side of Saint-Domingue was completed without official French sanction and has been described by historians as a calculated means of protecting himself from a land invasion.[45] In addition to eliminating or undermining successive French governors, agents, and commissioners Laveaux, Sonthonax, Hédouville, and Roume, Toussaint performed his greatest coup yet against French authority later that year. In response to the passage in 1799 of the Constitution establishing the Consulate and advocating "special laws" for the colonies, an ominous reference to the possible reestablishment of slavery,[46] Toussaint appointed a local assembly to create a constitution for Saint-Domingue. Reiterating the importance of "special laws" appropriate for colonial morals, customs, and needs in the *Discours préliminaire,* Toussaint recognized French sovereignty in the first article before declaring the permanent abolition of slavery in article 3. Proclaiming that "All men there are born, live, and die free and French," Toussaint reiterated his inclusive conception of French citizenship, while the rest of the document entirely bypassed French authority, placing all of the legislative and administrative power in Toussaint's hands, and naming him governor-for-life.[47]

## This Nationalism Which Is Not a Particularism

As we have seen, the enunciation of a universalist discourse of emancipation by Haitian revolutionaries was indissociable from a claim on French nationality; to speak the universal was to embrace the particularism which it betrayed, due not merely to the hegemony of one group of ex-slaves, but also to the particular culture that Republican universalism itself represented, which was embraced by the most powerful insurgent leaders. Yet although the claim on French nationality often served to justify limitations on definitions of freedom for the ex-slaves, its symbolic significance should not be missed. The universalist nationalism of the revolutionaries in Saint-Domingue represented an act of aggression on the terrain of the European universal, one that undermined the legitimacy of a racially exclusive notion of liberty, rationality, or sovereignty. During the radical phase of the Haitian Revolution, the mimicry of the Revolutionary leaders resembled an inverted form of mimicry as conceived by Homi Bhabha; that is, the process by which the agents of colonialism, in adapting the rhetoric and political forms of the Enlightenment to their purported civilizing mission abroad, reveal colonial reforms of native societies to be mechanisms of social control and political repression rather than tools for emancipation, as they profess them to be. In this way, argues Bhabha, colonial discourse alienates the values of Enlightenment from their prior meaning in Europe, thus destabilizing colonial authority.[48] Yet the case of Haiti demonstrates that mimicry enacted by anticolonial actors in the colonies is far more effective in disrupting colonial authority, since it exposes the limits and hypocrisies of European Enlightenment discourse both in the colony *and* in the metropole. The effect is to dissociate the ideal of freedom from the colonial state. In his famous letter to the Directory of November 5, 1797, Toussaint Louverture both praised France as the birthplace of liberty, and made clear that he would fight to the death if France ever dared to nullify that principle in Saint-Domingue: "France will not revoke her principles; she will not withdraw from us the greatest of her benefits. . . . But if, to reestablish servitude in Saint-Domingue, this were done, then I declare to you that this would be to attempt the impossible: we have known how to face dangers to obtain our liberty, we shall know how to brave death to maintain it."[49] Through an ironic admonition meant to underscore his suspicion that France planned to re-enslave its black citizens, Toussaint lifts his own mask of mimicry and declares that liberty is no longer an idea invented in France and benevolently exported to the colonies; it is, rather, a condition understood and protected only by those who have known true slavery and who have fought for their own emancipation.

During the war of independence following the French kidnapping of Toussaint Louverture and in the early postcolonial period, Haitian revolutionaries and their scribes pursued this logic, thoroughly overturning the earlier French nationalism of Toussaint, dissociating the idea of emancipation from France, and refiguring freedom as an abstract universal whose sole defenders were the inhabitants of Saint-Domingue. Essential to this ideology was the notion that France presented only a simulacrum of liberty, paraded merely as a means of duping the blacks in Saint-Domingue. Many of the earliest Haitian writers and historians make mocking reference, in particular, to the printed address in which Napoléon acknowledged the freedom of the inhabitants of Saint-Domingue but demanded their submission to French forces. This address was distributed by Leclerc and his representatives as they demanded entry into island ports in the winter of 1802.[50] Christophe and Toussaint pleaded with Leclerc to present written proof that the French were sincere in their promise to maintain freedom on the island, a request that Leclerc repeatedly refused to satisfy.

Nowhere is the theme of French treachery and deception more apparent than in the proclamation of independence written by Félix Boisrond-Tonnerre for and arguably with Jean-Jacques Dessalines, and delivered by Dessalines at Gonaïves on January 1, 1804. Entitled "Liberty or Death," the document reverses the terms of the colonialist binary of civilization and savagery, setting up the French as a barbarous, cruel, foreign race that seeks only to bring dissension and slavery to independent Haiti. Especially remarkable is the association of France with a rhetorical chimera of freedom, a *"fantôme de la liberté"* through which they attempt to deceive, divide, and resubjugate the ex-slaves. Admonishing those who succumbed to the discourse of Napoléon, Leclerc, and his French officers, Dessalines blames deceitful language, not French military prowess, for the prolonged war in Saint-Domingue: "What! Victims for fourteen years of our credulity and our indulgence; conquered not by French armies, but by the piteous eloquence of their agents' proclamations, when will we tire of breathing the same air as them?"[51] Here, the French idea of liberty is at best a degraded, racially bounded version of the freedom claimed by the slaves; at worst a rhetorical weapon used to manipulate and re-enslave those who would be free.

One might expect, therefore, the Haitian declaration of independence to mount a spirited defense of an ideal of universal freedom severed from French particularism. The Declaration at Gonaïves does exhort the people of Haiti, addressed as "citizens," to defend their freedom and their independence with their lives, so as to establish an "empire" and a "territory" of liberty: "we must . . . forever ensure the empire of liberty in the country that witnessed our birth; we must ravish from the inhumane government which has for so long held our minds in the most humiliating torpor, any hope of re-enslaving us; indeed, we must live free or die." Now that the French have betrayed their own values, they have themselves become captives: "Enslaved? . . . Let us leave this description for the French; they have conquered but are no longer free."[52] Yet, the very effort to detach the idea of liberty from the French, thus de-particularizing it, leads to a form of nationalism based on a rule of exclusion that equates the presence of French people with continued oppression and the condition of unfreedom. In this respect, Haitian Revolutionary nationalism expresses the paradox of universalism insofar as the universality of the condition of freedom is predicated upon the exclusion of a certain class or sector of humanity. As Ernesto Laclau explains, "for one estate to be par excellence the estate of liberation, another estate must conversely be the obvious state of oppression."[53] Similarly, Balibar has argued that all nationalisms rest upon the existence of visible or invisible barriers, materialized in laws and practices, designed to deny access to goods or rights to those considered foreign or alien to the national community.[54] In the case of newly independent Haiti, all French people are seen as the obstacle that must be purged in order for Haitian freedom, as well as its independence, to be realized. Hence the logic of extermination and recriminatory violence that pervades the document. The text moves quickly from an emphasis on difference and the lack of fraternity between the Haitians, defined at points as "natives," and the French, cast as foreign oppressors, to an all but explicit demand for Haitians to assassinate any remaining French people on the island: "Let them tremble when approaching our shores, if not from the memory of the cruelties that they carried out there, then from the terrible resolution that we will make to commit to death anyone born French whose profane foot sullies the territory of liberty."[55]

In this respect, early Haitian nationalism was based less on a particularism, than on a negative universalism. By that I mean a universalism distinct from that produced via the generalization of a particular explicitly defined (in the case of the French Revolution, for example, a certain idea of man conceived as an abstract individual but in fact bearing signs of particular gender, class, national, and/or racial status). Dessalines' proclamation instead produces an implicit notion of Haitian national identity via the *exclusion* of a particular from the human and from the community of citizens—the French. Haitians are above all those who have fought and will continue to fight the French, as compelled by their duty both to defend their liberty and to avenge their dead. Likewise, the construction of the Haitian nation is synonymous with the active and continued repudiation of France and of the French: "We swear to the entire universe, to posterity, and to ourselves, to renounce France forever, and to die rather than live under her domination." Just who the Haitians are remains highly ambiguous, however, for aside from their role as antagonists of the French, the document suggests virtually no positive basis upon which they might comprise a distinct national group. Although the periodic designation of Haitians as "natives" and claims of common "birth" in the island may well express a fantasy of genealogical unity in the Haitian people and of their ancestral link to the land, national independence is conceived not in terms of a nativist entitlement, but rather as a fight against slavery and for liberty, the latter of which is personified throughout the text as a body dying from French aggressions, and revived through the heroic actions and bloodshed of Haitian soldiers and generals: "Citizens, my countrymen, on this solemn day I have assembled those courageous soldiers who, on the verge of receiving liberty's last breaths, spilled their blood to save her."[56]

Dessalines' Constitution of 1805 provides further insight into the negative universalism of early Haitian nationalism, in part due to the lack of provisions regarding Haitian citizenship. There is the geographical reference to Saint-Domingue, the insistence in article 9 that "No one deserves to be Haitian who is not a good father, a good son, a good husband and above all, a good soldier," and the inclusion in article 7 of stipulations that make emigration a capital crime, but there are few provisions on how individuals can become citizens.[57] What we do have is a rather strict exclusion of white men of any nation, not from citizenship per se, but from becoming masters or owning property in Haiti, which presumably would prevent them from joining the social body (art. 12). Article 13 indicates that the previous article does not apply to white wives of Haitian men, who may be naturalized as Haitian by the government, thus suggesting that whites of both sexes would otherwise be excluded from citizenship. There are, however, no provisions on what such a naturalization might imply.

Yet Sibylle Fischer has shown that the lack of criteria for citizenship in the early Haitian constitutions may well index the transnational aspects of revolutionary antislavery in the context of the early nineteenth-century slaveholding Atlantic, insofar as the project of Haitian independence—freedom from slavery—could not be limited to the geographical boundaries of Saint-Domingue.[58] Of course, the framers of the 1805 constitution knew that the very existence of a state composed of a free nonwhite population posed a threat to the Atlantic colonial powers, and that any attempt to export the Revolution would provoke those powers to

retaliate militarily. Historians of Haiti maintain that this realization, together with the desire of Haitian leaders to gain the trust and recognition
of the international community, led to the insertion of noninterference
clauses in both the Gonaïves Declaration and the first Haitian constitution.[59] The Gonaïves Declaration in particular warns the Haitian people
against a "spirit of proselytism," which would destroy their achievement:
"Let us not, like revolutionary firebrands, erect ourselves into lawgiv-
ers for the Antilles, glorifying in our ability to disturb the peace of the
neighboring islands. They have not been soaked with the innocent blood
of their inhabitants, and they have no vengeance to claim against the
authority that protects them."[60]

Yet, such professions of satisfaction with the slave regimes of other
nations cannot be taken at face value, for the first legislators of the
Haitian state found more subtle ways to internationalize the project
of Haitian nationhood. The symbolic naming of the country "Haiti," the
assumed aboriginal term for the island Europeans called "Hispaniola,"
expressed both the break with France and the will to create a link with
the earlier resistance of indigenous populations to European colonialism and genocide, thus making Haitians the "avengers" of America, as
Dessalines had reportedly declared following his massacre of remaining
whites in 1804.[61] Just as important, however, Fischer identifies a crucial
relationship in the early nineteenth-century constitutions between the
affirmation of noninterference and the increasing specificity of asylum
provisions which suggest that "Haiti could become a refuge for those
subjected to racial slavery and genocide elsewhere." Reading backwards
from the 1816 constitution of Alexandre Pétion that guaranteed the right
of residence to anyone with African or Native American blood, she argues,
"the vagueness on citizenship in the early constitutions is a trace of the
transnational nature of radical antislavery. That the early constitutions
do not give criteria for citizenship . . . is evidence that the revolutionaries did not think of the new state along the lines of a new nation finally
liberated from the fetters of colonialism." She goes on to cite article 6
of the constitution of 1843, which declares all individuals of African or
Indian descent to be Haitian: "All individuals born in Haiti, or of African
or Indian descent, and all those born in foreign countries to a Haitian
man or a Haitian woman, are Haitian." What we have, then, is a case
in which Haitian nationalism is inseparable from a transnational identification; as Fischer argues, "the idea of transnational liberation itself
becomes part of a nationalistic rhetoric."[62] According to this evidence,
early nineteenth-century Haitian national identity was therefore rooted

in an identitarian claim that excluded white men and unified everyone
else in the Americas—blacks, mulattoes, and Indians—in part based on
assumptions of their historic or potential resistance to white colonial
domination and slavery.

I view this stance as a negative universalism insofar as Haitian identity is affirmed primarily through the exclusion, rather than the univer-
salization of, a particularity. I therefore read the assertion "all Haitians
are black" found in article 14 of Dessalines' Constitution of 1805 but
struck from subsequent versions, not as the generalization or universal-
ization of the identity of the dominant particular racial group, but rather
as an ironic parody of any attempt to define human beings in terms of
racial particularity at all. By calling all Haitians black, Haitian legislators
invalidated the biologist taxonomies through which colonial elites had
discriminated against people of color in Saint-Domingue.[63] Dessalines'
assertion of common blackness is at the same time an affirmation that
blackness names not a skin color but a political project of resistance to
slavery and colonial oppression, which replaces phenotypic or blood-based
categories as the essential trait of Haitian national identity. Once again,
it is the excluded term—whiteness—that conditions the political definition of the collectivity, seen as its opposite, the "black" other that was
previously reproved by white power and that now symbolizes not a biological essence but an absolute resistance to white racial supremacy. Thus
rather than reiterating the paradox that "the universal is typically derived
through a generalization of one of the particulars"[64]—in this case racial
blackness—the universal in post-Revolutionary Haiti was categorically different from the racial particularisms that had previously governed power
and prestige in the colony: the universal was derived from an opposition
to the logic of (racial) particularism itself, and from the exclusion of the
previously dominant group that had defined itself in racial terms.

ALTHOUGH DESSALINIAN nationalism was based on the exclusion of the
French from the Haitian social body, its narrative expressions conveyed
the absolute paradox such a project posed on the level of culture. The
breathtaking violence with which the French are treated in the declaration at Gonaïves bespeaks the immense anxiety aroused by Dessalines'
awareness that Haiti was itself indelibly French, its very birth enunciated
in the French language. Ironically, French culture is the enemy that has
yet to be vanquished, and that threatens never to be. Hailing the heroic
generals he has called before the people, Dessalines announces their work
to be incomplete: "Citizens . . . these generals who have led your efforts

against tyranny have still hardly done enough for your happiness . . . The French name still grieves [*lugubre*] our lands."[65] Scholars habitually point to the neologism *"lugubrer"* as an original expression of rupture with France through the willful subversion of the French language, but this interpretation tends to downplay more explicit references to the speaker's sense of powerlessness and awe before the indestructible French cultural edifice. He continues, "Everything here retraces the memory of the cruelties of this barbarous people; our laws, our habits, our cities, all still bear the trace of France. What can I say? There are French people in our island, and you believe yourselves to be free and independent of this republic that has fought all the nations, it is true, but that has never defeated those who wanted to be free."[66] Here French people come to stand for the French culture and language, seen as a colonizing rather than liberating influence, which Dessalines declares he has yet to obliterate, but that he himself propagates. It is as though by doing violence to the French, Haitians could successfully expel the other within and thus finally realize a radical break with France. At the same time, Dessalines recognizes and indeed memorializes the formative importance of French culture to the Haitian nation; not merely in the chosen language of expression, but also in the document's deployment of the rhetoric of citizenship, liberty, and nationhood. The rupture of the colonial relation is thus disavowed at the very moment of its enunciation, and Dessalines continues to speak the French universal.

This irony brings us back to the question of the role of universalism as an anticolonial discourse in the Haitian Revolution. As we have seen, revolutionary universalism in Saint-Domingue was initially wedded to the particularism of French national identity as leaders such as Toussaint Louverture framed the call for general liberty in terms of the Rights of Man and demanded access to citizenship in the French Republic. Although this particularization of liberty largely served to channel the desires and aspirations of the ex-slaves toward the interests of France, or those of the propertied, landowning sector of Saint-Dominguan society, it also served to undermine the exclusionary basis of French universalism by radically pluralizing the French idea of Man. Under Dessalines, however, Haitian Revolutionary universalism was severed from claims on French national identity, and transformed into an anticolonial discourse. What is fascinating is that the very paradoxical quality of universalism—that is, its fundamentally exclusionary basis—is precisely what enabled it to function as an anticolonial discourse. In declaring Haitians to be the founders and true defenders of the project of universal freedom, Dessalines rejected the

French as representatives of the universal and as members of the Haitian nation, conceived as a transnational and transhistorical unity of black and brown peoples radically opposed to European colonialism, slavery, and the ideology of white supremacy. However, the case of Haiti also demonstrates the doubly paradoxical nature of anticolonial universalism; for the desired exclusion of the colonizer is negated both by the discourse of universalism itself, which continually bears the trace of French Revolutionary rhetoric, and by the persistence of French language, culture, and social norms in the postcolonial state. Dessalines' declaration of independence and imperial constitution thus point up the impossibility of the project of universalist nationalism insofar as Haiti remained indelibly French, and the dream of exclusion a fantasy of the anticolonial imagination.

Yet, to recognize the limitations of anticolonial universalism is not to suggest the failure of the Haitian Revolution as an anticolonial movement. On the contrary, the discourses produced by various Revolutionary leaders demonstrate the significance of the Haitian Revolution as a declaration of belonging in precisely those forms of political modernity that colonialism, Enlightenment discourse, and European political institutions had engineered largely at the expense of the colonized and the enslaved, as well as an attempt to shape that modernity. Indeed, within ten years of Dessalines' declarations, Haitian publicists and historiographers such as Baron de Vastey and Juste Chanlatte were writing not in defense of a nativist or exclusionary Haitian identity, but rather in favor of the recognition of Haiti by the international community and its inclusion in the modern nation-state system on equal terms with the former colonial powers. In defending the Haitian Revolution and the right of Haiti to integrate the universal of modernity and the nation-state system, these early Haitian publicists sought at the same time to reconstruct and redefine the universal so as to reject those ideologies and intellectual premises they associated with slavery, namely racial prejudice. In this respect, Haitian intellectual discourse of the nineteenth century was largely concerned to imagine modernity and the universal through the exclusion, not of the former colonizer, but rather of the discourses and practices that made colonial slavery possible.

## Notes

The phrase *"légitime défense"* of my title refers to the phrase deployed by Pompée-Valentin, Baron de Vastey, to describe his discursive rebuttal to the negative propaganda war launched by France in denial of Haitian independence in *Réflexions politiques sur quelques ouvrages et journaux français, concernant Hayti,* xij. The expression was later picked up by avant-garde Caribbean writers Étienne Léro, René Ménil, Jules-Marcel Monnerot, and Pierre Yoyotte to name the oppositional literary journal they published in Paris in 1932.

1. Michel-Rolph Trouillot, *Silencing the Past,* 73–74.

2. Outside the rare reference to C. L. R. James's classic, *The Black Jacobins,* one finds almost no mention of Haiti in works such as Robert Young, *Postcolonialism;* Dipesh Chakrabarty, *Provincializing Europe;* Leela Ghandi, *Postcolonial Theory;* Ania Loomba, *Colonialism/Postcolonialism;* nor in the major theoretical works of figures such as Homi Bhabha and Gayatry Spivak. The notable exception is Edward Said, who examines at length C. L. R. James's revisionist, nationalist, and anti-imperialist account of the Haitian Revolution in *Culture and Imperialism,* 245–61. See also David Scott's critique of postcolonial thought through a reading of C. L. R. James's *The Black Jacobins* in *Conscripts of Modernity.*

3. Homi Bhabha, "Race, Time, and the Revision of Modernity," in his *The Location of Culture,* 244.

4. Young, *Postcolonialism,* 80–81.

5. Although elsewhere Young mentions in passing "the first black liberation war of 1791–1804, led by Toussaint L'Ouverture" as one of the "greatest" acts of anticolonial resistance, he provides no further examination of this war or of its political demands. Young, *Postcolonialism,* 161.

6. Aimé Césaire, *Toussaint Louverture: La Révolution française et le problème colonial* (1981 ed.), 24. Césaire's title nonetheless frames events in Saint-Domingue in terms of the French Revolution.

7. See, for example, Nicholas Thomas, *Colonialism's Culture,* 32–104.

8. Neil Lazarus, *Nationalism and Cultural Practice in the Colonial World,* 10–12.

9. Benedict Anderson, *Imagined Communities.*

10. See, for example, Partha Chatterjee's objection to Anderson's argument that postcolonial states have adopted models of nationalism already available in Europe and the Americas in *The Nation and Its Fragments,* 5. Chatterjee argues that the project of anticolonial nationalism is to "fashion a 'modern' national culture that is nonetheless not Western."

11. Eric Hobsbawm, *Nations and Nationalism since 1780,* 18–19; Étienne Balibar, "Homo nationalis: An Anthropological Sketch of the Nation Form," in his *We, the People of Europe?* 11–30. For an analysis of classical theories of nationalism by Hans Kohn, Ernest Gellner, John Plamenatz, and others in relation to questions of political liberalism and modernization, see Partha Chatterjee, *Nationalist Thought and the Colonial World,* 1–7.

12. Balibar, *We, the People of Europe?* 22.

13. On the development of nationalism during the French Revolution in relation to rights discourses and notions of popular sovereignty, see Conor Cruise O'Brien, "Nationalism and the French Revolution"; Brian Jenkins, *Nationalism*

*in France,* 3–25; and Jacques Godechot, "The New Concept of the Nation and Its Diffusion in Europe."

14. Étienne Balibar, "Constructing and Deconstructing the Universal," lecture at Northwestern University, February 15, 2005.

15. On Balibar's conception of the paradox of universalism, see his essays "Homo nationalis" and "Citizenship without Community" in *We, the People of Europe?*; and "The Ideological Tensions of Capitalism: Universalism vs. Racism and Sexism" and "Racism and Nationalism" in *Race, Nation, Class: Ambiguous Identities.* See also his "Ambiguous Universality," in *Politics and the Other Scene.*

16. Ernesto Laclau, "Identity and Hegemony,"especially 44–55.

17. On the various demands of insurgent slaves, see Carolyn Fick, *The Making of Haiti,* 113–17; Laurent Dubois, *Avengers of the New World,* 91–114, 132–93.

18. Quoted in H. Pauléus-Sannon, *Histoire de Toussaint Louverture,* vol. 1 (1938 ed.), 152.

19. Balibar, *We, The People of Europe?* 59.

20. Geggus, *Haitian Revolutionary Studies,* 125; Dubois, *Avengers of the New World,* 141.

21. Nathalie Picquionne, "Lettre de Jean-François, Biassou, et Belair, juillet 1792."

22. Léger-Félicité Sonthonax, Proclamation, August 29, 1793, quoted in Pauléus-Sannon, *Histoire,* 1:146.

23. Ibid., 147–48.

24. Ibid., 148.

25. Françoise Vergès, *Monsters and Revolutionaries,* 6.

26. See Dubois' reading of Julien Raimond's *Réflexions sur les véritables causes des troubles et des désastres de nos colonies . . .* (Paris, 1790) in Dubois, *A Colony of Citizens,* 185.

27. Pauléus-Sannon, *Histoire,* 1:148.

28. Geggus, *Haitian Revolutionary Studies,* 127.

29. Toussaint Louverture to the people of color at Le Cap, 25 August 1793, Archives Nationales, Musée de l'histoire de France AE II 1375, microfilm AE 38 D (XXV).

30. Toussaint Louverture to "brothers and friends," 29 August 1793, Archives Nationales, Section moderne AA 53/1490. This letter has been repeatedly misquoted and mistranslated by historians, as in Dubois, *Avengers,* 176; James, *The Black Jacobins,* 125; and Pauléus-Sannon, *Histoire,* 1:155.

31. Hobsbawm, *Nations and Nationalisms,* 9. Here Hobsbawm follows Ernest Gellner.

32. Susan Buck-Morss, "Hegel and Haiti," 822, 826, 830–31.

33. See, for example, Maximilien Robespierre's pamphlet, "Sur les principes de morale politique," in *Textes choisis III,* 113.

34. Toussaint Louverture, "Réponse à l'adresse faite par Jean François à ses

soi-disants frères du Dondon," 13 June 1795, Bibliothèque nationale, Manuscrits français 12103.

35. Toussaint Louverture to Pierre Dieudonné, 11 February 1796, Bibliothèque nationale, Manuscrits français, 12104.

36. Proclamation of 25 April 1796, in Gérard de Laurent, *Toussaint Louverture à travers sa correspondance* 391.

37. Laurent, *Toussaint Louverture*, 428, 336.

38. On Toussaint's ownership of land, see Pierre Pluchon, *Toussaint Louverture: Un révolutionnaire noir* (1989 ed.), 369–71.

39. Quoted in Laurent, *Toussaint Louverture*, 172.

40. See, for example, Toussaint Louverture, "Règlement relatif à la culture," by Toussaint Louverture, 12 October 1800, Archives Nationales, microfilm series CC 9B 18.

41. James, *The Black Jacobins*, 265. See also Schoelcher, *Vie de Toussaint Louverture*, 400–402, upon which James's account appears to be based. Schoelcher cites as his source the rare pamphlet by J.-Hippolyte-Daniel de Saint-Anthoine, *Notice sur Toussaint Louverture* (Paris: A. Lacour, 1842). Another mention of this project appears in Prosper Thomas Gragnon-Lacoste, *Toussaint Louverture, général en chef de l'armée de Saint-Domingue, surnommé le premier des noirs* (Paris: A. Durant et Pedone-Lauriel, 1877), 202–4. I thank Kenneth Carpenter for sharing with me his extensive bibliographical research on this question. I also thank Deborah Jenson and David Geggus for discussing the matter with me.

42. Balibar and Wallerstein, *Race, Nation, Class,* 62.

43. On the relation between French Revolutionary universalism, expansionist projects, and military interventions abroad, see O'Brien, "Nationalism and the French Revolution," 31–40; Jacques Godechot, *La Grande nation: L'expansion révolutionnaire de la France dans le monde, 1789–1799* (Éditions Montaigne, 1956). On ideas about the status of foreigners within French borders during the Revolution, see Sophie Wahnich, *L'Impossible citoyen: L'étranger dans le discours de la Révolution française* (Paris: Albin Michel, 1997).

44. Balibar and Wallerstein, *Race, Nation, Class,* 60–61.

45. James, *The Black Jacobins,* 240.

46. Pluchon, *Toussaint Louverture* (1989), 613; Victor Schoelcher, *Vie de Toussaint Louverture* (Paris: Paul Ollendorff, 1889 ed.), 302.

47. "Constitution de Saint-Domingue," 8.

48. Homi Bhabha, *The Location of Culture,* 86.

49. Letter to the Directory, 5 November 1797, in Pauléus-Sannon, *Histoire,* 3:35.

50. The proclamation is reprinted in Baron de Vastey, *Essay on the Causes of the Revolution and the Civil Wars of Hayti,* 28. See also Pauléus-Sannon, *Histoire,* 3:50. In *Reflections on the Blacks and the Whites,* Vastey attacks the French for willfully deceiving the ex-slaves with false promises of freedom. See also [Juste Chanlatte], *Histoire de la catastrophe de Saint-Domingue,* 46.

51. [Félix Boisrond-Tonnerre], "Liberté ou la mort," 20.

52. Ibid., 21.

53. Laclau, "Identity and Hegemony," 45.

54. Balibar, *We, the People of Europe,* 23.

55. [Boisrond-Tonnerre], "Liberté ou la mort," 20.

56. Ibid., 20, 21.

57. "Constitution d'Haïti, 1805," in Madiou, 546. For an English translation, see Sibylle Fischer, *Modernity Disavowed,* 275–81.

58. Fischer, *Modernity Disavowed,* 237.

59. David Nicholls, *From Dessalines to Duvalier* 36–38; Patrick Bellegarde-Smith, *Haiti: The Breached Citadel,* 70–75.

60. [Boisrond-Tonnerre], "Liberté ou la mort," 21.

61. Geggus, *Haitian Revolutionary Studies,* 207.

62. Fischer, *Modernity Disavowed,* 241.

63. Ibid., 232.

64. Ibid.

65. [Boisrond-Tonnerre], "Liberté ou la mort," 21. For the translation of *"lugubrer,"* I draw on Fischer, *Modernity Disavowed,* 201.

66. [Boisrond-Tonnerre], "Liberté ou la mort," 20.

II

# After the Revolution

Rethinking Emancipation, Postcolonialism, and Transnationalism

# "Charged with Sympathy for Haiti"

## Harnessing the Power of Blackness and Cosmopolitanism in the Wake of the Haitian Revolution

*Ifeoma C. K. Nwankwo*

THE HAITIAN REVOLUTION was a crucial turning point for Americans of African descent residing well beyond the new republic's coasts because it inspired new visions of the connections and disconnections between people of African descent in disparate locations.[1] As this essay illuminates, such new approaches to conceptualizing the bonds and the tensions among and across African American communities were posited not only by people of African descent, but also by white abolitionists and Atlantic governments. Here I undertake a close reading of the making of a Cuban of color into a "Black" hero by U.S. African American activist Martin Delany, and frame my reading with an explication of treatments of the same individual by the colonial Cuban government and a British abolitionist. Such texts, I am arguing, lay bare the extent to which the revolution in Saint-Domingue drove U.S. African Americans as well as American governments and white abolitionists to reconceptualize the grounds of "Black" community, and, by extension, the appropriate treatment of differences in those conceptualizations.

### White Fear and the Bounds of Black Identity

The Revolution, as has been repeatedly documented, created widespread panic among those in power across the Americas in particular, and the Atlantic world in general.[2] Above all, they feared that the Revolution would spread. They feared that their blacks would replicate the Revolution on their soil. Ultimately, they feared that their blacks would see themselves as "linked and interlinked" with the Haitian revolutionaries.[3]

This fear shows up particularly clearly in discourses from and on Cuba. For instance, in the wake of the Revolution, and throughout the bulk of the nineteenth century, the Cuban government was obsessed with keeping "foreign" blacks off the island. Government offices kept track of the travels of known foreign troublemakers, such as a "conspiring negro" who had been expelled from Charleston, and a Jamaican rebel who was said to be coming to Cuba.[4] Needless to say, "French" blacks appear most often as the greatest threat. Countless documents ranging from the 1790s to the 1870s reveal the Cuban ruling class's intense fear of the "hostile designs of blacks and mulattos in the French part of Santo Domingo."[5] In 1826 charges of sedition were brought against Salvador Lafrontaigne, described as a *"negro francés"* (French black).[6] In 1802, the government blocked the disembarkation of an insurrectionary black from Guadeloupe.[7] Even as late as half a century after the founding of Haiti, a U.S. State Department agent expressed his fear that without U.S. intervention Cuba would become another "'Black Empire' like Haiti, 'whose example they would be proud to imitate' in destroying the wealth of the island and launching 'a disastrous bloody war of the races.'"[8]

The panic among those in power had a profound impact on approaches of people of African descent to constructing and representing identity and community. I contend that in the decades after the Haitian Revolution whites' fear of its presumably contagious nature was so profound that people of African descent throughout the Americas, particularly those in the public and published eye, were forced to name a relationship to Haiti in particular and to a transnational conception of community in general.[9] On one level, then, the fear was a fear of actual violence. On another it was a fear of the unification of people of African descent across lines of class, color, and geography.

As a consequence of this fear, people of African descent in the public sphere had to decide whether to represent themselves as citizens of the black world, one that also included the revolutionaries, or to conceptualize identity and seek citizenship and equality in other ways. Some, like Frederick Douglass, met this challenge by not mentioning people of African descent in other countries in their narratives of enslavement—an implicit articulation of a relationship, albeit one of distance. Others, like James T. Holly, also from the United States, chose to embrace transnational racial community by emigrating to Haiti or using the Revolution to threaten those in power with the daunting prospect of its replication on U.S. soil. The uprising was significant, therefore, not only because it brought into being the first black republic in the Americas—one that became an enduring symbol for blacks throughout the hemisphere (as recalled by Césaire's oft-repeated celebration of the Revolution as the moment "where negritude rose for the first time")—but also because it inspired new visions of the possible grounds of intraracial relationality.[10]

## Enlightenment Cosmopolitanism, Black Cosmopolitanism

Texts by both free-born and formerly enslaved people of African descent in the Americas reveal that individuals' decisions about how and whether to mention or define themselves explicitly in relation to people of African descent from other parts of the Americas raise questions about the proper place of cosmopolitanism in the constitution and public articulation of African American (in the continental sense) identities. Cosmopolitanism —commonly understood to mean the definition of oneself through or in relation to the world—forms a particularly salient entry point for analyses of the approaches to identity represented in such texts because of its crucial place in nascent Enlightenment philosophies of (white and European) subjectivity and therefore also in the mechanisms used to dehumanize people of African descent in the Americas.[11]

The perception of people of African descent as less than human and as not worthy of being seen as equal to those of European descent operated in tandem with the construction of people of African descent as an antithesis of the modern. The desire of these supposedly "subhuman" people to be seen as equal was, therefore, always already bound up with their desire to be seen as modern. Statements made in the public sphere were consequently grasped firmly as opportunities to prove the individual's or the community's modernity. For a number of U.S. African American thinkers, the Haitian Revolution provided such an opportunity. James T. Holly, for example, celebrates the Revolution as "one of the noblest, grandest, and most justifiable outbursts against tyrannical oppression that is recorded on the pages of the world's history" during which "a race of almost dehumanized men—made so by an oppressive slavery of three centuries—arose from their slumber of the ages, and redressed their own unparalleled wrongs with a terrible hand in the name of God and humanity."[12] He presents the Revolution as evidence of people of African descent's humanity and civilization. He accomplishes his task through synecdoche: the part, Haiti, is meant to stand in for the whole, people of African descent across the continent, as well as humankind itself.

In contextualizing the Revolution as part of "the world's history," Holly constructs the uprising as an event that exemplifies humankind's potential for nobility, grandeur, and pursuit of justice. In his identification of the agents and beneficiaries of the Revolution as "a race of dehumanized men" rather than as "Haitians" or "people of Haiti," he opts for a more general term "race" that can be productively read as referring to both the people of Haiti, in particular, and all people of African descent more broadly. This blurring continues in his use of "their," because the subject (more specifically the possessing subject, since "their" is a possessive form) is "the race." The slumber and the wrongs, therefore, belong to the race—to all people of African descent, not just the people of Haiti. Evident in his celebration of the Revolution, then, are both a broad notion of racial community and a presumption that this particular event's value, for him and the world, is inherently linked to its suitability to stand in for the general. His presumption of the Haitian Revolution's universality, then, allows him to argue for a recognition of people of African descent as human, civilized, and, by extension, modern.

As a crucial element of modernity, cosmopolitanism was part of the ideology that drove the dehumanization of people of African descent. Imperialism and Orientalism were, in fact, forms of European cosmopolitanism—ways in which Europeans constructed their definitions of self and community in relation to and through their relationship to the world.[13] As part of this historical and ideological context, people of African descent evaluated the usefulness of cosmopolitanism for their own struggle to be recognized as human and equal (and modern). The approaches of people of African descent to public self-representation were born, in significant part, of the Atlantic governments' attempts to deny them access to a black identity that included the Haitians, that is to say, access to claiming their own cosmopolitan subjectivity. As the Cuban government's attempts to prevent the transnational movement of people of African descent exemplify, the white fear that arose in the wake of the Haitian Revolution was not only a fear of violence, but also a fear of people of African descent daring to engage beyond the boundaries drawn for them. This denial of access to cosmopolitan subjectivity coexisted with a denial of access to both national subjectivity and humanity, and, perhaps most significantly, with an emphasis on race, effectively determining the possible parameters of identity for people of African descent. The result was a uniquely tenuous situation. Race, nation, and humanity were three major referents through which individuals defined themselves and others in this Atlantic world so permeated by Enlightenment and French Revolutionary notions of subjectivity, but only one of the three referents was allowed people of African descent—race. Furthermore, even their ideas of what race and racial community meant were undercut because they frequently contradicted predominant characterizations of blacks. Consequently, this population often had to choose which of the parameters denied them they most wished to challenge, and by extension which referent they most wanted to have the right to claim.

As a result of this ongoing battle, texts that represent the identities claimed by or projected onto people of African descent in the wake of the Revolution posit particular perceptions of the appropriate definitions of and relationship between racial collectivism, national affinity, and cosmopolitanism. These perceptions include those that highlight race while negating the possibility of national affinity or citizenship (for example, that put forward by the Cuban colonial government); those that call attention to both a racial category and national affinity in the service of a transnationally framed goal (articulated by white abolitionists); and those that construct blackness as both a national and a transnational concept (embraced by Martin Delany).

This essay calls particular attention to a "cosmopolitanism from below" that came of age at the same time the forces of hegemonic cosmopolitanism in the Atlantic world were compelled to reconfigure themselves to deal with the new threats posed by the uprising in Haiti.[14] I contend that the Revolution instigated a battle of cosmopolitanisms. It created a crisis for the forces of hegemonic cosmopolitanism, making them recognize their dehumanizing cosmopolitanism's shortcomings, acknowledge the potential cosmopolitanism of those they sought to subjugate, and develop new ways to define and actuate their definitions of their own communities, as well as of those "below." At the same time it created the conditions for the rise of new approaches to engaging cosmopolitanism on the part of people of African descent themselves.

The remainder of the essay uses an analysis of one case to compare the perspectives on the place of cosmopolitanism in notions of racial community articulated by those above and those below in the wake of the Haitian Revolution. The case is that of Plácido, Cuban poet of color. The nature of representations of him in texts produced by the colonial government in Cuba, a white British abolitionist Joseph Soul, and a U.S. African American activist Martin Delany, reveal the mechanics and multiple agents of the construction of "Black" community during this period. All three envision a black community that transcends or transgresses national and social boundaries, to make their (very divergent) cases. In deciding to either highlight or downplay Plácido's racial and national identity, the Cuban government, white abolitionists, and black abolitionists, I am arguing, construct not only an individual but also a racial collective.

## Locating Plácido

Gabriel de la Concepción Valdés, commonly known as Plácido, a free Cuban poet of color, was executed in 1844 by the government in Cuba for allegedly leading what the government perceived as one of the largest conspiracies of slaves and free people of color against Cuban whites: *La Conspiración de la Escalera,* the Ladder Conspiracy, named after the torture tool for which the Cuban government was infamous. This unrealized uprising was supposedly planned to consist of simultaneous rebellions at multiple Cuban sites, culminating in the destruction of the Cuban slave system. Hundreds were executed for supposedly plotting this revolution that, according to the colonial government, even involved David Turnbull, the former English consul to Cuba.

Scholars continue to debate whether or not the conspiracy was a figment of the colonial Cuban government's active and fearful imagination.[15] There is consensus, however, on these key points: (1) the slave population in Cuba was increasing exponentially as more slaves were brought in to feed the boom in the Cuban sugar-based economy, (2) the colonial government was cognizant and deathly afraid of the real possibility of rebellions such as the Haitian Revolution, and (3) the abolition of slavery in the British colonies in 1833 increased the colonial government's fear while also creating pressure on Spain to move toward abolishing slavery. Regardless of the details of the conspiracy, the fact is that Plácido was executed by firing squad on June 28, 1844. Although before that point Plácido had been an important figure on the Cuban literary and political scene, on this date he became more powerful and dangerous than he could ever have been alive.

The absence of certitude in terms of the *Conspiración de la Escalera* itself mirrors the fact that many questions remain unanswered, and perhaps unanswerable, about Plácido's life. Although several accounts of his life have been written, there is disagreement between the authors in several areas, particularly among the nineteenth-century biographers.[16] There is significantly less disagreement among the mid- to late twentieth-century biographies.[17] They all generally concur that Plácido was born free in Havana in 1809. He wrote his first poems at the age of twelve, despite having only had a few sporadic periods of official schooling. He began to study literature more seriously with the support of the contacts he had made while a printer's apprentice. As more of his poetry was published he began to be invited to special events sponsored by Cuba's literati, and became a regular contributor to key literary magazines. His increased connections with the literati, many of whom were anticolonialists and slavery reform activists led to increased surveillance by the Spanish colonial authorities. It was perhaps this greater visibility that led to his being arrested for presumed participation in the Ladder Conspiracy, the arrest that led to the end of his life.[18]

## The Making of a Race Man, The Making of a Race

In death, Plácido became a symbol for both pro- and antislavery forces, inside and outside Cuba. From the perspective of these forces, his symbolic value resided, in large part, in his racial identity. Their representations of him not only ascribe a racial identity to him; they also either link him to or detach him from the Cuban nation in the service of achieving the authors' pro- or antislavery goals. Regardless of their differing motives, however, officials of the colonial government in Cuba, white abolitionists, and black activists were united in attributing to Plácido a belief in the predominance of racial consciousness over national identity.

Plácido was essentially made into a "race man." The concept is especially prevalent during this period, when the efforts of people of African descent to define their racial community and their fight to be recognized as men came to occupy a central position on the Atlantic stage. Scholarship on black leaders of the period (such as Frederick Douglass) illustrates that "race men" certainly did exist then, even though the term "race man" is most often used to describe twentieth-century figures and does not appear to have been in use during the period under study here.[19] I use the term to reflect the position of leadership ascribed to Plácido, and to spotlight both the racial and gender dimensions of the term. He is constructed as the representative and leader of a race, a race that can and must only be led by a man.[20] A battle over the humanity of people of African descent was fought, therefore, through dueling representations of Plácido as either a savage leader of an inhuman population, or a noble hero of an embattled collective.

## Pro-Slavery Discourse and the Construction of Black Community

The official discourses born of the fear that the Haitian Revolution would be replicated reveal the dialectical, dynamic, and dialogic relationship between views of the identities of people of African descent from above and from below. People of African descent acted together to foment uprisings, leading to official discourse about them as a collective. Yet I would argue that at the same time, the official perception (and treatment) of people of African descent as an undifferentiated (inhuman) mass instigated the uprisings and the notion of connectedness that produced them. The sentence imposed upon the *Escalera* conspirators, for example, displays a convoluted racial logic that simultaneously subsumes all people of African ancestry into one group—a group that wants to unite and make Cuba into another Haiti, and calls attention to their differences, based on a multipartite racial classification system.

The "conspiracy" was headed, as the officials repeat frequently, by Plácido, described as a free *pardo,* or person of mixed race. In the sentence against Plácido and his alleged fellow conspirators, the Cuban government describes the uprising repeatedly as "the conspiracy of the people of color ... for the extermination of ... the white population." Among their list of conspirators they specifically name *"pardos libres"* (free mixed-race people), *"morenos libres"* (free blacks), *"negros esclavos"* (black slaves), and *"las negradas"* (the slave masses),[21] thereby implicating and linking all racial groups with any named or claimed African ancestry. The conception of a connection between all the people of color of all classes is emphasized throughout the sentence, and reinforces the broad notion of black community indexed in the fear of the reproduction of the Haitian Revolution. The repetition of this phrasing ("the conspiracy of the people of color . . . for the extermination of . . . the white population") highlights for the white Cuban elite that the danger of this uprising lies, not simply in its existence, but more importantly in the coming together of people of color across various boundaries. It announces that the boundaries that are supposed to keep these people separated are crumbling, and that Haiti is beginning to happen here. As if to reiterate this point the document details how these different groups that are supposed to be separate came to unite.

In attributing disparate motivating factors to each group, the officials reveal a tension between the desire to negate differences between people of color, subsuming them into one group, and the drive to accord symbolic and social value to class and color differences. According to the government authors, the *pardos* joined the conspiracy with the object of gaining, through the movement, concessions that would improve their social condition. The *morenos* were reluctant to enlist because they were free and realized that they would not benefit from the plan. The authors felt no need to explain why the black slaves agreed to participate, but did note that their superior strength overwhelmed the *pardos.* In the government's view, the *pardos* seduced the *morenos,* the *morenos* seduced the *pardos,* the *negros* lent their brawn and tendency toward violence, then these races united and formed one, with the goal of the extermination and extinction of all whites, making themselves the owners of the island. This document, in effect, outlines the creation of a racial collective within which class and color differences are of minimal relevance.

Although in much of the text people of color are represented as coming together either at someone else's (namely the British consul's) behest, out of selfish consideration for their own subgroup, or simply out of their deep desire to exterminate the whites, it proves especially difficult for the government to completely deny Plácido's agency, and further to represent Plácido as anything other than a "race man." The government's version of events has Plácido present at the first meetings of conspirators from different regions of the island, but reduces the black insurrectionists to blank slates upon whom Turnbull, the British consul, wrote.[22] That representation is undercut by the fact that these men journeyed of their own accord from all over the country to meet and discuss the uprising, as well as by everything else the document goes on to say about Plácido. As the government tells the story, he did more work for the conspiracy than any of the others, serving as president of the principal junta, recruiter, instigator, one of the first agents of the conspiracy, elected official, and its first director.[23] All of these aspects of the government's approach to representing Plácido implicitly attribute to him a profound commitment to this united racial community, and thus lay bare that the government's ultimate fear is that united community. As the president of the conspiracy, and by extension as a leader of this new (trans)racial collective, he was therefore one of the greatest threats to the stability of the Cuban racial infrastructure, the fulcrum upon which the Cuban political and economic system rested.

## White Abolitionists, Black Martyr

Plácido also posed a major threat to the Cuban government even after his death, because his story and poetry traveled. London resident and British West Indian abolitionist Joseph Soul, for example, calls in an 1845 letter to the editor of the *Jamaica Guardian and Patriot* for the erection of a monument in Jamaica to honor Plácido.[24] Soul's letter, in addition to illustrating the danger to the stability of the slave system in Cuba inherent in interactions, whether representational, ideological, or material, between Cubans of color and the outside world (the danger being that they could be used by those who wish to overturn the system), also reveals the racialization of Plácido that Soul enacts as he makes this Cuban of color into an international abolitionist symbol. Like the governmental authors of the sentence, Soul makes Plácido into a type of "race man." In his case, he identifies Plácido unequivocally with "the African Race" throughout the letter. The term "African" would seem to mark this racialization as different from that of the sentence pronounced on Plácido, which focuses on designations based on proportion of African blood, such as *pardo, moreno,* and *negro.* These proslavery and abolitionist documents are clearly at odds in terms of both the descriptive terms for, and opinions of, people of color.

Given their opposing positions on the continued enslavement of people of African descent, we expect proslavery and antislavery discourses to differ in their perceptions of Plácido. Just as important, however, and perhaps even more significant for this discussion of nineteenth-century notions of black community in the Americas, is their fundamental similarity. Both discourses rest on a valuation of racial identity and a devaluation of (Cuban) national identity. Although the abolitionists' goal is clearly the opposite of the Cuban government's, and the terminology ("African race" vs. *"pardo"*) is different, indexing different systems of racial classification, the basic object of focus—his presumed connection to a broad-based community of color (whether defined in terms of his blood, continental origin, or color) is the same. Intracollective differences and (Cuban) national affinity are ultimately irrelevant to the racial community and the race man that the colonial government and Soul construct. The question that remains is whether and how U.S. African American writers who sought to use the transnational black identity the Revolution made possible as a weapon against Atlantic slavery diverge from white writers (whether pro- or antislavery) in their approaches to conceptualizing and representing Plácido.

## Brothers(?) in Chains? U.S. Black Abolitionists and Cubans of Color

Tales of the life and death of Plácido, as well as his poetry, spread widely after his execution in 1844. Among those who found the stories particularly compelling and useful were black abolitionists in the United States. The stories provided a clear way for the abolitionists to link the struggles of people of African descent in the United States and Cuba through the story of one well-known individual figure, rather than through statistical information or general reports of insurrections or mutinies. Inherent in the discourse on Plácido (then and now) is a tension between the view of him as an exemplar of the particularities of the Cuban context and the perception of him as a representative of the experience of the

African Diaspora in particular, and of humanity in general. Black abolitionists use representations of Plácido both to envision a basis for black
communal identity and to argue for the importance of differences in
location, language, identification, color, or class within the race. These
abolitionists, unlike either the Cuban colonial government or the white
abolitionists, consciously aim both to create and to elevate and uplift a
black community.[25]

It was in this spirit that U.S. African American political activist Martin
Robison Delany published a series of stories between 1859 and 1862
about the planning of a hemispheric black rebellion. They were later collected as the novel *Blake; Or, the Huts of America* (1970). *Blake* is clearly
meant as a threat to those in power, dramatizing a pan-Atlantic version
of the Haitian Revolution. The rebel leader and protagonist of the novel
is Henry Blake/Henrico Blacus, an African American/Cuban slave who
travels throughout the U.S. South and then to Cuba fomenting a transnational uprising, the ultimate goal of which is the overturning of the
entire Atlantic slave system.

The first part of the novel is set in the U.S. South. Henry's rebellious
anger takes root when his master sells his wife away to Cuba: "I'm tired
of looking [to] the other side . . . I want something on this earth as
well as a promise of things in another world. I and my wife have both
been robbed of our liberty and you want me to be satisfied with a hope
of heaven. I won't do any such thing; I have waited long enough on
heavenly promises; I'll wait no longer."[26] From this point forward, we
see Henry traveling from plantation to plantation across the deep South
attempting to stoke the fires of rebellion in the hearts and minds of those
similarly dehumanized by slavery. The second part takes place primarily
in Cuba. Henry enlists the help of a range of Cubans of color, including
his newly rediscovered wife and women and men of a range of colors and
class positions. The novel ends with the rebellion on the verge of actua-
tion on the island, with one of the Cuban characters, sword raised, shout-
ing, "Woe be unto those devils of whites, I say" (313). Included among
the many Cuban characters in the novel is Plácido. From Delany's perspective, Plácido was a Cuban version of his protagonist Henry, a vision
reiterated through his representation of Plácido as Henry's cousin.

An analysis of Delany's version of Plácido, and of his position in relation to Henry (the preeminent race man in the text), yields great insight
into both Delany's notion of black community and the place of differences in location, language, identification, class, or color within that
conception. In particular it enables us to see that despite the fact that

Delany's goal is to highlight the strength and power of a unified transnational black community and of a cosmopolitan, truly black leader, he parallels the Cuban government and the white abolitionists in his valuation of Placido's racial identity and allegiance. He also struggles to simultaneously acknowledge the potential impact of differences in location, national affinity, identification, color, and class within this transnational racial community he envisions while also effectively representing this unified collective's power.

## Delany's Plácido: Racial Identity and Ideology

In terms of appearance, Delany's Plácido is racially ambiguous. In his first appearance in the novel, Plácido is described as having an "orange-peel complexion, Black hair hanging lively quite to the shoulders, heavy deep brow and full moustache, with great expressive Black piercing eyes" (192–93). This ambiguity stands in sharp contrast to the emphasis throughout the text on Henry's obvious "Blackness" and purity of (African) blood: "Henry was a Black—a pure Negro—handsome, manly, and intelligent" (16). Plácido, in comparison to Henry, is less black. In addition, as is concomitant with Delany's (and the white abolitionists', and the Cuban government's) construction of true blackness as essentially male, Plácido is less masculine, described as also being "of slender form" and "sinewy" (16).[27] The effect of the racially ambiguous representation of Plácido is to emphasize Henry's position as the real man, the real (black) man, and the real race man. Delany's own racialist beliefs in the supreme importance of purity of blood are detailed in his text, *The Origin of Races and Color* (1879). Delany explicates his belief that there are only three pure races—yellow, black, and white—and that racial mixing will eventually result in the predomination of one of the races in the descendants. Although the offspring of an intermarriage "becomes a mixed race," "that mixed race is an abnormal race," and will eventually, with continued crossings, once again become one of the pure races.[28] Given these views, his initial representation of Plácido as racially ambiguous makes it difficult to tell whether that representation is meant to be positive, and perhaps more importantly, whether we are supposed to read Plácido as black.

Delany endeavors to quickly clear up this confusion, though. Despite Plácido's racially ambiguous appearance, Delany makes his Plácido one who embraces a broad notion of black community that crosses boundaries of color, class, and nation. Delany displays some flexibility here with respect to the physicality that is defined as black—surely forced, at least in part, by the descriptions of the apparently very fair Plácido circulating in the North American media—but absolutely no flexibility with respect to politics. Although Plácido does not share Henry's phenotypical blackness, he does share his ideological and political identity. Very early in the Cuba section of the novel, Henry and Plácido express their common commitment to (what Delany represents as) their race and begin to exchange information about what they have done and will do to remove the yoke of oppression that binds them. Plácido says: "'Give me your hand, Henry'—both clasping hands—'now by the instincts of our nature, and mutual sympathy in the common cause of our race, pledge to me on the hazard of our political destiny what you intend to do. . . . Heaven certainly designed it, and directed you here at this auspicious moment, that the oppressed of Cuba also may 'declare the glory of God!'" (195). To emphasize their connectedness, Delany includes several images and phrases that call attention to their bond: "clasping hands," "our nature," "mutual sympathy," "common cause," "our race." Through these images and phrases Delany ascribes to Plácido a definition of blackness that includes common blood and an activist political stance. Delany's Plácido believes wholeheartedly in the "common cause"—the cause of the overturning of the Atlantic slave system, and hopes only that "the oppressed of Cuba" should be partakers of it. This statement is the first of many such statements that Delany puts in the mouth of his Plácido that speak to a broad conception of racial community.

There is a tension in the text, however, between Delany's desire to impose that broad conception on all the characters and his recognition of the differences that exist in reality between such individuals and communities. That tension is clearly evident in his decision to make the "orange-peel" complexioned Plácido the cousin and second-in-command of the unmistakably black Henry, despite his own professed views of the abnormality and inferiority of mixed-race people. Although physical descriptions and representations of the historical Plácido vary in terms of his size, they share the characterization of his skin tone as definitely not dark.[29] Delany wants to claim Plácido as an exemplary black man (and race man), but must do something with the reality of Plácido's difference in order to do so. Delany chooses to make him politically, if not phenotypically, black.

It is no coincidence, then, that shortly after the physical description of a racially ambiguous Plácido, this same Plácido expresses radical antislavery politics. Delany's Plácido reads Henry a poem he has written for a meeting of revolutionaries in which he not only decries slavery, but also presents slaves' anger and violence against their enslavers as righteous. The poem is an explicitly political one in which the speaker dreams of killing his oppressors and enslavers. It reads, in part:

> Were I a slave I would be free!
>> I would not live to live a slave;
> But rise and strike for liberty
>> For Freedom, or a martyr's grave!
>
> One look upon the tyrant's chains
>> Would draw my sabre from its sheath
> And drive the hot blood through my veins
>> To rush for liberty or death."
>
>> (195)

Rather than live in slavery, the speaker vows that he would risk his life in a struggle for freedom. The shades of the Haitian Revolution are clearly present here. The poem is devoid of specific geographical references, thereby emphasizing the belief of Delany's Plácido that the oppressed everywhere share a common condition that binds them regardless of specific national or geographical location.

Delany, however, also spends substantial time in the novel parsing the differences between the Cuban and U.S. racial infrastructure. Although the novel is based on a presumption of a connection between these revolutionaries, a connection that is at least in part a racial one, Delany takes great pains to note differences in ideology and history between those who would participate in Henry's revolution. At one point he has his narrator call attention to differences in the ways people of African descent are identified in Cuba and the United States. As one part of the plan is beginning to be enacted, the narrator remarks that

> among the first few who appeared on the quay was a mulatto gentleman. There was nothing very remarkable about this, because were Cubans classified according to their complexion or race, three out of five of the inhabitants called white would decidedly be claimed by the colored people, though there is a larger number much fairer than those classified and known in the register as colored. To this class belonged the gentleman in question. (238)

Here he states explicitly that many individuals classified as white in Cuba would be "claimed by the colored people" in the United States. Henry has been working as a sailor on board a slave ship that has just returned from Africa with a shipment of slaves, and Plácido, the mulatto who appears on the quay, is secretly helping him to delay the auction and organize a mutiny. One of Plácido's major tasks is to spread "news" of the mutinous nature of the captives to discourage speculators from buying them. In addition, he hires fair-skinned people of color as agents for their political cause. They are to pretend to be slave buyers, purchase slaves, and take them to safety. Delany emphasizes these agents' color: "These agents were among the fairest of the quadroons, high in the esteem and confidence of their people, the entire cargo of captives through them going directly into Black families or their friends" (238). By acknowledging differences between racial infrastructures while simultaneously emphasizing common political action, Delany situates Plácido as part of a transnational black freedom network that cuts across racial infrastructures. He implies here that it is irrelevant whether Plácido and the others are fair, mulatto, classified as white, or classified as colored. What matters is that he and they are part of the push toward the common goal of freedom. Blackness is more about politics than it is about purity of blood.

Delany's racial logic here recalls, in curious ways, that of the Cuban government's sentence against the Ladder conspirators, and dramatizes the racial nightmare they imagined. Like the officials who wrote the sentence, Delany suggests that differences in color and classification are irrelevant when revolution is the issue. In his novel, as in the sentence, the *pardos, morenos,* and *negros* unite to plan this revolution. Delany's Black Cuban world reflects the diversity and complexity of nineteenth-century Cuba. It is populated by individuals of a wide variety of skin tones, occupations, classes, and origins from slaves like Henry, his wife Lotty/Maggie who came from the U.S. South, to Cuban Creole slaves like Dominico, to newly captured Africans like Mendi and Abyssa, to "educated, wealthy ladies" like Madame Cordora and her daughter, to the surgeon Pino Golias. All of these individuals unite, despite their differences, in the service of the freedom of all who have African blood. Delany's approach to portraying the character Gofer Gondolier, the palace caterer who can easily be thought of as the most violent figure in the novel given his "Cuban carver," a knife not meant for carving meats but rather for "carving of a different kind," makes this point powerfully (255). In fact, it is Gondolier, a dark-complexioned Cuban of color, who speaks the last and most threatening words of the novel: "Woe be unto those devils of whites, I say" (313). The point that Delany makes through his painting of Cuba is a powerful and clear one: people of African descent, regardless of their status, color, or national location, should have a common interest in the freedom of all members of the collective.

Despite the novel's predominant leaning toward this vision of black unity, though, it is still plagued by a tension between unity above all and the representation/recognition of differences similar to that which appeared in the sentence meted out by Cuban officials against the conspirators of *La Escalera*. Delany, through his narrator, does acknowledge that these revolutionaries represent a portion of the population, and that in the larger social structure divisions between classes of people of color are made and adhered to: "The four great divisions of society were white, Black, free and slave; and these were again subdivided into many other classes, as rich, poor, and such like. The free and slaves among the Blacks did not associate, nor the high and low among the free of the same race. And there was among them even another general division—Black and colored—which met with little favor from the intelligent" (276). Through Plácido and the other Cubans of color, Delany engages the differences between modes of identification, but is always sure to balance that attention with an emphasis on both the African blood that runs through all of their veins and on the common goal of freedom.

## What Is Cuba to Delany and His Plácido?

So far, I have noted the ways in which Delany has attempted to confront and represent the differences between Cubans of color and African Americans, while also constructing a community based on political and ancestral commonality. Delany's treatment of Plácido's Cubanness illustrates his attitude toward the place of nonracial national identity and difference in his idea of racial community, and more specifically in his conception of a race man. As previously mentioned, Plácido and Henry are represented as cousins. In fact, Henry is, as he puts it, "the lost boy of Cuba" (193). Both Henry and Plácido are Cuban, but they differ in their relationships to their Cubanness. Plácido is tied, geographically and culturally, to Cuba, whereas Henry simply has his origins there. As if to emphasize the irrelevance of national roots for a real race man, however, Delany strives to make the reader unsure about Henry's Cuban roots. Even though he identifies himself as "the lost boy of Cuba," at another point he describes himself as "African born and Spanish bred" (200). During the section of the text that takes place in the United States, Henry is only distinguishable from (what seem to be) his fellow African Americans by his speech.[30] Henry has no nation but the black racial nation.

In general, Delany constructs nonracial national affinities as irrelevant, and further as hindrances to the enactment of transnational black community. This point is illustrated on the very first page of the Cuba section when the first Cuban of color we see is referred to by the narrator as "a *Black* driver" (my emphasis; 163). Regardless of whether he is Cuban, he is, in terms of both phenotype and status, black from Delany's perspective, and Delany is sure to make that clear. Plácido is Cuban for Delany insofar as he was born, raised, and lives in Cuba and is wholly familiar with the political, social, and cultural dynamics of the Cuban context. From Delany's point of view, though, Plácido's Cubanness makes little difference for his vision of race. Plácido refers to the band of revolutionaries as "the army of emancipation of the oppressed men and women of Cuba," indexing his definition of the oppressed of Cuba as the people of color, as those who would be emancipated (241). Although we can read the fight for Cuban independence from the tyrannical rule of the Spanish crown that gained strength and eventually had its success during to the mid- to late nineteenth century into the absence of specific racial terminology from the poems and statements such as these, Delany does not use any words that speak specifically to the link between the fight for abolition and the struggle for Cuban independence.

As the historian Ada Ferrer notes, the two struggles were interwoven in the minds of many of the *mambises* of color who fought and died during the wars for Cuban independence.[31] The first war of Cuban independence began in 1868 with an armed uprising of black and white Cubans known as the Grito de Yara. The movement was led by a white Creole sugar planter and slaveholder, Carlos Manuel de Céspedes, who as part of his movement not only freed his slaves, but went so far as to address them as "citizens" and call them to "help 'conquer liberty and independence' for Cuba."[32] Cubans of primarily African descent were both participants and leaders in the Cuban wars of independence, making them an integral part of not only the birthing of the Cuban republic, but also, as Cuban historian Fernando Martínez Heredia explicates, the ideological and philosophical identity of the Cuban nation.[33]

Delany does, however, have Plácido display nonchalance about the Spanish Crown, and about what the whites in power consider to be Cuban culture and/or national events. At one point Plácido informs Henry that the next day will be "the celebration of the nativity of the Infanta Isabella," "a grand national fete" (240). Plácido exhibits no interest in actually celebrating with his countrymen, and instead (along with Henry) sees this day as a prime opportunity to actuate the revolution. Dana D. Nelson's theorization of the strategic value of being identified with a general class or based on one's own particularities is especially useful for thinking about Delany's treatment of Plácido's Cubanness. Nelson tells the story of white American political leader Benjamin Rush who has a dream in which he enters a grove filled with African Americans engaged in a religious celebration who are "cheerful and happy," until they see him, that is.[34] He asks them the reason for their great change from happiness to "general perturbation" and they respond, "We perceive you are a white man." For them, as they go on to explain, his whiteness, "which is the emblem of innocence in every other creature of God, is to us a sign of guilt in a man." They remind him of the atrocities that the black race has suffered at the hands of his group. As Rush begins to explain himself as a friend and advocate, one of the people recognizes him and calls him by his name and rushes up to embrace him. For Nelson, this dream exemplifies "white manhood's privilege, the liberal franchise of individual exceptionality." She points out that whereas he is "named, particularized, and recognized," we only learn the name of one of the Blacks. Delany simultaneously particularizes and generalizes Plácido. On one hand, through his construction of Plácido as an individual, exceptional figure, Delany claims this privilege for Cubans of color as well as other members of the African Diaspora. On the other, he does not choose to represent the Cuban particularities that might have resulted in a figure like Plácido having a different view of racial identity than Delany (or a figure like Henry), or actually feeling an affinity for La Infanta Isabella.

The historical details along with the expansive geographical scope of the novel, that includes ports, nations, seas, and peoples from a variety of sites in both hemispheres, is meant to ensure that the global white audience understands that they too are at risk. Delany wants them to know that their blacks could also be planning this revolution. He wants them to think about the fact that black sailors like Henry are crossing the seas on merchant vessels, and are not *only* working for the white captains and slave traders, even though they may seem to be. They are also working for their people by carrying information and fomenting multilocational rebellions. Mulattoes, like Plácido, who may appear to be happy to have a few of the privileges of being white, may actually be the ones who strike the ultimate death blow. Delany is saying to his audience, you may want to believe that the only radical blacks are those "voodoo ones" in Haiti, but if you do not want to die, I strongly encourage you to rethink that position. So on one level, Delany is employing Afro-Cubans as a synecdoche for all people of African descent everywhere. The fact of their Cubanness is simultaneously pivotal and irrelevant to their symbolic value for Delany. On one level, it allows Delany to talk back to the popular white view of Cubans of African descent as being at low risk for large-scale rebellion because they were divided by a multipartite system of racial classification, and because they were supposedly not as violent as their Haitian neighbors to the east who had taken their freedom with such violence or their Jamaican neighbors to the south who had used violence to force the British to emancipate them. Their Cubanness is also important because it allows Delany to play on the fears of the Africanization of Cuba that were rampant throughout the nineteenth century. In addition, during this period the United States was debating the annexation of Cuba and the Cuban elites were all too willing to acquiesce because the Spanish appeared to be succumbing to British pressure to end slavery on the island. This text, then, speaks specifically to the Cuban situation, warning the U.S. officials to make sure that they really understand the fight they would be getting into.

On another level, however, what is important to Delany is that there is a group of people of African descent in this hemisphere who are willing to unite and take their people's freedom by violence. He could just as easily have set the second half of the novel in Brazil during that period, or in any other part of the Americas before emancipation. Such a novel, however, would certainly not have had the same potential to inspire fear as this one because of the emphasis in contemporaneous discourse on Cuba in particular, and more generally on the volatility of that Western Caribbean triangle consisting of Cuba the slave society, free black Haiti on its right, and emancipated Jamaica to its south.

Clearly, for public figures of African descent like Delany, choosing to identify a person as black or as a member of a black community or of a community of color was about more than a simply phenotypical reference, a naming of origins, or a marking of individuals of "African descent who claim an identity with the race."[35] For people of African descent doing so, particularly in the wake of the Revolution, it was also a political action aimed at advancing specific goals, rather than the naming of an always already obvious identity. The political goals, however, do not erase the troubling contemporaneous and subsequent implications of the construction of transnational black community by way of the simultaneous subsuming and referencing of differences. The black activist discourse born of the Revolution must be understood as a complex, multivalent, dynamic one that indexes both the possibilities and perils of imagining black community while also confronting the reality of disparities in location, identification, color, and class. The Haitian Revolution created the conditions of possibility for imagining the kind of broad-based racial community analyzed here—one that could actuate a cross-color, cross-class, continent-wide revolution, one driven by a combination of local and cosmopolitan notions of racial community. At the same time, representations of and responses to it exposed the dangerous downplaying of difference that is inherent in the process of imagining such a community.

## Notes

Portions of this essay were originally published in my book, *Black Cosmopolitanism: Racial Consciousness and Transnational Identity in the Nineteenth-Century Americas* (Copyright © 2005 University of Pennsylvania Press), and are reprinted by permission of the University of Pennsylvania Press.

1. Carole Boyce Davies among others has pointed out the difficulty with descriptive terminologies for blacks in the Americas: *Black Women, Writing, and Identity*, 5. As a result I employ the terms *U.S. African American* and *U.S. black* to describe blacks who are born, raised, and have multigenerational roots in the United States, the terms *people of African descent in the Americas* and, less often, *African American* to refer to a broader continental community. I use *black* to connote not any inherent quality, but rather to index a way in which individuals or groups define themselves or are defined by others.

2. On the Revolution's impact on the United States, see Alfred N. Hunt, *Haiti's Influence on Antebellum America*.

3. Term taken from Frederick Douglass's description of his bond with his fellow slaves in *Narrative of the Life of Frederick Douglass*, 49.

4. Archivo Nacional de la República de Cuba, Asuntos Políticos, legajo 113, no. 58; legajo 117, no. 22. Unless otherwise indicated, translations in this essay are mine.

5. Ibid., legajo 99, no. 101.

6. Archivo Nacional de la República de Cuba, Reales, Cédulas, y Órdenes, legajo 31, no. 16.

7. Ibid., no. 50.

8. Quoted in Eric Sundquist, *To Wake the Nations*, 183.

9. I use *transnational* in the literal sense, meaning crossing national boundaries. *Cosmopolitan*, in my estimation, implies a weltanshauung, rather than simply a specific action or moment.

10. Aimé Césaire, *Notebook of a Return to the Native Land*, 15.

11. Space does not allow for a more detailed discussion of the predominant notions of cosmopolitanism during this period and beyond. For more, see Ifeoma Kiddoe Nwankwo, *Black Cosmopolitanism*; Thomas Schlereth, *The Cosmopolitan Ideal in Enlightenment Thought*; and Sankar Muthu, *Enlightenment against Empire*.

12. James Theodore Holly, "A Vindication of the Capacity of the Negro Race," 23.

13. See Edward Said, *Orientalism*, 12.

14. Here, I refer to the alternating cooperation and conflict between the dominant powers in the slaveocracies of the Americas over the appropriate approaches to preventing another Haiti. The ambivalent relationships between the colonial government in Cuba and the British and between the Creole elites in Cuba and the United States exemplify this vacillation.

15. Most biographies of Plácido, including that by Frederick Stimson, author of the foremost English-language biography of the poet, note increased travel throughout western Cuba, between Havana and Matanzas in particular, during 1843 and 1844, but are hesitant to present those movements as definitive proof of his involvement. Many scholars, Franklin Knight, author of the seminal text *Slave Society in Cuba during the Nineteenth Century* (1970), among them, question whether the conspiracy existed at all. Others state unequivocally that the conspiracy did exist. Robert Paquette has produced a thorough examination of the conspiracy. Using the archived documents in the Escoto collection among others, he argues, quite convincingly, that the conspiracy existed as several conspiracies, "each overlapping, if only in some cases at the margin, each dilating and contracting at particular times between 1841 and 1844." As I do here, Paquette also notes that regardless of the details of the conspiracy, it is clear that this conspiracy both reflected and produced a major change in the ideologies of both those who were beginning to consider themselves citizens of a nascent Cuban nation and those, officials in particular, who were agents of the Spanish crown. Frederick Stimson, *Cuba's Romantic Poet*, 67–75; Franklin Knight, *Slave Society in Cuba during the Nineteenth Century*, 81; Robert L. Paquette, *Sugar Is Made with Blood*, 263.

16. Nineteenth-century biographies or biographical sketches of Plácido include a remarkably substantive entry in Francisco Calcagano's *Poetas de color*, published one year after the official abolition of slavery in Cuba.

17. Twentieth-century biographies of Plácido include Domingo Figarola-Caneda, *Plácido*; M. (Manuel) García Garófalo-Mesa, *Plácido, poeta y mártir*; Jorge Casals, *Plácido como poeta cubano*; Jorge Castellanos, *Plácido, poeta social y político*. The first biography of Plácido published after the success of the 1959 revolution was Itzhak Bar-Lewaw Mulstock, *Plácido: Vida y obra*. Significantly, all these biographies construct Plácido as a symbol of the Cuban nation, although the character of the Cuban nation each biographer imagines him to represent differs. Vera M. Kutzinski, *Sugar's Secrets*; Enildo A. Garcia, *Cuba: Plácido, poeta mulato de la emancipación*; and the Instituto de Literatura y Lingüística's *Diccionario de la literatura cubana* also feature substantial biographical data on Plácido.

18. On this point, I agree with Jorge Castellanos and Frederick Stimson. Castellanos, *Plácido, Poeta Social y Político*, 99–141; Stimson, *Cuba's Romantic Poet*, 79. See chapter 3 of Nwankwo, *Black Cosmopolitanism*, for a more in-depth analysis of Plácido's life and poetry.

19. I would suggest that the idea of a "race man" was created during this period. For instance, the tug-of-war between Frederick Douglass and Martin Delany evidenced in Robert Levine's book on the two, I would argue, is fundamentally a battle over which of them was the better "race man." Robert S. Levine, *Martin Delany, Frederick Douglass.* For twentieth-century figures, see Hazel Carby, *Race Men,* 10, 12.

20. Among those who have called attention to such gender disparities is Jacqueline Nassy Brown, "Black Liverpool, Black America, and the Gendering of Diasporic Space."

21. Sentencia pronunciada por a Seccion de la Comision militar establecida en la ciudad de Matanzas para conocer de la causa de conspiracion de la gente de color. Archivo Nacional de la República de Cuba, Asuntos Políticos, legajo 42, no. 15, n.p.

22. Ibid.

23. Ibid.

24. "Comunicación dirigida por el Consul de España."

25. William Wells Brown, for example, includes Plácido in *The Black Man, His Antecedents, His Genius, and His Achievements* (1863). Plácido, for Brown, is unquestionably "Black" and, as such, advances his stated goals for the book—to "show that he [the Black man] is endowed with those intellectual and amiable qualities which adorn and dignify human nature." Brown, *The Black Man,* 88–90.

26. Delany, *Blake,* 16. Further references to this work will be made parenthetically in the text. Page references are to the 1970 edition.

27. For more on Delany's vision, see Maurice Wallace, "'Are We Men?',' 182–210.

28. Delany, *The Origin of Races and Color,* 92–93.

29. For a more detailed discussion of the verbal and artistic representations of Plácido, see Stimson, *Cuba's Romantic Poet,* 32–34.

30. Henry speaks standard English whereas they speak (Delany's version of) African American vernacular. Robert Levine's reading of *Blake* as reflective of Delany's elitism is instructive for reading this difference. Levine, *Martin Delany, Frederick Douglass,* 193.

31. Ferrer, *Insurgent Cuba,* 1–89.

32. Ibid., 15.

33. Martínez Heredia, "Nationalism, Races, and Classes in the Revolution of 1895 and the First Cuban Republic," 10.

34. Nelson, *National Manhood,* 179–80 (this and following quotations from Nelson).

35. Delany, *Official Report of the Niger Valley Exploring Party,* 121.

# "Is He, Am I, a Hero?"

## Self-Referentiality and the Colonial Legacy in Aimé Césaire's *Toussaint Louverture*

### E. Anthony Hurley

AIMÉ CÉSAIRE'S study of the Haitian Revolution in *Toussaint Louverture* (1962) forms part of a pattern that runs through Césaire's literary production, in which his creative imagination is stimulated to explore both the symbolic and the political significance of colonial heroes. This pattern is evident from the first reference to Toussaint in *Cahier d'un retour au pays natal* (1939), where Césaire's narrative persona, in attempting to list the component parts of his being ("what is mine"), is impelled to include "Haiti where negritude got up on its feet for the first time and said it believed in its humanity" (67).[1] This initial realization leads to the specific evocation of the Haitian hero, whose capitalized name, "TOUSSAINT, TOUSSAINT LOUVERTURE" (69), shouts from the text in a passage where the form of prose cedes to that of poetry for the recognition of the symbolic significance of Toussaint as the incarnation of the new awareness of "negritude" that Césaire was trying to articulate. The capitalization in the text emphasizes Toussaint's referential significance: he is the medium through which Césaire acquires self-knowledge and envisions the consciousness necessary for liberation within the context of colonization. In Césaire's account, the world of politics converges with that of literary representation to dramatize the historical and personal tragedy that colonialism inevitably produces, and Toussaint is the referent by means of which Césaire can assess his own viability as an anticolonial hero. This essay examines Césaire's *Toussaint Louverture* in relation to other Césairian works as a text in which one black leader (Césaire), concerned about the legacy of colonialism, reinscribes and analyzes the experiences of another colonized leader (Toussaint) whose attitudes and activities hold particular significance for him from his twentieth-century perspective. Since literary activity, for Césaire, is intimately connected

with political consciousness, my analysis will inevitably address both literary considerations and the related ideological and political aspects of
the work. Césaire's *Toussaint* is anomalous within the corpus of his literary production and, perhaps because of its difference, has received little
sustained critical attention. Apart from my own *Présence Africaine* study,
only Gloria Nne Onyeoziri has attempted a substantive, sensitive, and
insightful analysis of the text.[2]

Before Césaire composed his "history" of Toussaint, he had already
developed his theory of colonialism in the 1950 *Discours sur le colonialisme* (Présence Africaine edition, 1955), in which he suggested an essential opposition between colonialism and civilization, and proposed the
equation "colonization = thingification," the inevitable consequence of
which Césaire saw as "artistic magnificences wiped out, extraordinary
possibilities suppressed" (22). The politics of colonialism, therefore, had
for Césaire a profound creative, psychological, and spiritual significance.
Before *Toussaint*, Césaire had embarked on his exploration of anticolonial
rebel leaders in *Et les chiens se taisaient*, which appeared as a dramatic
piece in the poetic collection *Les Armes miraculeuses* (Présence Africaine,
1946; later published separately by Présence Africaine in 1956). This
self-proclaimed "tragedy" opens with the prophetic announcement "Of
course the Rebel is going to die," anticipating and suggesting that a revolutionary hero's life is destined to end tragically. Césaire's later representations of anticolonial heroes, *La Tragédie du Roi Christophe*, focusing
on another Haitian leader, and *Une Saison au Congo*, exploring the situation of the Congolese leader, Patrice Lumumba, continue this pattern.
Similarly, the Haitian Revolution serves to highlight in dramatic fashion
some of the contradictions experienced by a Caribbean individual such
as Césaire, particularly in relation to France both as a cultural center and
as a colonizing power.

Césaire's *Toussaint* purports, in Césaire's own words ("Introduction,"
23),[3] to supply an explanation for the success of the group of "*nègres,*"
the group of black slaves at the bottom of the colonial socioeconomic
scale comprising whites, mulattoes, and blacks, in conducting a successful anticolonial revolution, led by Toussaint. But how do we read this
text, in light of Césaire's stated purpose? The text does indeed supply the
explanation proposed by Césaire. It attempts to mirror the revolution it
is celebrating in the approach adopted by Césaire in allowing the various
participants, all of whom are involved in some form of "revolution" or
prerevolutionary consciousness or activity either in metropolitan France
or in Saint-Domingue, to speak in their own voices.

Yet certain aspects of the slant Césaire gives to his study reveal a self-referential preoccupation with an assessment of Toussaint as a revolutionary, anticolonial, hero within the context of colonialism, and the legacy his experience bequeaths to Césaire. In other words, despite the important difference of historical context between Toussaint Louverture and Aimé Césaire, in that Toussaint was involved in a direct military struggle against slavery while Césaire was fighting the legacy of the slavery experienced by Toussaint, Césaire's study is essentially a narrative of the experience and impact of colonization, centered on relationships between colonizers and colonized, and produced by a writer who is himself a product of the same colonizing process as the "hero" of his narrative. Césaire thus draws attention to the ironies and ambiguities of the language used in parliamentary debates and other documented sources. In this way not only is the constructed memory of the Revolution given documentary validity, but the reader is subtly made aware of the contradictions and limitations of Revolutionary rhetoric, particularly in the context of the relationship between France as colonizer and the groups of colonized people in Saint-Domingue.

Césaire's study, however, does more than explain the success of the group of *"nègres"* or of Toussaint himself. It suggests, in its presentation of the Haitian Revolution, that armed revolution is inadequate to erase the effects of colonization. The text is in effect the locus where the political and the symbolic coincide. For Césaire, the realm of past experience, or "history," functions as a mirror, both symbolically and in actuality, of his own contemporary situation. Toussaint, a real-life figure whose emergence to historical prominence is documented in the text, is represented both as a visionary himself and as an example and precursor for Aimé Césaire, who functions both as poet-narrator of the Toussaint trajectory and as a visionary anticolonial leader in his own similar Caribbean context. Thus the study points the way, however indirectly, to alternatives to armed revolution as a solution to colonial domination.

The title and subtitle of the Césairian text, *Toussaint Louverture: La Révolution française et le problème colonial* (Toussaint Louverture: The French Revolution and the colonial problem) exemplify in dramatic fashion the self-referential element that underscores the text. The associative field surrounding the title and the name of the individual (Toussaint Louverture) who serves as the reference point around which this narrative is written suggest some of the complexities of the Caribbean: a dominant European/Judeo-Christian tradition of veneration of the dead (in the name "Toussaint" or "All Saint"), that is perfectly compatible with West African belief systems, as well as the suggestion of a literal opening (in Toussaint's second name), an access to a new experience, and the implication in the elided definite article (Toussaint's last name is often rendered "L'Ouverture") of personal agency. It could be argued that Césaire's creative imagination was stimulated by the coincidence of a name (Toussaint Louverture) whose immense associative potential held special significance for the poet-politician. As a literary construction, however, the Toussaint Louverture of the title is not given independent agency, does not stand alone, but is connected through the subtitle to a larger historical context. In other words, this title subtly warns us against any expectation that the narrative will be a panegyric to Toussaint as a Haitian hero. Haiti and the Haitian Revolution are significantly absent from the title, and these absences raise questions about the notion of the Haitian Revolution itself and Césaire's views on the historical significance of this event, as well as about the literary revolution that it engendered for Césaire. The subtitle, "The French Revolution and the colonial problem," similarly invites reflection on the significance of the fact that focus is placed on the French Revolution rather than on the Haitian Revolution, and that the emphasis is displaced from Toussaint and Haiti to the colonizing power, France. Césaire does attempt explicitly to dissociate the Saint-Domingue revolution from the French Revolution: "The worst error would be to consider the Saint-Domingue revolution purely and simply as a chapter of the French Revolution" (*TL*, 22). It is for this reason that he is led to characterize the Haitian Revolution as essentially "a colonial type revolution"—in other words, an anticolonialist revolution (22–23). There is, however, an evident dissonance between the desire to distinguish between the two and the title and subtitle.

It is interesting to note that C. L. R. James's earlier (1938) study, *The Black Jacobins: Toussaint L'Ouverture and the San Domingo Revolution,* however "revolutionary" it might have been in recognizing the achievements of the black slaves of Haiti (James, in the preface to the first edition, calls it "one of the great epics of revolutionary struggle"),[4] betrays a similar ambivalence: the "black" in James's title is a mere qualifier; Toussaint and the Revolution are subordinated to the French signifier, "Jacobins," referring to members of the Revolutionary Republican society formed in 1789 which met in the Jacobin convent in rue Saint-Honoré in Paris. The titles of these two major studies of the Haitian Revolution by Caribbean intellectuals thus tend, ironically, to subvert the very achievement they purport to celebrate, not merely by insisting on the linkage to the colonial power, but in essence presenting the Haitian Revolution as an adjunct to European history.

The diminution of Toussaint's agency, I would contend, reflects Césaire's own sense of indebtedness to the French Revolution, which is, one may argue, an effect of the legacy of colonialism and the documented psychological complicity that develops between oppressor and oppressed. In a 1944 article, "Panorama," Césaire opens with a provocative statement about the condition of his native Caribbean, which he sees marked by a lack of revolution: "This country is suffering from a suppressed revolution. Our revolution has been stolen from us" (7). Césaire clarifies later in the article that "The Martinican Revolution will come about in the name of bread, of course; but also in the name of air and of poetry (which amounts to the same thing)" (9). In other words, for Césaire revolution consists of interconnected material (armed struggle) as well as spiritual (creative) elements. Toward the end of the article, the nature of the Caribbean revolution envisaged by Césaire is revealed in the statements: "I condemn any idea of *Caribbean independence*. . . . I know only one France. That of the Revolution. That of Toussaint Louverture" (10). Here, Césaire seems to be rejecting the idea of independence for his country unless it is achieved by armed struggle, as was the case in both France and Haiti. The juxtaposition of the terms "France," "Revolution," and "Toussaint" not merely indicates Césaire's trust in and attachment, even as a colonized subject, to the ideals of Revolutionary France, it also reveals his conception of Toussaint's historical and cultural debt to the colonizing power. The "real" France is, in Césaire's imagination, that of the French Revolution. Toussaint, who balked at the notion of independence for his country, somehow belongs to France. It would not be too great a stretch in logic to conclude that Césaire, in like manner, belongs to France. Thus, even though within the body of the *Toussaint* text Césaire credits Toussaint for his achievement in moving a rebellion to the point of a veritable "revolution" (299), it may be argued that Césaire's conflicted attitude toward colonial France and his admitted respect for the French Revolution are likely to color his analysis.

Césaire's attitude to the Haitian and French revolutions provokes further questions: How could Césaire reconcile the notion of revolution in the context of colonialism without political independence? How could there be a "Haitian Revolution" without Haitian independence? Césaire's study of Toussaint does not treat the final war of independence led by Dessalines, but he does offer an explanation (which will be discussed later) for Toussaint's ambivalence in relation to "liberty" and "independence" (*TL* 276). In his own career as a political leader, Césaire certainly had the opportunity, as early as 1946, to agitate, at home in Martinique and in the National Assembly in Paris, for Martinican independence. But he has never done so. Césaire's study of Toussaint was one way for him to attempt to understand the dilemma of the French Caribbean leader, confronted with the difficult choice of a fragile and uncertain independence or freedom within a France apparently committed to liberty, equality, and fraternity for all.

The problematic implicit in the title of Césaire's *Toussaint*—the displacement of focus from the Haitian to the French Revolution—assumes a different form in the structure of the study, which ironically parallels the social structure created by European colonization of Caribbean territories. The volume is divided into three "Books." Book 1, entitled "La Fronde des Grands Blancs" (The insurrection of the great whites), focuses on the actions of the group at the top of the colonial hierarchy. It discusses the insurrection of white colonists in Saint-Domingue against the bourgeoisie who had acceded to power in France through the Revolution, and who were now confronted with the complex problems of defining the relationships between the metropole and the colonies, of resolving the conflict between mulattoes and whites in the colonies, and of making a decision on slavery. Césaire follows the parliamentary action in Paris, leading to the decree by the National Assembly (March 8, 1790) to allow for the formation of colonial assemblies through which the wishes of the colonies would be expressed, and compares it to the action in the colonies, in Saint-Domingue and Martinique, where local white planters had already begun to form their own provincial assemblies, but who failed in the end to achieve meaningful autonomy for the colony.

Book 2, "La Révolte mulâtre" (The mulatto revolt), focuses on the middle group in the colonial hierarchy. In this section Césaire gives an account of the parliamentary debates in Paris, in particular the role played by Robespierre (February 25, 1791) in leading the National Assembly to "constitutionalize slavery" (114). Robespierre's speech in the Assembly asserted: "Since men of color are in this era equal to white men, it follows that they must have received the same rights and that the Revolution raised them up, by the very nature of things, to the same rank as white men, that is, to political rights" (97). Césaire points out what he designates as the "modern" reasoning of Robespierre in substituting class struggle for race struggle, in proposing that it was not according political rights to people of color that would shatter the slave system but precisely the opposite: "When you have given the same interest to all citizens of color who are landowners and (slave) masters, if you make only one party out of them, with the same interest in maintaining blacks in subordination, it is evident that subordination will be cemented in an even firmer way in the colonies" (99). The significance of these parliamentary debates for Césaire was, as he states, that "when the colonial question arose, the French Revolution had begun to face up to itself, and in confronting the principles from which it was born, it began to divide itself, hence to define itself" (103).

Césaire, in this section, also retraces the abortive attempt on the part of Vincent Ogé in Saint-Domingue to obtain full civil rights for free people of color. This group had their own organization, the Society of the Friends of Blacks, founded in 1783 with a two-pronged program: "immediate abolition of the slave trade; and civic equality for free people of color" (85). Their first shock came during the French parliamentary debate that started March 2, 1790, on the question of the formation of local assemblies in the colonies. The parliamentary document that emerged from this debate did not specifically include people of color among the eligible electors (89). When the leaders of this group, Vincent Ogé and Jean-Baptiste Chavannes, attempted to lead a revolutionary force in Saint-Domingue, they were arrested and publicly executed and beheaded on February 25, 1791 (91).

Césaire also traces the actions of disappointed mulattoes who tried unsuccessfully to use the 1791 slave uprising, on the one hand, to obtain voting rights for people of color and free negroes by the decree of April 4, 1792, and, on the other, to defeat the white planters militarily. Césaire indicates that when, in August 1791, the revolt of black slaves began as masses of them overran the plains of the North (132), the mulattoes decided to use this event strategically in a quasi-revolutionary manner. The result was the formation of a "combined army" (comprising whites and mulattoes), united against the black slaves (138). By spring 1793, however, it was evident that the class of the *"grands blancs"* (great whites) was no longer, politically or militarily, in charge in Saint-Domingue, since the combined army of mulattoes and whites were occupying Port-au-Prince. This group, as Césaire indicates, had in the short space of two years turned themselves into a class without which it would henceforth be impossible to govern (156).

The rise of the mulatto class, however, only highlighted the centrality of the group that had never been the focus of discussion in the official parliamentary debates (156). According to Césaire, the black masses in

Saint-Domingue had quickly understood that there was nothing to be expected from Paris and that they would have to rely on themselves to achieve freedom (159). Book 3, "La Révolution nègre" (The negro revolution), the longest by far of the three sections (it comprises eighteen chapters whereas books 1 and 2 comprise five and seven respectively), concentrates, therefore, on the activities of those at the bottom of the colonial social, political, and human ladder. It introduces Toussaint Louverture and traces his transformation of the revolt of the black slaves into a truly anticolonialist revolutionary movement.

For someone with the poetic sensibility of Césaire, who is acutely attuned to the semantic resonances of words, the progression in these three sections from "Fronde" (Insurrection) to "Révolte" (Revolt) to "Révolution," paralleling *"grands blancs"* (great whites), *"mulâtre"* (mulatto), and *"nègre"* (negro), must be read as intentional and significant.[5] The term *"Fronde"* occupies a peculiar place in French history, referring particularly to the seventeenth-century (1648–49) demonstrations against the harsh fiscal demands of Cardinal Mazarin and the relatively minor and unsuccessful military campaigns by some nobles against supporters of the Louis XIV monarchy. "Revolt" is intended to signify a more intense and extensive opposition, while "revolution" suggests an even more fundamental, organized, transformative, structured movement.

Thus, for Césaire, the Haitian experience of the late eighteenth century is profoundly, even ontologically, revolutionary in that it represented a successful challenge to and refutation of the validity of the "racial" politics constructed and institutionalized by European colonization. The Haitian Revolution was the culmination of struggles against the colonial power located geographically in Europe by the three predominant racial and economic affiliations and interests: local whites (Europeans accepting San Domingo as their preferred locus of identification), mulattoes (free persons of varying degrees of color with a recognized and visible biological European linkage), and so-called blacks. As Césaire explains, "This was colonial society: better than a hierarchy, it was an ontology: at the top, the white man—the *being* in the fullest sense of the term—, at the bottom, the negro, with no juridical personality, a piece of furniture; the thing, one may as well say *the nothing;* but between this all and this nothing, a formidable in-between: the mulatto, the free man of color" (31).

Césaire refers to the colonial structure as an ontology rather than a hierarchy, since this structure (in which the only "beings" were the whites) denied the very being of Africans. The distinctive features, however, of this new colonial structure were, on the one hand, the emergence of new beings, between being and nonbeing, and, on the other, the development of a new taxonomy to represent the previously unimagined varieties of combinations produced by the mixing of blacks and whites, such as *mûlatre, quarteron, métisse, mamelouque, quarteronné, sang mêlé, griffe, marabou,* and *sacatra,* among others (31).[6] For Césaire, the political and symbolic significance of this superficially ridiculous classification lay in the fact that these new designations constituted a serious social problem: the emergence within colonial society of a class of free persons of color, who, similar to the Third Estate in metropolitan France, would be aspiring to equal rights.

Césaire therefore provides information on the inadequacy and even stupidity of measures taken in France throughout the eighteenth century to deal with the untenable structure that France had created for its colonies. He references, for example, the 1766 legislation forbidding men of color to wear the same clothes as whites, to sit in the same churches, or to sit next to whites in theaters. Césaire notes that throughout the eighteenth century, while the material situation of free persons of color improved steadily, their legal situation got increasingly worse (33). By 1789, therefore, the "black question" constituted a veritable figurative and political gulf, an "abyss" (34), with which French society was confronted and which would inevitably take the form of a confrontation with the power that had artificially created the colonial class structure.

Thus the development of the revolutionary process within the territory that was to become Haiti ironically reflected for Césaire the racial and economic hierarchization created by European colonizers. For Césaire, one of the fundamental contradictions of the Haitian Revolution was precisely the success of the black masses and one of the questions to which Césaire seeks to find answers is precisely the riddle of the success of this group: "One may justifiably wonder why the whites failed at the start, why the mulattoes failed at the finish, and why the most deprived social group, the black group, the group with a 'general grievance,' succeeded" (23).

The referential significance of skin color is thus of primary interest to Césaire. He draws attention to the decision by white planters in 1789 in San Domingo to form a Colonial Assembly that they could dominate, and he underlines the fact that the choice they made was based on skin color distinctions: "It was perfectly understandable that such a policy would arouse the anger of the patriots. What is less understandable is the dividing line they chose: *the color question*" (68; Césaire's emphasis).

Césaire also cites a proclamation made by "patriots" in which the color distinction is expressly conflated with class: *"we have come with the firm resolve to compel a class of men whose absurd and shocking claims, unfortunately supported by the error of some of our brothers, have been the most fruitful source of the ills with which this colony is afflicted, to return to the respect and submission they owe to Whites"* (69; italics in original).

The revolution in Saint-Domingue therefore becomes, in Césaire's text, the occasion and location for the categorization of people according to variations in skin tone to be further entrenched as a political, social, and economic imperative. The importance attached to skin color in the context of the Haitian Revolution had earlier, in *Cahier d'un retour au pays natal,* stimulated Césaire to consciousness of his own "negritude." The economic importance of Saint-Domingue, however, should not be underestimated. As Césaire points out, "Saint-Domingue was more important to the economy of France in the eighteenth century than the whole of Africa to the French economy in the twentieth century" (*TL* 20). This association highlights what he considers as one of the primary motivations of European colonialist enterprise—raw profit, as significant in the context of Haiti as it is for the contemporary Caribbean. As he had previously asserted in *Discours sur le colonialisme* (Discourse on colonialism) (1955), moreover, Césaire sees eighteenth-century Saint-Domingue as a pivotal historical moment, one that triggered, concurrently with French (and American) republicanism, the birth of modern capitalism on the backs of enslaved Africans: "We know that major industry was born in France at the end of the eighteenth century; that it was then that capital, in the modern sense of the term, established itself, and large financial concentrations appeared" (*TL* 21).

It is also at this moment of French national debate that the enslavement of Africans becomes an intellectual embarrassment, impossible to justify without contortions of cartesian logic. Césaire's documentary references illustrate the ambiguity that was produced even in relation to lexical usage, as the politics of the colonizer compromised both linguistic clarity and moral integrity. Documents, particularly those recording the attitudes and ideas of the French, are shown to be revealing, hypocritical, untrustworthy, and deceptive. For instance, Césaire demonstrates Robespierre's lack of principle in substituting the words "non-free persons" for "slaves" in the decree by the National Assembly to the effect that "no law on the status of non-free persons can be made by the legislative body for the colonies except on the formal and spontaneous demand of the colonial assemblies" (114). Césaire interrupts his account of the parliamentary debates to underline the tragic hypocrisy of this measure: "This was a very serious thing: an assembly that had been elected to constitutionalize liberty had just constitutionalized the most abominable slavery" (114).

In addition to highlighting the implications of the linguistic contradictions, Césaire also provides a historical account of the colonial context in which these contradictions occur and illustrates the specific and significant political and economic tensions that characterized the relationship between Saint-Domingue and France in the final decades of the eighteenth century: the question of defining appropriate political links between metropole and colonies, complicated by an economic mercantilist policy which stipulated that the metropole controlled all commerce in the colony, as well as the fundamental existential problem of the status of the new varieties of human beings in colonial society (31).

One of the first political measures noted by Césaire is the move on the part of the (white) Saint-Domingue colonists toward integration and toward participation in the States General in France, contrary to the edict of Louis XVI which had never anticipated colonial representation (38). The colonists, however, insisted on forming electoral committees and in having representation at the national level. The question, from the perspective of Paris, became simply how many deputies to allow the colonists. But this question necessarily also raised the troubling question of the status of slaves, who were not considered as fully human, and whether it was appropriate for them to be represented by their masters. Despite the so-called colonial pact of mutual support between metropole and colony, the Revolution's proclamation of the Rights of Man, with the implicit recognition of equality and liberty for all men, without consideration of rank or color (47), contradicted its own logic in relation to the colonies. The Assembly, when confronted with this contradiction, as Césaire points out, could not deal with this fundamental flaw in the colonial pact. Césaire cites the intervention by Mirabeau (presumably the renowned orator, Honoré Gabriel Riqueti, who, though a noble, was ironically a spokesman for the Third Estate), whose comments underscore the complexity of the dilemma: "Do the colonies claim to rank their negroes and their people of color as men or as beasts of burden? But people of color are free, are landowners and taxpayers, and yet they have not been able to be electors. If the colonists want negroes and people of color to be men, let them free the negroes; let all of them be electors, let all be eligible to be elected" (41).

Césaire presents a chronological account of the competing political measures adopted by the metropole and colony which formed the context within which Toussaint was to emerge, not just as a revolutionary leader, but also as an inevitably tragic victim of the encounter between colonizers and colonized. The first colonial decree of the French Revolution was issued by the Constituent on March 8, 1790. This decree allowed for a colonial assembly, municipalities, and the right to make provisional laws, but refused the colony internal autonomy or freedom to trade (58). Saint-Domingue, however, as Césaire notes, had not waited on Paris. It had already exerted its political will by forming its own provincial assemblies that were eager to assume internal autonomy. Césaire draws attention particularly to a significant action taken by the Provincial Assembly of the North which demonstrated its power and its ideology by arresting a certain Dubois for declaring that the enslavement of blacks was contrary to natural liberty (62). Local assemblies, therefore, while challenging the political authority of the metropole, concurred with its hypocritical stance on black slaves. Thus, as Césaire notes, it was apparent as early as 1790 that the initiative was passing out of the hands of the great planter class, who had mounted an attack on the colonial system by launching a movement for local autonomy, but had abandoned the anticolonialist struggle in favor of compromise with the ultra-reactionary forces of the metropole. This left the way open for people of color and mulattoes to initiate their own revolt against the colonial system (85). According to Césaire, it was because of the incapacity of the whites to mount an anti-colonial struggle that the black slaves came to the fore as a revolutionary force (81).

It is important to recognize, however, that the caste of colonial whites did not constitute a politically unified group. There was, as Césaire points out, at least one significant division that existed among this group: on the one hand, the "merchants," typically capitalists and bankers, and, on the other, the planters, who were dependent on the merchants for financing capital. The merchants were patriots, supporters of the Revolution, while the planters, according to Césaire, were willing to do anything in their own interest. The most important point of contention between the two groups was the color question, with the patriots totally opposed to people of color (68). It became clear, however, by March 1791, that "the whites in Saint-Domingue were no longer a class on the attack, but a class on the defensive, and that the historical initiative had passed to other hands: those of the middle class of mulattoes" (80).

Césaire's prose appears to place special emphasis on the attitude of the leaders of the French Revolution toward blacks. For instance, he draws our attention to the fact that the French Revolutionary Convention issued what was in effect a Republican Black Code: "Do you know that there was a kind of Republican Black Code? It was published in Port-au-Prince on 5 May 1793 in a bilingual edition in French and Creole" (171). Césaire provides details of this decree: for instance, article 22 forbade slaves to bear arms, even sticks, under penalty of being whipped; article 27 imposed a severe penalty, death, on slaves for stealing horses, mules, oxen, or cows; article 30 ordered slaves who tried to leave the island to have their hamstrings cut; article 32 imposed a punishment of branding with the letter "V" (for *"voleur"* or *"thief"*) on the right shoulder for minor thefts; and article 34 ordered that runaway slaves, who had run away for a month, should have their ears cut off and a brand of the letter "M" (for *"maroon"*) on the left shoulder (172). As Césaire remarks with deliberate irony, "Very interesting reading!" (171).

Césaire's analysis underscores the understandable attitude of blacks in a context in which whites, who enjoyed political and economic privileges from which blacks were excluded, were on the whole insensitive to the desires and aspirations of blacks. Césaire notes that the black masses in Saint-Domingue had quickly understood that there was nothing to be expected from Paris and that they would have to rely on themselves (159). According to Césaire, the black slaves were not at all affected by the eloquence that marked the parliamentary debates in Paris; their suffering had made them ready, in fact had made them the only group ready, to fully comprehend the significance of the Revolution (177). Césaire, therefore, details the events within the movement of the black masses which projected Toussaint to the forefront.

Some of the significant details provided by Césaire include the vodou ceremony, led by Boukman, and attended by thousands of slaves, which took place in Cayman Woods on August 22, 1791, and sparked the first wave of mass revolt by blacks. Within a week, Césaire notes, two hundred sugar plantations and six hundred coffee plantations had been destroyed, hundreds of whites had been massacred, and the richest part of the island, the north plain, had been razed by fire and reduced to a smoking desert (179). When Boukman eventually fell, shot several times, he was decapitated, his body was burned, and his head was mounted on a stake. This event, according to Césaire, introduced a pause, a hesitation, in the advance of the slaves: "It was at this moment of stagnation that Toussaint

Louverture emerged to the forefront" (179), distinguished, according to Césaire, by "the firmness of his character" and by his "intellectual superiority" (180).

The figurative language used by Césaire in relating the transition in the black leadership from Boukman to Toussaint emphasizes what Césaire considers as the fundamental contribution of Toussaint and signals Césaire's perception of his own role: "The Boukman moment was the moment when the black insurrection, carried along on the tide of a single impetus, could have succeeded at one go; the moment of feverish inspiration and prophetism. The Toussaint Louverture moment was the moment of tomorrows of inspiration; the back to earth moment; the moment of cold reflection that corrects mistakes and rectifies methods" (180). Thus Césaire sees Toussaint's contribution as that of bringing discipline to the revolt and extending it, not merely militarily, but even more important, politically. And this political extension involved recognizing that "beyond men, it was a system that had to be destroyed. The goal, the sole valid goal, could only be liberty, liberty for all" (181).

It was this recognition of a profoundly political purpose that in Césaire's mind marks the transition from Toussaint Bréda to Toussaint Louverture—a transition into what Césaire characterizes as "the first great anticolonialist leader that history has known" (189). Toussaint's transition into this role was, according to Césaire, determined by the qualities that distinguished him from his predecessors: "what would be needed was something that neither Boukman nor Makendal had had: a political mind. Toussaint had no choice: he had to be that mind" (189).

The comparison between Toussaint's situation as viewed by Césaire and Césaire's situation in 1945 when he opted to enter the political arena formally and become the leader of a political party, the Parti Progressiste Martiniquais (Martinican Progressive Party), cannot be ignored. Césaire has asserted (in conversations with me) that he had not initially intended to enter formal politics or become a political leader, but that at that moment he too, like Toussaint, had felt he had no choice.

Thus Césaire can empathize with, and even admire, Toussaint's dedication to the single aim, the ideal of freedom for all, an ideal that Toussaint used to unify a band of black slaves and transform this band into an army. This legacy of fidelity to a single purpose is a reflection of Césaire's expressed desire in *Cahier*. The condition of being *"debout et libre"* (on his feet and free) achieved by Césaire's narrative persona toward the end of *Cahier* echoes and expands the condition of being *"debout"* (on its feet) (*Cahier* 67) associated earlier in the same text with the "negritude" manifested in the Haitian Revolution. Césaire's awakened and liberated persona commits himself at the end of his spiritual and cultural journey in *Cahier* to being "the lover of this unique people" (123). Thus Césaire can assert categorically in *Toussaint Louverture* that it is this dedication to a "precise ideal" that is the hallmark of Toussaint's heroism: "That is Toussaint's greatness" (191).

Césaire follows Toussaint as he conducts a propaganda campaign among the slaves, all the while acting as an ally of the Spaniards and speaking the formal language of counterrevolution and royalism in favor of general liberty: "Brothers and friends, I am Toussaint Louverture. Maybe you have heard of my name. I have embarked on vengeance. I want liberty and equality to reign in Saint-Domingue. I am working to make them come to pass. Join us" (191). Césaire argues that Sonthonax, in part as a result of the political pressure Toussaint is able to exert, is impelled to proclaim the abolition of slavery on August 29, 1793, with one of the articles stipulating: *"All negroes and mixed race people who are currently enslaved are declared free, to enjoy all the rights attached to the status of French citizens"* (195; italics in original).

Once again, the comparison between Césaire and Toussaint in their attempts to obtain "liberty" as citizens of France is striking. Césaire's decision to support departmental status for Martinique in 1946 echoes Toussaint's decision of 1793 to support France. According to Césaire, Toussaint was quite aware of the political implications of his actions in at first playing the royalist, pro-Spanish game. He was, Césaire asserts, "Mistrustful by nature. Mistrustful and perceptive" (196), but hoped to transform the local declaration of emancipation into a general principle, valid for all the colonies. Toussaint's actions of June 25, 1794, in pursuit of this goal, when he meticulously overran and slit the throats of the Spanish garrisons in Petite-Rivière, Dondon, and Gros-Morne, and raised the French tricolor, clearly demonstrated his allegiance to the French.

For Césaire, however, Toussaint's military strategy was always linked to and supported by another more basic interest, one that parallels Césaire's purpose: "For him, besides the military war with its display of violence, there is, underlying and orchestrating it, another war: that of the education of minds" (208). In other words, for Césaire, heroism, in the context of slavery and colonialism, is constituted not only by military and political achievement, but even more profoundly by the contribution of awakening the spiritual and psychological consciousness of enslaved and colonized people. Thus, as Césaire traces Toussaint's evolution over the next few years, he celebrates the birth of a leader of the blacks of

Saint-Domingue in terms that could serve as his own self-definition: "Clearly, a leader for the black people of Saint-Domingue was born: a revolutionary leader, that is, a man welded to the masses, discovering new dimensions in himself as events invested him with new responsibilities; a thinker, a doer, a diplomat, an administrator, all these qualities asserting themselves as they proved to be necessary—all that is Toussaint Louverture, and we shudder to think that his genius, unknown to men and useless, could have withered in slavery" (213).

Since the specter of assimilation was one Césaire himself had to confront in his own political life, it is understandable that he would find Toussaint's reactions to this political choice of particular interest. By the middle of 1796, Toussaint was effectively the leader of Saint-Domingue, and his authority was recognized even by the mulattoes. Césaire asserts that Toussaint's major concern, his major area of anxiety, was the fear that France would renege on the abolition of slavery decree. And as Toussaint listened to the rumblings coming from Paris, he received the impression that the dominant theme was to assimilate the colonies into the French Republic. Césaire comments, in a manner that signals the lessons he has learned from his own experience as well as from Toussaint's, that "[a]ssimilation, as always in history, was only, he [Toussaint] well understood, the mask for subjugation" (223). It is this realization, the futility for ex-colonized blacks of seeking to obtain liberation within the context of the French colonialist political machinery, that provides the strongest emotional and historical linkage between Toussaint and Césaire as anti-colonial heroes.

It is no surprise, therefore, that Césaire's analysis of the connection between Toussaint and France assumes a tone of regret tinged with bitterness, which signals the sadness that he himself, like Toussaint, may feel when he reflects on the political and existential disappointment they both experienced in relation to France. Toussaint, Césaire points out, is sadly forced to concede, in the latter part of 1796, that the general liberty that he sought would not be realized through or within the French parliamentary assembly but only through local methods and with his black army: "And thus the French experiment, in which Tousssaint had believed, to which he had committed himself completely, in which he had sunk all his intelligence, all his activity, and all his faith, revealed itself also to be merely a provisional compromise. And this was France, the France that he loved, and whose glory he had shared. Toussaint's sadness was immense" (226).

One could conclude that such a painful awakening is necessary for the colonial subject to move to the point of rejecting assimilation and compromise with the colonial master. It was this grief that impelled Toussaint to engage in what Césaire calls a "strategic reconversion," directing his efforts now against the authority of France, and it is for this reason that, on August 20, 1797, he orders his friend Sonthonax back to France. For Césaire this is a clear sign that Toussaint realized at that point that a break with France was inevitable and began to prepare for this eventuality. Césaire cites, in support of his hypothesis, a letter written by Toussaint to the Directory, in which he warns: *we have been able to face dangers to obtain our liberty; we will be able to face death to keep it* (229; italics in original).

Césaire exposes the ambiguity in Toussaint's thinking manifested in his use of the term "liberty" and his avoidance of the word "independence": "There is a magic word that Toussaint refused to say: the word *independence*" (275). It is this ambiguity that constitutes what Césaire refers to as Toussaint's "weakness" and resulted in the success Leclerc achieved through propaganda in affecting a separation between Toussaint and the black masses. Césaire suggests, however, that Toussaint did envision the future independence that he himself failed to achieve. Toussaint's surrender, Césaire notes, was predicated on preserving a military advantage that would eventually lead (presumably) to independence: "On the whole, Toussaint agreed to surrender, but not to compromise the future: the army would be safe and maintain its positions" (278).

In assessing Toussaint's role as a revolutionary hero, Césaire finds it necessary to confront Toussaint's attitude toward the idea of independence for his country. Césaire's failure to move Martinique toward political independence has raised the question of his own revolutionary leadership. Césaire asserts, however, that it is a false historical problem to ask whether Toussaint Louverture was or was not the founder of Haitian independence, since independence was already implicit in the treaty of Pointe-Bourgeoise of August 31, 1798, in which Saint-Domingue signed a separate treaty with England which was at war against France. Césaire notes that the English even offered to proclaim the independence of the island and proposed that Toussaint should wear the crown of Haiti, a suggestion that Toussaint rejected (233). Césaire calls this treaty Haiti's first act of independence.

Where Césaire offers some criticism of Toussaint is in relation to Toussaint's methods rather than his ideas. Césaire's experience permits him to assert that "[t]he most delicate problem for a revolutionary is his connection with the masses. . . . And it is there that Toussaint failed. . . . He thought he could resolve everything by militarizing everything" (243). The military option was in practical terms never available for Césaire, but it is evident that he can offer no alternative political solution to Toussaint's problem: "With colonialism defeated, peace restored, and the island independent, what would Toussaint's social policy have been? I have no idea" (247).

Césaire's study of Toussaint points, with an implicit self-directed irony, to the difficulty for the leader of a colonized people to develop a viable political strategy vis-à-vis the colonizing power. He notes that both Toussaint and Dessalines understood that Napoléon Bonaparte's recognition of the liberty of the people of Saint-Domingue was far from sincere and that they therefore had to be on guard against all proposals emanating from the metropole. So that when Bonaparte included in the new Constitution an article suggesting the creation of special laws for governing the French colonies, Toussaint called together an assembly to vote its own Constitution, which included (as article 3) the clause: "Slavery cannot exist in this territory; servitude is forever abolished. All men here are born, live, and die free and French" (251). The apposition between "free" and "French" underlines the notion that the principle of freedom for all, in this colonial context, may be inseparable from attachment to France.

Consequently, in light of Césaire's interest in exploring both the symbolic and the political significance of Toussaint's actions, he is faced with the task of explaining Toussaint's decision to place himself in the hands of the French in a way that does not present Toussaint as a passive victim of colonial conditioning, unconsciously attached to France, but rather gives Toussaint agency and insight. In this way, an apparent surrender is transmuted into a conscious act of profound symbolic and political significance: "This role of martyr, Toussaint accepted it, or better yet assumed it, because he really thought it was indispensable. . . . More than a mystical act, I see it as a political act. Yes, he conceived this journey that led him to captivity and death as his last political act, and without doubt, one of his most fruitful" (282–83).

Césaire's concluding chapter places emphasis on the political and economic imperatives, from the perspective of the colonizer, which led to the Haitian Revolution: "In order to maintain nine-tenths of the inhabitants of the island in slavery, a strong power was necessary. And the power could be strong only at the price of a general oppression: the oppression of all social classes, including the class of the privileged" (308). He also alludes to the irony of the French Revolution which "could not do justice to the claim for liberty by one class in colonial society without at the same addressing the problem of the very existence of colonial society" (308). So, for Césaire, the French Revolution made two significant contributions to colonial history: on the one hand, as a catalytic agent that accelerated the momentum of the Haitian Revolution, and, on the other, in its proclamation of the principle of the inalienable sovereignty of the people and of their right to organize and change the forms of their government (309). Césaire also emphasizes that no French revolutionary, even while proclaiming man's rights to nationhood, had envisaged the formation of a state by black slaves. Toussaint Louverture's contribution, in Césaire's view, was to serve as an "intercessor" on behalf of blacks: "Toussaint Louverture's fight was a fight for the transformation of formal law into real law, a fight for the *recognition* of man, and that is why he inscribes himself and inscribes the revolt of the black slaves of Saint-Domingue in the history of universal civilization" (310; italics in original). Césaire is very conscious, however, of the power of colonial conditioning, so that even though he admits that there may be "a negative side" to Toussaint's career, in that Toussaint "was more attached to deducing the existence of his people from a universal abstraction than seizing the singularity of his people in order to promote it to universal" (310), he nevertheless mitigates the criticism by explaining that that "negative" would have been difficult to avoid in the situation in which Toussaint found himself.

By way of conclusion, let us recapitulate and synthesize the group of concerns that exists at the core of Césaire's study of Toussaint and the Haitian Revolution: this study is fundamentally self-referential since studying Toussaint is for Césaire a means of studying himself as a black man and as an anticolonial leader, struggling to liberate himself and his people from the political, racial, and psychological domination of France. It is significant, therefore, that Césaire's trajectory has him retiring from the formal political arena which necessitated his constant presence in the metropole and devoting himself to nurturing cultural activities in his island.

My reading of Césaire's *Toussaint* leads me to offer the following reflections in relation to Toussaint and Césaire as both victims and heroes of French colonialism. In my view, Césaire's *Toussaint* suggests that total political and psychological independence from France is not really an option for the colonized, however revolutionary or heroic they may be; and neither Toussaint nor Césaire, nor any similar subject of French colonialism, can envisage a solution that excludes France. Césaire's *Toussaint* also implies that the defeat of colonialism is an illusion, and that heroism in such a context requires only participation in the struggle, because of the relativity of success and the inevitability of failure. I would further like to suggest that Toussaint and the Haitian Revolution survive and gain power not from the facts presented by Césaire, not from the historical details provided, but from the referential and signifying power that the historical data embody. Césaire's text, in my view, underscores the tragic power of colonial conditioning and indicates the vulnerability of all colonized people at the subconscious level. For historically grounded sociological and psychological reasons, it is awkward for a colonized Caribbean intellectual (such as Césaire or James), in the role of "historian," educated and trained within European traditions of intellectual enquiry, to reject completely the colonial conditioning that continuously reinscribes, at the literary and historiographical levels, the notion of the philosophical and moral rectitude of a nation that saw itself as representing the pinnacle of "civilization" in the modern era.

Thus, Césaire's *Toussaint* implicitly poses a question frequently asked but rarely answered convincingly throughout the twentieth century and into the twenty-first: How do the ex-colonized, living in a contemporary global community whose economic and political power is to some extent a product of the Saint-Domingue that necessitated the Haitian Revolution, avoid using Europe (or EuroAmerica) as the dominant referent? Just as both Toussaint and Césaire balked at the notion of independence from France, how many ex-colonized Caribbean and other writers and critics almost unconsciously continually pay tribute to European and EuroAmerican superiority? The acceptance of the primacy of European rationalism is the mark of the subliminal acceptance of European supremacy that is typically the inheritance of the descendants of the victims of European slavery, colonization, and imperialism globally. And it is this acceptance, the hesitation to create one's own literary and historical inscriptions, which marks much of the scholarship emanating from African diaspora scholars today. Césaire's *Toussaint* courageously foregrounds the dilemma that links author to protagonist and it is the lucidity and self-honesty of both figures that illuminate and underscore their heroism. At the same time, the legacy of the Haitian experience as documented by Césaire is the reminder that colonialism, with its capacity for duplicity and mutation, is far from over.

### Notes

1. In-text page references to *Cahier* refer to the 1956 Présence Africaine edition. Translations, unless otherwise indicated, are mine.

2. See Anthony Hurley, "Césaire's *Toussaint Louverture*," and Gloria Nne Onyeoziri, "Le *Toussaint* d'Aimé Césaire: Réflexions sur le statut d'un texte." Foster T. Jones's 1984 short article, "Césaire's *Toussaint*: A Metahistorical Reading," reads Césaire as a Marxist analysis through Hayden White's 1973 *Metahistory*. Nick Nesbitt's recent "Troping Toussaint, Reading Revolution" cannot be considered a major study of Césaire's *Toussaint* since the analysis of Césaire's text is subordinated to "the first great analysis of the Haitian Revolution, that of Hegel" (19). In fact, direct reference to Césaire's text occupies a mere two pages (28–30), and comes after extensive commentary on the ideas of Edmund Burke, Heidegger, Carl Schmitt, Alain Badiou, Ernst Cassirer, and Kant in relation to human rights in the introductory section (19–25), and "Hegel and Haiti" in the second section (23–28).

3. Page references to Césaire's *Toussaint Louverture* (abbreviated *TL,*) refer to the 1962 Présence Africaine edition.

4. See James's "Preface to the First Edition": "The transformation of slaves, trembling in hundreds before a single white man, into a people able to organise themselves and defeat the most powerful European nations of their day, is one of the great epics of revolutionary struggle and achievement. Why and how this happened is the theme of this book."

5. See Onyeoziri, "Le *Toussaint*," 92–93.

6. Some of these terms have no simple equivalent in English.

# Irrational Revolutions

## Colonial Intersubjectivity and Dialectics in Marie Chauvet's "Amour"

*Valerie Kaussen*

HAITIAN WRITER Marie Chauvet's trilogy of novellas, *Amour, colère et folie* (Love, anger, madness) has a legendary status in Caribbean literary history. Published in Paris by Gallimard in 1968, the trilogy, a bold critique of the dictatorship of François Duvalier, was effectively suppressed and nearly erased from the Haitian literary tradition shortly after its appearance: Chauvet's husband, fearing reprisals from Duvalier, and possibly ashamed of the damning portrait his wife painted of the Haitian bourgeoisie, bought up all copies before they could appear on Haitian bookshelves. Copies from abroad enjoyed a clandestine circulation in Haiti, and according to Chauvet's daughter, Erma St. Gregoire, *Amour, colère et folie* was Duvalier's "bedside reading," an indulgence that led the dictator to vow Chauvet his "eternal hatred."[1] *Amour, colère et folie* has only recently been reprinted and an English translation has never been published.

I open this essay on "Amour" (Love) by imagining a portrait of "Papa Doc" Duvalier secretly reading Chauvet's censored novellas behind the closed doors of his private *boudoir,* embroiled in a love/hate obsession with both the book and the bourgeois *mulâtresse* who wrote it. Suggested by a rumor, this tableau would be a fitting allegory for the racialized dynamics of desire and rage, madness and lucidity, privacy and performance that "Amour," a fictive diary, explores as the psychic condition of the postslavery, postcolonial society. Chauvet's critique of Duvalier's race totalitarianism exposes these psychic conflicts, by focusing not on the black "Africanist" dictator,[2] but on his putative enemy and other, the mixed-race "civilized" bourgeois woman. Obviously, one point of Chauvet's novella is to show the mirror relation between *macoute* and "whitened" mulatto, that each has internalized and is condemned to perform the same history: a persistent struggle between "master" and "slave," "white" and "black," whose origins lie in Haiti's history of French colonialism and slavery. More subtly, though, she suggests that the baleful intimacy linking masters and slaves constitutes the ground for any historical change, for revolution.

Despite a successful slave revolution and 1804 independence, in the twentieth century Haiti's sociopolitical model remained a colonial one, characterized by the effective dominance of the mulatto minority (who stepped into the shoes of the departing French colonizers after 1804). In the mid-twentieth century, representatives of the equally small black middle and upper classes, those who (like Duvalier) could claim to speak for the impoverished black majority, gained political power. In "Amour," one character voices a familiar Haitian aphorism to describe the historical cycle that has brought to power the novella's thinly veiled versions of Duvalier's *tontons macoutes:* "but the roles have only been reversed. Just like the Haitian saying goes, 'day for the hunter, day for the prey.'"[3] Indeed, under Duvalier's *noiriste* "revolution" Haiti's colonial structures remained intact, with Duvalier himself becoming the new "master" who effectively enslaved the Haitian population through a terror and violence that eliminated all dissent, real or imagined.[4]

While she was witness to the persistence of the colonial relation in postindependence Haiti, Chauvet, I will argue here, did not lose faith in Haiti's revolutionary project and the freedoms that it briefly made possible. As "Amour" shows, the promise of *liberté, égalité,* and *fraternité,* of universal freedom, that galvanized the revolt of Saint-Domingue's slaves paradoxically persisted, for Chauvet, in the colonial relationship. To imagine how revolution might once again erupt out of the colonial relation, in "Amour," Chauvet seeks to resuscitate the *process* of the master/slave dialectic. She suggests that this historical dynamic had been repressed and transformed into an antinomy by colonial ideologies (including *noirisme*). According to Chauvet, revealing how a dialectical process shapes individual subjects has the power to disrupt this antinomy, to produce revolutionary change. Chauvet represents this historical process in the sadomasochistic fantasies and obsession that her protagonist, Claire, a dark-skinned aging *bourgeoise* confesses in the private space of her personal diary. Claire's stated mission is to expose the hypocrisies of her own class, both their complicity in the violence that spreads through the country and relatedly, their disavowed sexual proclivities, repressed and hidden desires that they project onto the poor black "others" whom they continue to oppress. Claire's own confessions of her sexual obsession (in her case with her white French brother-in-law Jean-Luze) are intended to free her from the restrictions of her class education. But more importantly, Chauvet's narration of her protagonist's self-exposure gives voice to a psychic negativity that necessarily forms past of any revolutionary project. Chauvet's emphasis on the erotic, on "love," is finally an emphasis on the irrational unconscious, the site that reveals as primary the historical intimacy of black and white, master and slave. In "Amour," the subject's acceptance of complicity, of negativity, and of the master and slave within, has the potential to open up historical enclosures; through this narrative project, Chauvet posits an alternative to the condemnation to historical repetition represented by Duvalier's murderous regime.

### Eros and Recognition

"Amour" is written as the diary of Claire, a bourgeoise whose dark skin is the embarrassment of her "whitened" mulatto family. The patriarch is dead and the family, now impoverished, consists of three sisters who seek to uphold their social privilege. When the handsome white Frenchman Jean-Luze comes to the exotic island to test his fortune with the local American-owned Import-Export business, he marries Félicia, the whitest, blondest, and most racist of the three sisters. Claire, a kind of household domestic and a virgin at forty, develops a nearly violent obsession with Jean-Luze, whom she at first tries to seduce through a proxy, her sister, Annette. As this family romance unfolds within the Clamont household, women and beggars are being tortured at the nearby prison by another recent arrival, Calédu, a black police commander sent by the dictatorship to terrorize and dominate the town's racist mulatto elites. Claire's obsession with Jean-Luze is paralleled by Calédu's own obsession with mulatto "aristocratic" women, including Claire, who out of racial prejudice have spurned him. Claire's personal unrest grows with that of the community, and when rebellion finally breaks out, Claire, who at first plans to kill Félicia, decides to turn the knife on herself. At the last minute, however, she stabs Calédu, liberating the town from his tyranny.

As suggested above, in "Amour," Chauvet formalizes her meditations on Haitian history and its relationship to the Haitian subject by engaging one of her era's most important models, Hegel's master/slave dialectic. In this respect, she participates in the anticolonial francophone modernism of Aimé Césaire, Frantz Fanon, and others, all of whom rewrote Hegel's dialectic as a model for the worldwide relationship between colonizer and colonized and the struggle for decolonization. As Nick Nesbitt observes, Alexandre Kojève's reading of Hegel's dialectic (first made public in his seminars at the École Pratique des Hautes Études from 1933 to 1939)[5] was a crucial part of the formation of a whole generation of francophone Caribbean and African intellectuals working out of Paris, and it represented, in general, a form of a "symbolic capital" that was "the stamp of intellectual sophistication" of the day.[6] Though information on Chauvet's life is difficult to come by, we know that she was connected to the intellectual milieu surrounding Simone de Beauvoir (that included Fanon), and that through this contact she found a publisher for *Amour, colère et folie*, Gallimard, the same house that had published Kojève's seminars twenty years earlier.[7] Even without this publishing history, "Amour" makes clear that Chauvet, like Césaire and Fanon, was an heir of this particular intellectual tradition.[8] In particular, Chauvet engages Fanon's racialized version of the Hegelian/Kojèvian dialectic, which appears in *Peau noire, masques blancs* (1952) (*Black Skin, White Masks*, 1967). In this landmark text of the decolonization era, Fanon demonstrates that in the colonial context Kojève's dialectic of recognition between subjects is failed, halted, because of the inequality, and thus lack of reciprocity, between black and white.

Indeed, Chauvet also racializes the dialectic of recognition and she uses a heightened Kojèvian/Hegelian language throughout "Amour" to define as a struggle to be recognized Claire's sexual longing for the white Jean-Luze: "tonight . . . I will confess to him my love. He must reveal me to myself [*Il faut qu'il me révèle à moi-même*]" (178). Throughout "Amour" this language of recognition expresses Claire's desires for sex, for self-expansion, and, of course, for escaping the condemnation to playing out the role of the effaced and negated dark-skinned sister, the "old maid," who has never attracted a mate: "my life no longer satisfies me. . . . I want something else. Like you, like everyone else . . . I never knew how to make others recognize me [*s'imposer*] and life has passed me by" (34). Later, as Claire's confessions begin to result in a growing sense of agency, she writes with philosophical, even existentialist flourish: "yes, I've changed. . . . I'm becoming conscious of my worth. . . . This is a revolution. I feel ready to respond to the demands of my own being" (80).

Chauvet departs from Fanon and other male theorists of decolonization by representing the master/slave dialectic of recognition as an erotically charged quest, a drive to be sexually desired by the "other" and to have her own physical needs satisfied. By representing eros as the drive that fuels the quest for recognition, Chauvet emphasizes both its irrationality and the endlessness of the process of desire itself. As we shall see, she thus refuses rational teleologies through which the subject might escape unconscious impulses as well as the histories that have determined them.

In contrast, Fanon and Césaire could be said to work through the "madness" of the racialized dialectic in order to reach the teleology of mutual recognition between equal (male) subjects. In their heroic narratives, the black subject "wakes up" from an irrational colonial history and thereby asserts his agency and autonomy, the claiming of a healed subjectivity that becomes the necessary basis for organized political resistance, or decolonization.[9] In "Amour," Claire's "madness" is not uncovered in order to be rationally transcended; rather, revolutionary possibilities are immanent in the ambiguities of her desire, her love and rage. Based in processes that ultimately derive from histories of colonial contact, individual desire here remains resolutely historical and its effects, collective.[10]

Chauvet's narration, then, eroticizes the dialectic of recognition, but she does not abandon the ideal of collective revolution. In Claire's narrative voice, individual and collective revolutions are intertwined and inseparable. When Claire observes that her sister Annette, her stand-in, her substitute self in her fantasies of conquering Jean-Luze, has accepted his rejection, she writes: "then I will struggle. I'll never stand by and watch this affair finish so pitifully. If Annette gives up . . . then it shall be me who revolts" (34). And referring to the utopianism of her "love," she writes: "Ah! to march behind him in battle against who knows what fantasy [*chimere*]! . . . But how rejuvenating it is, this giving free reign to hope and to the building of a new and better world, if only in a dream" (151). Here, the battle for a dreamt-of "better world" is not an allegory for Claire's erotic quest; rather, Chauvet represents the erotic and the sociopolitical as intertwined and mutually determining drives whose intended objects are less important than the processes they incite. For both drives compel Claire to act and potentially lead her out of the stasis of the present into an unknown "chimeric" future.

## Modernism, Postmodernism, and the Haitian Revolution

In appropriating the language of militancy, Chauvet alludes to Haiti's own revolution, to the first mass movement for decolonization that was an exemplar for the global anti-colonial struggles that followed in the twentieth century. In this respect, Chauvet's novella also participates in Haiti's own modernist anticolonial tradition, which posited a continuity between the Haitian Revolution and twentieth-century decolonization. Jacques Roumain's *Gouverneurs de la rosée* (1944) (*Masters of the Dew*, 1947) and Jacques-Stephen Alexis's *Compère Général Soleil* (1955) (*General Sun, My Brother*, 1999) exemplify the Haitian engaged literary tradition, which in part through its Marxism, also appeals to the trope of the master/slave dialectic. Indeed, in the era that followed the U.S. occupation of Haiti (1915–34), Roumain, Alexis, and others theorized a genealogy that linked eighteenth-century colonialism to twentieth-century U.S. imperialism in the Caribbean. They theorized the historical and global scope of decolonization by applying Hegel's master/slave dialectic to the twentieth-century Caribbean, and specifically, to Haiti's growing numbers of displaced peasants, who were sold into indentured servitude on United States–owned plantations in Cuba and the Dominican Republic in a system that the laborers themselves termed the "slave trade."[11] For these writers, decolonization and Marxist internationalism both hearkened back to the Haitian Revolution with its cosmopolitan, universalist aims.[12]

Haiti's engaged literary tradition (in which I include Chauvet) could be said then to resituate Hegel's dialectic in the context that inspired its original formulation. Indeed Susan Buck-Morss, who has described the Haitian Revolution as "the crucible, the trial by fire for the ideals of the French Enlightenment,"[13] has also argued forcefully that Hegel wrote his allegory of modernity, the dialectic of lord and bondsman, as a response to the revolt of Haitian slaves. Haiti's Marxian writers return Hegel's dialectic to twentieth-century Haiti, to the historical landscape where the conflicts that inspired this theory continue to evolve, proliferate, and transform with the changing nature of world colonialism.

Chauvet sets "Amour" around 1940 in the period immediately following the U.S. occupation, the same period in which Roumain and Alexis set their own novels, and she likewise represents the new "slave trade" initiated by the American occupier. But in "Amour" colonial slavery and U.S. imperialism also inform Chauvet's representation of the history that could not be recorded by Roumain and Alexis: Duvalier's extreme black nationalism.[14] Witness to its rise, Chauvet has a different perspective on historical materialism and revolution and their relationship to the racially encoded positions of master and slave. In "Amour," Chauvet suggests that there are no heroes and no obvious victims, except perhaps the voiceless and hungry peasants whom she nonetheless refuses to idealize. Chauvet's emphasis on the subject, and in particular on the female subject, reflects her insistence that true universalism (and thus revolution) must necessarily attend to psychic negativity, e.g., to the unconscious impulses and desires that discourses of decolonization repress. For Chauvet, historical materialism is felt by the subject in the unconscious, in the irrationality reflected in dreams, fantasy, and desire. For her, historical change begins—but by no means ends—here.

Thus, while she writes her novel of revolution as the intimate diary of one woman, the scope of Chauvet's narrative seeks to be universal, that is, inclusive. On the one hand, "Amour" demonstrates that Chauvet, despite her awareness of decolonization's "failures" in Haiti and elsewhere, maintained a belief in the modern ideal of revolutionary change and liberation for which the slaves of Saint-Domingue fought, a project whose relevance was far from exhausted in her own time. But on the other, she was keen to the limitations of modernist notions of the subject's relationship to historical change, and she thus writes a version of Haitian revolution, of the struggle to decolonize, that includes subjects and desires not posited by Haiti's, and the francophone world's, Marxian modernist writers. Writing just prior to '68, Chauvet was surely inspired by the gathering energy that would explode in Paris, Haiti's former metropole, that same year, and she certainly saw the links between the sixties' Maoist, antiwar, women's liberation, and Black Power movements and the decolonization struggles that had so recently preceded them. Indeed, Kobena Mercer argues that the social movements of the late sixties must be understood in terms of the previous decade's decolonization struggles and the dissemination of the anticolonial discourse to new political subjects—women, gays, environmentalists—often located outside of the third world. Mercer categorizes as "postmodern" this expansion of the ethos of decolonization.[15] Following Ernesto Laclau and Chantal Mouffe, he identifies the fragmentation of the subject as necessary to and productive of these more inclusive models of resistance, often based on coalitions between diverse, shifting, and dispersed groups.[16]

Participating in this postmodern turn, Chauvet represents an inclusive form of revolutionary resistance that potentially includes the invisible and the abject: beggars, women, prostitutes, and the mad. Claire, a most unlikely revolutionary agent, calls herself, "one of the famished," and writes: "the needs of the flesh are normal. Can anyone live without eating or drinking? I writhe upon my bed prey to unquenchable desires" (17). Chauvet's analogy here is not intended to be parodic; in having Claire voice this personal, even narcissistic quest in terms of the political struggle of the impoverished, Chauvet both legitimates this woman's demands, and suggests how the bourgeoise old maid might legitimately speak for others. For once Claire can voice and accept the validity of her own (often negative) desires, she is able to recognize the links between her own demands and those of others, and act in solidarity, in coalition, with other groups and individuals who likewise pursue their freedom.

"Amour" challenges us to accept and acknowledge the necessity of this truly inclusive, rather than abstract notion of universality.

Chauvet's model of subjectivity and history in "Amour" can thus be termed "postmodern" in the historicized sense that Mercer defines it, and critics have often identified *Amour, colère et folie* as Haiti's first postmodern piece of fiction.[17] Indeed, in postmodern fashion, Chauvet represents Claire's subjectivity as fragmented and shifting, rendering inauthentic and impossible her forming any *essential* identifications or solidarities based on race, gender, nation, or any other category. Claire's race intersecting with her class and gender identities, she feels no sympathy for the extreme black nationalist regime and Calédu, its local representative. Indeed, Claire works to maintain her class privilege, also denying any kinship with the petit bourgeois black supporters of the new regime (whom she calls *"parvenus"*) or with the only other black member of her household, Augustine, the maid. Claire, the self-identified "old maid," does develop a sense of solidarity with other aging unmarried women of her class, principally because, like Claire, they are Calédu's favorite prey. But, in terms of gender, Claire's two younger light-skinned sisters, Annette and Félicia, are her enemies, and the household, despite the demise of the patriarch, is a battleground, especially for the "prize" of the white Frenchman, Jean-Luze. As Dayan diplomatically states the case, "it is not easy for women to read Claire. Her characteristics are so variable, and sometimes so similar to what she condemns that her preoccupations could be seen as 'nonfeminist.'"[18] Indeed, Claire, desperately in love with her brother-in-law, grovels at his feet to sweep up his cigarette ashes and fantasizes about stabbing her sister.

Yet, while in postmodern fashion, Chauvet posits a fragmented and unheroic political subject and resists essentialist notions of identity, the dialectic remains central to her model of subjectivity and history. In this sense she writes her novella on the cusp of the modern and the postmodern, philosophical and historical categories that she frames in both the global spread of decolonization to new subjects and in the specific context of a United States–supported dictatorship that manipulated an identitarian discourse to further entrench the master/slave sociopolitical model.

The (post)modern character of Chauvet's dialectics of recognition is perhaps best exemplified in her representation of Claire's relationship to Commandant Calédu, both her enemy-other and a mirror and emblem of what her redemptive love for Jean-Luze (whose name means "light") represses and negates. For as Claire pursues this "enlightened" love, this demand for recognition, her language and the fantasies they describe become ever more violent, so that in giving voice to her "love," she ultimately unleashes its repressions, at one point exclaiming: "Oh how love makes us sadistic and cruel! Am I not just like the torturers? I've suffered too much. What I need is a cease fire. . . . look at me becoming a criminal!" (103). Just as she calls herself one of the "famished," by proclaiming herself a "torturer" and a "criminal," Claire insists on her connection, not only to the "enslaved," the victimized, but also to the perpetrators of this violence. Claire has indeed been responsible for the death of innocent peasants when she managed her father's plantation, and Calédu taunts her with their likeness: "you and me, we both have death on our consciences. Mine trouble me little. And you?" (62). This history persists in Calédu's psyche as much as in Claire's, for Claire is indeed the primary object of his own quest to be seen as a "human," as an equal subject. While Claire has legitimate reasons for hating Calédu, her role as "master," as "white other" vis-à-vis the Commandant is indisputable: "In the street I pass Calédu. He greets me, but I pass with my head held high, haughty and disdainful; I pretend not to see him" (43).

Represented in tandem, Claire and Calédu's drives for recognition are clearly dialectical, but, conforming to the postmodern model, it is a dialectics of identity and power that cannot arrive at the resolution of "freedom" as mutual recognition. Instead, these proliferating dialectical relationships in "Amour" work to create a model of collectivity that is formed through the intersections and conflicts of individual trajectories of desire. The vocabulary of revolution emblematizes the inevitable historical underpinnings of these desires and their crossings. Thus, while Claire denies her identity with Calédu, in the multiple meanings of "love," "suffering," and "criminality," history speaks through her, and her psyche becomes a kind of Pandora's box. In unleashing her protagonist's furious desires, Chauvet exposes the dialectical inseparability of sexual obsession and history, and finally, individual desires and their collective effects, as we shall see.

## Fantasy, History, and Sadomasochism

Chauvet represents her dialectics of individual and collective history most vividly in scenes of often interracial sadomasochistic sexual encounters. As Linda Williams and Jessica Benjamin have shown, sadomasochistic encounters parallel in their structure Hegel's paradigm of master and slave: the master, while he gains recognition in the eyes of the slave, remains dependent upon this "inferior," who thereby enjoys a certain "mastery" over his lord. In a reading of the works of the Marquis de Sade, Dayan historicizes the connection between colonial histories and sadomasochism by arguing that Sade's "impure tales" of metropolitan libertines reveal the violent truths of slavery and colonial law, that which constitutes the Enlightenment's shadowy repressions, its unconscious.[19] Similarly, for Chauvet, sadomasochism dramatizes the psychic internalization of the "irrational" colonial master/slave relationship.[20] As such, sadomasochism, as a version of the master/slave dialectic, is the central analytic of Chauvet's novella, as s/m fantasy can expose the psychic and social dynamics that have determined Haitian history yet remain repressed in the discourses of both colonialism and decolonization.

Sadomasochism is the model with which Chauvet analyzes racialized colonial relations as primary, as experienced on the level of the subject's drives, impulses, and fantasies. Chauvet locates the original scene of Claire's racialized sadomasochistic yearnings in the family, in the domestic sphere, rather than in the public space of black/white encounters, the mise en scène that Fanon imagines as he formalizes his version of the racialized dialectic of recognition in *Peau noire, masques blancs*. Racial intersubjectivity as a dialectic between master and slave is played out in the Clamont "family romance" in which Claire is beaten by her father and unloved by her mother because of her dark skin. In her diary, Claire writes that her coming to consciousness as a subject is initiated by a violence that her parents practiced upon both their daughter and the servants and poor peasants who work their lands: "my first memories date from this time. For it's through the revelation of suffering that one becomes conscious of oneself" (104). Early in the novel, Claire relates her own "enslavement" within the Clamont family to that of the black peasants and servants who labor for them, as well as to Calédu's tortured prisoners: "at the sounds of their cries just like those of the prisoners, my blood boils and revolt cries out in me. Already, long ago, I hated my father for whipping the farmers' sons over the most minor offence" (15). As Claire writes the story of her own psychic formation, the event that marks her initiation into young adulthood is also a whipping by her father (110).

Claire's whip-wielding father assumes the conflated positions of bourgeois patriarch and colonial "master." Playing out his own internalized master/slave dialectic, Clamont also beats Claire into accepting her inheritance of the role of black "master." During his lifetime, Clamont continues to serve his black grandmother's *lwas*, or spirits, and when he tries to pass this inheritance onto his eldest daughter, she resists and is once again beaten for the offense. These primal scenes of the father/master's violence haunt Claire's sadomasochistic scenarios, as exemplified in a passage in which the colonial patriarch returns to disrupt Claire's fantasies and to remind her of her split identity as both black "other," or "slave," and black "master": "sometimes while imagining the most feverish scenes of love, I'm suddenly stricken by panic at the fleeting memory of my father beating me with his belt" (170). According to Chauvet, in the Haitian context, the postcolonial, mixed-race subject is split by a violence through which she is forced to internalize the positions both of mastery and servitude, "white" and "black."

As Williams observes in a reading of Freud's "A Child Is Being Beaten," sadomasochism is organized around complex structures of fantasy in which identifications are in flux between three roles: the beater, the beaten, and the spectator. Williams thus revises Freud's scenario to show that it represents bisexual desire, a movement between the positions of femininity, masculinity, mother and father, passive and active, identifications that are not necessarily sutured to their "opposites" as object choices.[21] Similarly, in Chauvet's version of sadomasochism, the positions of sadist/masochist, masculine/feminine, and master/slave are constantly in flux and cannot be fixed to particular gendered or raced subjects.[22]

Claire at first elaborates her intricate fantasy of conquering Jean-Luze by making herself the "spectator" and observing a developing flirtation between the Frenchman and her sister Annette. Assigning to Annette the fantasized colonial role of the licentious *mulattresse*, Claire at times masochistically effaces herself and hides behind the image: "sometimes I forget who I am and I believe that it's me whom Jean-Luze flees and then takes into his arms" (38); and at another point, she writes, "I felt terribly old and out of style, and I made a tremendous effort to forget myself and to identify completely with Annette" (61). Like the female cinematic spectator described by Mary Ann Doane and others, Claire masochistically identifies with a "screen" image through which she mediates her own desire.[23] Such mediation, though, also potentially leads to an empowered subjectivity, as Claire inhabits more and more, in fantasy, the "screen image" that she has in part created: "he often gives her long looks that make me shiver. I think I get more pleasure from his gaze than does she. She's not the recipient, but me. By what miracle?" (23).

As these moments suggest, Claire's intense voyeurism and masochistic self-effacement allow her to begin to recognize *herself* as a legitimate subject. Most importantly, Claire's taking on the role of the spectator as well as the masochist is the means by which she re-imagines her psychosexual primal scene. One scene marks this transformation fairly explicitly:

"I imagine them naked, holding one another, taking each other again and again. Then I get into bed mad with desire. I'm with them, in between them. No, I'm alone with Jean-Luze. Oh, how love cancels out all other feelings!" (31). Claire plays out a kind of Oedipal moment here, as she moves through the positions of the sadomasochistic scenario, from spectator to participant, at first loving and then suppressing Annette, the "mother," the object of identification, and using masochism as a vehicle that leads to a revelation of her own desires. Claire's shifting identifications temporarily release her from the social position that she inhabits within the domestic space and at times in relationship to Calédu (as "slave") and she imagines herself as the spectator who is also the torturer/master/patriarch demanding recognition through sex and violence: "I want him to rip you from your vulgar pleasures and throw you into an immense whirlpool of desire that will threaten your very life. . . . I want to torture you, both of you, until you cry out for mercy" (50). Claire, too, steps into a whirlpool in which she risks annihilation, as she plays out in sadomasochistic fantasy her desire to assume every role and to *have* every player in the drama: spectator, master, slave, torturer, victim. She writes variously: "it's me, Annette" (131); "I've suffered too much" (103); "Am I not just like the torturers?" (103); "I devour [Annette] with my eyes" (28), just as she devours with her gaze Violette, the town prostitute, desiring both to be and to have her (49). Yet Claire continues to be plagued by dreams in which Calédu taunts her with an "enormous erect phallus while a crowd cries out 'Kill her! Kill her!'"—a dream that reminds her of a recurring childhood nightmare in which her father, transformed into a beast, locks her in a cage and whips her while roaring like an enraged lion (145).

The psychic origin in trauma of Claire's split racial subjectivity paradoxically enables her to identify and empathize widely, and it is her promiscuous identifications that incite the expansion and transformation of her sexual proclivities for a collective project of revolution. Claire's "irrational" fantasies that turn around her identifications with both masters and slaves thematize the internalized histories that will eventually connect her to the collective sphere that lies outside her bedroom door. Sadomasochism, then, as an indeterminate dialectical process finally overtakes the teleology of the master/slave dialectic—recognition—and Chauvet imagines a different universal freedom produced out of the "irrational" interpenetration of self and other. For Chauvet, sadomasochism is the fantasy process that works through the irrational inheritance of racialized intersubjectivity in order to reach a different form of communion with the other, as we shall see.

To fully explicate Chauvet's use of sadomasochism as a means of transforming the racialized dialectic of recognition into an inclusive revolutionary dialectic, we must return to Fanon's *Peau noire, masques blancs,*
in which the author famously employs psychoanalysis, phenomenology,
and, as we've seen, Kojève's version of Hegel to analyze black subjectivity
in a colonial context. The most discussed chapter of *Peau noire, masques
blancs,* "L'Expérience vécue du noir" (The fact of blackness), is a non-
linear, subjective, and episodic work that represents with what could be
termed a postmodern aesthetic the (post)colonial subject's demand for
recognition from a white world. As Chauvet does in "Amour," Fanon
uses the first-person narrative to give form to the fantasies and the
"irrationality" created out of this racialized dialectic of identity: "since
no agreement was possible on the level of reason, I threw myself back
toward unreason. . . . here I am at home; I am made of the irrational;
I wade in the irrational."[24] Yet where Chauvet refuses to abandon this
"irrationality," the concluding chapter of *Peau noire, masques blancs*
demonstrates that the goal of Fanon's psychoanalytic "self-scrutiny" is
indeed to "disalienate," to heal the black colonized subject's fragmentation, thus freeing him from the irrationality of colonial history. *Peau
noire, masques blancs* closes with a moving declaration that evokes
Fanon's debt both to existentialism and humanist modernism: "I am my
own foundation . . . it is through the lasting tension of their freedom that
men will be able to create the ideal conditions of existence for a human
world. . . . Was my freedom not given to me then in order to build the
world of the *You*? At the conclusion of this study, I want the world to
recognize, with me, the open door of every consciousness."[25] As suggested in the move from the fragmented confessions and soul-searching
of the "Fact of Blackness" to the Sartrean existentialism of "By Way of
Conclusion," Fanon finally defines "freedom" as purchased by the rational, unified subject, whose liberation is predicated on a renunciation of
irrationality, the symptom of his internalization of an unequal dialectic
of identity *and* history.

In contrast to Fanon, Chauvet arrives at the universal, the "open door
of every consciousness," *through* the fantasies produced out of continuing colonial histories and intersubjectivity. Thus, like Fanon, Chauvet
performs, in the voice of her protagonist, a fictive "self-scrutiny," but her
goal is not to heal. Because, for Chauvet, when the irrational colonial
unconscious speaks it gives voice to both the "me" and the "you," and
thus to a kind of universal. For Chauvet, as for Fanon, in the unconscious
space of fantasy and dreams, history and the other take possession of the

subject, but for Chauvet, freedom lies in accepting this possession, this self-dispersal. Chauvet thus makes the epistemology of colonial irrationality the basis of her vision of universality and revolutionary change.

Chauvet's revision of the dialectic of recognition, her rejection of the notion that freedom is based on the transcendence of colonial splitting or irrationality is further evident when we examine the function of gender in *Peau noire, masques blancs*. Fanon's intersecting gender and race presuppositions come out forcefully in the chapter entitled "La Femme de couleur et le blanc" (The woman of color and the white man). This chapter is mostly devoted to an excoriation of Martinican novelist Mayotte Capécia's *Je suis martiniquaise* (1948) (*I Am a Martinican Woman*, 1997), which Fanon describes as a "vast delusion" in which "the most ridiculous ideas proliferat[e] at random."[26] Capécia's delusion, her "irrationality" is the same as Claire's in "Amour": to desire the love, admiration, and recognition of a white man, what Fanon describes as a desire for the black race's "lactification."[27] In Fanon's interpretation of Capecia's novel, he emphasizes this female author/protagonist's inability to transcend her pathology, her irrational love of the white other, and finally, he categorizes as feminine and feminizing the colonial irrationality and psychic conflict that impede historical change. By himself renouncing this "pathology," he designates a different other, the black colonized woman whose sickness damns all black colonized subjects to an irrational and static history. Fanon thus closes the chapter on Capécia with the frightful assertion that the willful fantasy of lactification is "the poison [that] must be eliminated once and for all."[28]

In "Amour," Chauvet rescues the "irrationality" of the woman of color who loves a white man, making it the basis of a universal consciousness. By formalizing the "illicit" love for the white other in terms of the master/slave dialectic, she legitimizes this form of desire (all desire, in fact) as carrying the potential for galvanizing collective historical change. And by using sadomasochism as a model for a dialectic of recognition, she insists that the interpenetration of self and other, master and slave, is not a pathology, but a lived and felt reality that cannot be overcome through rational teleologies. Rather, real freedom and revolution must potentially develop out of both anger and love, action and passivity, that is, the "irrational" desires of a dispersed collectivity of subjects, whose demands potentially intersect and can thus be marshaled for a collective project.

Four scenes in "Amour" trace how Chauvet uses sadomasochism to imagine the development of a collective revolution out of the psychic interpenetration of self and other, master and slave. In these scenes, Claire's drive for recognition from Jean-Luze is gradually redefined as a process that leads toward a revelation of the webs that link past to present, and by implication, collective and individual desires for liberation. The first scene takes place as Claire pursues her sexual fantasies while listening to Annette and Jean-Luze in the bedroom next to her own: "Oh how love cancels out all other emotions! Even screams from the prison could not grab my attention. Here I am, Annette, and I'm sixteen years younger. I didn't hear a thing except a horrible cry and the thump of a body. I don't wish to be witness to any embarrassing scene" (31).

At this point Claire's fantasy involves a total fusion with Annette's image. She both hears a scream and represses it, performed in the passage's sudden switch to the past tense by which Claire disavows her witnessing and rewrites the moment: "I didn't hear a thing." The scream could well have been from one of Calédu's victims, but it is in fact Félicia who cries as she discovers her husband and sister's adultery. In this scene, Claire refuses to be a witness; she refuses to look, to acknowledge the potential victims of her own actions.

In refusing to recognize Félicia's pain, Claire, here, remains locked within the illusion that the self, the private sphere of fantasy is a haven safe from collective determinations and effects. She duplicates the hypocritical refusal of the town's bourgeois class to act as witness, and she replays their repression of their own responsibility as historical subjects. Like the town's aristocrats, Claire refuses to recognize her own complicity in Calédu's violence. At this point, she mystifies the relationships between private and public, between past oppression and current terror, and between individual acts and their collective effects.

As Claire moves deeper into her fantasy life and feels her desires more violently and vividly, she begins to accept her complicity, the repressed others that she cannot help but hear in the expression of her own violent fantasies, in her own telling of history. This acceptance allows her to relate her own obsessions to the needs of other "starving beings," both past and present, not identical but linked to her own in flashes of unity. This acceptance is formalized in an episode whose setting parallels the scene quoted above; however here, Claire can no longer ignore the screams that erupt out of and into her own fantasies:

In my thoughts, Félicia is suppressed. Look at me becoming a criminal! I'm terrorizing myself. A long howl gives me a start. Someone calls for help in the dark and I run to the window. I hear the clicking of guns and the screams of a woman. I imagine my neighbors with ears pricked, like me, listening and trembling, and the handcuffed woman being led away by Calédu. I can't see anything or hear anything now either. . . . I'm surprised by my shaking hands and by the rage rising within me. (103)

In this passage, Claire's identifications, shifting according to the structure of sadomasochism, begin to express the social dimensions of her desire, emblematized by the scream of a woman. As Claire plays out the role of "master" or "sadist," calling herself a "criminal," she again hears the scream, and this time, she attends to, identifies with the "other" who is negated by her own and another's violent desires. For, while the scream indeed belongs to one of Calédu's victims, it also reinvokes the earlier episode and the pain that has been inflicted upon Félicia. The scream metaphorizes both the social underpinnings and the dispersed effects of the violent quest to be recognized, in part by revealing, once again, Claire's complex connection to both Calédu and to his victims.

Further, in the above scene, Claire's violent fantasies, moving between torturer, tortured, and spectator, become the means by which she feels the collective, including her neighbors whom she imagines to share this moment of witnessing. Without thinking, Claire stands up, opens the windows, and looks out for the first time in the novella, joining herself to the still shadowed crowd. Here, the fluid process of self/other identification thematized in sadomasochistic fantasy brings Claire into contact with others who likewise pursue their liberation. For Chauvet, the revolutionary moment takes place when individual desires coincide to create this flash of unity.

Toward the end of "Amour," members of the community begin to resist Calédu, and Claire has also acted in quiet resistance to both the commander and her own hypocritical class. Nonetheless, she has not abandoned her irrational project of gaining the love of Jean-Luze, and in fantasy, she plans the murder of her sister, the last impediment to her gaining recognition in the gaze of the white European. Cries from the prison, however, again remove Claire from her private machinations, forcing her to understand the collective dimensions of her personal quest: "I listen to the wails. . . . A strange shudder seems to shake the town like the muffled sound of wings soaring slowly over our heads. This shiver that runs through me cannot be personal, I know this now. Just like me everyone must work in secret to liberate themselves from duress and fear. I'm not alone. They're all there around me and we suffer together, obsessed with our certain deliverance" (177). Once again, Claire's imagining a violent act dialectically reveals what violence represses. But here, the repressed other is the entire community, which she feels as a "shiver," as a fleeting sense of unity. This "strange shudder" that is "like the muffled sound of wings soaring slowly over our heads" describes unity and universality as an unreachable horizon, a memory as well as a future that can only be grasped in flashes, an ideal that is only concretized in irrational moments of communion.

In the novella's final scene, Claire, who has planned to kill Félicia (she stabs the neighbor's cat for practice), at the last minute, decides to commit suicide. She plans her suicide as a stabbing—the ultimate performance in her internalized sadomasochistic fantasy. Bedecking herself in white silk for the spectacle, Claire looks into a mirror and sees a visual representation of her split subjectivity: "surprised, I discover that I have asymmetrical features: left profile: dreamy and tender; right profile: sensual, ferocious" (185). Claire's plan to inflict violence upon herself is a desperate attempt to heal this split. But her fragmentation cannot and will not be "healed," for it remains the basis of her gathering involvement in the struggle that surrounds her, and the suicide scene is interrupted once again by the presence of the collective narrative, emblematized by screams and cries in the street: "I'm lifting my arm and pointing it at my left breast when the cries of the crowd in revolt rip me out of my delirium. Holding the knife in my outstretched arm, I listen. Once again my attention has been diverted from its goal. Life, death, do they merely depend on mere chance alone?" (186). The answer is "yes," although, as the rest of the narrative has borne out, there is no such thing as mere chance. Ripped out of the "delirium" that has paradoxically permitted Claire to "know" the collective, she is now at one with the crowds in revolt, ready to act on the understanding revealed to her in her "irrational" fantasies of violence and recognition.

When Calédu stumbles under the gallery of Claire's house to escape the enraged crowd, Claire plunges the knife into his back. As Ronnie Scharfman writes, the end of "Amour" is "like a deep breath"[29] freeing the reader from the claustrophobia of Claire's obsessions, and from the novel's general atmosphere of suffocating paranoia. But what is crucial about this liberatory ending is that, although Claire has accomplished the murder, in effect liberating the town of its tyrant, she refuses the "reward" of Jean-Luze's affectionate embrace, his recognition. Chauvet represents Claire renouncing the heroic satisfaction, the triumphant turning of the tables that might perpetuate the continuing cycle of mastery and servitude. The novel closes with Claire silently retreating into her locked bedroom, from which she nonetheless contemplates the street, where "the doors of the houses are open and the entire town is standing up" (187).

The final lines of "Amour" return us to the anticolonial modernism of Chauvet's francophone predecessors. With seeming specificity, she refers here both to Fanon's universalist teleology in which the "door of every consciousness" is recognized, and to Césaire's evocation of the Haitian Revolution as the moment in which "*négritude* stood up for the first time." Summing up her narrative of obsessive love with these particular intertexts encapsulates Chauvet's project in "Amour": to reassert the revolutionary potential of the dialectical model but to revise it by showing that the violent master/slave struggle cannot be overcome through rational projects to transcend the past. For, if the colonized subject has internalized histories of unequal colonial contact, she has also internalized potential futures based precisely on feeling and thus understanding the other *within*. Finally, for Chauvet, the revolution that will bring true freedom to Haiti and the rest of the neocolonial world is a permanent one, based on the love of the ultimate other of the colonial project: the irrational, split subject who embodies the negativity that is history itself.

### Notes

1. Charles H. Rowell, "Erma Saint-Gregoire," 466.

2. Duvalier's regime was based on his ultra-nationalist cultural political theory, *noirisme,* in which he argued that Haiti's persistent problems were the result of the suppression of the "African" element of the Haitian psyche in favor of the European. See François Duvalier and Lorimer Denis, *Le Problème des classes à travers l'histoire d'Haïti* [The problem of social class throughout Haitian history] (Port-au-Prince: Collection "les Griots," 1959.)

3. Marie Chauvet, *Amour, colère, folie* (1968 edition), 96. Hereafter, page references will be made in text. All translations of this edition are my own.

4. For a discussion that characterizes Duvalier's regime in terms of the master/slave model, see Laënnec Hurbon, *Culture et dictature: L'Imaginaire sous contrôle* [Culture and dictatorship: The imaginary controlled].

5. See Alexandre Kojève, *Introduction à la lecture de Hegel.*

6. Nick Nesbitt, *Voicing Memory,* 119.

7. See Carrol F. Coates, "Translator's Note on Marie Chauvet's *Amour, colère, folie,*" 460.

8. For a discussion of Chauvet as a politically engaged activist/writer, see Rowell, "Erma Saint-Gregoire," 463–67.

9. See, for example, Aimé Césaire, *Cahier d'un retour au pays natal*; and Frantz Fanon, *Peau noire, masques blancs* For a discussion of these authors' modernist heroic paradigms of history, see J. Michael Dash, *The Other America.*

10. Similar to what I am arguing here, Anne Marty has recently asserted that Chauvet performs a "verbal play" between "I" and "We" in order to represent the universal as well as "individual emancipation, which is, in appearance at least, doubled with a collective emancipation." Anne Marty, "Naturelles correspondances entre l'univers haïtien et le 'moi' universel chez Marie Chauvet," 1 (translation mine).

11. Brenda Gayle Plummer, *Haiti and the United States,* 111. See also Hans Schmidt, *The United States Occupation of Haiti, 1915–1934.*

12. For a discussion of the Haitian Revolution as a universalist, pluralist, and cosmopolitan mass movement, see Sibylle Fischer, *Modernity Disavowed;* Laurent Dubois, *Avengers of the New World;* and Susan Buck-Morss, "Hegel and Haiti."

13. Buck-Morss, "Hegel and Haiti," 837.

14. Roumain died of natural causes in 1943. In 1961, Alexis was tortured and murdered by Duvalier's henchman after an unsuccessful attempt to invade Haiti and incite a rebellion. None of his four published prose fiction works deal directly with Duvalier's dictatorship.

15. See Kobena Mercer, "1968: Periodizing Postmodern Politics and Identity."

16. See Ernesto Laclau and Chantal Mouffe, *Hegemony and Socialist Strategy.*

17. See, for example, Dash, *The Other America,* 110; and Yannick Lahens, "L'Apport de quatre romancières," 36.

18. Joan Dayan, "Reading Women in the Caribbean," 233.

19. Joan Dayan, "Codes of Law and Bodies of Color."

20. For an extended discussion of sadomasochistic "play" and fantasy and its relationship to slavery, colonialism, and class in nineteenth-century England, see Anne McClintock, *Imperial Leather.*

21. Linda Williams, *Hard Core,* 215.

22. Ibid., 217.

23. Mary Ann Doane, *The Desire to Desire.*

24. Frantz Fanon, *Black Skin, White Masks* (Markmann trans.), 123.

25. Ibid., 231.

26. Ibid., 44. Dayan indeed argues that "Amour" must be read as a complex response to Fanon's "scathing indictment" of Capécia. "Reading Women," 231.

27. Fanon, *Black Skin, White Masks,* 47.

28. Ibid., 62. For an excellent discussion of gender in the chapter "The Fact of Blackness," see Gwen Bergner, "Who Is That Masked Woman?"

29. Ronnie Scharfman, "Theorizing Terror," 187.

# Chroniques de la francophonie triomphante

## Haiti, France, and the Debray Report (2004)

### Chris Bongie

There's nothing more strange and hypocritical than the language of
these Messieurs. It has to be read to be believed. Now that it's no longer a question of subjugating us by force of arms, nor of intimidating
us through terror, just see how they've changed their tune: no longer biting, imperious, ferocious, their tone is sweet as honey, almost
polite. Like a new Proteus, they present themselves to us in all sorts
of shapes: they no longer adopt the features of a dreadful monster
threatening to exterminate our race down to the last child; now they
are a siren whose melodious voice and seductive forms are inviting
us to throw ourselves into their arms. If they're to be believed, we no
longer have anything to fear from the French. Whatever bad things
they did to us were Bonaparte's fault; now it's simply a question of
starting over with us, embarking on a new course of action that will
be full of charming benefits and good deeds.

—Baron de Vastey, *Réflexions politiques* (1817)

IN FEBRUARY 2004, Haiti was the scene of yet another U.S.-
sanctioned coup d'état. To cite Aijaz Ahmad's bracing analysis of the
"current U.S. crimes in Haiti,"[1] a "'rebellion' was unleashed in order to
promote a social collapse that could then be portrayed in the media as a
prelude to a 'bloodbath' and that could be used as grounds for a 'humanitarian intervention,' a concept made popular in the Western imagination
by the human-rights industry" (41). The weeks leading up to this so-called
humanitarian intervention had been filled with sanctimonious rhetoric,
emanating not only from the United States but—and herein lies the focus
of this essay—from a France intent, after the self-serving pseudo-spat
over Iraq and its oil reserves, on making "eager amends for disloyalty

with a joint coup to oust another unsatisfactory ruler in the Caribbean."[2] Committed to "rebuild[ing] its bridges to the supreme imperial power," France—in Ahmad's words—"emerged as a firm and vocal ally of the U.S. in its occupation of Haiti, sending a contingent of its own troops, again on the pretext of providing 'security'" (41). As France's then foreign minister, Dominique de Villepin, put it only days before the coup, "everyone sees quite well that a new page must be opened in Haiti's history."[3]

It goes without saying that France's recent intervention in its erstwhile colony is, not only in world-historical terms, but also in terms of here-and-now realpolitik in Haiti, a puny thing, of little consequence when stacked up against the overwhelming fact of the supreme imperial power's mindlessly bullying foreign policy with regard both to Haiti and the greater Caribbean. However, that the French, two hundred years after their resounding, and indubitably world-historical, defeat at Vertières, were not only back in their former colony, but talking about it with the air of moral authority and possession characteristic of the deluge of printed matter they produced in the two decades immediately following upon the Haitian Revolution, is certainly a fact worthy of study by practitioners of French cultural studies, in their quest for an anthropological understanding of that quaintly self-universalizing European tribe and of the doggedly paternalistic relations it maintains with its former and present colonies in the Pacific, Africa, and the Caribbean. The recent resurgence of French interest in, and discourse about, Haiti also provides a useful cautionary reminder for those of us in the "progressive" field of francophone studies. France's recent military and discursive intervention in the former Saint-Domingue has a great deal to tell us about the neo-imperial underpinnings of a field of study that *legitimizes* the inclusion of Haiti within the confines of French departments in a way that is disturbingly analogous to the manner in which, as we will see, the concept of *la francophonie* helped legitimize France's latest "humanitarian" adventure in Haiti.

A comprehensive account of Franco-Haitian relations in the months leading up to the coup d'état would be a massive task, the world-historic puniness of the topic notwithstanding. Indeed, even were one to leave aside an engagement with the niceties of France's actual military intervention and focus only on the words through which that intervention was anticipated and justified by French politicians and the mainstream media in France—with their scandalized outcries against "this defrocked priest, this psychopath struck with the madness that comes from power and money" (to quote a bicentenary portrait of Aristide in *Le Figaro*)[4]—one would still have bitten off a great deal more than can be chewed here. At the risk of falling prey to the synecdochal fallacy, I will thus be limiting myself to a close reading of one highly visible part of the aforementioned discursive whole, a slim tome that can be plausibly identified as the single most important French text about Haiti to have been published during the bicentenary year: namely, the official report submitted to de Villepin on January 28 by the *Comité indépendant de réflexion et de propositions sur les relations franco-haïtiennes*, and published six weeks later (March 11) by La Table Ronde as a book, entitled *Haïti et la France*, under the signature of Régis Debray.

The Committee was organized by de Villepin as a direct response to Aristide's increasingly vocal calls in 2003 for a restitution, with interest, of the financial compensation paid out to France by Haiti, starting in 1825, as the price of its former imperial masters' officially recognizing the independence it had won on the battlefields in 1803. Aristide's call for restitution was first made at the bicentenary commemoration of Toussaint's death in April and involved a sum equivalent to $21,685,135,571.48 (U.S.). It was predictably rejected out of hand by the Chirac government, despite the fact that, as Peter Hallward notes, "unlike most slavery-related reparation demands currently in the air, the Haitian claim refer[red] to a precise and documented sum of money extracted in hard currency by the colonial power."[5] Aristide's demand did, however, indirectly result in the establishment, on October 7, of the aforementioned Committee headed by Debray—former companion-in-arms of Che Guevara, latter-day "arch-Gaullist," prolific "mediologist," and one of the more vocal French critics of pre- and post-9/11 U.S. foreign policy, which he has repeatedly characterized as "monocultural, monologizing, indeed monomaniacal."[6]

The stated goal of Debray's committee was "to reflect on the current situation in Haiti and on the state of Franco-Haitian relations, and to propose concrete actions capable of invigorating the Franco-Haitian connection and reorienting it, in such a way that it contributes, along with all Haitians of good will and with its regional partners and the OAS [Organization of American States], to eliminating the infernal circle in which that country is submerged."[7] We need not pause over the problematic phrasing of de Villepin's directive, with its invidious distinction between Haitians of good and bad *volonté* and its revealingly metaphorical talk about "infernal circles." Nor need we here go into any detail over the actual work of the Committee in the three-plus months between its creation and the delivery of a report that was based on interviews, mostly in Paris and Haiti, with over 150 notables, all listed at the back of it.[8] Rather, it is to the book version of this Report that we must now turn our attention.[9]

IT CANNOT be a question here of engaging in a comprehensive summary and critique of Debray's analysis of, and recommendations for, Haiti in the year 2004. In many respects, what he has to say differs little from the "common-sense" analyses provided by political scientists and historians the world over (which is another way of saying that Debray's account relies heavily on those analyses). His portrait of the predatory republic, his references to the long-standing disjunction between State and nation, his positive invocations of "civil society," his insistence on the need to lift sanctions and create "infrastructures of democracy" (roads, schools, etc.), are all familiar enough, as are his smug claims about "the stranding of messianic hopes" (36)—his attachment to the commonly held view that Aristide and the Lavalas movement succumbed to "the Haitian political 'habitus'" and took "unfortunate detours leading to multiple and obscure dead ends."[10] I will not be concerned here with the broad, "common-sensical" strokes of Debray's portrait of Haiti—a portrait that he pointedly identifies as "nonpartisan" in the Report's brief foreword (13), making the sort of rhetorical claims to neutrality with which he frequently lards his social-scientific work as a mediologist,[11] but that in the case of Debray's attitude toward Aristide are so clearly belied in interviews he gave shortly after the Report was published.[12] Rather, what I will be doing in this chapter is zeroing in on two symptomatic passages in the text where Debray appeals to (first) Haiti's francophone identity and (second) the particular memories that supposedly attach to this identity: in these passages, the ideological underpinnings of Debray's portrait of Haiti rise to the surface, revealing a "naïve and paternalist arrogance" that, elsewhere in the Report, he is careful to warn against (43).

The first passage on which I focus is, without question, the single most objectionable statement in the entire book. It is a statement that will ring alarm bells in the ears of anyone who has taken Poco Studies 101, but it is nonetheless essential to comment on it here, because the linguistic bias that it all too shamefully displays is that which alone makes it possible for Debray to speak of Haiti, to discover it on (and in) his own terms, and to render it an object of interest to his French audiences (to both his official *destinataire*, de Villepin, and the public at large). Reenacting what he himself refers to as "the rediscovery of Haiti under the rubric of *la francophonie*" in the 1970s (30), Debray envisions Haiti first and foremost as a place where French is spoken, and that is what for him primarily justifies the project of enhancing and consolidating Franco-Haitian relations. As he states early on in the Report, "the only officially francophone State in the 'hemisphere' is not for us Frenchmen simply a *half-brother* who has been left by the side of the road (too distant, too costly, too restless). Colonial empires pass on, their language and their law remain" (16).[13] Their (our) language—and, to be sure, their (our) law (the "Code Napoléon," no less, as Debray elsewhere reminds his readers [33]!)—is the anything-but-strange attractor that provides the rationale for, and legitimization of, France's ostensibly postimperial renewal of interest in its *demi-frère*. Haiti is, after all, as Debray noted in an interview shortly after the coup, invoking a time-honoured cliché, "the last remaining country where French is spoken."[14]

But, of course, at some point in his francophone-centric account of Haiti, Debray has to raise the issue of the language spoken by all Haitians, and not simply the "talented tenth." Midway through the Report, in the section entitled "École et culture, main dans la main," the issue of Creole is finally confronted head on, generating a statement well worthy of *MonsieurChauvin*. After reminding his readers that French is no longer the only official language in Haiti—"bilingualism was adopted by the Constitution of 1987, broadly ratified by the people, as a surety of personal dignity"—Debray admits that in Haiti

> French could not play a federative role joining together regional dialects, as was the case in France from the Revolution on, for Haiti's national unity is cemented in and by this original language, which cannot be reduced to a patois and a dialect. But Creole cannot provide access to the realm of international relations, to the data of universal knowledge [*aux données de la connaissance universelle*], nor to the culture of the legally constituted State. That is why, if education in Haiti aspires to be anything more than an apprenticeship in sequestration [*un apprentissage de l'enfermement*] (Creole only) or else an institutional ethnocide (everything in French), the two languages are called upon to cohabit, in a situation of mutual support. (56–57)

To state the obvious, it is a decidedly unequal cohabitation that Debray here envisions for Haiti's two official languages. Creole encloses, dooming its speakers to an eternal "apprenticeship," whereas French opens out onto the world of international relations, providing a gateway to the realm of "universal" knowledge and access to the rule of law. Personal dignity is one thing, but it is only to be expected that right-thinking Haitians will do whatever they can to give their children access to the "*données de la connaissance universelle,*" preferably at the Alliance française nearest them.[15]

For all its "originality," Creole is thus for Debray a "language" (not, he is careful to stress, a patois or a dialect) that functions in exactly the same way that the languages of the colonized so often did for earlier generations of colonizers. Creole's rightful, purely instrumental place in the linguistic hierarchy comes out especially clearly in the section of the Report devoted to the need to reinforce the French embassy in Haiti. In that section, he argues that functionaries working at the embassy should be encouraged to learn Creole: "*Creole* being a language currently and officially in use, it would seem judicious to extend its use. Those appointed to positions in the different French services in Haiti (embassy, French Institute . . .) could be urged even before taking up their positions, or at the very least when they arrive [in Haiti], to learn Creole, the principal mode of contact with the country's heartland [*le pays profond*]" (70–71). Such advice in no way diverges from the approach taken by colonial administrators in the days of the Third Republic. The "native" language becomes the key to accessing, and comprehending, the "heart" of the country. Such comprehension, in turn, is what makes documents such as the Report possible (even if its author does not himself know Creole), based as they are upon the assumption that an entire people can be not merely communicated with but brought within a "totalizing relation of 'comprehension,'"[16] of the sort that generates, for instance, Debray's portentous psycho-cultural comments about Haiti's "Janus-faced" attitude to other countries and its proclivity for what he dubs "victimary incrimination" (26–27).

What complicates, or at least seems to complicate, this blatant "othering" of Creole, its reduction to a "native" language, is the rhetoric of (re-)familiarization that is also deployed in the Report. Creole may not be a patois or a dialect, and its orthography may vary from the French model, we are told, but these two languages are nonetheless "*deux membres d'une même famille*" (75). If the family metaphor is to hold, of course, then Creole must here function as the younger sibling, living in the long shadow cast by a father masquerading as a big (half)brother. Simultaneously Other and part of the Same, Creole is brought back within the fold through the invocation of what Paul Gilroy has referred to, in a discussion of some of the less palatable ways in which Afro-diasporic identity has been figured, as the "trope of kinship."[17] Diaspora as a family affair, conceived here in linguistic as opposed to bio-political terms, draws a clear line of demarcation between inside and outside, us and them; this model of diaspora depends upon a boundaried vision of the world that is in a direct line of continuity with colonial discourse, rather than promoting the sort of "multiple identifications" and "plural identities" that are, or at least ought to be (according to the likes of Gilroy and Stuart Hall), the defining features of a less familiar, postcolonial experience of diaspora as historical "dissemination" of the margins as opposed to mythic "return" to the center.[18]

Although family is not the only metaphorical model through which Debray attempts to (re)assert France's integral relation with Haiti,[19] it is an especially revealing one inasmuch as it assumes the *organic* nature of that relation. Organic matter, to be sure, has a determinate lifespan: it lives and dies, and Debray is enough of a "realist" to recognize the possibility that members of the francophone family may expire, if not provided with the necessary life-support system. Only a page after his assertion that *"les deux langues sont appelées à cohabiter, en s'épaulant"* (as is only "natural" for members of the same family), he thus introduces the dystopian possibility that the family, and its values, might be under threat in Haiti, given the equally natural (but *inorganic*) "gravitational pull" of English-as-a-second-language. Of thirty available television stations in Haiti, he notes, "only two are French-language" (*deux seulement sont francophones*), and it is an indisputable fact that "there are already more Haitians, in the world, capable of 'functioning' in English than in French (from bank directors to street sweepers). *La francophonie* does not have eternity ahead of it. How many more generations are left?" (58). Given this situation, how can one, as he puts it, "equilibrate the law of gravity?" Debray seems confident that it can be done, "with help from the Europeans and the vast francophone club" (58)—for instance, by spearheading an intensive attack on illiteracy, which ideally would be facilitated by "a certain number of foreign partners (Africans, Maghrebians, Québécois, Belgians, etc.)" (54); or by ensuring a greater role for Haiti's cultural workers in "the institutions of *la francophonie internationale,*" which must take care that Haitian writers, musicians, and professors find in such countries as France, Belgium, and Switzerland "as warm a welcome as they do in North America" (61). It is not, however, the solutions Debray offers to the "gravitational pull" of "the big neighbor" to the north—a pull reinforced by Haiti's location within the mainly "Anglo-Saxon" Caribbean basin (*"un bassin à coloration majoritairement anglo-saxonne"*; 79)—that are of interest to us here, or the various jibes against the "Anglo-Saxon" world elicited by this pull.[20] Rather, the very fact of *la francophonie*'s possible mortality is the vital point to register here. Just as, within the logic of colonial discourse, tropes like the "primitive" and the "exotic" are substantiated through appeals to their extinction or disappearance,[21] so here the projected death of *la francophonie* merely serves to corroborate and consolidate its real existence. If it can die off, then what greater proof could there be that such a thing once lived?

That Haiti's organic relation with *la francophonie* might, at some point in the future, go the way of all flesh is thus acknowledged by Debray and deployed as yet one more reason for increasing France's profile in the country. However, such a scenario of extinction is only raised once in the Report, which everywhere else foregrounds the other, optimistic side of what is, when all's said and done, the very same francocentric coin. If Debray is not as confident as was the director of the Archives de France in 1953, when he proclaimed, as part of the sesquicentenary commemoration of Toussaint Louverture's death, that "in Haiti, the French language has never been more alive [*plus vivante*] than today,"[22] he is nonetheless buoyed by the knowledge that, to quote from another recent book of his, language is "the most tenacious of all group memories."[23] Indeed, and here we come to the second main thread of my argument, the issue of language for Debray is inseparable from the memories associated with it: memories that, in the case of the former Saint-Domingue, inevitably include those, be they negative or positive, of the colonial era; memories that, as we will now see, exercise a disturbingly strong gravitational pull of their own on the author of *Haïti et la France*.

IT IS, NO DOUBT, of little consequence that the name Saint-Domingue is used at several points in the Report, as well as on the map that precedes it (14), as a synonym for "la République Dominicaine": perhaps the ghostly presence of Saint-Domingue on a map of the present-day Caribbean merely serves as a tribute to what the author approvingly identifies as that Spanish-speaking country's "francophile sentiments" (71). Be that as it may, colonial memories certainly haunt this text and, indeed, continue to provide a rationale for action in the present. Nowhere is the continued relevance of such memories more blatantly, and absurdly, asserted than in the section entitled "France-Allemagne," where Debray comments on the need for the European Union to become more involved in Haiti. Given that his own country "finds itself, in this francophone space, better situated than others to catalyze the efforts of the European Union" (68–69), it would, Debray remarks, be appropriate to combine its resources and personnel with those of other large European countries (*de grands pays européens*), notably Germany. He expands upon this remark by suggesting one symbolic and practical measure in particular that might help stimulate European cooperation in Haiti: "It would be worthwhile for Paris and Berlin to look into this possibility, for one cannot help thinking about the advantages, and they would not be merely symbolic advantages, to be gained by establishing in Port-au-Prince a *joint diplomatic mission* between France and the Federal Republic of Germany . . ." So far so good. But the sentence does not end there. Tit requires tat when it comes to the relations of the *grands pays européens,* and so Debray's local suggestion immediately takes on a more global dimension:

> . . . a *joint diplomatic mission* between France and the Federal Republic of Germany—the natural counterpart of which would be [*à laquelle ferait naturellement pendant*], on the other side of the Atlantic, the establishment of a *Germano-French mission,* for example at Windhoek, in Namibia, or elsewhere. In this way the respective linguistic affinities and historical heritages would be balanced. It is worth noting that our ambassador in Haiti, Thierry Burkard, happens to be perfectly conversant with German culture. (69)

The postcolonial critic can do little but cringe in the face of this Cartesian delusion, this neocolonial *combinatoire* that so readily establishes an "equilibrium" between two vastly different colonial histories. There is no need to do statistical research into the question of how many German speakers are still to be found in the former German South-West Africa, to weigh the two "heritages" on the historical balance and see just how commensurable they are,[24] or—more to the point—to demonstrate the ways in which this pathetic suggestion is part and parcel of a cynical instrumentalization of Africa that surfaces at more than one point in the Report, providing a mirror image of what Debray claims is Aristide's cynical tendency to play Africa off against the West (68).[25]

That the suggestion is pathetic is not the point that needs to be made here—there are other such suggestions in the Report. (This is a document, after all, which concludes by recommending the creation of "a high-level French Institute for sport with a regional orientation" that would promote "soccer, track and field, cycling—sports that are popular in Haiti, the Caribbean, and France" [94], and the final sentence of which calls for a *tour de l'île* that would supplement the "cycling competitions in Guadeloupe, Martinique, Guyana" [94–95]!) The point, rather, is to suggest that, just as the repeated invocation of *la francophonie* in the context of this official document should give the postcolonial critic pause whenever he or she is tempted to use "francophone" as a code word for "resistant" discourse, so Debray's memory-induced *combinatoire,* with its unconsidered appeal to "historical heritages" (and their necessary link to "linguistic affinities"), should serve to make us wary *both* of the seemingly sensible and sensitive invocations in the Report of the "duty to remember" (*devoir de mémoire*), to which I now turn, *and* (although this is only an argument I can gesture toward here) of the possible epistemic complicity between Debray's colonial memories and our own insistence as postcolonial critics on the unquestionable value of counter-memories that might be thought to offer premonitions of, and a foundation for, a decisively transformed future.

At one point early on in the Report, Debray evokes the *devoir de mémoire* (26)—a concept that has become a veritable mantra in recent years on both sides of the Atlantic, including Haiti, whenever the issue of colonialism, slavery, and their aftermaths comes to the fore (as, for instance, during the 1998 sesquicentenary commemorations of the abolition of slavery in the French colonies).[26] The Report begins with an extended analysis of the ways in which France has forgotten Haiti's central role in its history, and insists in no uncertain terms on the need to remember the links between "our amnesiac modernity" and the colonial history that made it possible, "this somewhat embarrassing intimacy that goes beyond the well-known relations of love/hate between a *métropole* and its former colony" (17). The historical relations between France and Haiti have, Debray asserts, been subject to erasure: "we have all *repressed* the deed of the first black Republic of the world"; Haiti in particular, and slavery in general, have disappeared from "the story we tell about ourselves" (*notre roman national*) through a process of repression that is nothing less than Freudian (19). Rather than remain in this state of repression, the memories of Haiti must be allowed to rise to the surface and perform their therapeutic task; rather than "disengage once and for all" from a country with no strategic interest to France (15), "we" need to maintain and strengthen "our" relations with Haiti, as part of the necessary process of transforming it from a place that has long been marginalized in France's *history* into one that is firmly ensconced in its *memory*.[27] The bicentenary, in particular, provides an ideal occasion for facilitating this transformation, for insisting upon the "privileged historical link" between France and Haiti (66), for rejoining "the threads of an intermingled destiny" (20). The "utility of commemorative dates," Debray points out, is that "by bringing buried memories to the surface, they permit each of us to reconcile himself to the loss of his humiliations as of his triumphs [*de faire son deuil de ses humiliations comme de ses triomphes*]." They provide an opportunity to "exorcise one's demons so as to face up to the demands of the future, but with full knowledge of the root-cause(s)" (as recently happened, he adds, with Algeria, 2003 having been officially designated "Algeria Year" in France) (20–21).

One must give Debray's argument its "due." There would appear to be little to quibble with regarding such general claims about the virtues of memory, claims which resonate so strongly with the counter-memorial impetus of much postcolonial criticism. And yet, looked at closely, the passages I have just cited are rather less straightforward than they might at first appear, and not just because the *therapeutic* dimension of the *devoir de mémoire* seems here less a matter of creating new relations (in Glissant's sense of the word) with Haiti than of providing the former colonizer with a fresh start, a no longer haunted conscience. Debray's explicit and repeated insistence on the value of this particular bicentenary commemoration turns out to be inseparable from a certain ambivalence, or even disavowal, which surfaces in curious phrasing or seemingly incidental comments in the text.

The subtle (il)logic of Debray's prose, which continually undermines what it appears to be asserting, can be seen, for instance, in another sentence where he openly welcomes the bicentenary (*"Bienvenu ce bicentenaire . . ."*), this time on the grounds that it "reminds us of the slow and roundabout passage from the ideal to the actual (the rights of man don't travel well [*n'ont pas le pied marin*])" (18). This apparently straightforward sentence is in fact doing rhetorical double duty. It may well refer, at one level, to France's failure to export its ideals, its failure to respect the universal rights of man in its relations with the colony of Saint-Domingue from 1789 to 1794 (when slavery was finally abolished) and after 1802 (when Napoléon launched his failed attempt at reimposing slavery). But Debray's reference to this process of historical degradation, in which the actual fails to match up with the ideal, is suitably vague enough for the statement to become also, and even primarily, an indictment of post-Revolutionary Haitian history—and this reading is reinforced by the curious parenthetical statement with which the sentence ends. That statement subtly relocates the object of commemoration, drawing our attention away from the triumph of Haitian independence (the glorious defeat of the French), and triumphantly, if surreptitiously, returning our admiring gaze to the mother-country, France: for, if the rights of man have trouble crossing the ocean, lacking *le pied marin,* this suggests not only that those ideals failed to take root in Haiti but also that they have maintained, as it were, a lasting foothold in the land of their birth.

That the preceding paragraph offers a niggling, or even perverse, reading of what might be simply unconsidered phrasing on Debray's part could well be argued. One does not, however, have to engage in such micro-readings of the text to get a sense of just how anxiously manipulative Debray is when it comes to bringing this colonial memory to the attention of his "amnesiac" audience. He may insist on the need for France to remember Haiti (and, of course, for Haiti not to forget France!), but he lays out very clear rules of conduct regarding the possible uses to which this long-repressed memory can be put: what obligations do and do not attach to it; what appeals to it are and are not legitimate. Thus, Debray's first practical move in the Report, after his opening dithyrambs regarding the *devoir de mémoire* and the welcome opportunity provided by the bicentenary to fulfill that duty, is to reject the Haitian government's demand that France remember Haiti *in a particular way* by paying back, with interest, the indemnity imposed by its former colonial rulers in 1825 as the price for officially recognizing Haitian independence—a demand that, as we saw, was a prime stimulus behind the formation of Debray's "independent" Comité de réflexion.

No doubt, Debray admits, the occasion of the bicentenary *legitimates* certain solicitous gestures on the part of France and its European allies with regard to Haiti: "the bicentenary of Haiti and the fact that the year 2004 has been dedicated to the commemoration of the struggles against slavery and of its various abolitions . . . would go far toward *legitimizing* [*seraient de nature à légitimer*] a special gesture on the part of Europe," he states in a discussion of European sanctions and the possibility of lifting some of them (64; my italics). However, Aristide's call for restitution, his recourse to "legal wrangling, doubled by aggressive demonstrations and oneiric bookkeeping," has dirtied the waters of Franco-Haitian relations, and in a "childish" way: this call for restitution is the product of what Debray labels "victimary incrimination," which renders a "fair-minded collaboration *between adults*" impossible (26; my italics). Whatever commemorative gestures France makes will be "according to a logic of solidarity and not of reimbursement," Debray proclaims; the *"devoir de mémoire,"* after all, "is not a question of repentance but acknowledgement [*n'est pas repentance mais reconnaissance*]" (26).

In countering the legitimacy of Aristide's call for restitution, Debray trots out the usual arguments one hears whenever the subject of reparations for crimes against humanity, such as slavery, gets raised. He notes that there is no "juridical foundation" to such claims, daring Haiti to take France to the International Court of Justice at the Hague; and then he mockingly asks how far back one is supposed to go when it comes to making right the wrongs of history ("The Camisards? The Saint Bartholomew

Massacre? The Albigenses? The Crusades? The Battle of Alésia?" [23]).
While admitting to being scandalized by the fact that Haiti "had to, in a
manner of speaking, purchase in gold its international recognition after
having conquered its independence at the cost of its blood," Debray is
quick to remind his readers that the right to self-determination of peoples
did not exist at the time the debt was incurred (23).

In any case, he continues, shifting gears, the responsibility for this debt
can be largely traced to the Haitians themselves:

> We have proposed to our interlocutors the establishment of a mixed commis-
> sion of historians to establish the chain of events and their exact circumstances,
> in which one would remark [où l'on verrait] with a certain surprise that the
> idea of an indemnification for the massacred French colonists (15,000) or
> for those forced to flee (15,000) originated with the Haitian presidents them-
> selves, Pétion and Boyer. There has, for the moment, not been any follow-up
> by the Haitian side to our offer of cooperative investigation, on a scholarly
> basis [sur une base scientifique]. (24)

This is, of course, a tendentious statement, both from an historical and
a grammatical point of view. As history, it fails to make any mention of
the indisputable fact that, although the original idea of paying France
may have come from Pétion and his successor Boyer (leaders of Haiti's
francophilic mulatto elite, which governed the entire former colony of
Saint-Domingue after the death in 1820 of the staunchly anti-French
Henri Christophe, who would never have accepted the idea),[28] the decision to engage in this "indemnity shakedown," and the reckoning of its
amount, was taken unilaterally by Charles X and backed up by several
dozen gunboats lying in wait outside the harbors of Port-au-Prince.[29] The
history offered in the Report, and in the appendix specifically devoted to
the history of the debt, is a partial one, to say the least.[30]

But even more interestingly, for the purposes of our close reading of the
Report, is the peculiar use of tenses here, in which the results of the never-
formed "mixed commission of historians" are announced in advance
("où l'on verrait"): the commission, before it even meets, is destined
to place the blame for the idea of indemnities squarely on the Haitians
themselves, who are, in turn, subtly cast adrift from the world of rational
inquiry by virtue of the fact that they have yet to agree to work with the
French "sur une base scientifique." What use such a "scientific" inquiry
into the origins of the indemnity would be, given the supposed lack of a
"fondement juridique" for Haiti's request for restitution is, of course,
a question that Debray does not address. Emphasizing the "unscientific"

nature of that request is the sole rhetorical purpose of this part of his response to the question he poses in the title of the section that contains it: *"Quelle sorte de dette?"* (21).

What sort of debt? One that has no basis in science or in law, if we are to believe Debray. One that need have no *material* consequences, apart from those that the former colonizer, in its philanthropic wisdom and retaining its status as *agent*, deems justified in the form of foreign "aid," of which Haiti, we are assured, gets its fair share—admittedly less than Togo or Cameroon "but more than Mexico or Brazil, which have ten times the population" (25). Rather than open up "the Pandora's box of indemnifications," the appropriate response to such historical inequities is, we are informed, a *symbolic* one, similar to what happened at the World Conference against Racism held at Durban, South Africa, in September 2001, when France "expressed its *regrets*" for its role in the slave-trade (25). That this is the only reasonable response to the case of Haiti, Debray argues, is further substantiated by the fact that most of the people interviewed by the Committee, and certainly no one "in the democratic opposition," took Aristide's call for restitution seriously, with the notable exception of "the excellent Paul Farmer" (22).[31]

Most of his interviewees, Debray remarks with satisfaction, "could adopt as their own the position of René Depestre, the great Franco-Haitian writer"—a position that is, understandably, quoted at length:

> To try and settle the scores of a past that has gone by in an historical context that is no longer that of General Rochambeau's iniquities, or the no less murderous responses of the founders of our national identity, does not seem to me to be the most serene, the most intelligent, or the most civilized way of lending an international lustre to the celebration of Haiti's origins. What is at stake for us in the ongoing process of globalization ought rather to encourage Haitians of 2003–4 to devise, in close and friendly consultation with the France of the twenty-first century, forms of cooperation and of solidarity that would be just the opposite of the colonial relations of yesteryear. (Quoted 22–23)

In the serene vision of this willing witness for the prosecution, the old colonial language of "civilization" conveniently combines with the supposed imperatives contained within the latest hegemonic buzz word, "globalization," to create a situation in which the only "intelligent" form that Franco-Haitian relations and the bicentenary commemoration can take is one in which the violence of colonial repression and anticolonial struggle are treated as equally "murderous" and in which this troubling violence is exiled to the margins of the very memory it made possible.

(With good press like this, incidentally, it is small wonder that Depestre quickly returned the favor and, in the April edition of *Le Monde diplomatique,* effusively praised the Report as part of his plea for Haiti and its "martyred people" to assume their rightful place in a globalizing world, in tandem with "a France that no longer measures the world simply according to the standard of its hexagonal myths.")[32]

The Debray Report is awash with suggestions, such as the aforementioned *tour de l'île,* for largely symbolic "forms of cooperation and solidarity" that can respond to the (therapeutic) imperatives that the *devoir de mémoire* imposes on France. Two such suggestions are of particular interest to us here, and provide a fitting conclusion to my close reading of the Report, because of the exemplary manner in which, marginal as they might be to the text, they display its characteristic (il)logic, the double gesture of affirmation and erasure that is at its rhetorical heart.

The first example of this simultaneous invocation and disavowal of the bicentenary celebrations of France's defeat at the hands of Haitian insurgents comes in the section where Debray discusses the possibility of reconstructing the Institut français and suggests that this project is worth considering not only for practical reasons but because of its "political and symbolic significance" (87). After noting that the Institute was "created in 1945, on what is called the Bicentenary site (after the founding of Port-au-Prince)," and that it has been "property of the French State since 1949," he reminds his readers that "the French Institute has always been more than just a center for teaching (1,500 students per term), lectures, and performances: it has been the symbol of Haitian cultural life as well as a hotbed of historical resistance through which a good number of the country's notables have passed" (86). It is, of course, highly ironic that the supposed symbol of Haitian cultural life should be *French property,* but what particularly strikes me in this sentence is the way in which *another* "Bicentenary," one that does not threaten but instead confirms the French "foundations" of Haiti, is brought to the fore here. The founding of Port-au-Prince in 1749 is an historical memory on which France can place its "optimistic wager on the future" (87) with far more self-assurance than on that other memorial site marked by the date 1804, which belongs not to the French but to those who defeated a band of genocidal colonizers in order to found their postcolonial nation.

A second example in which the bicentenary is symptomatically both remembered and forgotten comes during Debray's discussion of the desirability of improving Haiti's lamentable network of highways by creating a "new route of friendship," modeled on the *Route de l'amitié* between

Port-au-Prince and Jacmel. The "route Port-au-Prince/Hinche/Port-de-Paix," he suggests, "could be called . . . the *Route du Bicentenaire*" (85). However, he immediately adds, if the necessary "freeing up of multilateral funding cannot be arranged, it would fall to France to propose bilateral financing and in that case the Route Nationale 3 would become the 'Franco-Haitian,' thus reflecting the renewal of relations between the two countries" (85). The micromanaging obsession with nomenclature on display in this hypothetical passage from the *Bicentenaire* to the *Franco-haïtienne* sums up the double-dealing logic of the Report, its repeated erasure of the Haitian agency it is nonetheless compelled to recognize, its risibly neocolonial obsession with restoring a privileged form of bilateral relations between France and its former colony in which, despite inevitable protestations of equality, the founding father always comes first (*Franco*-haïtienne). With each and every such assertion of mastery, be it trivial, as here, or glaring, as in the clear line he draws between what the *devoir de mémoire* does and does not entail, Debray reasserts the dominion of an "amnesiac modernity" that he is ostensibly arguing against.

If the problems with Debray's tellingly amnesiac embrace of memory and the duties it supposedly entails are thus clear enough, that which is rather less evident is whether the commemorative logic generating his seemingly positive invocations of the need to remember *"la face noire des Lumières"* (19), the need to pay tribute to the "other" side of the Enlightenment, is in any respect significantly different from or opposed to that generating the countless appeals of postcolonial critics to the virtues of remembering other-wise. While it is doubtless preferable to recall the overthrow of French colonialism in Saint-Domingue as something more than "the sad bicentennial of a once fabulous sugar colony,"[33] to restore it from the margins to which it has been exiled in order to "rescu[e] the idea of universal human history from the uses to which white domination has put it,"[34] one cannot help questioning what practical value the rescuing of such counter-memories might have. How, to put it bluntly, does an ostensibly anti-hegemonic emphasis on the resistant memories of yesteryear contribute toward helping bring about social justice in the Haiti of today?

As Robert J. C. Young has recently reminded us, "postcolonial politics seeks to change the inequitable power structures of the world."[35] What role, if any, do counter-memories have to play in promoting and enabling this necessary politics? Debray's pious assertions regarding the need to remember the central role of the Haitian Revolution in human history show the extent to which hegemonic thinking can absorb the symbolic ramifications of even the most dramatic memories of anticolonial resistance. Exemplifying the institutional emphasis in France on the *devoir de mémoire* as a cure-all fetish, the Debray Report is prime evidence that those in France who benefit most from "the inequitable power structures of the world" have learned the lesson that it is as easy to acknowledge as to repress whatever memories are at odds with the official (hi)story a nation has become accustomed to telling about itself. Debray is surely right to point out that the epistemological question of acknowledgment is not the same as the ethical question of repentance. And those actively engaged in the attempt at transforming the power structures of the world are surely also right to question what, if anything, can come from any and all symbolic gestures of acknowledgment that are not accompanied by substantive *acts* of repentance. That which remains altogether less sure, though, from the activist standpoint of "postcolonial politics" as defined by Young, is whether the postcolonial critic's pious insistence on an "other" world of anti-hegemonic counter-memories can in any significant way be differentiated from the dutiful appeals to that very same world which, as we have seen, are such a prominent feature of Debray's manifestly hegemonic text. How does what the postcolonial critic asks us to remember differ from what is on offer in the Debray Report? How do postcolonial critics remember differently, and for whom are they remembering? What form might the *act* of repentance take for them . . . and for us?

THE TITLE of this essay plays off that of another book by Debray that was published in 2004: *Chroniques de l'idiotie triomphante,* a collection of journalistic interventions written in the years 1990–2003 on the subject of "terrorism, wars, diplomacy"—and specifically on the two Gulf Wars. In it, Debray time and again criticizes the United States for "a dramatic incompetence in the handling of crises in the Third World" that can in large part be attributed to the absence in the Yanqui corridors of power of something that, he asserts, is present in Europe: namely "an historical vision of human history," a readiness to acknowledge that "there exist other memories, other histories apart from its own" (82). Europe's "culture of time" (as opposed to North America's "culture of space"), he argued in 1991, cannot become "the hostage of this proven incompetence" (83). Twelve years later, responding to the manner in which the States "have chosen France as scapegoat" for not having blindly followed George Bush and his gang of thugs into the killing fields of Iraq (134), Debray claims that Europe no longer possesses the "euphoric arrogance" of the United States. "It has reconciled itself to the loss of the Absolute. . . .

It has outgrown the age of ultimata, of protectorates at the antipodes, and the white man's burden" (138). The White House, by contrast, is constantly being led into geopolitical cul-de-sacs by its "indifference to differences" (197), its "inability to conceive that one can conceive of the world in another way than it does [*incapacité à penser qu'on peut penser le monde autrement qu'elle*]" (195). In neither of the two Gulf Wars has the United States acted *intelligently*, for "intelligence," Debray reminds us, consists in the ability "to break out of one's own system, to break out of the limits of one's ways of thinking and living" (57), "to vanquish one's own myth and to cleanse one's vocabulary" (59).

In a world of global empire in which, as Tariq Ali notes, "the Monroe Doctrine ha[s] now been extended to the whole world,"[36] it is indeed hard to overlook the "idiocy" of U.S. foreign policy, and one can certainly not fault Debray for putting the case so clearly. Yet, as we have had ample occasion to see, the Francophone Doctrine undergirding Debray's Franco-Haitian intervention is equally lacking in "intelligence," equally committed to a national myth it cannot vanquish, a colonial vocabulary it cannot cleanse, a "way of thinking and living" that is not, in any vital respect (bicycling competitions aside), different from or incompatible with the triumphant idiocy this one-time *compañero* of Che Guevera denounces in the case of Iraq. Indeed, Debray implicitly admits as much in the section of his Report entitled "Concertation avec les Etats-Unis," where he stresses the need for France and the United States to work together in Haiti, in a relation of "coordination without subordination" (65). "Many people," he notes, imagine that when it comes to the relations between these two world powers "it is a question of rivalry, when it is actually a question of complementarity, and although it is the case that our means of influence do not overlap, they nonetheless can and indeed must reinforce one another, for the good of the Haitian nation" (64). This Franco-American *combinatoire*, he adds, in one of his disconcertingly specific asides, currently has all the more chance of succeeding because of "the presence in Port-au-Prince of an eminently capable French ambassador and of a top-quality American ambassador, French-speaking [*francophone*], with an open and imaginative mind" (66).

If the proposed *tour de l'île* and countless other of the Report's stated desiderata remain as yet sadly unrealized, the same cannot be said with regard to Debray's call for a rapid determination of "the modalities and the spirit of this *combinatoire*" (64). Only weeks after the publication of the Report, Debray's insistence on the desirability in theory of a coordinated Franco-American strategy with regard to Haiti would find its practical realization in the events of late February 2004, when the former colonial and present-day neocolonial masters of Haiti worked in tandem to rid themselves of that country's troublesome, and no doubt deeply flawed, democratically elected president and replace him with eminently pliable, and equally flawed, members of the self-styled and anything-but-"democratic opposition." Just over a month after the coup-knapping, in mid-April, the French defence minister Michèle Alliot-Marie would become the first French government official to visit Haiti since 1803—a visit to be quickly followed in May by the brief stopover in Haiti of de Villepin's successor, France's newly minted foreign minister, Michel Barnier. During her visit, Alliot-Marie praised the one thousand French troops on Haitian soil for "creating a relationship of trust with the population," which had helped stabilize the country; "it is," she reminded them, in a disarmingly amnesiac statement, "one of the characteristics of the French armed forces to be able to create such relationships."[37] With impeccable timing, only a few days after the delivery of these comments, the newly installed prime minister of Haiti, Monsieur Gérard Latortue, officially dropped the Haitian government's demand that France make restitution for the debt it had imposed on his country in 1825: stressing that Haiti wanted to have good relations with France, Latortue dismissed a claim that had been so closely associated with Aristide with the assertion that "it was illegal, ridiculous, and had been made only for political reasons."[38]

If, as Noam Chomsky wrote, days after the coup, "the right way for the US and France to proceed is very clear[: t]hey should begin with payment of enormous reparations to Haiti (France is perhaps even more hypocritical and disgraceful in this regard than the US),"[39] then Latortue's convenient dismissal of the demand for restitution is a sure sign, as if any were needed, that the hypocrisy and disgrace which have for several centuries now characterized the "idiotic" policy of these two countries when it comes to the troublesome subject of Haiti will continue for the foreseeable future. A close reading of the Debray Report has the unquestionable virtue of sensitizing us to this disgraceful hypocrisy, but from the standpoint of "postcolonial politics" it has to be asked, in closing, what more can such a reading accomplish than to demonstrate the various textual strategies through which the "wrong way" is made to seem right? After all, such neocolonial documents, and critical (re-)readings of those documents, have been in circulation ever since Haiti gained its independence, as my epigraph from Baron de Vastey, Haiti's first postcolonial intellectual, attests.

Personal secretary to King Henri Christophe, Vastey was a tireless oppo-
nent of Pétion's efforts, after the fall of Napoléon, at restoring "normal"
relations with the former colonial master by paying massive compensation to France for the loss of its precious colony and the emancipation of
its human property. Vastey wrote his *Réflexions politiques* of 1817 in response to the new, "softer" approach adopted toward Haiti by the Bourbon monarchy after its restoration in 1814.[40] With a prescience for which
he has never been given enough credit, Vastey provides in that book an
in-depth rhetorical analysis of the writings of the French government's
propagandists, offering a withering deconstruction of France's purported
desire to "start over with us" on a new and more equitable footing.
Vastey's critique of French neocolonial discourse remains as scathingly
relevant as it was two centuries ago for any reading of the Debray Report,
which laid the intellectual groundwork for the latest French military intervention in Haiti, supplying the intellectual rationale for its bicentenary
expedition to the far reaches of "francophone space." Debray and his
associates are indeed but the latest manifestation of a neocolonial Proteus that has stalked Haiti's dangerously postcolonial crossroads for the
last two hundred years; *la francophonie* is indeed but the latest master
signifier in the "strange and hypocritical" language through which alone
France, along with its transatlantic successor and collaborator the United
States, has been able to speak of and remember the independent black
republic of Haiti. These are the obvious but essential conclusions that can
be legitimately drawn from a close reading of the Debray Report. After
such necessary conclusions have been reached, however, a discomfiting
question remains—one that any analysis of the sort offered by Vastey or
those postcolonial epigones of his, such as myself, who have inherited
his textualizing bias must surely provoke: now that we have, yet again,
exposed the triumphant idiocy of a colonialism that will never find the
"right way to proceed," what can, and must, be *done* to end it?

## Notes

1. Aijaz Ahmad, "Haitian Tragedy and Imperial Farce," 44. Hereafter page
numbers are given in text.
2. Perry Anderson, "Dégringolade," *London Review of Books*. This and
some of the other articles cited are available both in print and on the Web. All
Web addresses cited in this essay were last verified on 16 April 2007.
3. Quoted in Christopher Marquis's *New York Times* article, "France Seeks
UN Force in Haiti."
4. "La République haïtienne trahie par ses élites."

5. Peter Hallward, "Option Zero in Haiti," 43.

6. See, for example, Régis Debray, *Chroniques de l'idiotie triomphante*, 198. For a brief overview of Debray's life and work, see Keith Reader, *Régis Debray: A Critical Introduction*.

7. France Diplomatie, "Comité de réflexion et de proposition sur Haïti."

8. Régis Debray, *Haïti et la France*, 113–19. (Hereafter, the Report. Further page references to this work will be made in text. Translations are mine.) As far as the real-world repercussions of the Committee's visits to Haiti are concerned, however, it should be noted that shortly after the coup Aristide, who had received Debray twice in late 2003, cited him—along with fellow committee member Véronique de Villepin-Albanel, sister of the French foreign minister—as among those legally responsible for his ouster. The story of Aristide's "coup-knapping," and the ways in which it replayed events from two hundred years ago, has been insightfully told by Deborah Jenson, in "From the Kidnapping(s) of the Louvertures to the Alleged Kidnapping of Aristide."

9. For reasons of space, I have omitted here an extended close reading of the book's paratextual materials, notably its preface by Denis Tillinac, editor of La Table Ronde and a self-styled *militant de la francophonie*. Tillinac's repeated emphasis, in this luridly exoticizing preface, on the virtues of *la francophonie* prepares the ground for Debray's own, similarly militant and territorializing, appeals to "francophone space" in his decidedly more soberly written Report.

10. Robert Fatton, Jr., *Haiti's Predatory Republic*, 11, 208.

11. E.g., "The mediologist is content . . . with even-handed understanding." Régis Debray, *Transmitting Culture*, 30.

12. Mireille Nicolas, a French novelist who has spent time in and written about Haiti, has ably criticized Debray's post-coup comments about Aristide's departure, reacting specifically to an interview he gave (France Culture, 21 April 2004), in which he stated that "Aristide left of his own free will; he himself made the request to the Americans. Now he's keeping mum; he has every reason for doing so. I met with Aristide on several occasions. Alone. I told him that things were going to get nasty for him. I have respect for what he once was; I proposed to him that he resign, while staying on the scene and playing a role in political life. The opposition was refusing to speak with him; when it became clear to me that he wasn't credible, that he was being showered with insults, I told him to do what Allende should have done, what De Gaulle did. That was the precaution I called on him to take." For Nicolas's response to Debray's astounding shrug of the shoulders with regard to Allende's democratic reforms in Chile, see her "Mais bien sûr, M. Debray!"

13. It is well worth citing, and commenting on, what in Debray's Report immediately follows this appeal to Haiti's francophone identity. Haiti, we are told, "also bears *witness*—first, to what any trailblazing and prosperous country [*n'importe quel pays précurseur et prospère*] can wind up becoming, when its elites have reneged on their responsibilities and the State does a disappearing act"

(16; emphasis in original). When, we might well ask, was Haiti ever "prosperous"? What we find here, sutured together in this Janus-faced statement, are an acknowledgment of the precursory virtues of the Haitian Revolution and a nostalgic invocation of prerevolutionary Saint-Domingue, most prosperous colony of the New World in the eighteenth century. This interpretation of the sentence is confirmed a few pages later by Debray's explicit invocation of the "Pearl of the Antilles" trope: "May our Haitian friends assume their share of the responsibility for the inconceivable collapse which over the course of two centuries has reduced the 'Pearl of the Antilles,' the richest colony in the world, which provided a third of France's foreign trade—the Kuwait of the Age of Voltaire—to a level of Sahelian malediction" (20).

14. In this interview (France Culture, 21 April 2004), speaking of Aristide, Debray remarked: "He's a very cultured man. Haiti is the last country where French is spoken. He's not someone to be despised. He's not an ignoramus [*Ce n'est pas une brute*]: right up to the end he was quoting the Bible to me; mystic by day, bandit by night." The revealing, to say the least, logical slippages at work in his statement (culture = speaking French = non-brutishness = quoting the Bible) are ably interrogated by Nicolas in her scathing critique of this interview, "Mais bien sûr, M. Debray!"

15. "The demand for French also comes from the parents of the poorest children, for whom Creole would mean social exclusion. The rising attendance at the six Alliances françaises, spread across the country, is testimony to the fact that this sentiment is not just the view of the upper classes" (57). This (for Debray) natural "demand" for French can, of course, readily be traced to the lingering effects of colonial ideology, as Christophe Wargny, for one, lucidly argues in a discussion of the debilitating effect of "the French-Creole baggage" on education in Haiti. See his *Haïti n'existe pas*, 113–14.

16. I take this phrase from Doris Garraway's favorable gloss on Emmanuel Levinas in her *The Libertine Colony*, 90. Against such ethnographic "comprehension," Levinas opposes an "ethical" dialogue that respects "the strangeness of the Other."

17. See, e.g., Gilroy, "It's a Family Affair," 192–207.

18. On these two competing models of diaspora, see Stuart Hall, "Creolization, Diaspora, and Hybridity," 189–91.

19. The most egregious of these other models in the Report transforms Haiti into a *text* that has been, and continues to be, coauthored by France: "The French remain, for better and for worse, the *coauthors* of this sophisticated pariah, Christian *and* Vodou, straddling Guinea and Manhattan, nationalist *and* nomadic, premodern *and* postmodern" (17).

20. The subtle biases at work in Debray's representations of the languages spoken in Haiti are exemplified by his portrait of it as a "strange country where the subtlest of scholars lines up alongside the illiterate, as do Latin quotations and American pidgin" (53). Here, the parallel antitheses establish a rhetorical

equation between Haitian illiteracy and Haitian English, reducing the latter, moreover, to the status of a "pidgin."

21. See my *Exotic Memories,* 99 and passim.

22. See Jacques de Cauna, ed., *Toussaint Louverture et l'indépendance d'Haïti,* 19.

23. Debray, *Transmitting Culture,* 56.

24. For a relevant analysis of Namibia's ongoing relations with Germany, which include recent reparation calls for massacres the Germans committed in the first decade of the twentieth century, see the chapter "Herero" in Edouard Glissant's novel *Sartorius,* 287–98.

25. Debray's instrumentalization of Africa is most visible in the section of the Report immediately preceding "France-Allemagne," which is devoted to the OIF (Organisation internationale de la Francophonie). The "mediation of several top-ranking African personalities," Debray notes, could have a positive effect "on this American country that often claims a connection with black Africa" (68). Given Aristide's (supposed) tendency to play Africa off against the West, the OIF has a role to play in Haiti; even non-francophone countries such as South Africa can be enlisted in the work of the OIF, all the more so since the South African authorities have "already shown, in a true spirit of friendship with France, a deep personal engagement with a country that is symbolic in their eyes" (68). No doubt it was in the spirit of that *amitié* that on February 29, President Mbeki sent a military plane loaded with weapons to Haiti, in support of Aristide's belea-guered regime—a plane that, of course, never arrived at its destination, for by the time it landed in Jamaica, the "coup-knapped" Aristide was already crossing the Atlantic in the other direction. (See BBC News, 15 March 2004, http://news.bbc .co.uk/2/hi/africa/3513006.stm.)

26. See my "A Street Named Bissette." 215–57.

27. Debray's distinction between history and memory is the Report's most important "theoretical" contribution: "If *history* is the critical and distanced re-construction of what actually took place, [then] *memory* is the refractive lens brought to bear on these events, forged for identitarian ends, the sacred story handed out at school, in textbooks and museums, to give a human grouping the highest level of self-esteem—each people, as we know very well in Europe, carves out a glorious place for itself in the turpitudes of its neighbor" (19).

28. Yves Benot, *La démence coloniale sous Napoléon,* 128.

29. See, e.g., Jean Métellus, *Haïti, une nation pathétique,* 38. The phrase "in-demnity shakedown" is taken from Paul Farmer, "What Happened in Haiti?" 19.

30. Authored by French historians François Blancpain and Marcel Dorigny, the Report's second appendix, "'Restitution de la dette de l'indépendance'?" (101–4), provides a sketchy, evasive account of the events leading up to and fol-lowing upon Charles X's *ordonnance,* the acceptance of which "*liberated* Haiti from the ostracism of foreign countries, who, from that point on, struck up dip-lomatic relations with it" (103, my italics). The appendix says absolutely nothing

about the actual demand for restitution of the "debt of independence," and concludes by noting that the Haitians "impeccably kept their commitments": "Haiti honored its signature and paid back the entire 90 million francs," we are told, as if there were something honorable about paying a debt that was arbitrarily imposed upon Haiti by a bloody-minded European colonial power as the price of its independence!

31. Farmer, among the most vocal critics of U.S. foreign policy in Haiti, made a cogent case in support of restitution to the Committee, noting that "the great majority of the population, desperate with the country's terrible situation, is in favor of this process." See "Twelve Points in Favor of the Restitution of the French Debt [to] Haiti." Farmer was, of course, by no means alone in publicly supporting the call for restitution. Christophe Wargny, in *Haïti n'existe pas*, supported restitution in theory, but noted that "the endemic corruption of the Haitian executive makes it a very poor spokesperson for, and an impossible recipient of, it." This corruption, he went on to note, with a sigh, "permits France, end of 2003, to create an official committee to reflect on the relations between the two States, presided over by Régis Debray. Which will in turn issue forth a set of recommendations . . ." (59).

32. In this article, which was subsequently incorporated into his collection of essays *Encore une mer à traverser,* Depestre asserted that "there can be a renewal of hope, for Haitians of the twenty-first century, through the hope of the entire Francophone world [*dans l'espérance de toute la francophonie*]," adding that this "burst of optimism" came to him after reading the Debray Report: "I feel the urge to place my hope, that of a Franco-Haitian writer, in the implementation of the timely measures that Debray has proposed to the authorities of my country of adoption for the 'salvation' of my land of origin" (144–45).

33. To cite the revealing title of an article from *The Economist,* 18 December 2003. The online version of this article at Economist.com has recently had its title changed to the decidedly more neutral "Haiti's Sad Anniversary." See http://www.economist.com/world/la/displayStory.cfm?story_id=2303369.

34. Susan Buck-Morss, "Hegel and Haiti," 836, 865.

35. Young, *White Mythologies,* 31.

36. Ali, *Bush in Babylon,* 173.

37. Haiti Democracy Project: "France Promises to Help Rebuild Haiti," Agence France Presse 15 April 2004, Haiti Democracy Project Web page item #2170, 18 April 2004, http://www.haitipolicy.org/content/2170.htm.

38. See the entry for 18 April in "The 2004 Removal of Jean-Bertrand Aristide," Center for Cooperative Research, http://www.cooperativeresearch.org/timeline.jsp?timeline=the_2004_removal_of_jean-bertrand_aristide.

39. Chomsky, "The 'Noble Phase' and 'Saintly Glow' of US Foreign Policy," in Chomsky et al., *Getting Haiti Right This Time,* 9.

40. Vastey, *Réflexions politiques,* iii–iv. For more on Vastey, see my "'Monotonies of History,'": 75–88.

III

# Literary Representations of
# the Haitian Revolution

# Recuperating the Haitian Revolution in Literature

From Victor Hugo to Derek Walcott

*A. James Arnold*

## Romantic Utopias and Dystopias

As a LITERARY SUBJECT, the Haitian Revolution is contemporaneous with European Romanticism, which turned its back on the proprieties of neoclassicism in favor of excess of every sort. Romanticism, Victor Hugo assured the world, would combine the grotesque with the sublime. No wonder then that one of his first efforts, at age sixteen, was the novel *Bug-Jargal,* 1826, which he set in Saint-Domingue in 1791. The eponymous hero is a noble savage, a slave of royal blood who magnanimously saves Hugo's narrator from the massacre of the whites. Nonetheless, and through an unfortunate concatenation of circumstance, Bug-Jargal is executed. His unjust end haunts the narrator-protagonist for the rest of his days. Bug-Jargal is a black Ruy Blas or Hernani, a pure incarnation of Romantic revolt. The author's motivation is anything but disinterested, however. Hugo's maternal grandfather had been a sea captain operating between Nantes and Saint-Domingue and he himself stood to gain from the indemnity that Haiti paid France after 1825. Léon-François Hoffmann has demonstrated how Hugo framed the Haitian Revolution so it could serve as a vehicle for the Bourbon restoration's insistence on financial reparations.[1] All the traitors in Hugo's novel are mulattoes, a plot device that reveals racial prejudice against what was then thought of as miscegenation. This racial bias would alternate with its variant, the attraction of the beautiful but doomed "tragic mulatto" woman throughout the nineteenth century and well into the twentieth. *Bug-Jargal* presents two further plot devices that were to have a very long life indeed: an idealistic appeal to the noble savage, on the one hand; and, on the other, a gory depiction of mindless violence. In terms of literary modes these are versions of Utopia and Dystopia. Like the extreme limits of the pendulum's swing, these two contrary modes of imagining the Haitian Revolution are used by writers in Europe and the Americas to recuperate its meaning for their own time, place, and social values.

Even before Victor Hugo, a German Romantic writer recognized the potential for *Sturm und Drang* (storm and stress) that the Haitian Revolution afforded. Heinrich von Kleist, the master of Romantic short fiction in German, published his story "Die Verlobung in Santo Domingo" (Betrothal in Santo Domingo) in 1812. Like Hugo's novel, it combines the sublime and the grotesque. For Kleist's readers, however, Napoléon was still the foremost figure in European politics. In 1806 he had brought an end to the Holy Roman Empire and forged the Confederation of the Rhine. Two further examples will serve to illustrate the tendencies present throughout Europe in the first quarter of the nineteenth century. A special place must be reserved for the novella *Ourika* by the Duchess of Duras, Claire-Louise Lechat de Coëtnempren de Kersaint. Since the MLA published the French-language edition prepared by Joan DeJean and Margaret Waller in 1994, the Duchess of Duras has been turned into an early exponent of feminism and an abolitionist. Both attributes would have astonished the duchess herself as well as her friends and her early readership among the inner circle of the reactionary Bourbon court. Her mother was a Martinican who inherited her wealth from family sugar interests that depended ultimately on chattel slavery. As émigrés during the early years of the French Revolution, she and the future Duchess of Duras traveled to Martinique "to recover Mme de Kersaint's considerable inheritance."[2] Roger Little's edition of the novella, which has a fuller critical apparatus, takes essentially the same position on this short story from 1823–24. In the English translation by John Fowles, the African-born heroine, who had been educated in aristocratic society as though she were a titled lady, gives this appreciation of the revolution in Saint-Domingue:

> About this time talk started of emancipating the Negroes. Of course this question passionately interested me. I still cherished the illusion that at least somewhere else in the world there were others like myself. I knew they were not happy and I supposed them noble-hearted. I was eager to know what would happen to them. But alas, I soon learned my lesson. The Santo Domingo massacres gave me cause for fresh and heartrending sadness. Till then I had regretted belonging to a race of outcasts. Now I had the shame of belonging to a race of barbarous murderers.[3]

By placing these words in the mouth of her heroine, the Duchess of Duras renders the authors of the 1791–92 events in Saint-Domingue directly responsible for the melodramatic fate of Ourika. She is condemned to isolation, melancholy, and an early death, less because of her African birth than because slaves in Saint-Domingue had murdered whites like those who had raised her exactly as they did their own children. The author used Ourika to write back from a white Creole perspective against the revolution that had dispossessed her class in Saint-Domingue and had threatened to do likewise in the other sugar islands. *Ourika* was published a year before the last Bourbon monarch, Charles X, finally recognized Haitian independence in exchange for a crippling indemnity. Hugo's *Bug-Jargal*, which he had written in 1818, was published in a revised text two years after *Ourika*. By the mid-1820s the court was again interested in things Haitian, not out of any magnanimity, but so as to recoup the State's financial losses. Our contemporary ideology of political correctness has obscured Duras's political positioning of narrative point of view in *Ourika* and rendered its meaning opaque.

In her examination of Cuban responses to the Haitian Revolution, Sibylle Fischer quotes a member of the Domingo del Monte circle in Havana, Félix Tanco y Bosmeniel, who wrote in 1836: "And what do you say about *Bug-Jargal*? I would love it if among us a novel was written in that kind of style."[4] No literary work written in Cuba did so; however, Gertrudis Gómez de Avellaneda did write the novel *Sab*, 1841, in Spain, in a decidedly Romantic vein.[5] As Fischer puts it, "Bug-Jargal, who had joined the rebel army in Saint Domingue, is turned into Sab, who renounces insurrection."[6]

In the English-speaking world the best-known contribution to the Romantic treatment of the Haitian Revolution is surely Wordsworth's sonnet "To Toussaint Louverture." The text itself dates the poem to 1803, the year of Toussaint's death:

> Though fallen thyself, never to rise again,
> Live, and take comfort. Thou hast left behind
> Powers that will work for thee, air, earth, and skies:
> There's not a breathing of the common wind
> That will forget thee; thou hast great allies;
> Thy friends are exultations, agonies,
> And love, and man's unconquerable mind.[7]

Wordsworth appeals to all Nature, personified as a divine force, enlisting it on the fallen hero's behalf. Wordsworth shares with early Haitian interpreters of their revolution the sense of universal meaning it holds forth to humanity. In the same collection, immediately following his sonnet

"To Toussaint Louverture," Wordsworth printed a sonnet entitled, very simply, "September 1, 1802." I find this sonnet much more modern and, ultimately, more touching. From a historiographical standpoint it speaks to the fundamentally different ways in which Haiti and the remaining French West Indies experience the first half of the century:

> Driven from the soil of France, a female came
> From Calais with us, gaudy in array,
> A negro woman like a lady gay,
> Yet downcast as a woman fearing blame;
> Meek, destitute, as seemed, of hope or aim,
> She sate, from notice turning not away,
> But on our proffered intercourse did lay
> A weight of languid speech,—or at the same
> Was silent, motionless in eyes and face.
> Meanwhile those eyes retained their tropic fire,
> Which, burning independent of the mind,
> Joined with the luster of her rich attire
> To mock the outcast—ye heavens be kind!
> And feel, thou earth, for this afflicted race![8]

This sonnet speaks to the immediate consequences of the Haitian Revolution in the Lesser Antilles and in France itself. In May 1802 General Richepanse, dispatched by the First Consul to stem the slave revolts in Guadeloupe and Martinique, succeeded in putting down the last armed military resistance by mulatto officers and black troops of the French army and navy. The latter blew themselves up at Fort Matouba on Guadeloupe, rather than surrender and suffer re-enslavement. Wordsworth reminds us that the fallout of this sad period re-enslaved black people living in France as well. His anonymous Negro woman is fleeing Napóleon's France for England before the reestablishment of slavery strikes her along with all those blacks whom the French Revolution had freed nearly a decade earlier.

The reimposition of slavery in Guadeloupe, Martinique, and French Guiana in 1802 has caused the literature of those overseas *départements* of France to treat the Haitian Revolution as a ghostly companion or revenant, a reminder of what was not achieved in their own region.

## From Universalism to Racial Particularism in Haiti

Throughout the nineteenth century, writers and poets in Haiti constructed a pantheon of heroes of the Revolution in odes of neoclassical perfection that formally and ideologically contradict Romantic dystopias. In the same year that the Duchess of Duras published her novella, Eugène Séguy Villevaleix penned a heroic ode to Jean-Pierre Boyer, who had succeeded Alexandre Pétion in the presidency in 1818 and had reunited the country at the death of Christophe in 1820. Haiti addresses France:

> Appear now, you whom my glory annoys,
> You whom deadly delirium to vengeance excites!
> What can your impotent anger do?
> This lone hero stands guard at my frontier;
> His aegis and his strong arm my only buckler,
> Tremble, for his thunder is upon you.[9]

In this "Ode to Independence," Boyer's strong arm and buckler will suffice to protect Haiti's frontier from any possible incursion by the former colonial master.

Already under the reign of Henri Christophe, Pompée Valentin, Baron de Vastey, had declaimed in *Réflexions sur . . . les Noirs et les Blancs:* "Fortunate land, I salute you! Land of predilection! O Haiti! O my fatherland! Sole haven of liberty where the black man may raise his head and contemplate the gifts of the universal father of all men, I salute you."[10] Haitian literary works of this period are difficult to read today because of their neoclassical poetics, which literary historians influenced by the Modernist tradition have long relegated to the prerevolutionary past. However, from the beginning to the end of the nineteenth century, Haitian writers undertook to present their revolution not as unique in human history but as the harbinger of freedom for oppressed peoples everywhere. They missed no opportunity to counter every attack on blacks or Africans anywhere in the world. The great issue was, of course, slavery; Haiti remained a threat to those nations that retained an economic system based on the peculiar institution. The Caribbean planter class and its commercial allies in Europe and the Americas published frequent diatribes or scurrilous attacks on the great men of the Haitian Revolution. From Bryan Edwards's *Historical Survey of the French Colony in the Island of St. Domingo,* first printed in London in 1797, to Sir Spencer Saint-John's *Hayti or the Black Republic* in 1884, the dominant note did not change: Haitians are primitive savages who are unable to govern themselves. The French translation of *Hayti or the Black Republic* was published in 1886 and was a best seller.

Haiti produced a truly incredible output of serious literature throughout the nineteenth century. The fact that most of it was imitative of French models is much less important than its very existence. The Haitian elite that emerged rapidly after the Revolution had no illusions about the great republic to the north. In a poem entitled "Slavery" Jean-Baptiste Chenêt in 1846 urged his compatriots to: "flee contact with the shores of America / Where Washington was born. There the child of Africa / Humiliated, tortured, knows of humanity / Only its ills, its pains, and its reduced capacity."[11] Haitians had no doubt whatever that their nation held the promise of the regeneration of the African race. Haitians would be Afro-Latins, infinitely more civilized than the materialistic Anglo-Saxons of the new United States of America.

These views, which certainly flattered the French sense of superiority over the English-speaking world, were nonetheless rarely returned in kind. French writers were scarcely more indulgent toward the Haitian Revolution than were those in England or the United States. Among other reasons, France retained chattel slavery until its second revolution of 1848, a socioeconomic fact that created the major division between Haiti and the remaining French West Indies. Two historical figures who played a prominent role in 1848 deserve our special attention, the Alsatian parliamentarian Victor Schoelcher and the poet-parliamentarian Alphonse de Lamartine. The former was primarily responsible for conditioning parliamentary opinion to accept abolition; the latter was to sign the official emancipation document as minister for foreign affairs of the Second Republic. Schoelcher's biography of Toussaint was published only in 1879, although the documentation for it dates from a trip to Haiti in 1841. He also used such English sources as Harriet Martineau and the Rev. John Beard, both of whom had written a biography of Toussaint, the former in 1840, the latter in 1853. Martineau and Beard were Evangelical Christians who were active in the antislavery movement. Schoelcher sometimes seemed to answer directly, at a distance of seventy-five years, the charges of bloodthirsty revenge that DuBroca had leveled against Toussaint at the time of the Leclerc expedition in 1802. This is especially evident in chapter 29, part 3, where Schoelcher cites both Martineau and Beard in defense of Toussaint's repeated and apparently well-known appeals for leniency against the enemy.

Lamartine's dramatic poem was staged in Paris at the Théâtre de la Porte Saint-Martin on April 6, 1850, before a packed house that included François Arago, who had contributed to the struggle to abolish slavery definitively only two years earlier, and Louis-Napoléon Bonaparte, then president of the republic. Lamartine's play had been written as a contribution to the abolitionist cause; indeed its interest today is more historical than dramatic. The Romantic dramatist makes of Haiti a snow-capped volcanic island where tigers roam beneath date palms. He took considerable liberties in the presentation of Toussaint's family, including the sort of heinous crime that made the pulse beat faster in an audience familiar with the conventions of nineteenth-century melodrama. Régis Antoine has abundantly detailed Lamartine's historical and geographical failings, which I need not belabor here.[12] More importantly for our purposes, Léon-François Hoffmann found only twenty-nine plays, out of some eight thousand produced in Paris between 1831 and 1850, that featured a black character. Of those, only two were situated in Saint-Domingue or Haiti. The vast majority depicted black characters as comic figures. Prior to the production of Lamartine's *Toussaint Louverture,* no black character on the nineteenth-century French stage had a serious dramatic or tragic dimension.[13] That French society was not entirely ready for this humanistic challenge to institutional racism is evident from the abundance of scurrilous attacks on Lamartine and his play in the Paris press. Léon-François Hoffmann in his edition of *Toussaint Louverture* provides a wealth of material to demonstrate that journalists were parroting the pseudoscientific notions of the day to the effect that Africans and their descendants everywhere were congenitally inferior.[14] The French public, on the other hand, made the play a success on the Paris stage. It was published in Brussels as well as Paris in 1850, and two German editions appeared that same year, one of them in French.[15] Not long thereafter a grand opera by Gottfried Herrmann, based on Lamartine's play, premiered in Lübeck.[16] A Spanish translation of the play was published in Madrid in 1853. The Haitian writer Demesvar Delorme, writing in 1860 in *L'Avenir,* a paper published in Cap-Haïtien, found in Lamartine's *Toussaint Louverture* "the justification of the Haitian revolution and the glorification of our political independence."[17] Notwithstanding this initial success in 1850, Lamartine's play had never been revived in France up to the point when Hoffmann was preparing his 1998 critical edition. In 1987 Yves Benot wrote that France had a shameful record of suppressing all reference to the Haitian Revolution in the context of its own revolutionary past. He offered a number of titillating examples. Benot made the point that France's overseas empire made the circumstances of the "loss" of Saint-Domingue a particularly touchy subject.

In Haiti the memory of Lamartine's tribute to Toussaint-Louverture has been regularly revived. On the occasion of the first centennial celebration of Haiti's independence, the city of Les Cayes staged the play on January 5, 1904. Fifty years later the French Institute in Haiti was the scene of another revival of *Toussaint Louverture* on April 6, 1954. Five years earlier, Haiti sent an official delegation to represent the nation when Lamartine's body was removed from Passy to Burgundy in 1949, thereby signifying that the gratitude of the nation was both sincere and enduring.[18] Posterity has not been kind to Lamartine's *Toussaint Louverture* as a drama. In his general study of the Romantic theater in France, W. D. Howarth wrote in 1978 that "the means of dramatic expression are those of the melodrama. . . . It is not difficult to imagine the same play written in prose by Pixérécourt."[19] Critics who have looked at the play ideologically, as a prefiguration of Negritude specifically, have been far more generous. E. Freeman in his edited volume *Myth and Its Making in the French Theatre* wrote that Lamartine's hero "anticipates by a hundred years . . . many of the views of Césaire, Senghor, Fanon and Sartre."[20] Léopold Sedar Senghor obviously agreed, when he wrote on the occasion of the centennial of Lamartine's death that, in his *Toussaint Louverture,* "with rare lucidity and an astonishing sense of the future he argued in favor of racial equality, stigmatized slavery, and contributed to the spread of new ideas on the condition of black people. . . . [His] generous ideas . . . make of him a forerunner of the struggle for Negritude."[21]

The occupation of Haiti by the U.S. Marines from 1915 to 1934 shook to its foundations the faith Haitians had placed in the Enlightenment values that previous generations of literary nationalists had enshrined in their revolution. Michael Dash has demonstrated in considerable detail how two generations of Haitian intellectuals, the Indigenists and the Griots, turned away from rationalism to a spiritual construction of racial identity:

> The Griot movement did not immediately follow Indigenism (the journal *Les Griots* was not published until 1938), but was facilitated by certain ideas and influences that emerged in the 1930s. The most important of these is interest in race which existed at this time. The study of African survivals and the ethnic uniqueness of Haitian culture is directly linked to the anti-rational tradition that is evident in Indigenism. Ethnological works which supported the myth of the organic and instinctive features of African culture are directly responsible for the racialist obsessions and Messianism of Africanist ideology.[22]

The Haitian brand of literary modernism that the Griot movement fostered did not privilege revolutionary themes. Therefore we need not examine it in detail here, especially since Dash (1981) and Hoffmann (1995) and have treated it so thoroughly. However, its main features were to resurface among the Caribbean counter-modernists, notably Carpentier and Césaire, who will be treated in the final section of this article.

## Pétion and Latin America: Persistent Ambiguity

Literary reflections of the Haitian Revolution abroad represent Dessalines, Christophe, and Toussaint, especially the latter, but rarely if ever Pétion or Boyer. The omission of Pétion is curious because of the role he played in supporting Simón Bolívar in his successful invasion of Venezuela in 1816. Within Haiti, support for Bolívar is periodically advanced as proof of the universalist claims Haitians consistently made for their successful revolution from 1804 through the 1920s. The Haitian geographer Dantès Bellegarde is typical of this trend in his 1938 book *La nation haïtienne,* where he sums up Pétion's contribution to the liberation of Spanish America and, most importantly for Haiti, the emancipation of slaves held in the Spanish colonies of South America. He relates in detail Bolívar's two sojourns in Haiti, before and after his temporary defeat at the hands of general Morales on July 10, 1816, and the very considerable contribution President Pétion made in arms, supplies, and volunteers to the successful campaign that began in December of the same year. The same author cites a letter written by Simón Bolívar in which the Libertador expressed the desire to name Pétion "the author of American freedom."[23] Pétion's modesty prevented him from accepting, according to this relation of events, and he requested only that the "general liberation of the slaves" be proclaimed in every state Bolívar would liberate. Bellegarde notes that a statue to Alexandre Pétion was erected in Caracas to commemorate his contribution to Venezuelan and Spanish American independence.

One might expect that Pétion and the early Haitian republic would therefore figure importantly in Latin American history and literature. The record, however, is spotty at best. José Ramón Medina's 1993 history of Venezuelan literature in the twentieth century makes no mention of Pétion, and Christopher Conway's 2003 *Cult of Bolívar in Latin American Literature* mentions only his "backing" of the Libertador's successful campaign in late 1816.[24] *The Cambridge History of Latin America,* volume 3, *From Independence to c. 1870,* contains one mention of Pétion's "support for [Bolívar's] cause."[25] Similarly the *Encyclopedia of Latin American History and Culture* in its entry for "Bolívar, Simón," mentions "help from the Haitian government" but does not name Pétion. Even the great Pablo Neruda, in his *Canto General,* failed to make the connection. Book 4, "Los Libertadores," contains an ode to "Toussaint Louverture" but makes no mention whatever of Haiti's part in the liberation of the continent.

The Colombian playwright Enrique Buenaventura in 1963 published a trilogy devoted to the colonial period that included *La tragedia del Rey Christophe* (The tragedy of King Christophe), which is dated March 1962 at the end of the text. His play in five acts is more a historical chronicle of the period 1791–1820 than a tragedy in the dramatic or aesthetic sense. The dramatis personae include thirty-eight distinct roles of varying importance. Although the historical sweep of the play includes the period of Pétion's presidency, the focus on the career of Henri Christophe allows the Colombian dramatist to exclude Pétion completely from this treatment of the Haitian Revolution and its aftermath. By so doing, he also elided completely the link between Pétion and the independence struggle in South America.

In an effort to understand and explain this systematic forgetfulness, Ineke Phaf-Rheinberger and Matthias Röhrig-Assunção have given a detailed account of the interrelations between Haiti under Pétion and events in Curaçao and Venezuela. Manuel Piar is commemorated in Venezuela among the ten companions of Bolívar in the national pantheon. He was a mulatto born in Curaçao around 1777, raised on the Venezuelan coast, who became a ship's captain. "Piar is reported to have been a very close friend of Alexandre Pétion . . . and to have been [in Haiti] when Miranda, the most militant and famous Venezuelan patriot, came to Haiti in 1806."[26] Piar undertook a strategy of conquering Venezuelan Guyana (the province of Cumanà) from 1812 to 1817, contrary to the strategy of the *jefe supremo,* Bolívar. Piar was eventually tried for insubordination and betrayal, and he was executed in October 1817 in Angostura (today's Ciudad Bolívar). For Phaf-Rheinberger and Röhrig-Assunção, Piar was a scapegoat: "One must also consider that his friend and idol Pétion had always been strongly opposed to the killing of the whites in Saint Domingue and to all black nationalist acts of revenge. Thus, by charging Piar with fomenting racial conflicts, the Bolívar group projected onto him its own dread of a Haitian-style revolution, which might entail the physical elimination of the white elite by so-called black patriots."[27] Phaf-Rheinberger and Röhrig-Assunção have compared the treatment of this revolutionary saga in five novels written in Venezuela, Colombia, and Curaçao in the 1980s: Manuel Trujillo's *El gran dispensador,* 1983, and Francisco Herrera Luque's *Manuel Piar: Caudillo de dos colores,* 1987 (both published in Caracas); Gabriel García Márquez's *El general en su laberinto,* 1989 (published in Madrid); and Tip Marugg's *De morgen loeit weer an,* 1988, and Boeli van Leeuwen's *Het teken van Jona,* 1988 (both published in the Netherlands). They conclude, rather pessimistically as regards Curaçaoan culture, "There is no place for history, not even for Piar, in contemporary Curaçaoan literature as it reflects on Latin America. . . . It would appear that Piar's execution must increasingly be questioned in fictional historiography on the mainland."[28] One might add, still more pessimistically, that the scapegoat role these literary historians find assigned to Piar by his more famous contemporaries explains the growing silence surrounding Pétion and Haiti in rewritings of the revolutionary period on the mainland of South America. Historians in the United States from the mid-twentieth century have been more generous. Gerhard Masur, in his intellectual and historical biography of Simón Bolívar, relates Pétion's importance to the Libertador's efforts in terms that Dantès Bellegarde would not have disavowed. Indeed, he confirms the claim that Pétion himself asked Bolívar not to liberate the slaves in South America in his name. Masur does add, however, that Pétion in so doing may have cautiously attempted to avoid the wrath of the United States. He further reveals that the money raised for Bolívar's cause came not from the Haitian state treasury but from a wealthy English businessman, Robert Sutherland. Shorter histories, such as John Johnson's from 1968, usually reduce this chapter to a sentence or two on the connection between the aid Pétion gave Bolívar and the latter's promise to free slaves in Spanish America.

## Toussaint, The Black Napoléon

Literary treatments of the Haitian Revolution in the nineteenth-century United States were in all cases overdetermined by the author's position and class values regarding the enslavement of Africans in the New World. The pseudoscience and, indeed, the theology that underpinned the institution were themselves determined by those same class values. In this respect the United States presents the same pattern of denigration of the Haitian Revolution by the planter class and the merchants who supported them, whereas the abolitionists—Northerners and primarily Evangelical Christians—praised the heroes of the Revolution and blamed the planters rather than the former slaves for the murderous excesses that occurred on both sides during the conflict. In 1861, on the eve of the U.S. civil war, the eminent abolitionist Wendell Phillips delivered a resounding speech that tied the fate of slaves in the United States directly to the Haitian Revolution:

> And you may also remember this—that we Saxons were slaves about four
> hundred years, sold with the land, and our fathers never raised a finger to end

that slavery. . . . There never was a slave rebellion successful but one and that was in St. Domingo. Every race has been some time or other in chains. But there never was a race that, weakened and degraded by such chattel slavery, unaided, tore off its own fetters, forged them into swords and won its liberty on the battlefield, but one, and that was the black race of St. Domingo. God grant that the wise vigor of our government may avert that necessity from our land—may raise into peaceful liberty the four million committed to our care and show under democratic institutions a statesmanship as far-sighted as that of England, as brave as the Negro of Haiti![29]

In purely literary terms, Phillips's pairing of Toussaint with Napoléon is more important today than his warning against civil war, which went unheeded: "I would call him Napoleon, but Napoleon made his way to empire over broken oaths and through a sea of blood. This man never broke his word. 'No retaliation,' was his great motto and the rule of his life; and the last words uttered to his son in France were these, 'My boy, you will some day go back to St. Domingo; forget that France murdered your father.'"[30]

Lamartine had already set the stage for this archetypal drama of warring brothers that would reach its apogee in the semifictional biography published by Percy Waxman in 1931, *Black Napoleon*. This topos, which extends far beyond the limits of the present essay, has itself generated a rather considerable literature. Without exhausting the list we would have to cite the following, among twentieth-century treatments: in German, Karl Otten's *Der schwarze Napoleon;* in English, John W. Vandercook's *Black Majesty;* and in French, Raphaël Tardon's *Toussaint-Louverture, le Napoléon noir.* David Geggus, the historian who may have contributed more than any other to our current understanding of the Haitian Revolution, has himself paid possibly involuntary homage to this tradition in *Haitian Revolutionary Studies:* "Late in 1799, France, like Saint Domingue, acquired a military strongman for a ruler. Napoleon Bonaparte and Toussaint Louverture had much in common. Both were seen as defenders of basic revolutionary gains of the previous decade, particularly of new land settlements. Both were autocrats who extinguished all political liberty in their respective countries. Both were destroyed by their own ambition."[31]

All the preceding examples owe a debt to Romantic drama and historiography, which stressed the heroic action of larger-than-life figures in the shaping of modern history. Over against this monumentalizing of the great man, the tradition of melodrama placed an evil antagonist, the

Demon who is eventually vanquished by the Angel. More importantly, from the standpoint of Caribbean writers, Romantic historiography involved setting the Haitian Revolution in the context of the European wars that were sparked by the French Revolution, continued by Napoléon into the First Empire, and ultimately brought about a restructuring of the European world-system and its colonial dependencies.

### Caribbean Counter-Modernists: Carpentier, James, Césaire, Glissant, Walcott

From the mid-twentieth century onward Caribbean writers have sought to extricate themselves from the binary oppositions that the Romantic worldview had enshrined in poetics, aesthetics, and historiography. History (with a capital H) was not their history; the novel, the drama, and the long poem had to be reconceptualized so as to present the Haitian Revolution from a perspective set within the Antillean archipelago. Their aesthetic position was, in its broadest outline, a Counter-Modernism, to borrow Theo D'haen's term.[32] D'haen has argued persuasively that, in the late phases of Caribbean colonialism and the early period after independence, Caribbean writers pressed the expressive means of European Modernism into service against the colonial masters, in effect writing back against the aesthetic imported from Europe. It is in this context that one can best understand the implications of Alejo Carpentier's *El reino de este mundo* (*The Kingdom of This World*), which was first published in 1949. His novel spans the period from 1751 to approximately 1832. Events are depicted through the very limited vision of the slave Ti-Noel. Carpentier foregrounds the exploits of Macandal and Boukman. He makes the former a traditional African healer, who apparently learned his art as a maroon. His Boukman is a *vodún* priest who, in the historiography sponsored by the Indigéniste group in Haiti during the U.S. occupation of 1915–34, was primarily responsible for leading the slave revolt in 1791. With respect to the major stages of the Haitian Revolution, Carpentier has left the heroic period completely out of consideration in this novel. From late 1791 to 1816 Ti-Noel lives in Santiago de Cuba, where his owner, M. Lenormand de Mézy, has taken him. When Ti-Noel returns alone to squat on his dead master's former plantation, Haiti is independent; Toussaint is long dead; Dessalines has been assassinated; and Christophe rules despotically over the northern plain. Although a free man, the already old Ti-Noel is conscripted into a labor gang in 1817 and is made to work like a slave on Christophe's citadel until the emperor's death in 1820. In Ti-Noel's perspective, one form of slavery has replaced another. When Boyer comes to power, Ti-Noel is living again on the former Lenormand de Mézy plantation, amid plunder from Christophe's Sans Souci palace.

None of these events are dated in the text, which carefully avoids historical representation. The narrative mode is mythic but, as Barbara Webb has described it, different from European Modernism: "Although the mythic imagination with its fusion of time and space in which everything is possible . . . is the model for Carpentier's experiments with time and space in this novel, his use of the culture myth of the African slaves also serves another function."[33] At the end of part 1 of the novel, Carpentier relates the events of Macandal's death twice, first from the perspective of the black slaves, then from the perspective of the white authorities. A narratological analysis suggests that the second version is a correction of the first. Enthusiasts of Magic Realism have systematically overlooked the question of the narratee in favor of the author's focus on *vodún*. In Barbara Webb's assessment: "The invocation of the African loas Ogun . . . and Damballah . . . proved powerful weapons against the 'civilized' decadence of the slaveholders and the European 'Goddess of Reason.' In *El reino* Carpentier suggests that the Europeans' failure to understand the role of vodún stemmed from their general contempt for the humanity of the slaves."[34] This is no doubt true, but it does not warrant a treatment of the Haitian Revolution that makes *vodún* its one necessary and sufficient cause. By reading out of the plot the military and political exploits of Toussaint, Dessalines, and Pétion, Carpentier has undercut the narrative of the Revolution as the triumph of the Enlightenment that Haitian historians themselves long championed. Furthermore, the exclusive focus on the most egregious of Christophe's failures does little to present the Haitian Revolution as a beacon of light to oppressed peoples everywhere. Moreover, concerning the central importance accorded to Boukman, David Geggus points out that before the Indigéniste movement reinterpreted the Haitian Revolution, early historians never stressed the Bois Caïman ceremony in their accounts. He concludes that Léon-François Hoffmann was mistaken in claiming that the ceremony never took place; but he tempers the claims of such Indigénistes as Dantès Bellegarde who wanted to rehabilitate *vodún* as part of a revitalized national myth. According to Geggus, "There is . . . no evidence for Dantès Bellegarde's assertion that the leaders of the uprising were chosen at Bois Caïman and that Toussaint Louverture was present."[35] In sum, "it served to sacralize a political movement that was then reaching fruition. The decision to launch a rebellion, taken seven days earlier at the elite meeting of slave-drivers and coachmen, was at Bois Caïman directly communicated, to a perhaps predominantly African group of field slaves, in a religious setting calculated to mobilize support."[36] The stress Carpentier placed on *vodún*, to the exclusion of political motivations among the principal revolutionaries —who do not play a role in his account—has the net effect of undercutting the Revolution's meaning for the nineteenth century.

A decade after *El reino de este mundo,* Carpentier published *El siglo de las luces,* which John Sturrock translated in 1963 as *Explosion in a Cathedral,* thereby writing out of the title the clear reference to the Enlightenment project of progressive liberation of humanity. *Explosion in a Cathedral* follows the career of the French Revolutionary Victor Hugues from Saint-Domingue, which he flees when the insurrection burns his business in the colony, to Guadeloupe—where he sets up the guillotine as the agent of the Revolution—then to Cayenne—the island colony off the coast of French Guiana—where he likewise represents the Revolution. Late in the novel (part 4, chapter 32) in a quite Voltairean conversation in Cayenne, the reader is treated to this anti-black harangue by an abbé who had refused to pledge allegiance to the Republic:

> When Sonthonax thought that the Spanish were going to attack San Domingo, he took it upon himself to proclaim the freedom of the negroes. This took place a whole year before you all wept with enthusiasm in the Convention, and declared that equality was established between all the inhabitants of French possessions overseas. In Haiti they did it to get the Spaniards off their backs, in Guadeloupe to make sure of chasing out the English, here to give the death blow to the rich land-owners and the old Acadians, who were very ready to ally themselves with the Dutch or the British, if that would stop the Pointe-à-Pitre guillotine from being brought to Cayenne. Colonial politics—that's all![37]

Another participant in the conversation adds somberly: "All the French Revolution has achieved in America is to legalise the Great Escape which has been going on since the sixteenth century. The blacks didn't wait for you, they've proclaimed themselves free a countless number of times."[38] There follow two pages of details concerning major slave uprisings throughout the Caribbean, Mexico, and South America that culminate in a brief evocation of Boukman and the Bois Caïman ceremony. The reader is thus invited to open up the narrative of *Explosion in a Cathedral* onto the perspective of *The Kingdom of This World,* which s/he may be expected to know already. If the novel can be said to set the Haitian Revolution in the context of slave revolts throughout plantation America, it also undeniably empties it of its historic specificity.

In 1948, the year before Carpentier published the novel that launched *lo real maravilloso americano*, Derek Walcott was an eighteen-year-old undergraduate at the University of the West Indies in Mona, Jamaica. At the invitation of his twin brother Roderick, he wrote a play he entitled *Henri Christophe* that dramatized the struggle between Dessalines and Christophe after the death of Toussaint. The play—the first of three in which Walcott would treat the Haitian Revolution—turned out to be a family affair when it was staged the following year in St. Lucia. The author's mother, Alix, a local schoolteacher, designed the costumes. The narrator was played by George Lamming. Besides the narrator, the principal characters are Christophe, Dessalines, Vastey, Brelle (Christophe's confessor), and old general Sylla. The young Walcott also owed a considerable debt to Modernism—not the Surrealist variety that Carpentier had absorbed, then repudiated—but the variety Eliot had already spread throughout the English-speaking world. Although this play—which belongs among the Nobel laureate's juvenilia—reads like a Shakespearean drama of kingship, I agree with Charles Pollard who has argued recently that "Walcott recognizes . . . that the modernism of Pound, Joyce, or Eliot could be useful to a Caribbean writer precisely because it expresses deep doubts about the 'European model of history,' including the 'notions of progress and temporal closure'."[39] Walcott's early Modernism deserves to be reconsidered seriously in the Caribbean context that includes Carpentier and Césaire.

The latter is frequently quoted for having written in his *Cahier d'un retour au pays natal* (Notebook of a return to the native land), 1939, that "Haiti, where negritude rose for the first time and stated that it believed in its humanity . . . is mine."[40] For Césaire, and for so many other Caribbean writers and intellectuals in the twentieth century, the major effort would be to make the Haitian Revolution their own. Theirs has been the task of creating a "prophetic vision of the past," as Édouard Glissant would put it in the introduction to his play *Monsieur Toussaint*. Césaire would return twice more to the Haitian Revolution, in the historical essay *Toussaint Louverture*, 1961, and in the play *La tragédie du Roi Christophe*, in 1963. *Toussaint Louverture* treats the entire revolutionary period from the early 1780s to 1803, the year of Toussaint's death. It is a Marxist treatment of the subject, with ethnoclass values carefully embedded in a dialectical movement. The three parts of the essay are entitled "The Resistance of the White Planters," "The Mulatto Revolt," and "The Black Revolution." Césaire puts Toussaint's captivity down to a combination of betrayal on the part of the mulatto caste in

Saint-Domingue and to General Brunet's treachery in inviting Toussaint to come aboard his ship for a parley. Clearly Césaire saw the black slaves as the sole repository of the revolutionary cause in Saint-Domingue, but he interpreted that role in terms of values that were those of the white world turned inside out. As he wrote of Toussaint's death in his *Cahier/Notebook*:

> What is mine
> a lonely man imprisoned in
> whiteness
> a lonely man defying the white
> screams of white death
> (TOUSSAINT, TOUSSAINT LOUVERTURE).[41]

The Negritude vision could only see the freedmen of Saint-Domingue as an illegitimate third group, between the white masters and the black slaves, that was destined to disappear into the dustbin of History, to paraphrase Marx. As long as Caribbean intellectuals continued to reason in this manner—to fail to imagine a more inclusive nation—conflict in the newly independent Caribbean was bound to fester and explode periodically after 1960.

Three years before Césaire published his long poem in Paris, C. L. R. James staged a play in London on the theme of "The Black Jacobins" in which Paul Robeson played Toussaint. James is, of course, best known today for his essay, likewise titled *The Black Jacobins,* which was first published in 1938. His vision is pan-African, but Trotskyite; in his view Toussaint ultimately failed because he lost contact with the black masses.[42] James has the highest praise for Césaire's *Notebook* in his revised second edition of 1963: "[Césaire] discovers a new version of what the Haitians . . . had discovered, that salvation for the West Indies lies in Africa, the original home and ancestry of West Indian people."[43] Twenty-five years on, in the heady days of African independence, James himself had tilted quite far in the direction of Negritude and away from a Marxist vision of History. The primacy of race had displaced the primacy of class. In successive editions of *The Black Jacobins* we see James gradually aligning himself with the Negritude intellectuals.

Césaire's play on the reign of Henri Christophe in the north of Haiti from 1807 to 1820 was staged in Salzburg, Berlin, and at the Venice Biennale in 1963. *The Tragedy of King Christophe* has often been interpreted as a warning to the newly independent African states to avoid one-man rule. More significant, I think, is the role of *vodún* in bringing about

Christophe's downfall. Césaire interprets the emperor's stroke, which Christophe suffered during the religious festival of the Assumption, as the revenge of the African gods—the *loas* of *vodún*—on the ruler who had forsaken them for the God of the Europeans. Politics doesn't enter into Henri Christophe's downfall, which is portrayed by Césaire as a cultural tragedy. Like Carpentier in this, he interprets events in the Haitian Revolution as a clash of cultures, which he represents as African versus European. The point to be made here is that no discursive space is left by Césaire for the process of creolization, which over the centuries has made the Caribbean neither African nor European, but a syncretic society of a new and unique type. In this respect at least, we must acknowledge that Césaire had not succeeded in breaking out of the binary opposition of black/white, Africa/Europe. Papa Doc was in full control of Haiti in 1963, with the support of international capital, notably from the United States, and his *noiriste* ideology was consonant with the message of Christophe's tragedy, as depicted by Césaire. Originally a member of the group of Indigéniste scholars who in the 1930s had labored to restore to respectability the black peasant culture of Haiti, François Duvalier used all aspects of blackness—and most importantly *vodún*—to undergird a regime that made of the mulatto ethnoclass the villains of Haitian history. I do not mean to suggest that Césaire in any way supported Duvaliérisme, but that Negritude, like the ideology of the Indigénistes, could be hijacked for unspeakable political ends.

It was left to a Martinican of the next generation, Édouard Glissant, to think through the logical trap that Negritude set for itself and to point the way to creolization as the process of original incorporation of all the elements that go into constituting the societies of the region. In his long poem *Les Indes,* which dates from 1955, the section entitled "Les Héros" includes poems devoted to Toussaint and Dessalines. Of Toussaint he wrote: "And history closed over this betrayed warrior the forgetful trapdoor of winter / Let him die, let him die, that the forest may live."[44] And of Dessalines, "Shadow of blood, sprung from a lake of blood, pitiless, that's Dessalines."[45] Of Christophe, not a word. Six years later, at precisely the moment when Césaire was bringing out his historical essay on the Haitian Revolution, Glissant undertook to problematize both time and space in his treatment of Toussaint-Louverture's death in the Fort de Joux. By staging the drama on the eve of Toussaint's death, in an atmosphere where his physical and mental state were compatible with dream or hallucination, Glissant has the hero dialogue with his wife, Dessalines, Christophe, a number of other historical figures of the period,

Macandal, who died when Toussaint was a young boy, and a priestess of *vodún* whom Glissant has introduced, Maman Dio. Historical events, Toussaint's self-critique, and the commentary of the entire supporting cast create a dialogic environment within which it is impossible to lodge a master plot. Glissant is at pains to dismantle both the master plot of European revolution, within which events in Saint-Domingue would play a secondary role, as well as the countervailing master plot of Negritude, which would have privileged the role of the maroon figures who, in the Indigéniste version of the Haitian Revolution, led the war against the French. As Michael Dash put it in his general study of Glissant:

> The imprisoned father of Haitian independence is anything but the roman-
> ticized liberator. Rather, he is a man caught between icy prison and island
> space, the hills of the maroons and the sea that took him away, the flames of
> Makandal's pyre and the terrible cold of the Jura mountains. The play is con-
> structed, not in terms of linear chronology, but according to a complex inter-
> twining of present tragedy, historical reality and imaginary dialogue between
> Toussaint and those who are dead or merely absent. . . . There is a sense in
> which no one in this play is right or wrong but each character takes positions
> within the movement of history.[46]

One can gauge how far Glissant's vision is from Carpentier's and Césaire's by this observation: "The debate between Makandal and Toussaint pits the inward-turning maroon fighter against the man turned towards the outside world, modernity, and the mainstream of world history. It is this desire not to form a maroon enclave but to participate in a world culture of modern technology and democratic freedom that drives Toussaint."[47]

Dash further notes that "In this play, all of Glissant's major preoccu-pations are evoked—the lure of the universal, the individual and collec-tive destiny and . . . the complex relationships that make up the history of the Americas."[48] I would add that the ghost-like presences who dialogue with Toussaint in the play suggest the nightmare of History that Glissant has attempted to disentangle over the past half-century.

I should like to conclude by returning to Derek Walcott who, in 1984, revised his creative understanding of the Haitian Revolution in the play *The Haitian Earth*. A man of the theater in a sense that neither Glissant nor Césaire ever was, Walcott opens his play with a Creole-speaking Dessalines caught in a life-and-death struggle with a wild boar, which foreshadows his own death at the hands of Christophe's stooges. The plot turns on the success of the Revolution, the execution of Ogé and Chavannes, the fate of Toussaint, the betrayal of Dessalines by Christophe, and Christophe's own demise, all in a theatrical telescoping of historical time. This summary may sound a bit cluttered, but Walcott moves the plot along so well that one is struck by the dramatic intensity, not the implausible chronological reach from 1792 to 1820. He leaves us with a chorus of peasants and Pompey, who returns the body of his wife Yette to the Haitian earth. The satisfying blend of St. Lucian Creole, which is very close to Martinican, and creolized English helps the audience grasp that this version of the Haitian Revolution is seen from below, by the most humble participants. Walcott took a long time to work out his version of Nation Language, as Kamau Brathwaite would call this idiom, but the result is consonant with Glissant's desire to demythologize the great men of the struggle for Haitian Independence. He shows them to us, not clothed in heroic postures and spouting fancy rhetoric, but warts and all, speaking the language of the people.

## Notes

1. Léon-François Hoffmann, "Victor Hugo, les Noirs et l'esclavage."

2. Claire de Duras, *Ourika,* edited by Joan DeJean and Margaret Waller, vii.

3. Duras, *Ourika, an English Translation,* translated by John Fowles, 21.

4. Sibylle Fischer, *Modernity Disavowed,* 114.

5. Carlos Alonso, "Fiction," in *A History of Literature in the Caribbean,* vol. 1, 144.

6. Fischer, *Modernity Disavowed,* 115.

7. William Wordsworth, *The Poetical Works,* 170.

8. Ibid.

9. Villevaleix in Léon-François Hoffmann, *Littérature d'Haïti,* 79. (My translations unless otherwise indicated.)

10. Vastey, ibid., 81–82.

11. Jean-Baptiste Chenêt, ibid., 436.

12. Régis Antoine, *Les écrivains français et les Antilles,* 257–64.

13. Léon-François Hoffmann, "Introduction," *Toussaint Louverture,* by Alphonse de Lamartine, xxiv–xxv.

14. Ibid., xxv–xxviii.

15. Bibliographic information in Lamartine, *Toussaint Louverture,* 153–54.

16. Gottfried Herrmann, *Toussaint Louverture,* libretto of a "grand opera in five acts."

17. As quoted in Hoffmann, "Introduction," xxxiii.

18. Ibid., x–xi.

19. W. D. Howarth, *Sublime and Grotesque,* 347–48.

20. Freeman, *Myth and Its Making,* as quoted in Lamartine, *Toussaint Louverture,* xxxvi.

21. Léopold Sedar Senghor, "Lamartine, homme de pensée et d'action," 67–69.

22. J. Michael Dash, *Literature and Ideology*, 100.

23. Dantès Bellegarde, *La nation haïtienne*, 102.

24. Christopher B. Conway, *The Cult of Bolívar in Latin American Literature*, 22.

25. Leslie Bethell, *The Cambridge History of Latin America*, vol. 3, *From Independence to c. 1870*, 137.

26. Ineke Phaf-Rheinberger and Matthias Röhrig-Assunção, "History Is Bunk!" 164.

27. Ibid., 166.

28. Ibid., 173.

29. Wendell Phillips, in Mercer Cook and Dantès Bellegarde, eds., *Haitian-American Anthology* 14–15.

30. Ibid., 15.

31. David Patrick Geggus, *Haitian Revolutionary Studies*, 23.

32. Theo D'haen, "Modernist and Counter-Modernist Caribbeans," 309–12.

33. Barbara J. Webb, *Myth and History in Caribbean Fiction*, 29.

34. Ibid., 33.

35. Geggus, *Haitian Revolutionary Studies*, 90.

36. Ibid., 91.

37. Alejo Carpentier, *Explosion in a Cathedral*, 230. Page references are to 1979 edition.

38. Ibid., 231.

39. Charles W. Pollard, *New World Modernisms*, 19.

40. Aimé Césaire, *Collected Poetry*, 47.

41. Ibid.

42. C. L. R. James, *The Black Jacobins*, 2nd ed., 321–22.

43. Ibid., 399.

44. Édouard Glissant, *Poèmes complets*, 154.

45. Ibid., 154–55.

46. J. Michael Dash, *Édouard Glissant*, 103.

47. Ibid., 104.

48. Ibid., 105.

# Toward New Paradigms in Caribbean Studies

## The Impact of the Haitian Revolution on Our Literatures

*Jean Jonassaint*

ALTHOUGH THE echo of the Haitian Revolution in American literature extends from Victor Séjour ("Le Mulâtre," 1837) to Madison Smartt Bell (*Master at the Crossroads,* 2000) through Harriet Beecher Stowe (*Uncle Tom's Cabin,* 1852) and Eugene O'Neill (*The Emperor Jones,* 1920) or William Faulkner (*Absalom! Absalom!* 1936), with the exception of some recent scholarship on nineteenth-century literature from the United States, the relationship between the Haitian Revolution as historic or mythical grand narrative and Haitian and Caribbean or American literatures at large has not been the subject of well-known studies.[1] Some critics such as Daniel-Henri Pageaux and Carmen Velasquez have pointed out the key role of Haiti in Carpentier's concept of *"lo real maravilloso";* and Abiola Irele, in his annotations of *Cahier d'un retour au pays natal* (1939; *Return to My Native Land,* 1968), has recalled the importance of Haiti for Césaire.[2] But to the best of my knowledge, until now no one has shown the debts of Alejo Carpentier (1904–1980) and Aimé Césaire to Haitian historians like the Baron de Vastey (?–1820) and Verniaud Leconte (1866–1932) for *El Reino de este mundo* (1948; *The Kingdom of This World,* 1957) and *La Tragédie du Roi Christophe* (1963; *The Tragedy of King Christophe: A Play,* 1969); or of C. R. L. James (1901–1989) to Pauléus Sannon (1870–1938) for his *Black Jacobins* (1938).[3] As well, it seems that little attention has been paid to the transtextual relationships between Édouard Glissant's *Monsieur Toussaint* (1961; *Monsieur Toussaint: A Play,* 2005) and *Toussaint au Fort de Joux* (1896) by Vendenesse Ducasse (1872–1902); or between *Dessalines ou la passion de l'indépendance* (1983) by Vincent Placoly (1946–1992) and *L'Empereur Dessalines* (1906) by Massillon Coicou (1867–1908) or *Dessalines, ou le Sang du Pont-Rouge* (1967) by Hénock Trouillot (1923–1988).

Besides, since Lilyan Kesteloot's thesis of 1963, *Les Écrivains noirs de langue française: naissance d'une littérature* (translated into English by Ellen Conroy Kennedy under a more accurate title, *Black Writers in French: A Literary History of Negritude*, 1974), there has been a general presumption that the Negro-African works (to use a term of the 1960s and 1970s) before the only issue of *Légitime Défense* (1932), or even Negritude, are solely imitations of European models without link or tie to indigenous or national realities or issues relating to their contexts of production. Yet, beyond the fact that the question of imitation is a false problem, or at the very least a bad question (literature is always rewriting/transformation/adaptation/imitation), nothing could be further from the truth. Indeed, as Alain Baudot pointed out in his 1977 article, "Antilles et Guyane," Kesteloot misapprehended "Haitian literature (and even the literature of the lesser Antilles prior to the 1930s)."[4] But the myth is alive, and still now, for the huge majority of francophone critics, the negro-African literatures (if not all francophone literature outside of Europe) were born in the 1930s–1940s with the Césairian and Senghorian negritudes. Therefore, the impressive Haitian corpus of the nineteenth century which foreshadowed forthcoming anticolonialist and anti-imperialist or nationalist francophone discourses of the 1960s has been erased or forgotten.

The first aim of this essay is to open the gates for a rereading of the Haitian corpus of the nineteenth and twentieth centuries (mainly between 1810 and 1940) by showing, among other things, how the Haitian Revolution forms the raw material and is a major source text for those works—in other words, their deepest *hypotext* in a Genettian sense. Mainly, I will show how Haitian works of all types are indebted to the very first Haitian written expression of this revolution, the so-called Proclamation of Gonaïves by Dessalines, which ten years later was echoed by another less well known but equally important and much more elaborate proclamation, the *Manifeste du Roi* (1814) by Henri Christophe ("The Manifesto of the King" [1816]),[5] as well as by a large range of Caribbean texts in French, English, and Spanish. On the other hand, I will try to explain why, even though the independence myth is widespread at all levels of society, and omnipresent in poetry, theater, and of course historical or political essay, it is more often absent from Haitian fiction as motif, anecdote, or storyline. For, it seems to me, we have there a means of better understanding Haitian poetics. Last but not least, I will to the extent possible highlight some works of the Americas that echo the Revolution's narrative and show its impact on our literatures.

This essay, which is rather exploratory, with provisional conclusions for the sake of further inquiry and exchange, includes two parts: first a descriptive one which, up to a certain point, gives the state of the corpus; and a second shorter and rather interpretive one, which presents some (tentative) responses, even though, at least for now, my explanations, though very plausible, cannot be validated. Indeed, our ignorance of the wide corpus of the nineteenth century in Haiti and the Caribbean at large (the texts of which are so often difficult to find and have very rarely benefited from critical or annotated editions) and their transtextual relationships with eighteenth- and nineteenth-century French literature, is one of the main gaps of francophone studies. That is an important field to explore, which would undoubtedly need more than one thesis like Roger Toumson's *La Transgression des couleurs* (1989).

Before proceeding further, let us recall that it is not always apparent how to comment on the glorious Haitian past, nor to rightly frame a time period for the Haitian Revolution, that huge event also called by Haitian politicians the "Epic of 1804." Although this last expression is more precise on the temporal axis by its formulation, it is also ambiguous and misleading. Indeed, since November 1803, the Indigenous Army had defeated Napoléon's troops, and the Declaration of Independence pronounced in Gonaïves on the first of January 1804 is the accomplishment of more than ten years of intense battles between the Indigenous (blacks, mulattoes, and even whites) of the Revolutionary Army and the French expeditionary forces or other European troops. Thus, this former French colony became the second independent state in the Americas after the United States, and the third republic of modern time, after the assassination of the Emperor Jean-Jacques Dessalines (October 17, 1806) with the presidency of Alexandre Pétion (1807–18).

Hence, whatever the expression used, we must specify what we call the Revolutionary era, for it is not a simple given fact, but a construction. For our study, we can say that it goes from 1791 to 1820, in other words from the general slave insurgency following the "Ceremony of Bois Caïman" to the unification of the country following the suicide of the King Christophe. But the advent of Haitian Independence occurred on January 1, 1804. On this day, Boisrond-Tonnerre, a secretary of Dessalines, managed to get the approval, by the chiefs of the Indigenous Army, of two very important and famous documents: one known as Haiti's Independence Act, and the other known as Dessalines' Proclamation of Gonaïves.

This latter document of 1,181 words is one of the first texts written by a Haitian and, together with the Independence Act, is the starting point of the national literary canon. Indeed, it is reproduced *in extenso* in the very canonical *Histoire de la littérature haïtienne* by Berrou and Pompilus, which is a revised and extended version of the first and only Haitian literary history to be approved by the Department of Education for the high school curriculum, *Manuel illustré d'histoire de la littérature haïtienne* (1961),[6] and for a long time the main literary textbook in Haiti. More than any other Haitian text, Dessalines' Proclamation of Gonaïves is a founding document of both the country and its literature, showing the main features of almost all forthcoming national expressions. For the sake of our demonstration, I will quote and comment on parts of Dessalines/Boisrond-Tonnerre's text, which show us some peculiar features of Haitian literature in the nineteenth and twentieth centuries. Indeed, in this document we retrace four main features, which are all very common in Haitian texts.

1. The first feature is the real taste for linguistic innovation, or better, for the creolization or haitianization of French language in order to express more adequately the national reality. In other words, a French language that wants to be different from hexagonal French, translating a peculiar relationship, mostly ambiguous, of the Haitian with the French, both, the language and the people, of which *Gouverneurs de la Rosée* (1944; *Masters of the Dew*, 1947) by Jacques Roumain (1907–1944) is the most notorious example. The very first compelling example of this literary feature is the famous phrase of Dessalines' Proclamation, *le nom français lugubre encore nos contrées,* that we can translate as "the French name still glooms our countryside." The first systematic use of this Haitian French or French Haitian in a narrative was by Justin Lhérisson (1873–1907) in his *audience* (short story),[7] *La Famille des Pitite-Caille* (1905). However, according to Gouraige and Cornevin, since the nineteenth century, Haitian theater has mixed Haitian Creole and French, and included dialogues in Haitian French, as in *Place vacante* (date unknown) by Vendenesse Ducasse in collaboration with Georges Sylvain (1866–1925), who published the first book in "Haitian Creole," an adaptation of La Fontaine's fables, *Cric? Crac! Les fables de La Fontaine racontées par un montagnard haïtien et transcrites en vers créoles* (1901).[8] Hence, the quest for a national Haitian expression in Haitian French, even in Haitian, has been a long and constant process of literary commitment for Haitian writers, long before the Haitian indigenous movement or the

Negro-African negritude of the 1930s–1940s, and of course the so-called *créolité* of the 1980s.

2. The second point to highlight is the dialogic form of the communication, a very rhetorical usage, in which the orator questions his audience in a quite intimate and authoritative manner, which, at the same time, allows him to dissociate himself from others (I/You), and associate himself with his interlocutor(s) (We), both facing the same enemy, They/Them. A convincing illustration of this second feature in the Proclamation is the passage where Dessalines is encouraging the people to take revenge on the French, but at the same time he is questioning them on the reason to act in this way, as in the following excerpt:

> Indigenous citizens, men, women, girls and children, bear your regards on all the parts of this island; look for yourself, your spouses, your husbands, yourself, your brothers, you, your sisters; *what do I say?* Look for your children, your children that are being breast fed! *What have they become? . . . I tremble to say it . . .* the prey of these vultures. *Instead of these interesting victims, your dismayed eye can only perceive their assassins;* those tigers that are still dripping with their blood, and whose horrible presence reproaches your insensitivity and your slowness to avenge them. *What are you waiting for to appease their souls?* (Italics, my emphasis)

Indeed, as the online edition of the *Oxford English Dictionary* defines "dialogism," Dessalines is arguing for the killing of the French colonizers "under the form of a dialogue" with the people, "[imputing] ideas and sentiments" to his audience. This dialogic rhetoric is also one the main features of both popular narratives like *kont* (tales), and novels of Haitian tradition.[9] To be convinced, one can recall, among others, the famous "Prologue" of *Compère Général Soleil* (1955) by Jacques Stephen Alexis (1922–1961), especially the passage where, in one of the rare times in a Haitian novel, the legendary figure of Dessalines is evoked:

> The night was still breathing heavily, like an elderly grandmother.
>
> *His Aunty Christiana would have said "for ages and ages."* SHE WAS A REAL BLACK WOMAN, AUNT CHRISTIANA, A GOOD WOMAN, A SISTER—YES, BROTHER! *For ages and ages. Ever since the war of barrel hoops, the war of all the blacks of Haiti,* THE WAR OF DESSALINES, WHO DID NOT WANT TO SEE ANY WHITES IN THE COUNTRY—AT LEAST NOT THE BAD WHITES. *For ages and ages—depi ti konkonm tap goumen ak berejen—as they say jokingly. We blacks joke all the time. . . .*

*What was I saying? Oh yes, the side of a shack. I talk too much—shut up!*
. . .

> *A rooster had just begun crowing. It was Ti-Luxa's fighting cock, tied a the*
> *back of his courtyard. A good cock to bet on.*
> "*Cock-a-doodle-doo!*"
> *You can bet on Ti-Luxa's cock with confidence. Every cock in Port-au-*
> *Prince answered. In Port-au-Prince, cocks sing all night long.*[10]

3. The third feature is the warning or caution, which is a prescription/
prohibition forecasting a tragedy, as in the novels of Haitian tradition. In
the last paragraphs of Dessalines' Proclamation, the shadow of the "Pont
Rouge," where the founding father was assassinated in 1806, and similarly, the Haitian disaster, is apprehended: "And you, people who have
been disadvantaged for so long , . . . if for whatever reason you refused
or received while grumbling the laws that the genius that watches over
your destiny will dictate to me for your good fortune, you would deserve
the fate of ungrateful peoples." In other words, one can say, you will be
damned. However, Dessalines adds: "But let me do away with [*loin de
moi*] this horrible idea. You will be the support of the liberty that you
cherish, the support for the chief who commands you." Thus, for first
time we may observe a specific feature of Haitian tragedy, which, contrary to Greek tragedy, offers a choice to the individual. The prohibition
or warning (*mise en garde*) is not only a prospective narrative, it is also
an option, an alternative for the character or the reader. But Dessalines'
first premonition of his fatal loss is (was) the right one, not his second
(optimistic) thought. The Emperor will be assassinated at the Pont Rouge,
and the country will sink into civil war and division. It is a scenario more
or less similar, but reversed, that Roumain repeats in *Masters of the Dew*.
Indeed, in his fiction, Roumain made of the assassination of Manuel the
sacrifice that allows for the reunification of the village of Fonds-Rouge.
But whatever the outcome, in both cases the subjects had the choice to
escape from their tragic death, or their assassins had the option not to
sink into damnation. The warning was also (part of) a cautionary tale.

At this point, it is useful to note VèVè Clark's insightful comment on
the Haitian Revolution as a cautionary tale for the Third World leader
in the 1960s, which seems to prove that the impact of this event goes
beyond the Caribbean and Americas, and of course beyond the literary
scene. Indeed, she wrote:

> From 1796 through 1975, a total of sixty-three plays concerned with the Haitian
> Revolution were either performed or published. Playwrights from Africa, the

Caribbean, Europe, Scandinavia, and the United States have provided diverse interpretations of the event and its principal leaders, the Black Jacobins. . . .

By focusing attention on Toussaint Louverture and Henri Christophe, the playwrights examine universal motifs associated with armed resistance and post independence strategies during the years from 1791 to 1820. In this period of Haiti's tragic overture, Toussaint died in a Swiss prison [*sic*], and his two most trusted lieutenants, who became his successors, each died abruptly. Dessalines, who ruled from 1804 to 1806, was hacked to death; Christophe, who ruled from 1807 to 1820 committed suicide. The tragic endings of these three leaders from Haiti's revolutionary era established an ambiguous code of behavior that during the 1960s provided a cautionary tale for future heads of decolonized states in the Third World.[11]

4. Finally this Proclamation features a distinctive vocabulary focused on two semantic fields: on the one hand, the fight to build a nation like a great family with its chief, its protective parents, its obedient and grateful children, their ancestors and gods; and on the other hand the dichotomy *We* (Haitians free from slavery, and *civilized people*) and the *Others* (the French and other European colonizers, and *barbarous people*). This reversal of the terms of negativity is central in the new Haitian counter-discourse, which, of course, recalls the American counter-discourse of the American War of Independence, and that of the French Jacobins in the late eighteenth century. Indeed, as Gouraige put it in his history of Haitian literature: "The influence of the French Revolution and its speeches from the tribune is not negligible in the writings of that era. The Declaration of Independence, which is the first work of Haitian literature, is quite impregnated by that, and its author Boisrond-Tonnerre, by writing it, seems to have remembered that event and its discourses."[12] But what is very different and new is that for the first time, the counterpart who claimed his humanity against barbarity, to recall the famous line by Césaire ("Haiti where negritude stood up for the first time and swore by its humanity"), is the one to whom all humanity was and is still denied. The most recurrent key words of this Dessalinian reversal and vocabulary in Haitian patriotic poetry of the nineteenth century, at least in the poems reproduced by Berrou and Pompilus in their textbook, include the following: independence, country, liberty, free, law, people, blood, nation, France, glory, fight, death, soul, cherish, children, Haiti, and their derivatives.

For this last feature—a distinctive vocabulary around two semantic fields: the fight to build a nation like a great family, and the dichotomy

*We* (Haitian people) and the *Others* (the Frenchmen and other European colonizers)—which is the starting point of our description of the Haitian literary corpus as it appeared in Berrou and Pompilus's textbook, the "Cantate à l'Indépendance" (Cantata to Independence) published in 1821 by Juste Chanlatte (1766–1828), is one of the most relevant pieces of the period.[13] It is one of the few available examples of Haitian poetry from the early 1800s, and it shows the obvious influence of the web of Dessalinian words. But one must be aware that even though Haitian critics consider that Haitian literature was born with Haitian Independence, they do not agree on the importance of the first thirty years of literary production of the country. Indeed, for a very influential Haitian scholar like Ghislain Gouraige, works before the so called "École de 1836," or Haitian Romanticism, are very marginal. Indeed, in his history of Haitian literature (1960) as well as his anthology of Haitian poetry and prose (1963),[14] Gouraige made almost no mention of pioneers like the poet Chanlatte, or the famous secretary and historian of King Christophe, Baron de Vastey, one of the very few Haitian writers of the nineteenth century whose works were translated and commented on in English.[15]

Hence, our reading of the Haitian corpus could be more or less different if it was based on Gouraige's textbooks, for example. However, our finding of a very strong transtextual link of Haitian writings in the nineteenth century with the Proclamation of Gonaïves and the Independence Act is consistent with Gouraige's statement about the influence of French Revolutionary rhetoric on Haitian literature of the first four decades of independent Haiti. Indeed, Chanlatte's title repeats the key word of Dessalines' speech, *independence*, with its consequence, *freedom*, and the main actor or character of this epic saga, the *people*. All those words are among the most recurrent in Haitian patriotic poetry of the nineteenth century, as in this line of the poem: "Un peuple qui connaît sa liberté chérie,"[16] which echoes this phrase of the Dessalines Proclamation: *"You, the people, you will be the support of the liberty that you cherish"* (italics, my emphasis). Moreover, Chanlatte's title is part of a well-established tradition of Haitian poem titles of that period, such as "Hymne à la liberté" (Hymn to Freedom) by Antoine Dupré (?–1816), generally considered as the very first Haitian poet, and "Hymne à l'*Indépendance*" (Hymn to Independence) by Jean-Baptiste Romane (1807–1858),[17] written after the recognition by France of Haitian Independence (1825).

Both texts are very patriotic, even though the last line of Romane's Hymn, *"Vive Haïti! Vive la France!"* (italics in original) is quite paradoxical, and contradicts Dessalines' profession of "anathema to the French name!" and his cry of "Eternal hatred to France!" But as Edgard La Selve, a French commentator of this time, remarked, France's recognition of Haiti's independence in 1825 by Charles X "cause[d] in Haiti a true frenzy of enthusiasm, which burst in numerous couplets where the Independence is a pretext for the refrain: *Long live Haiti! Long live France!*"[18] On the other hand, strange as it may be, this refrain also repeats or rewrites in a less equivocal manner another ambiguous and paradoxical passage from Dessalines' Proclamation, on the problematic relationship of Haitians to France. Moreover, it seems to me that this "Eternal hatred to France!" in the very French language is per se contradictory. How can Dessalines adopt the other's language, if his relationship with him is only hatred? Besides, is not hatred a part of love or envy? Dessalines' relationship to France and to the French (the people and the language), or at least Boisrond-Tonnerre's relation to French, since he was the ghostwriter of the Gonaïves Proclamation, was not as univocal as this cry of hatred might suggest. It was more complex. Indeed, on January 21, 1793, after the execution of King Louis XVI, Boisrond-Tonnerre demonstrated in the streets of Paris with a suburban crowd. According to Pascal Trouillot, from this historical day on, he developed long and close ties with the most radical Jacobins, those of the Parisian suburbs.[19] Hence, more than any other of Dessalines' secretaries, he knew the principles and the rhetoric of the French Revolution, and that France was not monolithic. That is precisely what Baron de Vastey recalls in the conclusion of his essay, *Le Système colonial dévoilé* (1814), when he praises Wilberforce and Grégoire, and calls for his right to denounce and fight the colonist slave-owners and the merchants of human flesh.[20]

Finally, one must be reminded that Dessalines excluded from the death penalty those French people who, by their science or their action, were able to help the new country. In addition, he knew very well that all the French in the colony were not Rochambeau, and that a significant number of French Jacobins were openly against slavery. Indeed, it is not by chance that the first history of Haitian literature by Duraciné Vaval (1879–1953?), *Histoire de la littérature haïtienne* (1933), is dedicated to Abbé Grégoire, a French "member of the first Society of Friends of the Blacks," author of, among other titles, *Epître aux Haïtiens* (1827) and *De la littérature des nègres* (1808; *On the Cultural Achievements of Negroes*, 1996). Grégoire never visited Haiti, but as Jean-François Brière reminds us, he was so popular and admired in the country that his death, on "5 September 1831, . . . was marked in Haiti with a national day of mourning that included a 21-gun salute."[21]

Hence, what Dessalines seems to argue at the very beginning of his Proclamation is quite complex. For, at the same time that he acknowledges a French legacy in independent Haiti, he warns his people about this presence, demonstrating the doubly ambiguous relationship of Republican France with the slaves of Saint-Domingue, and vice versa, that of the new free Haitian citizens with the French. Indeed, Dessalines states: "it is not enough to have put a brake on these ever reviving factions which take turns play-acting this liberty, like a ghost that France had exposed before your eyes." Then two paragraphs further, he says: "defeated, not by the French armies, but by the shamefaced eloquence of the proclamation of their agents; when will we tire of breathing the same air as them?"

So, it is not by chance that we find in the same Proclamation this uncanny statement: "our laws, our customs, our cities, all bear the French imprint; what do I say? There are French in our island, and you believe yourselves to be free and independent of that republic which fought all nations, it is true, but which has never been victorious over those who wished to be free." What, we may ask, did Dessalines/Boisrond-Tonnerre mean by that statement?

First of all, in the new nation "laws, customs, cities, all bear the French imprint." So, up to a certain point Haiti is French. A controversial Haitian intellectual, under the pseudonym of D'Ussol, a century later, will restate this idea more frankly to argue that "Haiti does not have literature, and it could not have a national literature." Indeed, according to Gouraige on February 5, 1905, in *Haïti littéraire et sociale*, D'Ussol wrote: "all [the] essential features [of a national literature] are missing in Haiti. Our language is French, French are our customs, our ideas, and whether we want it or not, French is our soul!"[22]

Second, the Proclamation seems to say that the French presence in Haiti is incompatible with the independence of the nation, or at least constitutes a threat for Haitian Independence and liberty. That is a first reading of this huge question: *"There are French in our island, and you believe yourself to be free and independent?"* But there is another more complex reading, and it may be more in line with Dessalines' thoughts. In my opinion, what Dessalines/Boisrond-Tonnerre, and especially Dessalines, wanted to say here is that one cannot accept on Haitian soil citizens who are not Haitians, or worse who are white colonizers and proslavery advocates. This reading finds its foundations in the first truly Haitian Constitution of 1805, which stipulates in its "Preliminary Declaration" (article 14): "Any distinction of colour or race among the children of one and same family, of whom the chief of the State is the father, being necessarily to cease, the Haitians shall henceforth be known only by the generic appellation of Blacks." And, in the same section, by its article 13, this constitution grants all rights of Haitian citizenship to "white women naturalized by the government," and their children, as well as the "Germans and Polish naturalized by the government."[23]

Moreover, one can argue that Dessalines, and especially Boisrond-Tonnerre, who was associated in France with the (antislavery) radical Jacobins, whatever the hesitations of some agents of Revolutionary France, knew well the debt of the Haitian to the French Revolution of 1789. It is clearly what Tertulien Guilbaud (1856–1937) stated in his poem, "Dix-huit cent quatre" (1881), when, highlighting the foundations of such paradoxical relations, he wrote:

> Your unbeaten soldiers, invincible soldiers,
> France! we have defeated them!
>
> .   .   .   .   .   .   .   .   .   .   .
>
> If cruel oppressors have come to us from your shores,
> What do we not owe to your divine thinkers?
> Our victory is also yours.
> . . . if our warriors had, to confront the horror of deadly cannons
> Such a disdain for death and this proud audacity,
> It is because they knew how to sing the proud Marseillaise![24]

Briefly, in those lines by Guilbaud, we have to stress two points: first, the Haitian Indigenous Army defeated the French invincible soldiers (*Your unbeaten soldiers, . . . France, we defeated them*). Second, according to Guilbaud, this Haitian victory is also a French victory (*Our victory, it is also yours*), for the Haitian soldiers sang the national French anthem, *La Marseillaise,* and more broadly, Haitians have a debt to great French thinkers. Indeed, what was true in 1803 at Vertières was still true in 1881, and even today, for the Haitian flag, motto, and symbol are all borrowed or derived from the French Revolution. Indeed, the fidelity of the Haitian Republic to the French Revolution was so deep that, as Jean-François Brière noted, "Under the Restoration, the Haitian Republic thus remained the only country in the world to use the emblems of the French Revolution. In 1826, the government of Charles X, deeply irritated by this, demanded that the Haitian authorities stop sending correspondence on letterhead showing the Phrygian cap and the motto 'Liberty-Equality.'"[25] President Boyer promised to use only plain paper, instead of changing the Haitian emblem and motto, one should add.

I could multiply the evidence of praise for the Revolution in the nineteenth century, but it would be more tiresome than efficient. So, let us recall with Berrou and Pompilus that up to the development of Romanticism in Haiti after 1860, patriotic poetry was still alive, as indicated by book titles such as *Patrie* (1885) by Tertulien Guilbaud (1856–1937), *Poésies nationales* (1892) by Massillon Coicou (1867–1908), and also poems like "Dessalines" by Ignace Nau (1808–1845), or more eloquently the last quatrain of "Épopée des aïeux" (1900) by Oswald Durand (1840–1906).[26] In those lines, the national bard of Haitian beauties shows himself to be both a great poet and a passionate patriot. He writes:

> This is the *bloody* epic of our elders
> My voice, in order to sing it, cries and roars in vain
> I would need the lute of the divine blind man
> Or Dante's quill dipped in pure *blood*!
>
> (my translation; italics, my emphasis)

Again, we have here a clear recognition of European influence on Haitian life, mainly through the use of European poetics, but also a clear commitment to Haitian patriotic rhetorical tradition, for the last line of the poem is a rewriting by metaphorical and metonymical shifts of the very famous (or maybe infamous) request by Boisrond-Tonnerre to use *white blood as ink, and a bayonet as a pen to write the Independence Act.* We also see the repetition of a key word in the Gonaïves Proclamation, *sang* (blood) and its derivative, *sanglante* (bloody).

This impassioned rhetoric is not only a feature of nineteenth-century Haitian poetry; it also shapes the theater, in which a great number of the plays borrow their argument from national history, as indicated by some very evocative titles such as *Nehri* (ca. 1812?), the anagram of Henri, King Christophe, by Juste Chanlatte, a drama praising the victory of Haitian troops over the French Army, which inspired "the love of independence and the horror of European tyranny," according to Hérard Dumesle in his *Voyage au Nord d'Haïti,* quoted by Vaval;[27] *La Fille de l'Empereur* (1860) by Liautaud Éthéart (1826–1888), which dramatizes the tragic love affair of Dessalines' daughter, Célimène, with the captain Chancy; *La Dernière nuit de Toussaint Louverture* (1877) by Alcibiade Pommayrac (1844–1908), a short verse monologue of twenty pages in its first edition, according to Bissainthe,[28] of Toussaint's last night; *1804* (ca. 1896) by Vendenasse Ducasse; and *Liberté* (1894) by Massillon Coicou. Indeed according to Robert Cornevin, from whom I mainly borrow the abstracts of those plays, almost half of Haitian dramas published between 1804 and 1915 are historical, and Anna Paola Mossetto is right to speak of an "obsession with history in Haitian theater."[29]

Since most of those dramas were unpublished, or are difficult to find, it is almost impossible to analyze them as a whole, or even any large number of them. But the few of them available today, such as *Toussaint au Fort du Joux* (1896) by Vendenesse Ducasse[30] and *Ogé ou le préjugé de couleur* (1841) by Pierre Faubert (1803–1868),[31] highlight the magnanimity and greatness of the fighters for Haitian Independence in contrast to the brutality and savagery of the colonists; or the cupidity and perfidy of Napoléon and his generals in contrast to the dignity of the Haitian heroes, as clearly expressed in the last words of Toussaint in Ducasse's play: "A bas les égorgeurs, VIVE L'INDEPENDANCE!" (Down with the cut-throats, LONG LIVE INDEPENDENCE),[32] or in *Ogé*, by Faubert, the rigorous and fair trial of the white planters by the colored people in contrast to the parody of justice of the colonists toward the mulatto insurgents.[33] In a way, both dramas replicate (duplicate) Dessalines' Proclamation, and King Christophe's *Manifesto*, which is more graphic in its description of the crimes perpetrated by the French expeditionary army in Saint-Domingue and by the colonist slaveowners in general. Indeed, this latter document is probably the one, which, for the first time, emblematized Rochambeau, the son of the famous general who led French troops in the American War of Independence, as a "monstrous agent of Bonaparte [who] surpassed in cruelty the most accomplished villains of ancient or modern times . . . [and] invented a new machine of destruction, in which victims of both sexes, heaped upon one another, were suffocated wholesale amidst sulfur smoke." Moreover, adds the *Manifesto,* "In his insensitive rage, he procured from Cuba, at a great expense, human blood-hounds, . . . and the human race was delivered to be devoured by dogs that will partake of the frightful immortality of their masters."[34] This last scene was voiced loudly by Wendell Phillips in his famous 1861 lecture, "Toussaint L'Ouverture," then rewritten by C. R. L. James, *Black Jacobins* and Carpentier, *The Kingdom of This World,* among others.

Since the first quarter of the twentieth century, Haitian poetry has tried, even up to a certain point managed, to move away from patriotism, mainly with the so-called *poètes de la Ronde,* a group of young intellectuals united around the journal *La Ronde* (1898–1902); and later on in the 1960s–1970s, with the poets of *Haïti littéraire* like Davertige (1940–2004), Jean-Richard Laforest, and Serge Legagneur, who reacted against the hegemonic indigenous discourse of the 1930s–1950s.[35] In contrast, Haitian theater in French was significantly patriotic up to the end of the twentieth century. Authors of different perspectives or backgrounds continue to find inspiration for their dramas in the pre-Colombian, colonial, or revolutionary eras. To name a few: the playwright and historian Verniaud Leconte (1866–1932), who praises Christophe in his *Le Roi Christophe* (1901); Charles Moravia (1876–1938), who evokes the war's decisive historical battle in *La Crête-à-Pierrot* (1908); Isnardin Vieux (1865–1914), who in *Mackendal* (1925) portrays the legendary chief of the maroons (whose name is now part of vodou mythology, and the literature of French Louisiana, with the novel, *Le Macandal: Épisode de l'insurrection des noirs à St. Domingue* [1892] by Tante Marie); Marcel Dauphin (1910–1982), whose *Boisrond-Tonnerre* (1954) recalls for us a key figure of Haitian Independence; the poet and diplomat Jean F. Brierre (1909–1992), who raises the issues of Haitian and French relationships with *Adieu à la Marseillaise* (1955), or the prolific historian Hénock Trouillot who, in response to Massion Coicou's play on the Emperor, dramatizes the destiny of this founding figure in *Dessalines, ou le Sang du Pont-Rouge* (1967).

The tradition of borrowing arguments or stories from the Haitian Revolutionary era is so well rooted in the Haitian theatrical tradition that, even the poet René Philoctète (1932–1995), one of the thinkers of the experimental Haitian literary movement, "spiralism," framed what he called his "best play," *Monsieur de Vastey* (1975), in the historical kingdom of Henri Christophe in order to target the Duvalier regime without naming it.[36] Similarly, in 1974, in order to discuss the political situation in Haiti, the former New York–based Haitian Avant Garde theater group, Kouidor, produced its reading of the assassination of Dessalines, *Quelle mort tua l'Empereur?* (What death did kill the Emperor?) And it is amazing to note that to write, from New York in Haitian language, his critical account of Haitian history, *Ti difé boulé sou istoua Ayiti* (1977), Michel-Rolph Trouillot borrows the popular theatrical form of storytelling. Thus, up to a certain point, he reinforces the idea that, for Haitians, their history cannot be *narrated*, only acted or dramatized. It is interesting to note that performance and theater are also central in what is probably the single Haitian novel about Dessalines, *L'Année Dessalines* (1986), by the Franco-Haitian physician and prolific writer Jean Métellus, who is a very preeminent figure of the commitment to this tradition of patriotic historical theater, or the theatricalization or dramatization of the Haitian past. As Ginette Adamson notes, Métellus "consciously conceived a great project to show [Haitian] History"[37] with a set of plays, which dramatizes all periods of the Haitian past from the pre-Columbian era to the post-independence Haiti: *Anacaona* (1986), *Le Pont Rouge* (1991), *Colomb* (1992), *Toussaint Louverture* (2003), *Henri le Cacique* (2005).

The essay genre also does not escape this patriotic fever. On the one hand, generally, the books are replies to the detractors of Haiti or the black race, as in the 665 pages of *De l'égalité des races humaines: anthropologie positive* (1885) by Anténor Firmin (1850–1911), which is precisely a refutation of the racist thesis of Arthur de Gobineau (1816–1882) in his *Essai sur l'inégalité des races humaines* (1853). At this time, Firmin's book was probably the unique monograph of its scope on this very sensitive issue of racial equality, one that Carolyn Fluehr-Lobban, in her introduction to the English translation, *The Equality of the Human Races* (2000), compares favorably with E. B. Tylor's *Anthropology* (1881). We can also recall the 636 pages of *La République d'Haïti et ses visiteurs* (1883) by Louis-Joseph Janvier (1855–1911); or the 736 pages of *De la réhabilitation de la race noire* (1900) by Hannibal Price (1841–1893).

Up to a certain point, those works repeat the dialogic rhetoric of the Gonaïves Proclamation around the opposition *We* (Haitians or blacks) / *You* (colonists or whites), reversing the opposition barbarian (savage) / civilized in favor of the Haitians, even though they attribute to Europe in some cases a great part of civilization, which it must share with Africans or others. But this plea for sharing the "enlightenment" of civilization with Africa, and other lands of the savage world (including some parts of Europe), is of course indissociable from the vigorous condemnation of colonization, and especially slavery which, according to Baron de Vastey, has just one goal: to abuse people for profit, that is, enrich the colonists and their allies in Europe at the expense of the colonized people (Africans, Native Americans, and so on).[38]

This literary polemical tradition, this commitment to a literature of ideas, rooted in the French lampoonist revolutionary tradition, goes back to the Gonaïves Proclamation, and more particularly to the *Manifesto of the King,* and the *Système colonial dévoilé* (1814) by Baron de Vastey, which was echoed in the twentieth-century Caribbean by writers like C. L. R. James, Frantz Fanon (1925–1961), René Depestre, and Aimé Césaire. For example, the long list of colonial horrors drawn by Baron de Vastey foreshadows Fanon's testimonial rhetoric in his presentation of four series of mental-health problems in colonized Algeria, "Guerre coloniale et troubles mentaux," (Colonial war and mental disorders) in *Les Damnés de la terre* (1961),[39] and Fanon's famous chapter title, "l'Algérie se dévoile" in *L'An V de la révolution algérienne* (1959), recalls the Baron's *Le Système colonial dévoilé*. Of course, at first glance, Fanon's title, "l'Algérie se dévoile" (Algeria unveiled),[40] refers to the Islamic veil, but it seems obvious to me that Fanon employs also the verb "dévoiler" (to unveil) in the metaphorical sense of "to reveal," "to unmask," which is the meaning of Baron de Vastey's title, "the colonial system unveiled." This reading of the Fanonian title is as important, or even more important, than the first one of the unveiled Algerian women. For this unveiling is awakening and revelation, particularly of the incredible capacity of the women of Algeria to fight. Above all, it is this fight for independence, for freedom, which is the object of this work, as is apparent from its original title, *L'An V de la révolution algérienne* (The fifth year of the Algerian Revolution), which is probably less evident from the English title, *A Dying Colonialism*.[41]

In addition, some of the key expressions (or their derivatives) of Césaire's negritude were already part of Baron de Vastey's vocabulary: "l'homme noir" (the black man), "nos frères africains" (our African brothers), "la civilisation de l'Afrique" (the civilization of Africa), "système colonial" (colonial system), "liberté" (liberty), and so on and so forth. Saying that does not imply that Fanon or even Césaire, with certainty, read the Baron's works. But one cannot avoid seeing the similarities between Baron de Vastey's, Fanon's, and Césaire's texts, as Chris Bongie, among others, has pointed out.[42]

On the other hand, the Haitian literature of the nineteenth century is quite dominated by historical books, or essays on Haitian history and politics. Moreover, this last category of works has probably encompassed the most considerable, and even the most famous and impressive Haitian books. According to a foreign commentator at this time, Edgard La Selve, who published the first monograph on Haitian writings, with the second half of the nineteenth century the Golden Age of Haitian literature started, especially with three genial historians Thomas Madiou, Beaubrun Ardouin, Céligny Ardouin.[43] Indeed, how could one not be impressed by the eleven volumes of *Études sur l'histoire d'Haïti* (1853–60) by Beaubrun Ardouin (1796–1865) or the three tomes of *Histoire d'Haïti* (1847) by Thomas Madiou (1814–1884)?

But, with the exception of the allegorical novel by Émeric Bergeaud (1818–1858), *Stella* (1859), which is the very first in Haitian literature but never really accepted as a "true Haitian novel" by contemporary Haitian criticism, mainly because it is not a realistic account,[44] and two or three short stories, there is no Haitian fictional narrative of the Revolution in the nineteenth century. The few novels published in volume are rather *exotic,* focused on "European characters and spaces." On the other hand, if the novel of the twentieth century describes Haiti and Haitians, it not historical at all. The works where the Haitian Revolution or the colonial period are narrated or even evoked are rare. The very few titles we can retrace never really had a prominent status in the Haitian canon, neither *La Danse sur le volcan* (1957) by Marie Chauvet (1916–1973), translated into English (*Dance on the Volcano,* 1959) and published in both languages by important French and American publishers (Plon and W. Sloan Associates); nor *L'Année Dessalines* by Jean Métellus, also published by a great Parisian imprint, Gallimard (1986); nor *Aube tranquille* (1990) by Jean-Claude Fignolé, published by le Seuil; and even less *Le Vieux piquet* (1884) by Louis-Joseph Janvier (1855–1911) or *Mémoires d'une affranchie* (1989) by Ghislaine Charlier. Indeed, those books received very little attention, in some cases no attention at all. For example, of some twenty articles about Chauvet's work listed on the MLA Bibliography online on September 5, 2006, only one of them tackles *Dance on the Volcano,* which, at its release, was reviewed in *The New York Times.*[45] In fact, since 1959, only Anne Marty and Lucienne J. Serrano seem to have analyzed this text.[46] As for *L'Année Dessalines* by Métellus, only two articles comment on it; if Charlier's novel is dealt with in part of a chapter of *Framing Silence* by Myriam Chancy,[47] it has not really been studied elsewhere. In all the cases, it is obvious that Haitian criticism is rather silent on these works. One very rare exception is a recent article by Marie-Denise Shelton on Haitian women's historical novels."[48]

However, one must recognize that historians of Haitian literature did not pay attention to the absence of the Revolutionary war's memory in Haitian fiction, nor did they wait for my demonstration to take the first day of Haiti's independence as the starting point of Haitian literature, the frontier between national literary production of Haiti by Haitians and non-national literary production of Saint-Domingue, whether the works are by whites, mulattoes, or blacks. On this issue, the Haitian choice of the postindependence era, or Haitianness, as the key factor in the recognition or canonization of an author is very different from those of Quebec or the French Antilles, where colonial production is part of the national literature. On the other hand, it seems that up to now nobody has studied the Gonaïves Proclamation in relation to Haitian literature, or more precisely, how this speech prefigured a great part of the Haitian corpus of the nineteenth and twentieth centuries and also forecasted the country's forthcoming disasters. But after all, this is not the most important point.

On the contrary, to me the really uncanny fact that needs explanation is the duplication or reproduction, at least partially, in Haitian fiction of the Dessalinian discursive model, which is a tragic discourse like Haitian narrative, even though the figure of General-in-Chief or Emperor, who is the very first tragic figure of Haitian history, as well as other characters of the Revolution, is rather absent from those narratives which I call the novels of Haitian tradition.[49] Nevertheless those historical figures are very present, even omnipresent in other literary genres as well as in other artistic expressions, like painting or sculpture (see "The Square of the Unknown Maroon" in Port-au-Prince), and widespread in everyday Haitian discourse, as attested by a very common expression like *"lwa Desalin li monte l"* (he is ridden or driven by Dessalines' spirit), which is used to say that someone reacts very strongly.

Why such an absence of the Revolutionary or the colonial past in Haitian fiction through the centuries? That is the question.

My first guess was to argue that to some extent, for Haitian writers, the colonial as well as the so-called postcolonial question does not entirely make sense in their history. It may be that the postindependence "massacre of French slaveowners" has played the role of a collective psychoanalysis liberating the national memory from the slave-colonial trauma, present-day struggles becoming more relevant than past glories or miseries. Indeed, to some extent, since the alma mater Africa shared the responsibility of the slave trade with Europe, slavery's memory goes beyond the era of colonization, and of white or European domination—we have only to think about the zombi myth and the famous Haitian proverb "Negroes are eating Negroes since Africa." But, above all, the passage from colonial slavery to indigenous *tyranny,* from white masters to negro rulers, from slavery to zombification, from maroons to "cacos," "piquets," "zobop," or even present-day so-called "chimères" (thugs), created a huge never-ending struggle for power, which monopolizes all Haitian resources and, of course, all narratives from the most common *lodyans* to the more innovative novel through quite effective *télédyòl* or other popular narratives like *Bouki's stories.*[50]

Now, let us go back to our argument about the absence of revolutionary and colonial memories in Haitian novels. First of all, I must confess that as eloquent as my previous explanation could be, it is not entirely relevant, for it cannot explain why Haitian writers feature or recall the Revolutionary plot in their plays. Or why Haitian painters used to portray heroes of the Independence, or sensitive sites of this glorious past. So, I had to revise my hypothesis, review my analysis. Now I think that even though the urgency of the contemporary Haitian situation forced Haitian novelists to avoid or erase the Revolutionary war narrative or the colonial slavery past in their books, there is a more imperative and relevant reason that explains why there are very few novels framed in the Revolutionary era (1791–1820); it is the Haitian narrative tradition per se.

Indeed, the Haitian narrative (oral or written) is a tragic narrative, hence it does not allow for the narration of an epic story like that of the Haitian Independence. Moreover this Haitian narrative tradition implies a kind of implicit or explicit dialogue between all instances of the narration (narrator, narratee, and characters), who must share some common knowledge about the story (locations, characters, etc.), which is an account of and for their present time. So, it is clear that the Revolution as well as the colonial era are too distant, and above all, slaves, heroes, and independent Haitian citizens no longer shared the same concerns. Since complicity or even a common "identity" of all instances of the narration is an important feature of Haitian narrative tradition, how could the story of those slave or heroic ancestors be narrated or fictionalized? The task is impossible, incompatible with Haitian narrative structure, and that is probably why, compared to theater—which is mostly dramatic with the tragic figures of Toussaint, Dessalines, Christophe, Ogé—we have very few novels of the colonial or Revolutionary era in Haiti.

Finally, we must add that the Haitian novelistic tradition is also a realist one. For example, one has only to recall the very Balzacian surtitle of Fernand Hibbert's novels, *Scènes de la vie haïtienne* (Scenes of Haitian life). Hence, it is more focused on the present time of narration than the past. Its very realistic or testimonial nature, like other French Caribbean novels, should also explain its reluctance to tackle the colonial or the Revolutionary past, unless in the manner of Jean Métellus (*L'Année Dessalines*) or Jean-Claude Fignolé (*Aube tranquille*), and its tendency to look at them through the lens of current events or contemporary characters. Indeed, we can see some similarities with French Caribbean writers who also have not narrated or fictionalized the glorious Haitian past, but have dramatized it in some very well-known plays like *Monsieur Toussaint* by Glissant, *The Tragedy of King Christophe* by Césaire, or *Dessalines* by Placoly. Now, in contrast, in so many great novels like Simone Schwarz-Bart's *Pluie et vent sur Télumée Miracle* (1979; *The Bridge of Beyond*, 1974), Daniel Maximin's *L'Isolé, Soleil* (1981; *Lone Sun*, 1989), Edouard Glissant's *La Case du commandeur* (1981), Maryse Condé's *Moi, Tituba, sorcière . . . noire de Salem* (1986; *I, Tituba, Black*

*Witch of Salem,* 1992), French Caribbean writers narrate their own colonial fights, their own colonial past, which is also a present, for to some extent the French Antilles are still a colony (a modern colony, but a colony). But another literary question remains: why in this first decade of the twenty-first century, do Haitian writers seem to be interested in fictionalizing their colonial or Revolutionary memories? Why now are so many Haitian novels set in the Revolutionary era, like *La Deuxième mort de Toussaint-Louverture* by Fabienne Pasquet (2001), *Rosalie l'infâme* by Evelyne Trouillot (2003), or *Moi, Toussaint Louverture . . . avec la plume complice de l'auteur* by Jean-Claude Fignolé (2004)?

I would venture a quick, provisional answer as follows: the post-Duvalierism trauma with the very long and painful transition to "democracy," the pressure of the independence bicentennial, and so on, could be one key reason. So, we can say that the narration does take place in a context of proximity, of immediacy, of burning issues, as a response to an emergency or a crisis. Indeed, not so far from the oral situation of *lodyans* or *teledyòl* performances. But that is speculation, hypothesis for the sake of dialogue. What is sure is the real impact of this revolution and its discourse on all kinds of Haitian texts, and beyond Haiti on a great number of important writers of the Americas (*Nuestra América,* to recall José Martí's title): Carpentier, Césaire, Faulkner, James, O'Neill, Phillips, Beecher Stowe, Derek Walcott, to name a few. On the other hand, what matters also is how this revolution introduced into the French-speaking world a new significance to words like "Indépendence" and "Liberté." For if "Independence" as a political act and word found its English roots in the American Revolution, it is only with the Haitian Revolution that it becomes a political paradigm in French, and we can say that Boisrond-Tonnerre/Dessalines coined it on the first day of January 1804 in the city of Gonaïves, at the same time they truly universalized the word "Liberty": two key concepts of our time.

### Notes

1. See, among others, Susan Belasco, "Harriet Martineau's Black Hero and the American Antislavery Movement."

2. See Daniel-Henri Pageaux, *Images et Mythes d'Haïti,* 11–25, 61–80, 84–98; Aimé Césaire, *Cahier d'un retour au pays natal,* edited, with introduction, commentary, and notes, by Abiola Irele (2000), 73–75, note 45.

3. For more bio-bibliographical data on Haitian writers and statesmen studied or cited here, see Raphaël Berrou and Pradel Pompilus, *Histoire de la littérature haïtienne;* Daniel Supplice, *Dictionnaire biographique.* For the other

francophone Caribbean writers and intellectuals, see Île en île: http://www
.lehman.cuny.edu/ile.en.ile/antilles/index.html; Jacques Corzani, *La Littérature
des Antilles-Guyane;* Auguste Viatte, *Histoire littéraire de l'Amérique française.*
All URLs cited in this essay were last verified on 2 May 2007.

4. Alain Baudot, "Antilles et Guyane," in *Guide culturel,* 196–97.

5. Henri Christophe, "The Manifesto of the King," in *Haytian Papers,*
115–32.

6. See Berrou and Pompilus, *Histoire de la littérature haïtienne,* vol. 1, 62–67;
Frères de l'Instruction chrétienne, *Manuel illustré d'histoire de la littérature haïtienne.* Both documents, the Proclamation of Gonaïves as well as the Independence Act,
are available online, in French at http://www.upmf-grenoble.fr/Haiti/Dessalines
.htm; in English translation at http://www.geocities.com/CapeCanaveral/9972/
independ.htm (The Proclamation), and at http://thelouvertureproject.org/wiki/
index.php?title=Act_of_Independence (Independence Act). All my quotes in English of those texts are borrowed from those translations.

7. On this "specific" Haitian form, see Jean Jonassaint, *Des romans de tradition haïtienne,* 130–32, 220–24.

8. See Ghislain Gouraige, *Histoire de la littérature haïtienne,* 91; Robert
Cornevin, *Le Théâtre haïtien,* 116.

9. See Jonassaint, *Des romans,* 130–63.

10. Jacques Stephen Alexis, *General Sun, My Brother,* 4–5; the small caps
are mine, but the italics are not. For the original French version of this passage,
see *Compère Général Soleil,* 9–10.

11. VèVè A. Clark, "Haiti's Tragic Ouverture," 240.

12. Gouraige, *Histoire,* 14 (my translation).

13. Juste Chanlatte, "Cantate à l'Indépendance," in Berrou and Pompilus,
*Histoire,* vol. 1, 26–29.

14. See Gouraige, *Histoire,* 13–16, and *Les Meilleurs poètes et romanciers
haïtiens.*

15. See David Nicholls, "Pompée Valentin Vastey: Royalist and Revolutionary"; Baron de Vastey, *An Essay on the Causes of the Revolution and Civil Wars
of Hayti* and *Reflections on the Blacks and Whites.*

16. Chanlatte, "Cantate," 27.

17. Antoine Dupré, "Hymne à la liberté," and Jean-Baptiste Romane,
"Hymne à l'Indépendance," in Berrou and Pompilus, *Histoire,* vol. 1, 20–22;
52–53.

18. Edgard La Selve, *Histoire de la littérature haïtienne,* 45 (my translation).

19. See Ertha Pascal Trouillot and Ernst Trouillot, *Encyclopédie biographique
d'Haïti,* vol. 1, 124–25.

20. See Baron de Vastey, *Le Système colonial dévoilé,* 95–96.

21. Jean-François Brière, "Abbé Grégoire and Haitian Independence," 34.

22. Gouraige, *Histoire,* 165 (my translation).

23. See 1805 Constitution: http://web.upmf-grenoble.fr/Haiti/Dessalines.htm (French); http://www.webster.edu/~corbetre/haiti/history/earlyhaiti/1805-const.htm (English).

24. Tertulien Guilbaud, "Dix-huit cent quatre," in Berrou and Pompilus, *Histoire*, vol. 1, 406–9 (my translation).

25. Brière, "Abbé Grégoire and Haitian Independence," 38.

26. Ignace Nau, "Dessalines," and Oswald Durand, "Épopée des aïeux," in Berrou and Pompilus, *Histoire*, vol. 1, 129–30, 359–61.

27. Duracinée Vaval, *Histoire de la littérature haïtienne*, 244.

28. See Max Bissainthe, *Dictionnaire de bibliographie haïtienne* 283, notices 3520–21.

29. See: Robert Cornevin, *Le Théâtre haïtien*, 253–54, 260–69; Anna Paola Mossetto, "Pour ne pas perdre son ombre," 49–63.

30. This play is mostly known under this title, *Toussaint au Fort du Joux,* but it was published more than fifty years after the death of Ducasse under the title of the manuscript, which is, according to the publisher, *Fort de Joux: les derniers moments de Toussaint Louverture.*

31. For a detailed analysis of this play, see Anna Brickhouse, "The Writing of Haiti: Pierre Faubert, Harriet Beecher Stowe, and Beyond."

32. Ducasse, *Fort de Joux*, 36.

33. See Pierre Faubert, *Ogé, ou le préjugé de couleur,* 71–83, 101–4, 109–13.

34. Henri Christophe, *Manifeste du Roi,* 11–12; "Manifesto of the King," 171–72.

35. See Davertige, *Idem et autres poèmes;* Jean-Richard Laforest, *Le Divan des alternances;* Serge Legagneur, *Textes interdits* and *Textes en croix.*

36. See René Philoctète, *Callaloo* interview, 623–27.

37. See Ginette Adamson, "Jean Métellus ou l'écrivain en partage," 369–70.

38. See Baron de Vastey, *Le Système,* 11–18.

39. See Frantz Fanon, *The Wretched of the Earth,* 249–310; Baron de Vastey, *Le Système,* 39–62.

40. See Frantz Fanon, *A Dying Colonialism,* 35–67.

41. This radical change of perspective in Fanon's title translates the tendency of Anglo-American scholars and intellectuals to look at the Third World or the South from the colonizer or colonial perspective, as it is expressed at its best (or its worst) by the wide-spread term "postcolonial," instead of "postindependence" as in French. Moreover, the last two paragraphs of the appendix to this chapter are very clear on this point:

> The woman's place in Algerian society is indicated with such vehemence that the occupier's confusion is readily understandable. This is because Algerian society *reveals itself* [my emphasis] not to be the womanless society that had been so convincingly described.

Side by side with us, our sisters do their part in further breaking down the enemy system and in liquidating the old mystifications once and for all. (Fanon, *A Dying Colonialism,* 67)

42. See Chris Bongie, "Monotonies of History," 77–80.

43. See La Selve, *Histoire,* 58–59.

44. *Stella* is a fictional account of the Haitian independence war featuring five highly symbolic characters: Le Colon (the colonizer); two brothers, a black and a mulatto, Romulus and Rémus; their mother, a slave woman, L'Africaine (the African); and the "white" Stella, a "divine force," very instrumental in the fight of Romulus and Rémus for Liberty. For more details on this work, see Léon-François Hoffmann, "The First Haitian Novel: Émeric Bergeaud's Stella," in his *Haitian Fiction Revisited,* 213–27.

45. Review by Judith Quehl, *New York Times,* January 18, 1959, p. BR31.

46. Anne Marty, "Naturelles correspondances," 76–79; Lucienne J. Serrano, "La Dérive du plaisir," 95–113.

47. See Myriam Chancy, *Framing Silence,* 72–103.

48. Marie-Denise Shelton, "L'écriture de l'histoire," 71–81.

49. Indeed, as in the Greek tragedies or in the novels of Haitian tradition, Dessalines in his Proclamation of Gonaïves forecasts a "fatal loss" (Aristotle's "change of fortune from good to bad"), which is a prospective narrative (of his assassination), but also, and that is the *tragic,* a caution, a warning or, better, a *mise en garde* to the Haitian people ("And you, people who have been disadvantaged for so long , . . . if for whatever reason you refused . . . you would deserve the fate of ungrateful peoples"). Such a *mise en garde,* with its counterpart, the *mise au point* (clarification or explanation of the denouement) are the main features of the tragic narratives. See Jonassaint, *Des romans,* 167–275.

50. *Lodyans:* a story about someone who is quite well known by the witness narrator and the audience. *Télédyòl:* a kind of widespread political or social rumor to harm someone in power. *Bouki's stories:* a popular series of tales about a loser who seems to represent the fellow Haitians.

# "The First Epic of the New World"

## But How Shall It Be Written?

*Paul Breslin*

WHEN AIMÉ CÉSAIRE, during an interview with René Depestre, said that "The first epic of the New World was written by black Haitians, Toussaint, Dessalines, and Christophe,"[1] he used the word "epic" in its colloquial sense, figuratively equating action with writing. But, as Césaire well knew, events do not write themselves, and those who write them inevitably intervene by selecting and arranging incidents, framing events in available narrative patterns. For the writer confronting the Caribbean past, whether as an historian, novelist, playwright, or poet, narration—never a simple matter under any circumstances—becomes additionally vexed. For the experience to be represented is, by the testimony of Caribbean writers themselves, especially resistant both to mnemonic recovery and formal narrative shape.

### In Theory: The Obstacles to Representation

#### *The Trouble with Epic*

One might begin with the genre evoked by Césaire, turning from its colloquial to its literary sense. As David Quint argues, epic has been associated with the celebration of victorious empire, and its narrative conventions cannot be fully disentangled from this theme:

> Epic draws an equation between power and narrative. It tells of a power able to end the indeterminacy of war and to emerge victorious, showing that the struggle had all along been leading up to its victory and thus imposing upon it a narrative teleology. . . . The epic victors both project their present power prophetically into the future and trace its legitimating origins back into the past. . . . [T]he ability to construct narratives that join beginnings purposefully to end is already the sign and dispensation of power.[2]

On the other pan of the scale, "epic's losers," "the enemies of empire," can only "embody a potential, indeed inevitable, collapse of narrative." The confident plotting of epic teleology dissolves into "endless war" or "the circuitous wanderings of romance." Indeed, "from the perspective of epic, romance is a narrative representation of the nonnarratable." And yet, the epic of the victors includes the counter-narrative of wandering and chaos: "the epic narrative projects episodes of suspension and indirection in order that it may overcome them and demonstrate its ultimately teleological form. When these episodes expand or multiply to disrupt narrative unity and closure, epic may be suspected of going over to the side of the losers, as it does in the anti-Virgilian poems of Lucan and his successors."[3] In this accounting, every Virgil contains (almost in the Cold-War sense of the word) a pent-up Lucan, every epic its suppressed doppelgänger, romance.

Quint makes two observations about the "losers' epic" that prove suggestive for the plays considered here: that it dwells on the imagery of ruins, and that it veers toward the conventions of romance, with an emphasis on geographical displacement and questing, travel. Walcott, in his essay "What the Twilight Says,"[4] figuratively compares Jean-Jacques Dessalines and Henri Christophe to ruins, alluding to Christophe's Citadel at Ferriere: "Their tragic bulk was massive as a citadel at twilight. They were our only noble ruins." In commenting on his own quasi-epic *Omeros* (1990), which evokes yet finally disavows epic parallels to Caribbean experience, he would later speak of *The Odyssey* as "the story of some man who wandered around." Epic, to be viable, must be extricated from its implications of a triumphal march to a "manifest destiny" and adapt itself to engagement with historical damage (ruins) and displacement (wandering around).[5]

If we accept Quint's hypothesis that epic tells the story from the point of view of victory and romance from the standpoint of defeat, which narrative belongs to the Haitian Revolution? In one respect, the Revolution was an astonishing victory, unique in recorded history: a revolt in which slaves overthrew their masters and created an independent state. But we all know that the story since 1804 has not been a happy one, and to read Michel-Rolph Trouillot's *Haiti: State against Nation* is to become painfully aware of how the totalitarianism of the Duvalierist state was "an outcome—albeit not an inevitable one—of [the] nation's historical evolution."[6] Alex Dupuy, in his paper for Northwestern's symposium on the Haitian Revolution (2004), called it a "Pyrrhic victory," which the Encarta World English Dictionary glosses, conveniently for my purposes, as "a victory won at such great cost to the victor that it is tantamount to a defeat." Formal national sovereignty has not brought political freedom or economic prosperity. Haiti is still bound—to borrow a phrase from Walcott—in its "swaddling cerements." Seen in this light, the Revolution seems less the stuff of imperial epic than matter for what Quint calls romance—or for tragedy, which is the genre Césaire explicitly assigns to his play on Henri Christophe.

## Problems of "Emplotment"

One could try to position the revolutionaries as victors by a fairly simple stratagem of what Hayden White calls "emplotment":[7] from the open-ended succession of events in chronicle, one cuts a segment, choosing the beginning and ending so as to create a narrative trajectory. So, for instance, Marie Vieux Chauvet's *Dance on the Volcano* ends with Minette's death just after the announcement of Sonthonax's proclamation of freedom for the slaves. She is able to die with a sense that her hopes have been vindicated. But as we know, and Chauvet knew, the revolutionary conflict would continue for another ten years, with much death and misery still to come; the French would restore slavery in their other colonies and were prevented from doing so in Saint-Domingue only by the combined effects of their susceptibility to yellow fever and the fierce, if hastily organized, resistance of a people no longer united behind Toussaint Louverture. One might contrast Chauvet's emplotment with Alejo Carpentier's in *The Kingdom of This World*, in which Ti-Noël, leaving Saint-Domingue in the early days of the Revolution for Santiago de Cuba, returns during the post-Revolutionary reign of Henri Christophe and, driven into forced labor on Christophe's citadel and palace, wonders why things remain so much as they were in the pre-Revolutionary regime of slavery. For Ti-Noël there has been no victory, no progress, only "this endless return of chains."[8] Even after his revelatory "lucid moment," he can say only that "a man never knows for whom he suffers and hopes" (184) and that the suffering and hoping have to be projected blindly into an uncertain future; the metamorphosed spirit of Macandal hovers as a sign of an unfinished and unfinishable aspiration.

If one looks at the emplotment in literary representations of the Revolution, what has been selected for inclusion and exclusion, one finds with surprising frequency a pattern that resembles Carpentier's in the elision of large stretches of time or seemingly crucial events. Césaire writes a play on the post-Revolutionary kingship of Henri Christophe, but deals with Toussaint in nonfictional prose. Walcott's early play *Henri Christophe:*

*A Chronicle in Seven Scenes* begins at the moment when reports of Toussaint's death reach Saint-Domingue, which signals the beginning of a disastrous plunge into unrestrained cruelties and internal division among the revolutionaries themselves. Toussaint's name reverberates through the play as the standard of morality and wisdom by which his successors are judged and found wanting. Glissant's *Monsieur Toussaint* is set entirely in the prison cell of Fort Joux, after Toussaint's actions in Saint Domingue are already finished; Langston Hughes's play *The Emperor of Haiti* presents Jean-Jacques Dessalines in the August rising of 1791, then jumps to the last days of his rule, with everything in between left out. Is it that these works present the Revolution as futile, leaving us to contemplate the gap between its promising beginnings and its unhappy aftermath? Or is the Revolution itself so disturbing, or so resistant to representation, that it can only be faced indirectly, like the reflection of Medusa in the shield of Perseus? If so, might that be a reason why so few narratives of the Haitian Revolution have been produced by Haitians, in whom whatever is disturbing in this history will cause the most pain?

## Metamorphosis of Epic

It may help in understanding these works to juxtapose Quint's account of epic with some remarks of Édouard Glissant in *The Poetics of Relation,* which offer a somewhat different way of conceiving the relations between teleology and narrative, one that has developed from a specifically Caribbean perspective on the literary canon and the power relations of empires and their colonies. Glissant begins the essay "Expanse and Filiation" by claiming that "In the Western world the hidden cause (the consequence) of both Myth and Epic is filiation, its work setting out upon the fixed linearity of time, always toward a projection, a project."[9] By "filiation" he means the attempt to ground the legitimacy of the "projection" in a narrative of origin and continuous descent to the present and beyond, into the future. Like Quint, he sees epic as involved in the legitimation narratives of conquest or empire. In "Errantry [*Errance*], Exile," however, he observes that despite this impulse, "the great founding books of communities, the Old Testament, the *Iliad,* the *Odyssey,* the *Chansons de Geste,* the Islandic [*sic*] *Sagas,* the *Aeneid,* or the African epics, were all books about exile and often about errantry." Consequently, "within the collective books concerning the sacred and the notion of history lies the germ of the exact opposite of what they so loudly proclaim."[10] And just as Quint finds that "the absence of an organizing teleology" proposes, as the answer to the question "who has won," that "nobody wins,"[11] Glissant believes that a "modern epic and a modern tragedy" would be no longer "rooted in any specific legitimacy," but rather "directed toward a continuum (in expansion)."[12] Neither side's "legitimacy" triumphs; instead, the continuing results of their encounter, intextricably mingled, have to be represented without the armature of an organizing master-plot.

If we think of epic's mutations in twentieth-century British and American literature, in the hands of writers as diverse as Ezra Pound, H. D., W. C. Williams, Hart Crane, James Joyce, Basil Bunting, or Charles Olson, to name just a few, one already finds an attenuation or dissolution of narrative linearity, and with it a less confident assertion of ideological commitments (even in those such as Pound with a fatal attraction to ideological vehemence). So in this respect, Caribbean quasi-epics such as Césaire's *Notebook of a Return to the Native Land*, Walcott's *Omeros*, Glissant's *The Indies*, or Brathwaite's *The Arrivants* are not uniquely Caribbean in their nonlinearity. They participate in a growing skepticism about legitimation narratives, a skepticism that Glissant finds already nascent in earlier epic and tragedy. Whenever ambition for power "culminated in the thought of an empire . . . poetic thought went on the alert: beneath the fantasy of domination it sought the really livable world."[13]

Very well, then; the term "epic" can take us only so far. Few, if any, narratives of the Haitian Revolution will comfortably fit Quint's model of the winner's epic, with its projection of a legitimating teleology that extends from the moment of founding into the present and future. They may seem, at first, to comport more readily with the loser's epic, with its collapse of linear narrative into romance conventions of wandering, digression, and suspended resolution. Nonetheless, as Betsy Wing argues in defending her translation of Glissant's *"errance"* as "errantry" rather than "wandering," there is still "a sense of sacred motivation," of going *toward* something, though without the "arrowed" certainty of what the objective is that characterizes the conqueror or empire-builder. But Quint's description of epic mutating into romance when its teleology collapses helps account for what we find in narratives of the Haitian Revolution. If *errance* is more nearly "errantry" than "wandering," "errantry," as in knight-errantry, is the stuff of romance narrative. And the deferral of resolution, the frustration of linear narrative progress, describes the kinds of narrative gaps and displacements we encounter in the representations of the Revolution.

## The Caribbean Past: "Nonhistories"

To the general suspicion of tidy linear narratives in modern and postmodern literature we must add the difficulties of representation specific to the Caribbean past. One famous (though notoriously disaffected) Caribbean writer, V. S. Naipaul, has simply declared the Caribbean past unnarratable: "The story of the islands can never be satisfactorily told," he claimed in his embittered 1962 travel book, *The Middle Passage.* "Brutality is not the only difficulty. History is built around achievement and creation; and nothing was created in the West Indies."[14] The second part of his objection, to a perceived void in West Indian culture, echoes the sentiments of James Anthony Froude, whose dismissive judgment of 1887 that "there has been . . . no hero unless philonegro enthusiasm can make one out of Toussaint," and that "[t]here are no people there in the true sense of the word, with a character and purpose of their own," provides Naipaul with his epigraph.

"Brutality" may not be the only problem, but it matters. The brutality of the slavery regime on Saint-Domingue's sugar plantations, and the counter-brutality with which the rebellious slaves finally requited it, are hard to represent without indulging in the aestheticizing of violence. As an illustration, one might take a passage near the beginning of Madison Smartt Bell's *All Souls' Rising,* in which the humane Dr. Hébert, just arrived from France, happens upon a dying slave woman who, as a punishment, has been nailed naked to a post: "Pulling against the vertex of the nail, her pectoral musculature had lifted her breasts, which were taut, with large aureoles, nipples distended."[15] The clinical detachment of the diction ("vertex," "pectoral musculature") cannot quite neutralize the incipient prurience in the description. Bell's ambitious, serious trilogy of the Revolution is marred by its almost voyeuristic treatment of violence and sexual degradation. In displaying the horrors of slavery (and the counter-brutality of the revolutionaries) for the reader's shocked condemnation, Bell also invites the reader to enjoy the stylistic invention and graphic particularity lavished on these scenes, with an effect that sometimes verges on pornography.

Apart from "brutality," there is the sheer discontinuity of Caribbean history to be reckoned with. Édouard Glissant has described the Caribbean past as a "nonhistory," though unlike Naipaul, he sees the problem not as a lack of significant event, but as a result of the fact that so much of what happened was initiated by colonial power rather than the actions of Caribbeans on their own ground. As a result, "Our historical consciousnesses could not be deposited gradually and continuously like sediment, as it were . . . but came together in the context of shock, contraction, painful negation, and explosive forces. This dislocation of the continuum, and the inability of the collective consciousness to absorb it all, characterize what I call a nonhistory."[16] The most obvious example of such trauma is the Middle Passage, but further dislocations, shocks, and arbitrary dispositions of fate continued long after arrival. Consider, for instance, the divergent outcomes for Haiti, Guadeloupe, and St. Lucia after the French Assembly temporarily emancipated its colonial slaves in 1794. St. Lucia's slaves enjoyed a year of freedom (1795–96), but in May 1796 the English wrested the island from the French, at which point the re-enslaved blacks launched a guerrilla war of resistance that continued for a year and a half before they were defeated. When the French tried to restore slavery in 1802, the revolutionaries in Haiti were able to resist successfully, but the resistance of Delgrès in Guadeloupe was crushed. So after the treaty of 1814, Haiti, already independent, remained free; St. Lucia, awarded to Britain, remained enslaved till 1838; and Guadeloupe, still under French rule, had to wait for emancipation until 1848. C. L. R. James's play, *The Black Jacobins,* dramatizes one of these sudden moments of transformation dictated from across the sea. During the very meeting in which Toussaint is sealing his alliance with the Spanish, Moïse brings word of the French proclamation of emancipation. Immediately Toussaint reverses course, declares himself a loyal French subject, and takes the Spanish negotiators prisoner.[17] His sudden turnabout provides a great theatrical moment, but James has a hard time developing a through-line of plot for the entire play; he presents a sequence of short scenes, temporal cross-sections of a historical period spanning several years.

Because Glissant is considering the Caribbean past not primarily as a historian but as a writer, he is especially attuned to the challenge of nonhistories to the available resources of literary representation. Both in *Caribbean Discourse* and in his later volume, *Poetics of Relation,* he seeks alternatives to realistic, chronological narration. For experimentally inclined writers such as Glissant, narrating Caribbean history requires distancing from the chronicle-like portrayal of events in the order of their occurrence (common to epic and the realistic novel), and from the conventions of realistic fiction. Glissant meets the demand of European modernity for universal, rational transparency with a "counter-poetics" that claims "for each community the right to a shared obscurity." As a consequence of "the erasing of memory in all of us," Caribbean people, attempting to reclaim their history, "do not see it stretch into our past and calmly take us into tomorrow"; rather, "it explodes in us as compact mass, pushing through a dimension of emptiness where we must with difficulty and pain put it all *back together.*" The sense of historical relation to the world is expressed less as a linear temporal sequence than through a "language of landscape." The Caribbean writer's "quest for the dimension of time will . . . be neither harmonious nor linear. Its advance will be marked by a polyphony of dramatic shocks, at the level of the conscious as well as the unconscious, between incongruous phenomena or 'episodes' so disparate that no link can be discerned."[18]

Glissant finds the sense of temporal rupture evident in the New World imagination of space, as if landscape were petrified time. He contrasts the European "intimate relation to landscape," established over centuries of continual dwelling, to American space ("American" in the inclusive sense), which is "open, exploded, rent"; there is "something violent in" the "American sense of literary space."[19] The awareness of a disrupted history impinges with sharp immediacy on a displaced people seeking to conceive the New World environment as their home rather than a place of exile and oppression.

Wilson Harris's sense of the Caribbean landscape as a palimpsest to be examined for its almost-erased marks of past historical violence resonates with Glissant's, despite the differences between the mainland landscapes of Harris's Guyana and those of Glissant's insular Martinique, as well as the differences between anglophone and francophone Caribbean cultures. "The native and phenomenal environment of the West Indies," says Harris, "is broken into many stages in the way in which one surveys an existing river in its present course while plotting at the same time ancient and abandoned, indeterminate courses the river once followed." To "reconcile the broken parts" of the West Indian's "enormous heritage," he urges minutest attention to immediate surroundings, so that "the smallest area one envisages, island or village, prominent ridge or buried valley, flatland or heartland, is charged immediately with the openness of imagination."[20] Like Glissant, he rejects narration of the past as temporal sequence mapped by sequential narrative, instead conceiving of history as a violent, discontinuous, and opaque presence in the consciousness of each moment.

## The Haitian Revolution as "Non-event"

If, as Harris and Glissant maintain, Caribbean history in general resists narration, the Haitian Revolution presents the writer with additional difficulties of its own. Sibylle Fischer and Michel-Rolph Trouillot have remarked on the silence or, in Fischer's term, "disavowal" shrouding the Revolution in modern memory. Even now, one finds that otherwise well-educated Americans, who know something about their own revolution and the one in France, usually lack even basic knowledge of the Haitian counterpart. Some of this neglect may have to do with the lack of documentation by the revolutionaries themselves: whereas the leaders of the French and American revolutions wrote copiously and articulately, most leaders in the Haitian Revolution had been slaves, seldom gaining access to literacy. As a result, the surviving contemporary documents, apart from Toussaint's letters, are for the most part written by colonial officials or indignant French planters. But David Geggus notes that although "[t]he source material for studying the revolution is very extensive, as befits a 15-year conflict to control the most important colony of its time," it has been, at least until very recently, strangely underutilized, so that among historiographers, "the Haitian Revolution has been the subject of a great deal of writing and controversy but relatively little archival research."[21] Fischer's term, "disavowal," to be understood "both in its everyday sense as 'refusal to acknowledge,' 'repudiation,' and 'denial' (*OED*) and in its technical meaning in psychoanalytic theory as a 'refusal to recognize the reality of a traumatic perception,'" is helpful in understanding this curious avoidance. For disavowal is not the same thing as total amnesia; it entails the nagging awareness that there "is *something* that is being disavowed," so that "as Freud explains, disavowal exists alongside recognition."[22] Disavowal, then, requires an active but never quite successful attempt at forgetting, because the irritant of that which is to be suppressed keeps generating new evasive maneuvers to keep it quiet.

Michel-Rolph Trouillot, in *Silencing the Past*, insists that "silence" is not mere absence of speech, but "an active and transitive process: one 'silences' a fact or an individual as a silencer silences a gun. One engages in the process of silencing." The silencing process, he maintains, can occur at several stages of historical record-keeping: "Silences enter the process of historical production at four crucial moments: the moment of fact creation (the making of *sources*); the moment of fact assembly (the making of *archives*); the moment of fact retrieval (the making of *narratives*); and the moment of retrospective significance (the making of *history* in the final instance)."[23] It follows that silencing in early stages makes recovering that which was silenced more difficult in later stages, since what is missing may not have received any contemporary acknowledgment as a fact, or if it did, the relevant documents may not have been selected for archival preservation and organization. Trouillot argues that the inadequacy of even the most progressive Western discourse to encompass the Haitian Revolution's radical challenge to the ideological legitimations of slavery silenced it from the outset, while later developments reinforced this silencing, so that even a modern reference text such as the Larousse *Great Events of World History* (1992) omits the Haitian Revolution altogether, and even a progressive historian such as Eric Hobsbawm barely mentions it in his study, *The Age of Revolution: 1789–1848*. This silence, then, is independent of the conscious political commitments of the writer: "what we are observing here is archival power at its strongest, the power to define what is and is not a serious object of research and, therefore, of mention."[24]

Trouillot calls one of his chapters "An Unthinkable History: The Haitian Revolution as a Non-event." He observes that although progressive thinkers in Europe and America were troubled by the idea of slavery, they could never quite conceive of blacks as fully human; the idea of blacks as property, and the discourse of property rights, kept confusing the issue, resulting in incoherent compromises such as the agreement, in the United States, to count a slave as "three-fifths of a man" in determining proportional representation, or in the Haitian planters' attempt to count slaves in the census in order to acquire more seats in the French Assembly, while denying them any participation in the selection of the representatives. When slaves ran away, colonial explanations always blamed some atypical circumstance or abuse, rather than the slave's desire to escape slavery altogether. Even on the eve of the 1791 revolt, planters were writing back to France that the slaves were "tranquil and obedient," so that "[a] revolt among them is impossible." When reports came to France that the impossible had happened, "the most common reaction among interested parties was disbelief." Either the reports were false, or something other than the will of the slaves themselves had caused the events: meddlesome outsiders or poor management by the planters. The Revolution was "unthinkable even as it happened." For the most part, its ideological premises remained unthinkable and therefore "unspoken among the slaves themselves"; although they challenged "Western philosophy and colonialism" by their deeds, "the revolution was not preceded or even accompanied by an explicit intellectual discourse." In short, *the events that shook up Saint-Domingue from 1791 to 1804 constituted a sequence for which not even the extreme political left in France or in England had a conceptual frame of reference*" (Trouillot's emphasis). The ostracism of Haiti through most of the nineteenth century, and the economic and political decay partially caused by that ostracism, reinforced the initial silencing, so that finally "the revolution that was unthinkable became a non-event."[25]

Though immensely suggestive, such explorations of the Caribbean past as nonhistory and of the Haitian Revolution as nonevent tell us more about what narrative forms are inadequate to Caribbean historical narrative than about what might work, or what actually has. We would expect, from the accounts of Glissant, Harris, Fischer, and Trouillot, that accounts of the Haitian Revolution would inevitably be formally complex and opaque. Why wouldn't the retrieval of a "non-event" buried within a "non-history" demand radically experimental and challenging narrative form?

## The Desire for Simplicity

Despite all the reasons for expecting literary representations of the Revolution to be dauntingly obscure, in practice this is not the case. Glissant's own play, *Monsieur Toussaint,* is not especially difficult to follow, despite the dreamlike apparition of living and dead characters in Toussaint's prison cell; his poems are more difficult. Other well-known writings that depict the Revolution and its aftermath, by Aimé Césaire and Derek Walcott, are among their authors' relatively accessible works: compare Césaire's *The Tragedy of King Christophe* with *Notebook of a Return to the Native Land,* or any play in Walcott's *Haitian Trilogy* with *Dream on Monkey Mountain.* Marie Vieux Chauvet's *Dance on the Volcano* is a formally conventional novel, whatever the power and originality of its characterization and social insights. Even Alejo Carpentier's *The Kingdom of This World,* noted as an early instance of "magical realism," is not his most demanding book.

Although I cannot prove my hunch, my guess is that the massive cultural significance of the Haitian Revolution, its iconic role as *the* central emblem of the Caribbean quest for liberty, exerts a counterpressure on narrative toward clarity and simplicity, even as the elusiveness of the events and their significance pressures it toward tortuous indirection. The meaning of the Revolution, including both its exemplary goal and the cautionary lessons to be drawn from its bitter aftermath, have to be made legible to all, not merely to an avant-garde elite. If the difficulties of representing the Caribbean past in general, and the Haitian Revolution in particular, push toward a complication of literary form, the sense that this story, above all others, is a collective legacy pushes toward a simplification. At this point, we may circle back to Césaire's characterization of the Haitian Revolution as "the first epic of the New World." Is some form of epic, perhaps a mutant strain, viable for the narration of this event? After all, epic typically narrates a story that is the common property of a people, on which their collective identity is founded. Or, if epic is not viable, might some other form stressing the communal remain possible? It's notable how many of the well-known versions are plays: C. L. R. James and Édouard Glissant, prolific in other genres, wrote only one play each, and those plays are both about the Haitian Revolution. Walcott has written three plays on the Haitian events but no poem, though he is equally productive in both genres. If epic's communal grounding stresses the past, then that of drama stresses the present: actors present the play as if it were happening now, in front of an audience drawn from the community. It is a good choice of genre for the writer who wants to pose the question: what can this story mean to us, together, now?

## In Practice: How Texts on the Revolution Actually Work

### Temporal Elision and Displacement

The classic literary treatments are centrally concerned with the cultural meanings of the Revolution, but most of them, as noted earlier, approach the central events from an oblique angle—Chauvet's heroine in *A Dance on the Volcano* dies in 1794; Carpentier's Ti-Noël spends most of the Revolution in Cuba. Similarly, Walcott's *Henri Christophe* begins with news of Toussaint's death reaching Saint-Domingue; it treats Toussaint as an absent presence by which the actions of his successors must be judged. Césaire, too, chooses Christophe for hero and begins his narrative after the Revolution is over. Glissant's *Monsieur Toussaint* is set inside the captured hero's prison cell in Fort de Joux, when his work as Revolutionary leader is already done. And Langston Hughes's *The Emperor of Haiti* resembles these Caribbean works in its radical omission or elision of seemingly crucial historical events. It begins with the August 1791 rising, placing Dessalines in the forefront (though no evidence proves that he was), and then skips to the declining days of Dessalines' postwar rule as emperor, ending with his assassination in 1806. His choice of Dessalines as protagonist might have been harder to sustain had not the plot jumped from 1791 to 1806, conveniently leaping over Dessalines' harshly authoritarian policies, his possible connivance in the betrayal of Toussaint to the French,[26] and his slaughter of the whites early in 1805—an act condemned by C. L. R. James not out of any sympathy for the planters, but as a gratuitous act of revenge that only "degrade[d] and brutalise[d]" those who performed it.[27] In all of these works, what might seem the most central events have been pushed to the edge of the canvas, like the falling Icarus in Brueghel's famous landscape. This displacement is the most obvious sign of something in the historical materials that resists direct representation.

### Who Is the Protagonist?

The elision of incident, as we have seen in the case of Hughes's treatment of Dessalines, is related to the simplest question of all: since narratives, despite the decline of the "great man" school of history, still require heroes or antiheroes, who should the protagonist, or protagonists, of the narrative be? In Glissant's *Monsieur Toussaint,* Walcott's *Henri Christophe: A Chronicle in Seven Scenes,* and Césaire's *La Tragédie du roi Christophe,* the emphasis falls, as the titles suggest, on a single figure. In their plays choosing Christophe, Walcott and Césaire also choose a tragic perspective: they describe the overreaching, decline, and suicide of one of the Revolution's heroes, and the division of the country into warring factions after independence. As Edward Baugh remarks of Walcott's early *Henri Christophe,* "nothing would have seemed amiss if Walcott had called this play a tragedy instead of a chronicle."[28]

    In choosing Toussaint Louverture, Glissant takes a more hopeful view, affirming the value of Toussaint's example despite the flaws that his interlocutors, living and dead, mercilessly fling in his face; even as they quarrel with him, they nonetheless revere him as "papa," and the ghost of Macandal, leading him across the divide between life and death, affirms that his "name will mount to the stars."[29] It is significant that there is no play on Dessalines of a stature and reputation comparable to these. In the folk tradition, as Joan Dayan points out,[30] he may be the most important figure of the three; only he has been added to the vodou pantheon. Walcott treats him unsympathetically as gratuitously violent, cruel, and impatient. He does not appear in Césaire's play, having been assassinated before the action begins, but he is remembered as a cruel despot. Pétion, explaining why the powers of the president have been restricted, tells Christophe: "you can hardly be unaware that there is one danger which a people that has had to live under Dessalines fears more than any other. Its name is tyranny."[31] Only Glissant treats him with admiration: he sees Dessalines as necessary to the completion of the Revolution. In his introduction to the play, he explains that he has taken, from James's *Black*

*Jacobins* and Césaire's nonfictional *Toussaint Louverture,* the idea that Toussaint deliberately allowed the French to capture him; having lost touch with the people, and "perhaps convinced that his presence would make reconciliation between the Negroes and Mulattoes impossible . . . sacrificed himself to the common cause and found in this sacrifice the consummation of his political action" (*MT,* 15). Unlike Toussaint, Dessalines "carries no master in his head"[32]—he has more completely freed himself from the internalization of the slave identity.

Some treatments of the Revolution seem determined to move away from the notion of a central hero toward what Edward Baugh, discussing Walcott's *Haitian Trilogy,* calls "heraldic men" and "heraldic women." He borrows the adjective "heraldic" from Walcott's *Another Life.* In contrast to heroes, "towering men, larger than life," the "heraldic men would be simple, ordinary persons . . . close to the earth, the elements, who, by their experience and integrity, become icons of the generality, the common people, just as figures in heraldry, as on coats of arms, are symbolic, representative of a group, in some cases a nation."[33] The "heraldic" common figure, not yet present in the early *Henri Christophe,* emerges in *Drums and Colours,* both in the person of Mano, the Carnival reveler who organizes the pageant as a play within a play, and in the characters of Pompey and Yette, who are prominent in the final Jamaican episode. Walcott then revives these two characters, or at least recycles their names, in *The Haitian Earth,* where the story of their courtship, quarrels, and reconciliation to each other and to a life of working the "Haitian earth," receives equal billing with the exploits of Toussaint, Dessalines, Christophe, and Napoléon himself; as Baugh suggests, their fictional story finally emerges as more crucially important than the heroics of the historically based figures. As Yette, condemned to death by Henri Christophe for inflicting vodou spells on him, says of Pompey: "He is the sweat and salt of the earth, this man. / And I prouder of him than if he was a king."[34]

## Transnational vs. Nationalist Discourse

Fischer remarks that one way of disavowing the transnational antislavery discourse of the Revolution was to subsume it to a nationalist rhetoric.[35] One indeed notices a tension between nationalist and transnationalist aspirations that troubles the narratives, especially in Césaire's *The Tragedy of King Christophe.* Metellus, a rebel whom Christophe is about to execute, contrasts the aspirations of Toussaint to those of Christophe's monarchy:

We were going to build a country
   All of us together!
Not just to stake out this island!
A country open to all the islands!
To black men everywhere. The blacks of the whole world!
                                        (*TKC*, 30)

That sounds more like *négritude* than nationalism, and if one takes into account the peculiarly circular definition of blackness in post-Revolutionary Haiti, by which all Haitian citizens were declared black regardless of phenotype, it begins to resemble universalism.

Christophe, in contrast to the open-border policy of Metullus, is obsessed with fortifying the island against any possible European attempt to reclaim and enslave it. His tragic flaw, even more than hubris, is his inability to claim the independence the Revolution has won. He continues to worry about European responses instead of addressing the needs of the fledgling country. His supporter Vastey justifies his insistence on being king rather than president of a republic by arguing that Europe will only respect a monarchy. He builds the Citadel because he wants to be able to hold out against any European attack. He also compulsively repeats the European identification of the king's body with the body of the nation; he sees no irony in pressing the newly liberated slaves into forced labor on his fortress, since it is "the citadel, the freedom, of a whole people. Built by the whole people, young and old, men and women, and for the whole people" (*TKC*, 44). But of course the whole people cannot fit inside it. Christophe and his court might take refuge there for years, but little good that will do those who toiled to raise it. Christophe describes the citadel in mythified terms, as the people's triumph "against fate, against history, against nature" (*TKC*, 44). As readers of Césaire's other work will immediately recognize, the desire to go "against nature" is for him a white man's disease, which Christophe has managed to contract. Christophe's description of the Citadel is also loaded with phallic images of vertical rigidity; the gender politics of this play are a topic for another time, but Christophe's hypermasculinity ("if the husbands let him, he wouldn't be every Haitian's godfather, he'd be their father," quips Hugonin [*TKC*, 22]) is of a piece with his reactive character: it is a reassertion of manhood against the insults of slavery.

Walcott's three plays touching on Haiti, though retroactively collected as a "trilogy," are really separate works. The latter two were written for occasions with public symbolism attached to them. *Drums and Colours* was composed on commission for the ceremonies inaugurating the short-lived West Indies Federation in 1958, while *The Haitian Earth* commemorates the 150th anniversary of Emancipation (1834–1984) in the British territories. *Drums and Colours* is committed by its very occasion to a pan–West Indian program, rather than single-island nationalism. It is federalist in form as well: Walcott's prefatory note indicates that "the scenes are so arranged that interested producers can excise shorter, self-contained plays from the main work" (*HT,* 133); I have seen a St. Lucian collection of plays for students that excerpts the Haitian section in this way.

Federalist ideology, as expounded by such leaders as Norman Manley and Eric Williams, argued that the West Indies would show the world that people from many races and many nations could harmoniously combine; it drew on Enlightenment universalism for its rhetoric. Manley, at the 1947 Caribbean Labour Conference, hoped that "we, with our many strands, from Africa, from India, from China, from an assorted variety of European territories—we are capable of welding the power of that diversity into a united nation."[36] This is nationalism, but in the bygone spirit of what Peter Alter calls "Risorgimento nationalism," in which fragmented local communities combine into a nation state and enter into the universal history of humankind[37]—as opposed to the micronationalism that has been the fate of the Anglophone Caribbean since the dissolution of the Federation, and of so many other parts of the world in the second half of the twentieth century: the former Czechoslovakia, the former Soviet Union, the former Yugoslavia; the former regions of India now called Pakistan and Bangladesh.

Unlike the other plays considered here, *Drums and Colours* had an assigned ideological job to do: it had to affirm the Federation (a Federation, we should remember, to which Haiti, unlike all of the other locations in the play, did not belong; the Haitian Revolution simply must appear because it looms as *the* iconic event in the West Indian quest for freedom). Walcott, concerned not to erase the regional history of violence, contrasts the present with "the painful birth of democracy" in the times of "rebellion" (*HT,* 120). But in portraying those times, he looks for moments when oppressor and oppressed can suspend hostilities and attempt mutual recognition. We meet the colonizers in moments of vulnerability: Columbus as he is sent home in chains, or Sir Walter Raleigh during his last, desperate expedition, about to go home to an ignominious death. In the Haitian portion, Toussaint encounters his former master, Armand Calixte-Breda, alone in the woods. Before Dessalines arrives and persuades the reluctant Toussaint to kill him, the former master confronts the former slave. Calixte-Breda accuses Toussaint of "butcheries," calling on God to "give me strength to shoot this monster." To which Toussaint replies, "Where was God in those years / When we were whipped and forced to eat our own excrement, / Were peeled alive, pestered with carnivorous ants?" (*HT*, 246). In the end, both concede that events have swept beyond their control.

Although the play does not absolve the colonizers of their guilt, it refuses to demonize them; indeed, the least sympathetic character in the Haitian episode is probably Dessalines rather than any of the whites. Nonetheless, when Toussaint accedes to the demand for Calixte-Breda's death, he tacitly acknowledges that Dessalines' implacability is necessary: to let his old master off the hook would undermine his own authority and compromise the integrity of the Revolution.

One can see the impulse to affirm a transnational, perhaps even (to use that suspect word) universal, principle of human relation when Glissant engages Toussaint in conversation with Manuel, one of his guards, about land. Manuel launches into a lyrical description of the countryside in his region of France, and Toussaint, who has not spoken to him prior to this point in the play, continues his description, as if seeing it in his mind's eye. Manuel, pleased and astonished, pays him the compliment of calling him "a real peasant" (*MT*, 115). Of course, the land that Toussaint has known and worked on is very different from Manuel's French farmland, yet they meet, in Baugh's terms, as "heraldic men," both "close to the earth, the elements." This kinship overrides distinctions of black and white, guard and prisoner, metropole and colony. Manuel, a common soldier, has a simplicity and earthiness that his officers Langles and Amyot lack. In Walcott's *Haitian Earth*, too, despite the nationalistic overtones of the title, the earth is earth first, Haitian earth second; the bond to Haiti has less to do with political allegiances than attachment to the land as the soil of earth, that by which we sustain our lives.

### The Resources of Dramatic Form

In *Drums and Colours*, and indeed in all of the plays I am concerned with here, we find one advantage of drama as a mode of historical representation: its many-voicedness. As the playwright and novelist Michael Frayn remarks in a current *New Yorker* profile, "in prose, however detached the exposition, there cannot help but be some sort of narrative voice, whereas in plays the characters seem to speak for themselves more convincingly."[38] Although a good historian will quote from actors on opposing sides of a conflict, it is the historian's single narrative voice that shapes the account as a whole, and that interprets and adjudicates the competing claims. In epic, too, the narrating "I" typically intervenes and judges, sometimes, as in Milton's *Paradise Lost,* quite aggressively: we are constantly reminded of what a bad lot the devils are. But as the German playwright Friedrich Hebbel said, in an aphorism quoted by Frayn, "in a good play, everyone is right"—not that we must morally approve of all of them, but that the playwright must not take sides.

To be sure, the playwright lurks offstage, writing the speeches and moving the actors, but direct juridical intervention breaks the dramatic frame. Bakhtin, in his discussions of heteroglossia, focuses on the novel, but a play can make powerfully literal his idea that any new word is refracted through the surrounding ambience of previous speech and writing, and releases its meaning only as it is changed by its passage through that medium. For any character, all the others provide that medium. Any speaker must contend with the others, and what the audience constructs as the meaning of the play is not under any one character's uncontested control. Different interpretations of actions and motives, different evaluations of outcomes, all have their turn to speak. Dramatic form is well suited to acknowledging the mediated and incomplete status of historical knowledge.

The other attractive feature of dramatic form is its use of living human actors to represent the long-dead, absent persons of the past. It is possible, of course, that this illusion of presence can be exploited to hypnotize the audience into thinking that the actor playing Toussaint, Dessalines, or Christophe is a literal incarnation of the historical personage, and that we are seeing the past, in Ranke's famous phrase, *wie es eigentlich gewesen.* That was what Bertolt Brecht sought to disrupt in devising an "epic theatre" based on an "alienation effect," which requires the actors to step outside of their roles and make visible their non-identity with the characters they represent.

In addition to Brecht's conception of theater as a form of epic, one must consider the venerable dramatic form, tragedy. Walcott's comment on Christophe and Dessalines imagines them as tragic figures, and Césaire's play on Christophe is explicitly labeled a tragedy. At the opposite extreme, Fischer speaks of "melodrama," with "its heightened emotions, its stress on the virtues of the lowly, and its distaste for mediations and rank," as "a narratological rendition of Kojève's version of the master-slave dialectic."[39] And indeed there are strong traces of melodrama—and what a musician might call its relative major, farce—in the plays chosen for discussion here. Immediately following the cockfight and prologue, Césaire instructs the actors in his tragedy: "Tout ce premièr acte est en

style bouffon et parodique, où le sérieux et la tragique se font brusque-
ment jour par déchirures d'éclair." (This entire first act is in a clownish
and parodic style, in which the serious and the tragic abruptly dawn
in flashes of lightning.) This directive, inexplicably omitted from Ralph
Manheim's English translation, is crucial to establishing the turbulent
clash of tragic and farcical tones in this play.[40] They correspond, roughly,
to dignified self-assertion and ridiculous colonial mimicry, which prove
hard for Christophe and his court to disentangle from each other.

In her attempt to reconstruct, from fragmentary evidence, a description
of theater in Saint-Domingue just before the Revolution, Fischer remarks
that without such venerable metropolitan institutions as the Comédie
Française to sustain convention within the increasingly creolized culture
of the colony, "submission to the traditional rules would have seemed out
of place," leaving "a bastardized, transculturated type of performance
in which the original genres of comedy and tragedy mixed," in a manner "reminiscent of Bakhtin's account of Carnival."[41] The sophisticated
and widely traveled Glissant, Césaire, and Walcott should not be con-
fused with obscure eighteenth-century colonial dramatists, but the idea
of Caribbean theater as carnivalesque, and generically mixed, survives;
indeed, Walcott's *Drums and Colours* frames its dramatization of Caribbean history as an improvised performance during Trinidad carnival.

Brecht's term "epic theatre" nonetheless helps characterize these plays,
which retain something of the collective purpose of epic within the multi-
voiced medium of drama. And there is, moreover, either a Brechtian "alienation effect" or some kindred form of narrative self-consciousness (the
cockfight as play within a play in Césaire's *Tragedy of King Christophe*,
the chorus-like role of Maman Dio in Glissant's *Monsieur Toussaint*) at
work in all of them.

### Ogun vs. Rousseau: Representing Incommensurable Cultural Frames

Several treatments of the Haitian Revolution, most notably those by
Carpentier, Glissant, and the U.S. novelist Madison Smartt Bell, concern themselves with the clash between modern and premodern world
orders within Revolutionary Haiti. They raise the question of whether
the Revolution was a matter of "black Jacobins," in James's famous
phrase, holding the feet of the French to the fire of their own principles,
and thus appropriating Enlightenment ideologies of natural rights, or
rather something grounded in Afro-Creole religion and practice: were
the slaves inspired by Rousseau or Ogun—or, like the metaphysical poets

as described by Samuel Johnson, did they manage to yoke these opposites by violence together? That question receives prominent treatment in
Glissant's *Monsieur Toussaint*. It also informs Carpentier's use of "magical realism" in *The Kingdom of This World* and the radically separate
narrative voice that Bell assigns to Riau, an uneducated vodou *serviteur*
in *All Souls' Rising* and the ensuing volumes of his fictional trilogy.

In the very first sentence of his *Postethnic Narrative Criticism*, Frederick
Luis Aldama asks whether the term "magical realism," so often indis-
criminately applied to Caribbean narrative, identifies "a subtype of basic
prose epic genre, a storytelling style, or an ethnopoetics." He argues that
discussions of this term, and of Caribbean narrative literature generally,
have been much hampered by "a conflation of the literary form with ethnographic content: a confusion of narrative with ontology."[42] He thinks,
it appears, that remarks like Césaire's description of the Haitian Revolution as an "epic" do not merely use a convenient shorthand, but set an
all-too-widely followed precedent for confusing the events represented with
the mode of representation. So too with the argument that magicorealism
is simply the faithful representation of a marvelous Caribbean reality. He
argues that magicorealism, when it does not sink to a cheap exoticism
for export, must be understood as a narrative form with its own artful
conventions, not a special Caribbean mode of experience. He asks critics
to "be careful with theories of the hybrid Other that often conflate narrative fictions with actual facts"; otherwise, they may "primitivize" the
"subaltern peoples" whose cultural autonomy they claim to defend.[43]

Thus cautioned, one nonetheless can't help noticing that when Alejo
Carpentier imports Franz Roh's term *"Magic-Realismus"* for the description of something uniquely "American," it is his stay in Haiti, and especially his visit to the ruins of Christophe's Citadel at La Ferriere, that trig-
gers the identification. It is also significant that Carpentier structures his
first essay on "the marvelous real" not around the notion of encounter
with a mysterious Other, but that of *return* from encounters with several
other cultures. Some of these—China and "the world of Islam"—are
so completely different, in language and traditions of thought, that he
despairs of understanding them at all. Then he considers Prague and Len-
ingrad, European cities somewhat marginal in relation to the western
Europe of Paris (in which Carpentier spent much of his life), Rome, Berlin,
or London. These cities are part of Europe, but it is Europe with a difference. These off-center cities begin to suggest the notion of the marvelous
real, which is strange and yet ordinary. But only with his arrival in Haiti,
which is still not home, but a place very close to home, does the idea

come into focus. This narrative suggests that for Carpentier, magicorealism is the result of defamiliarization: one must go away and then see "home" with new eyes.

Carpentier's implication that awareness of the marvelous real derives from travel and comparison clashes with his insistence that it is a way of seeing uniquely connected to the juxtapositions of New World history, and also with his insistence that "the phenomenon of the marvelous presupposes faith."[44] The first contradiction can be resolved by saying that what Carpentier discovers by straining to encompass the cultures of China or Islam is the need for a similar imaginative effort to encompass the discontinuities within the culture of home. He adumbrates what Antonio Benítez-Rojo has argued: that the salient feature of Caribbean experience is the simultaneous presence of premodern, modern, and postmodern cultural phenomena. Benítez-Rojo sees this situation as a fertile abundance: in the Caribbean, cultural change means addition of new elements, never the replacement of one thing by another.[45] Carpentier, in a second essay on magicorealism, associates the mode with the baroque, a style associated with abundance ("a horror of the vacuum")[46] and multiple centers of energy, if one likes it, or with wretched excess and clutter if one does not. (Carpentier may be the only writer to claim Mozart's *Magic Flute* as a baroque work,[47] while never mentioning J. S. Bach—his point is that the baroque is an always-available attitude toward the world and artistic form, not a style confined to one historical period.)

The entry into "faith" is more difficult than Carpentier's essay allows, as any reader of *The Lost Steps* will recognize: there, the sophisticated student of cultures stumbles on an unselfconscious paradise to which, once he has left it, he can never return. Nor am I sure that the narrative stance in *The Kingdom of This World*, the novel to which "The Marvelous Real in America" served as preface, can be described as "faith" so much as willing suspension of disbelief. The dream of returning to some sort of premodern unselfconsciousness haunts much of modern literature, and Carpentier's remark about "faith" belongs to a modernist discourse of nostalgia. Carpentier's own language betrays his anxiety: to argue that poets and artists must "bet their souls on the terrifying card of faith" is to concede that this is a frightening and extreme step, not easy for an educated and cosmopolitan Cuban author to take.

When Jacques Stephen Alexis introduces "marvelous realism" into a specifically Haitian context, he insists more singlemindedly than Carpentier on the identity between magicorealist narration and the consciousness of the people: since the Haitian people believe in "the Voodoo gods" and invoke them in their folklore, the Haitian artist must follow their lead: "creating realism meant that the Haitian artists were setting about speaking the same language as their people. The Marvellous Realism of the Haitians is thus an integral part of Social Realism, and in its Haitian form it follows the same preoccupations."[48] This is a thirties Marxist defense of magicorealism, in which the artist supplies the "realism" by accurately mirroring the consciousness of the people, who in turn supply the "magic" by their religious practices and storytelling. This account, even more than Carpentier's, is susceptible to Aldama's criticism that literary form has been conflated with social content.

Nonetheless, in reading *The Kingdom of This World*, I take Carpentier's matter-of-fact narration of the world as seen through Ti-Noël's eyes, a world in which Macandal escapes death by metamorphosis into a mosquito, where the *loa* enter their *serviteurs*, not so much as an uncritical mirroring of an allegedly uniform consciousness of the people, but as dramatizing the irreconcilable split between the Enlightenment rationalist suppositions of the colonists and the animist beliefs of the slaves. For Carpentier gives us not only the "magical realist" account of Macandal's death, in which "[o]nce more the whites had been outwitted by the Mighty Powers of the Other Shore" (*KW*, 52), but also the white colonists' dismissal of it: "But could a civilized person have been expected to concern himself with the savage beliefs of people who worshipped a snake?" (*KW*, 79). Even if the slaves' belief in the metamorphosis and survival of Macandal is from a rational standpoint mistaken, it sustains the faith that eventually fuels the rising of 1791 and the subsequent Revolution. An "objective" rational analysis of the situation would have concluded that revolt was likely to fail, thus discouraging action. In this sense, their belief, though unfounded according to modern criteria of evidence, has practical and psychological value. Moreover, the inability of the whites to comprehend the belief system of the slaves puts them at a tactical disadvantage. By burning Macandal in public, they think they have intimidated and crushed resistance, not understanding that where they saw a man tortured and killed, the slaves saw something else, the triumph of Macandal's magic over white brutality.

Of the other works considered here, the one that has most overlap with magicorealist conventions is *Monsieur Toussaint*, in which dead and living characters mingle in a dream space centered in Toussaint's prison cell in Jura; among the characters is Mama Dio, a vodou priestess. In his preface to the first edition of the play, Glissant remarks: "It may be useful to point out that Toussaint's relations with his deceased companions arise from a tradition, perhaps particular to the Antilles, of casual communication with the dead" (*MT*, 18). Nonetheless, because Toussaint's colloquys with the dead occur, until the end of the play, only when he is alone, and because his jailers wonder why he is silent in their presence, we are constantly aware of the white, French perspective: these men do *not* believe in talking with the dead, but would rather discuss rum, firewood, or missed opportunities for service under Napoléon. The juxtaposition of the supernatural premise of the play with a secular point of view keeps the post-Enlightenment skeptic awake within the audience, rather than lulling it into a trance of suspended disbelief.

Most crucially, the conflict between premodern and modern consciousness is played out within Toussaint himself. The character most critical of Toussaint is Macaïa, who considers himself a maroon and an African; he has not appropriated, as Toussaint has done, the French Revolution's rhetoric of natural rights. Toussaint has been a suppresser of vodou and has insisted on military discipline on the European model. Yet as he dies, he speaks Creole for the first time and cries out to the warrior god Ogun (*MT*, 121). Does he, in the extreme moment, experience a conversion and return to his origins? Or does he tear away what has always been a tactical mask, revealing the transplanted African under the Black Jacobin? The play, to its credit, does not answer the question, but leaves us to wonder how Toussaint managed to engage the Europeans in European terms while still commanding the loyalty of people whose sense of how the world works often had more to do with Ogun and Legba than with The Rights of Man.

### Conclusion

The cluster of twentieth-century narratives of the Haitian Revolution discussed here come—with the exception of Chauvet's—from elsewhere in the Caribbean, during its period of decolonization: a process that Haiti, uniquely, had completed (formally, at least) in 1804. These writers seem drawn to the story as a mirror for the conflicts of their own time. Although their narratives include no text as daunting as, say, Wilson Harris's *Guyana Quartet*, Patrick Chamoiseau's *Texaco*, or Robert Antoni's *Divina Trace*, the disjunctions and opacities of the historical record emerge in them as off-center emplotment, as slices of chronicle separated by narrative gaps, or as stylistic registration of disparate worldviews among the characters. The medium of drama allows a combination of communal, public representation with the many contradicting points of view of characters, each endowed with a distinctive voice, on the stage. Most of these works are well made and compelling, yet it must be said that none of them ranks among the very finest works of Caribbean literature. Walcott's full scope is best seen in his poetry and a few of his other plays; Césaire's masterpiece is the *Notebook,* and Glissant's reputation rests more on his poetry and novels than on *Monsieur Toussaint.* Although the Revolution calls to the imagination, it also frustrates it to a degree. Or it may be that the story cannot satisfy until it receives the happy ending it has been denied: that is, until the "first epic" begun in deeds over two hundred years ago arrives at a nonrepressive and tolerably prosperous Haiti, a time when the chains finally cease to return.

## Notes

1. Joan Dayan, *Haiti, History, and the Gods,* 3.
2. David Quint, *Epic and Empire,* 45.
3. Ibid., 46.
4. Derek Walcott, *What the Twilight Says: Essays,* 11.
5. Article in *South Atlantic Quarterly* 96, no. 2, 235.
6. Michel-Rolph Trouillot, *Haiti: State against Nation,* 15.
7. Hayden White, "The Historical Text as Literary Artifact," 395–407. I find White's argument for the constitutive power of emplotment suggestive and partially persuasive but overextended. See Michel-Rolph Trouillot, *Silencing the Past,* 1–30, for a persuasive critique of White's relativism.
8. Carpentier, *The Kingdom of This World* (abbreviated *KW*), 1957 ed., 177. Hereafter, page references will be given in text.
9. Édouard Glissant, *Poetics of Relation,* 47.
10. Ibid., p. 15.
11. Quint, *Epic and Empire,* 47.
12. Glissant, *Poetics of Relation,* 55.
13. Ibid., 28.
14. V. S. Naipaul, *The Middle Passage,* 29; Froude quoted p. 10. Derek Walcott, in an interview, once remarked: "Perhaps it should read that 'nothing was created *by the British* in the West Indies." See Edward Hirsch, "The Art of Poetry XXXVII" (1985), rpt. in William Baer, *Conversations with Derek Walcott,* 107.
15. Madison Smartt Bell, *All Souls' Rising,* 11.
16. Édouard Glissant, *Caribbean Discourse,* 61–62.
17. C. L. R. James, *The Black Jacobins,* in the *C. L. R. James Reader,* 73–77. One might add that in this case, Toussaint, by changing as quickly and capriciously as the policy-makers in Paris, is able to seize agency for himself, turning nonhistory into history, at least for the time being.
18. Glissant, *Caribbean Discourse,* 161–62, 145, 106–7.
19. Ibid., 145.
20. Wilson Harris, *Selected Essays,* 141–42.

21. David Patrick Geggus, *Haitian Revolutionary Studies*, 31, 43.

22. Sibylle Fischer, *Modernity Disavowed*, 37–38.

23. Trouillot, *Silencing the Past*, 48, 26.

24. Ibid., 99, 72, 90.

25. Ibid., 88–89, 82, 98.

26. C. L. R. James, *The Black Jacobins* (2nd ed., 1963), 333. Carolyn E. Fick doubts that Dessalines (or even Christophe, who had deserted) played a role in Toussaint's capture: *The Making of Haiti*, 212–13.

27. James, *The Black Jacobins*, 373.

28. Edward Baugh, "Of Men and Heroes," 48.

29. Glissant, *Monsieur Toussaint* (abbreviated *MT*), Dash-Glissant 2005 translation, 98.

30. Dayan, *Haiti, History, and the Gods*, 17, 30.

31. Césaire, *The Tragedy of King Christophe* (abbreviated *TKC*), 12.

32. Glissant, *Monsieur Toussaint*, 75. This translation uses the 1961 French text. The Dash-Glissant translation, using a recent revision that I could not obtain in French, has this line as "The Tiger has no Lord in his head!" (96). The French, in the Gallimard 1998 reprinting of the Éditions du Seuil text of 1986, reads: "Le Tigre ne porte aucun Seigneur dans sa tête" (119). If both translators are working from the same French words, the capitalization of "Seigneur" favors the Dash-Glissant version, though one could construe the word as meaning either an earthly master or the Christian Lord, capital L.

33. Baugh, "Of Men and Heroes," 46–47.

34. Walcott, *Haitian Trilogy* (abbreviated *HT*), 433. Hereafter, page references will be given in text.

35. Fischer, *Modernity Disavowed*, 104–5, 225.

36. Norman Manley, "West Indian Federation," 166.

37. Peter Alter, *Nationalism*, 55–91.

38. Profile of Michael Frayn, *New Yorker*, October 25, 2004, 70.

39. Fischer, *Modernity Disavowed*, 30–31.

40. Aimé Césaire, *La tragedie du roi Christophe*, 1970 ed., 18. Mannheim was working from the 1963 edition, but the identical stage direction also appears there; for whatever reason, he simply left it out.

41. Fischer, *Modernity Disavowed*, pp. 209–10.

42. Frederick Luis Aldama, *Postethnic Narrative Criticism*, 1, 3.

43. Ibid., 108.

44. Alejo Carpentier, "On the Marvelous Real in America," 86.

45. Antonio Benítez-Rojo, *The Repeating Island: The Caribbean and the Postmodern Perspective*, 2nd ed. (1996), 23, 151–52.

46. Alejo Carpentier, "The Baroque and the Marvelous Real," 93.

47. Ibid., 94.

48. Jacques Stephen Aléxis, "Of the Marvellous Realism of the Haitians," 197.

# Bibliography

**Archival Sources**

*Archives d'outre-mer, Aix-en-Provence*
  Série F3

*Archives nationales de France*
  Section Moderne, AA
  Section Musée de l'histoire de France, AE II
  Série Colonies CC9

*Archives nationales de Paris*
  Série AF

*Archivo del Ministerio de Asuntos Exteriores, Madrid*
  Sección Política, República Dominicana

*Archivo del Museo de la Ciudad de la Habana*
  Actas Capitulares

*Archivo General de Indias, Seville*
  Papeles de Cuba
  Sección Estado

*Archivo General de Simancas, Simancas, Spain*
  Sección Guerra Moderna

*Archivo Histórico Nacional, Madrid*
  Sección Estado

*Archivo Nacional de Cuba, Havana*
  Fondo Asuntos Políticos
  Reales, Cédulas, y Órdenes.

*Bibliothèque nationale de France*
Section manuscrits français

*Servicio Histórico Militar, Madrid*
Colección General de Documentos, Reel 65

**Primary Printed and Electronic Sources**

1805 Constitution d'Haïti: http://web.upmf-grenoble.fr/Haiti/Dessalines.htm [French]; http://www.webster.edu/~corbetre/haiti/history/earlyhaiti/1805-const.htm [English].

Acte de l'Indépendance: http://www.upmf-grenoble.fr/Haiti/Dessalines.htm (French); http://thelouvertureproject.org/wiki/index.php?title=Act_of_Independence (English).

Alexis, Jacques-Stephen. *Compère Général Soleil.* Paris: Gallimard, 1955.

———. *General Sun, My Brother.* Translated by Carrol F. Coates. Charlottesville: University Press of Virginia, 1999.

———. "Of the Marvellous Realism of the Haitians" [1956], rpt. in *The Post-Colonial Studies Reader,* edited by Bill Ashcroft, Gareth Griffiths, and Helen Tiffin. London: Routledge, 1995.

Anon. *Histoire de Mesdemoiselles de Saint-Janvier, les deux seules blanches sauvées du massacre de Saint-Domingue.* Paris: J. J. Blaise, 1812.

Bell, Madison Smartt. *All Souls' Rising.* New York: Penguin, 1995.

[Boisrond-Tonnerre, Félix]. "Liberté ou la mort." In *Littérature Haïtienne,* vol. 1, *Les Pionniers à L'École de 1836,* edited by Christophe Ph. Charles. Port-au-Prince: Éditions Choucoune, 1998. (See also Proclamation des Gonaïves.)

Brown, William Wells. *The Black Man, His Antecedents, His Genius, and His Achievements.* New York: Thomas Hamilton; Boston: R. F. Wallcut, 1863.

Carpentier, Alejo. "The Baroque and the Marvelous Real," rpt. in *Magical Realism: Theory, History, Community,* edited by Lois Parkinson Zamora and Wendy B. Faris. Durham, NC: Duke University Press, 1995.

———. *Explosion in a Cathedral* [*El siglo de las luces,* 1962]. Translated by John Sturrock. New York; London: Colophon Books. Harper and Row, 1963, 1979.

———. "On the Marvelous Real in America" [*De lo real maravilloso americano,* 1949], rpt. in *Magical Realism: Theory, History, Community,* edited by Lois Parkinson Zamora and Wendy B. Faris. Durham, NC: Duke University Press, 1995.

———. *The Kingdom of This World* [*El reino de este mundo,* 1949]. Translated by Harriet de Onís. New York: Alfred A. Knopf, 1957.

Césaire, Aimé. *Les armes miraculeuses.* Paris: Présence Africaine, 1946.

———. *Cahier d'un retour au pays natal.* [1939] Paris: Présence Africaine, 1956, 1968, 1971.

———. *Cahier d'un retour au pays natal.* Edited, with an introduction, commentary, and notes, by Abiola Irele. Columbus: Ohio University Press, 2000.

————. *The Collected Poetry [of] Aimé Césaire.* Translated and edited by Clayton Eshleman and Annette Smith. Berkeley, Los Angeles, London: University of California Press, 1983.

————. *Discours sur le colonialisme.* [1950] Paris: Présence Africaine, 1955.

————. *Et les chiens se taisaient.* [1946] Paris: Présence Africaine, 1956.

————. *Notebook of a Return to the Native Land.* Translated and edited, from 1947 French edition, by Clayton Eshleman and Annette Smith. Middletown, CT: Wesleyan University Press, 2001.

————. "Panorama." *Tropiques* 10 (February 1944): 7–10.

————. *Return to My Native Land.* Translated by Emile Snyders. Paris: Présence Africaine, 1968, 1971.

————. *Return to My Native Land.* Translated by John Berger and Anna Bostock, with an introduction by Mazisi Kunene. Baltimore, MD: Penguin, 1969.

————. *Toussaint Louverture: La révolution française et le problème colonial.* Paris: Présence Africaine, 1961, 1962, 1981.

————. *La Tragédie du roi Christophe.* Paris: Présence Africaine, 1963, 1970.

————. *The Tragedy of King Christophe.* Translated by Ralph Manheim. New York: Grove Press, 1969.

————. *Une saison au Congo.* Paris: Editions du Seuil, 1967.

[Chanlatte, Juste]. *Histoire de la catastrophe de Saint-Domingue.* Edited by A. J. B. Bouvet de Cressé. Paris: Librarie de Peytieux, 1824.

Chauvet, Marie. *Amour, colère et folie.* Paris: Gallimard, 1968.

————. *La Danse sur le volcan.* Paris: Plon, 1957.

————. *A Dance on the Volcano.* Translated by Salvator Attanasio. London: Heinemann, 1959.

Chenêt, Jean-Baptiste. *Études poétiques ou Chants du Barde glanés chez les muses.* Paris: Paul Dupont, 1846.

Christophe, Henri. *Manifeste du Roi.* Cap-Henry: P. Roux, Imprimeur du Roi, 1814.

————. "The Manifesto of the King." In *Haytian Papers: A Collection of the Very Interesting Proclamations, and other Official Documents; together with some Account of the Rise, Progress, and Present State of the Kingdom of Hayti,* edited by Prince Saunders. Westport: Negro Universities Press, [1816] 1969.

"Comunicación dirigida por el Consul de España en la isla de Jamaica al Capitán General de Cuba, fecha Kingston 2 junio 1845, adjuntándole un periódico donde se publica un artículo en el cual se trata de elevar un monumento en dicha Isla al poeta Gabriel de la Concepción Valdés (a) Plácido." (Communication directed by the Spanish Consul in Jamaica to the Captain General of Cuba, dated Kingston 2 June 1845, with a newspaper article attached on the elevation of a monument in Jamaica to the poet Gabriel de la Concepción Valdés, a.k.a. Plácido.) *Boletín del Archivo Nacional de la República de Cuba* 18, 83.

Constant, Benjamin. *Journaux intimes.* Edited by A. Roulin and C. Roth. Paris: Gallimard, 1952.

"Constitution de Saint-Domingue." In *Les Constitutions d'Haïti, 1801–1885,* edited by Louis Janvier. Paris: C. Marpon et E. Flammarion, 1886.

"Constitution d'Haïti, 1805." In Thomas Madiou, *Histoire d'Haïti,* vol. 3. Port-au-Prince: Éditions Henri Deschamps, 1989.

Davertige. *Idem et autres poèmes.* Paris: Seghers, 1964.

Debray, Régis. *Chroniques de l'idiotie triomphante: Terrorismes, guerres, diplomatie—1990–2003.* Paris: Fayard, 2004.

———. *Haïti et la France* (The Report). Paris: La Table Ronde, 2004.

———. *Transmitting Culture.* Translated Eric Rauth. New York: Columbia University Press, 2000.

Delany, Martin R. *Blake; Or, The Huts of America.* [1859, 1861–62] Boston: Beacon Press, 1970.

———. *Official Report of the Niger Valley Exploring Party.* New York: Thomas Hamilton, 1861.

———. *The Origin of Races and Color.* 1879. Baltimore: Black Classic Press, 1991.

Depestre, René. *Encore une mer à traverser.* Paris: La Table Ronde, 2005.

Descourtilz, Michel Étienne. *Voyages d'un naturaliste . . . à Saint-Domingue.* 3 vols. Paris: Dufart, 1809.

de Vastey. See Vastey.

Douglass, Frederick. *Narrative of the Life of Frederick Douglass,* 1845. New York: Dover, 1995.

DuBroca, B.-M. J. *La Vie de Toussaint Louverture.* Paris: DuBroca, 1802.

Ducasse, Vendenesse. *Fort de Joux: les derniers moments de Toussaint Louverture.* [1896] Port-au-Prince: Éditions Vétéran, 1957.

Du Morier, Joseph-Pierre. *Sur les troubles des colonies.* Paris: Didot Jeune, 1791.

Duras, Claire de. *Ourika.* Edited by Joan Dejean and Margaret Waller. New York: MLA, 1994.

———. *Ourika.* Edited by Roger Little. Textes littéraires CV. Exeter, UK: University of Exeter Press, 1998.

———. *Ourika, an English Translation.* Translated by John Fowles. MLA Texts and Translations. New York: MLA, 1994.

Edwards, Bryan. *An Historical Survey of the French Colony in the Island of St. Domingo.* [1797] London: 1801.

Fanon, Frantz. *Black Skin, White Masks.* Translated by Charles Lam Markmann. New York: Grove Press, 1967.

———. *A Dying Colonialism.* [1965] Translated by Haakon Chevalier. New York: Grove Press, 1967.

———. *Peau noire, masques blancs.* Paris: Editions du Seuil, 1952.

———. *The Wretched of the Earth.* [1963] Translated by Constance Farrington. New York: Grove Press, 1965.

Faubert, Pierre. *Ogé, ou le préjugé de couleur, drame historique suivi de Poésies figutives et de notes.* [1841] Paris: C. Mallet-Schmitz, 1856.

*Gaceta de Madrid,* 1791–1805.

García Márquez, Gabriel. *El general en su labirinto.* Madrid: Mondadori, 1989.

Garran, J.-Ph. *Rapport sur les troubles de Saint-Domingue,* 2 vols. Paris: Imprimerie nationale, 1797–1799.

Glissant, Édouard. *Caribbean Discourse: Selected Essays.* Translated, with introduction, by J. Michael Dash. Charlottesville: University Press of Virginia, 1989.

———. *Monsieur Toussaint.* Paris: Seuil, 1961.

———. *Monsieur Toussaint* (playscript edition). Fort-de-France: Acoma, 1978.

———. *Monsieur Toussaint: version scénique.* Paris: Éditions Gallimard, 1986, 1998.

———. *Monsieur Toussaint.* Translated and edited by Joseph G. Foster and Barbara A. Franklin, with an introduction by Juris Silenieks. Washington: Three Continents Press, 1981.

———. *Monsieur Toussaint.* Translated by J. Michael Dash and Édouard Glissant. Boulder, CO: Lynne Rienner, 2005.

———. *Poèmes complets.* Paris: Gallimard, 1994.

———. *Poetics of Relation.* Translated by Betsy Wing. Ann Arbor: University of Michigan Press, 1997.

———. *Sartorius.* Paris: Gallimard, 1999.

Gonaïves Declaration. See Proclamation des Gonaïves.

Gros, *Isle St.-Domingue, province du Nord. Précis historique, qui expose dans le plus grand jour les manoeuvres contre-révolutionnaires employées contre St.-Domingue; qui désigne et fait connoître les principaux agents de tous les massacres, incendies . . . qui s'y sont commis . . .* Paris: L. Potier de Lille, 1793.

Harris, Wilson. *Selected Essays.* Edited by Andrew Bundy. London: Routledge, 1999.

Herrmann, Gottfried. *Toussaint Louverture.* Libretto. Grosse Oper in 5 Aufzügen. Lübeck: Rahtgens, [18??].

Holly, James Theodore. "A Vindication of the Capacity of the Negro Race for Self-Government and Civilized Progress as Demonstrated by Historical Events of the Haytian Revolution; and the Subsequent Acts of That People Since Their National Independence," in *Black Separatism and the Caribbean, 1860,* by James Theodore Holly and J. Dennis Harris. Edited by Howard H. Bell. Ann Arbor: University of Michigan Press, 1970.

Hugo, Victor. *Bug-Jargal. Bug-Jargal.* Paris: J. Hetzel, 1826.

James, C. L. R. *The Black Jacobins* (play, 1936). Rpt. in *The C. L. R. James Reader,* edited by Anna Grimshaw. Oxford: Blackwell, 1992.

Kleist, Heinrich von. "Die Verlobung in St. Domingo." *Sammler* (Vienna) 79–87 (2–20 July 1812).

Laforest, Jean-Richard. *Le divan des alternances*. Montréal: Nouvelle Optique, 1978.

Lamartine, Alphonse de. *Toussaint Louverture*. [1850] Edited by Léon-François Hoffmann. Exeter, UK: University of Exeter Press, 1998.

Laurent, Gérard de, ed. *Toussaint Louverture à travers sa correspondance*. N.p., 1953.

Leborgne de Boigne, Claude-Pierre-Joseph. *Nouveau système de colonisation pour Saint-Domingue, combiné avec la création d'une compagnie de commerce pour rétablir les relations de la France avec cette isle; précédé de considérations générales sur le régime des européens dans les deux Indes*. Paris: Chez Dondey-Dupré, 1817.

Le Brasseur, J. A. *De l'etat actuel de la marine et des colonies*. Paris: L. P. Couret, 1792.

Leclerc, Charles Victor Emmanuel. *Lettres du général Leclerc, commandant en chef de l'armée de Saint-Domingue en 1802*. Edited by Paul Roussier. Paris: Société de l'histoire des colonies françaises et Librairie Ernest Leroux, 1937.

Legagneur, Serge. *Textes en croix*. Montreal: Nouvelle Optique, 1978.

———. *Textes interdits*. [Montreal]: Estérel, 1966.

Louverture, Toussaint. *Toussaint Louverture à travers sa correspondance*. Edited by Gérard de Laurent. N.p. 1953.

Madiou, Thomas. *Histoire d'Haïti*. [1847–48] Port-au-Prince: Éditions Henri Deschamps, 1989.

Manley, Norman. "West Indian Federation: A Cause Vital to Our Progress." In *Manley and the New Jamaica: Selected Speeches and Writings 1938–1968*, edited by Rex Nettleford. Trinidad and Jamaica: Longman Caribbean, 1971.

Maximin, Daniel. *L'isolé soleil*. Paris: Seuil, 1981.

———. *Lone Sun*. Introduction by Clarisse Zimra. Charlottesville and London: CARAF Books. University Press of Virginia, 1989.

Métellus, Jean. *Haïti, une nation pathétique*. Paris: Maisonneuve et Larose, 2003.

Métral, Antoine. *Histoire de l'expédition des français à Saint-Domingue, sous le consulat de Napoléon Bonaparte*. Paris: Fanjat ainé, 1825.

Michelet, Jules. *L'Oiseau*. Paris: Hachette, 1857.

Naipaul, V. S. *The Middle Passage: Impressions of Five Societies—British, French and Dutch—in the West Indies and South America*. New York: Vintage, 1962.

Neruda, Pablo. *Canto General*. Buenos Aires: Losada, 1968.

Phillips, Wendell. "Toussaint Louverture." *Speeches, Lectures and Letters*. Boston: James Redpath, 1863.

Proclamation des Gonaïves: http://www.upmf-grenoble.fr/Haiti/Dessalines.htm (French); http://www.geocities.com/CapeCanaveral/9972/independ.htm (English). See also Boisrond-Tonnerre, Félix.

Réimpression de l'Ancien moniteur, seule histoire authentique et inaltérée de la Révolution française depuis la réunion des États-généraux jusqu'au Consulat. [nivose an VI (January 1799)] Paris: Plon, 1854.

Robespierre, Maximilien. "Sur les principes de morale politique qui doivent guider la Convention nationale dans l'administration intérieure de la République." In *Textes choisis III,* edited with preface and notes by Jean Poperen. Paris: Éditions sociales, 1974.

Roumain, Jacques. *Gouverneurs de la rosée.* [1944.] Paris: Le Temps des cérises, 2000.

Tarbé, Charles. "Rapport sur les troubles de Saint-Domingue, fait à l'Assemblée nationale, par Charles Tarbé, député de la Seine-Inférieur, au nom du comité colonial, le 29 février 1792." Paris: Imprimerie nationale, 1792.

*Toussaint Louverture à travers sa correspondance.* See Laurent, Gérard de.

Trujillo, Manuel. *El gran dispensador.* Caracas: Fundación CADAFE para la difusión de la cultura, 1983.

Vastey, Pompée-Valentin, Baron de. *An Essay on the Causes of the Revolution and Civil Wars of Hayti, Being a Sequel to the Political Remarks Upon Certain French Publications and Journals Concerning Hayti.* Translated from the French by W. H. M. Exeter: Printed at the Western Luminary Office, 1823; 2nd ed. New York: Negro Universities Press, 1969.

———. *Reflections on the Blacks and Whites. Remarks upon a Letter Addressed by M. Mazeres, a French Ex-colonist, to J. C. L. Sismonde de Sismondi, Containing Observations on the Blacks and Whites, the Civilization of Africa, the Kingdom of Hayti, etc.* London: J. Hatchard, 1817; 2nd ed. Liverpool: F. B. Wright, 1817.

———. *Réflexions politiques sur quelques ouvrages et journaux français concernant Haïti.* Sans-Souci: Imprimerie royale, 1817.

———. *Réflexions sur une lettre de Mazières, ex-colon français adressée à M. J. C. L. Sismonde de Sismondi, sur les Noirs et les Blancs, la civilisation de l'Afrique, le royaume d'Hayti, etc.* Cap-Henry: P. Roux, 1816.

———. *Le Système colonial dévoilé.* Cap-Henry: P. Roux, imprimeur du Roi, 1814.

Walcott, Derek. *The Haitian Trilogy: Henri Christophe, Drums and Colours, The Haitian Earth.* New York: Farrar, Straus and Giroux, 2002.

Wordsworth, William. *The Poetical Works.* The "Chandos Poets." London: Frederick Warne and Co., 1880.

### Secondary Sources

Adamson, Ginette. "Jean Métellus ou l'écrivain en partage: une esthétique de vie et d'écriture." In *Écrire en pays assiégé—Haïti:Writing under Siege,* edited by Kathleen M. Balutansky and Marie-Agnès Sourieau. Amsterdam and New York: Rodopi, 2004.

Ahmad, Aijaz. "Haitian Tragedy and Imperial Farce," *Canadian Dimension* 38, no. 3 (2004). (Originally published in *Frontline.*)

Aldama, Frederick Luis. *Postethnic Narrative Criticism: Magicorealism in Oscar "Zeta" Acosta, Ana Castillo, Julie Dash, and Salman Rushdie.* Austin: University of Texas Press, 2003.

Ali, Tariq. *Bush in Babylon: The Recolonisation of Iraq*. London: Verso, 2003.

Alonso, Carlos J. "Fiction." In *A History of Literature in the Caribbean*, vol. 1, *Hispanic and Francophone Regions*, edited by A. James Arnold, Julio Rodríguez-Luis, and J. Michael Dash, 141–53. Amsterdam and Philadelphia: John Benjamins, 1994.

Alter, Peter. *Nationalism*. Translated by Stuart McKinnon-Evans. London: Edward Arnold, 1989.

Anderson, Benedict. *Imagined Communities: Reflections on the Origin and the Spread of Nationalism*. London: Verso, 1983.

Anderson, Perry. "Dégringolade," *London Review of Books* 2 September 2004, http://www.lrb.co.uk/v26/n17/ande01_.html.

Antoine, Régis. *Les Écrivains français et les Antilles*. Paris: Maisonneuve et Larose, 1978.

Antonin, Arnold. "Bolivar y los principios haitianos." *Revista de Occidente* (Madrid) 30–31 (1983): 70–77.

———. *Les Idées haïtiennes et la révolution sud-américaine*. Pétion-Ville: Centre Pétion-Bolivar, 1990.

Ardouin, Beaubrun. *Études sur l'histoire d'Haïti*. Port-au-Prince: François Dalencour, 1958.

Arnold, A. James. "D'Haïti à l'Afrique: *La Tragédie du roi Christophe* de Césaire." *Revue de littérature comparée* 60, no. 2 (1986): 133–48.

Baer, William. *Conversations with Derek Walcott*. Jackson: University of Mississippi Press, 1996.

Balibar, Étienne. "Ambiguous Universality." In *Politics and the Other Scene*, 146–76. London: Verso, 2002.

———. "Citizenship without Community." In *We, the People of Europe?* 51–77.

———. "Homo nationalis: An Anthropological Sketch of the Nation Form." In *We, the People of Europe?* 11–30.

———. "The Ideological Tensions of Capitalism: Universalism vs. Racism and Sexism." In Balibar and Wallerstein, *Race, Nation, Class*, 29–36.

———. "Racism and Nationalism." In Balibar and Wallerstein, *Race, Nation, Class*, 37–68.

———. *We, the People of Europe? Reflections on Transnational Citizenship*, translated by James Swenson. Princeton: Princeton University Press, 2004.

Balibar, Étienne, and Emmanuel Wallerstein. *Race, Nation, Class: Ambiguous Identities*. London: Verso, 1991.

Bancel, Nicolas, Pascal Blanchard, and Françoise Vergès, *La République coloniale*. Paris: Albin Michel, 2003.

Bar-Lewaw Mulstock, Itzhak. *Plácido: Vida y obra*. Mexico D.F.: Ediciones Botas/Impresora Juan Pablos, 1960.

Basknell, David. "Bolívar, Simón." *Encyclopedia of Latin American History and Culture*, vol. 1. Edited by Barbara A. Tenenbaum, 360–62. New York: Scribner's, 1996.

Baudot, Alain. "Antilles et Guyane." In *Guide culturel: civilisations et littératures d'expression française,* edited by André Reboullet and Michel Tétu. Paris: Hachette, 1977.

Baugh, Edward. "Of Men and Heroes: Walcott and the Haitian Revolution." *Callaloo* 28 (1).

Belasco, Susan. "Harriet Martineau's Black Hero and the American Antislavery Movement." *Nineteenth-Century Literature* 55, no. 2 (2000): 157–94.

Bellegarde, Dantès. *La Nation haïtienne.* Paris: Gigord, 1938.

Bellegarde-Smith, Patrick. *Haiti: The Breached Citadel,* Revised edition. Toronto: Canadian Scholars' Press, 2004.

Benítez-Rojo, Antonio. *The Repeating Island.* Translated by James Maraniss. Durham, NC: Duke University Press, 1992, 1996.

Benot, Yves. *La Démence coloniale sous Napoléon.* Paris: La Découverte, 1992.

———. *La Révolution française et la fin des colonies 1789–1794.* Paris: La Découverte, 1987, 1989.

Bergner, Gwen. "Who Is That Masked Woman? Or, the Role of Gender in Fanon's *Black Skin, White Masks.*" *PMLA* 110, no. 1 (Jan 1995): 75–88.

Berrou, Raphaël, and Pradel Pompilus. *Histoire de la littérature haïtienne illustrée par les textes.* 3 vols. Paris and Port-au-Prince: Éditions de l'École, 1975–77.

Bethell, Leslie, ed. *The Cambridge History of Latin America,* vol. 3, *From Independence to c. 1870.* Cambridge, London, New York: Cambridge University Press, 1985.

Bhabha, Homi. *The Location of Culture.* London: Routledge, 1994.

Bissainthe, Max. *Dictionnaire de bibliographie haïtienne.* Washington: Scarecrow Press, 1951.

Blackburn, Robin. *The Overthrow of Colonial Slavery, 1776–1848.* London: Verso, 1988.

Bongie, Chris. *Exotic Memories: Literature, Colonialism, and the Fin de Siècle.* Stanford: Stanford University Press, 1991.

———. "'Monotonies of History': Baron Vastey and the Mulatto Legend of Derek Walcott's *Haitian Trilogy,*" *Yale French Studies* 107 (2005): 75–88.

———. "A Street Named Bissette: Memory, Nostalgia, and the *Cent-cinquantenaire* of the Abolition of Slavery in Martinique (1848–1998)," *South Atlantic Quarterly* 100, no. 1 (2001): 215–57.

Brickhouse, Anna. "The Writing of Haiti: Pierre Faubert, Harriet Beecher Stowe, and Beyond." *American Literary History* 13, no. 3 (2001): 407–44.

Brière, Jean-François. "Abbé Grégoire and Haitian Independence." In "Haiti, 1804–2004: Literature, Culture, Art," special issue, *Research in African Literatures* 35, no. 2 (2004): 34–43.

Brierre, Jean Fernand. *Pétion y Bolívar y El adios a la Marsellesa.* Buenos Aires: n.p., 1955.

Brown, Jacqueline Nassy. "Black Liverpool, Black America, and the Gendering of Diasporic Space." *Cultural Anthropology* 13, no. 3 (August 1998): 291–325.

Buck-Morss, Susan. "Hegel and Haiti." *Critical Inquiry* 26, no. 4 (Summer 2000): 821–65.

Buenaventura, Enrique. *Teatro: Un requiem por el Padre Las Casas; La tragedia del Rey Christophe; En la diestra de Dios Padre.* Bogotá: Ediciones Tercer Mundo, 1963.

Calcagano, Francisco. *Poetas de color.* Havana: Militar de la V. de Soler, 1878.

Carby, Hazel. *Race Men.* Cambridge, MA: Harvard University Press, 1998.

Casals, Jorge. *Plácido como poeta cubano: Ensayo biográfico critico.* Havana: Publicaciones del Ministerio de Educacion Dirección de Cultura, 1944.

Castellanos, Jorge. *Plácido, poeta social y político.* Miami: Ediciones Universal, 1984.

Cauna, Jacques de, ed. *Toussaint Louverture et l'indépendance d'Haïti: Témoignages pour un bicentenaire.* Paris: Karthala and La Société française d'histoire d'outre-mer, 2004.

Chancy, Myriam. *Framing Silence: Revolutionary Novels by Haitian Women.* New Brunswick: Rutgers University Press, 1997.

Chakrabarty, Dipesh. *Provincializing Europe: Postcolonial Thought and Historical Difference.* Princeton: Princeton University Press, 2000.

Chartier, Roger. *Lectures et lecteurs dans la France d'Ancien Régime.* Paris: Seuil, 1987.

Chatterjee, Partha. *Nationalist Thought and the Colonial World: A Derivative Discourse.* 1986. Minneapolis: University of Minnesota Press, 2004.

———. *The Nation and Its Fragments: Colonial and Postcolonial Histories.* Princeton: Princeton University Press, 1993.

Childs, Matt. "'A Black French General Arrived to Conquer the Island': Images of the Haitian Revolution in Cuba's 1812 Aponte Rebellion." In *The Impact of the Haitian Revolution in the Atlantic World,* edited by David Geggus. Columbia: University of South Carolina Press, 2001.

Chomsky, Noam, Paul Farmer, and Amy Goodman. *Getting Haiti Right This Time: The U.S. and the Coup.* Monroe, ME: Common Courage Press, 2004.

Clark, Vèvè A. "Haiti's Tragic Overture: (Mis)Representations of the Haitian Revolution in World Drama (1796–1975)." In *Representing the French Revolution: Literature, Historiography, and Art,* edited by James A. W. Heffernan. Hanover, NH: University Press of New England, 1992.

Coates, Carroll F. "Translator's Note on Marie Chauvet's *Amour, colère, folie.*" *Callaloo* 15, no. 2 (1992): 460–61.

Cohen, William B. *The French Encounter with Africans: White Responses to Blacks, 1530–1880.* Bloomington: Indiana University Press, 1980.

Conway, Christopher B. *The Cult of Bolívar in Latin American Literature.* Gainesville: University Press of Florida, 2003.

Cook, Mercer, and Dantès Bellegarde, eds. *The Haitian-American Anthology: Haitian Readings from American Authors.* Port-au-Prince: Imprimerie de l'État, 1944.

Cornevin, Robert. *Le Théâtre haïtien des origines à nos jours.* [Montréal]: Leméac, 1973.

Corzani, Jacques. *La Littérature des Antilles-Guyane.* 6 vols. Fort-de-France: Éditions Desormeaux, 1978.

Dash, J. Michael. *Édouard Glissant.* Cambridge Studies in African and Caribbean Literature. Cambridge: Cambridge University Press, 1995.

———. *Literature and Ideology in Haiti, 1915–1961.* Totowa, NJ: Barnes and Noble, 1981.

———. *The Other America: Caribbean Literature in a New World Context.* Charlottesville: University Press of Virginia. 1998.

Davies, Carol Boyce. *Black Women, Writing, and Identity: Migrations of the Subject.* New York: Routledge, 1994.

Dayan, Joan. "Codes of Law and Bodies of Color." *New Literary History* 26, no. 2 (Spring 1995): 283–308.

———. *Haiti, History, and the Gods.* Berkeley: University of California Press, 1995.

———. "Paul Gilroy's Slaves, Ships, and Routes: The Middle Passage as Metaphor." *Research in African Literatures* 27, no. 4 (1996): 7–14.

———. "Reading Women in the Caribbean: Marie Chauvet's *Love, Anger and Madness.*" In *Displacements: Reading Women in the Caribbean,* edited by Dejean and Miller. Baltimore: Johns Hopkins University Press, 1991, 228–53.

D'haen, Theo. "Modernist and Counter-Modernist Caribbeans." In his "(Post)Modernity and Caribbean Discourse," *A History of Literature in the Caribbean,* vol. 3, *Cross-Cultural Studies,* edited by A. James Arnold, 303–21. Amsterdam and Philadelphia: John Benjamins, 1997.

Doane, Mary Ann. *The Desire to Desire: The Woman's Film of the 1940s.* Bloomington: University of Indiana Press, 1987.

Dorigny, Marcel. "Aux origines: L'indépendance d'Haïti et son occultation." In *La Fracture coloniale: La société française au prisme de l'héritage colonial,* edited by Pascal Blanchard, Nicolas Bancel, and Sandrine Lemaire. Paris: La Découverte, 2005.

Dubois, Laurent. *Avengers of the New World: The Story of the Haitian Revolution.* Cambridge, MA: Harvard University Press, 2004.

———. *A Colony of Citizens: Revolution and Slave Emancipation in the French Caribbean, 1787–1804.* Chapel Hill: University of North Carolina Press, 2004.

Dubois, Laurent, and John D. Garrigus. *Slave Revolution in the Caribbean 1789–1804: A Brief History with Documents.* Boston: Bedford / St. Martin's, 2006.

Ely, Rolando. *Cuando reinaba su majestad el azúcar.* Buenos Aires: Editorial Sudamericana, 1963.

Farge, Arlette. *Le Goût de l'archive.* Paris: Editions du Seuil, 1989.

Farge, Arlette, and Jacques Revel. *The Vanishing Children of Paris: Rumor and Politics before the French Revolution.* Cambridge, MA: Harvard University Press, 1991.

Farmer, Paul. "Twelve Points in Favor of the Restitution of the French Debt [to] Haiti," 3 Nov. 2003, Embassy of the Republic of Haiti in Washington D.C., http://www.haiti.org/general_information/farmer.htm.

———. "What Happened in Haiti? Where Past Is Present," in Chomsky, Farmer, and Goodman, *Getting Haiti Right This Time*.

Fatton, Robert. *Haiti's Predatory Republic: The Unending Transition to Democracy*. Boulder, CO: Lynne Rienner, 2002.

Ferrer, Ada. *Insurgent Cuba: Race, Nation, and Revolution 1868–1898*. Chapel Hill: University of North Carolina Press, 1999.

———. "La société esclavagiste cubaine et la révolution haïtienne," *Annales*, March–April 2003, no. 2, especially pp. 346–56.

Fick, Carolyn. *The Making of Haiti: The Saint-Domingue Revolution from Below*. Knoxville: University of Tennessee Press, 1990.

Figarola-Caneda, Domingo. *Plácido*. Havana: Imprenta "El Siglo XX," 1922.

Fischer, Sibylle. *Modernity Disavowed: Haiti and the Cultures of Slavery in the Age of Revolution*. Durham, NC: Duke University Press, 2004.

Fouchard, Jean. *Les Marrons du syllabaire: Quelques aspects du problème de l'instruction et de l'éducation des esclaves et affranchis de Saint-Domingue*. Port-au-Prince: Henri Deschamps, 1988.

France Diplomatie, "Comité de réflexion et de proposition sur Haïti: Allocution du Ministre des Affaires étrangères, M. Dominique de Villepin," 7 October 2003, http://www.france.diplomatie.fr/actu/bulletin.asp?liste=20031008.html.

Franco, José Luciano. "La conspiración de Aponte." In *Ensayos históricos*. Havana: Editorial de Ciencias Sociales, 1974.

———. *Las conspiraciones de 1810 y 1812*. Havana: Editorial de Ciencias Sociales, 1977.

Frayn, Michael. "Profile." *New Yorker*, October 25, 2004.

Freeman, E., ed. *Myth and Its Making in the French Theatre*. Cambridge: Cambridge University Press, 1988.

Frères de l'Instruction chrétienne. *Manuel illustré d'histoire de la littérature haïtienne*. Port-au-Prince: Henri Deschamps, 1961.

García, Enildo A. *Cuba: Plácido, poeta mulato de la emancipación*. New York: Senda Nueva de Ediciones, 1986.

García Garófalo-Mesa, Manuel. *Plácido, poeta y mártir*. México: Ediciones Botas, 1938.

Garraway, Doris. *The Libertine Colony: Creolization in the Early French Caribbean*. Durham, NC: Duke Univerity Press, 2005.

Geggus, David Patrick. *Haitian Revolutionary Studies*. Bloomington: Indiana University Press, 2002.

———. *The Impact of the Haitian Revolution in the Atlantic World*. Columbia: University of South Carolina Press, 2001.

Genovese, Eugene D. *From Rebellion to Revolution: Afro-American Slave Revolts in the Making of the Modern World*. Baton Rouge: Louisiana State University Press, 1979.

Ghandi, Leela. *Postcolonial Theory: A Critical Introduction*. New York: Columbia University Press, 1998.

Gilroy, Paul. *The Black Atlantic: Modernity and Double Consciousness*. Cambridge, MA: Harvard University Press, 1993.

———. "It's a Family Affair: Black Culture and the Trope of Kinship." In *Small Acts: Thoughts on the Politics of Black Cultures*. London: Serpent's Tail, 1993.

Godechot, Jacques. "The New Concept of the Nation and Its Diffusion in Europe." In *Nationalism in the Age of the French Revolution*, edited by Otto Dann and John Dinwiddy. London: The Hambledon Press, 13–26.

Gouraige, Ghislain. *Histoire de la littérature haïtienne (de l'Indépendance à nos jours)*. Port-au-Prince: Imprimerie Théodore, 1960.

———. *Les meilleurs poètes et romanciers haïtiens*. Port-au-Prince: Imprimerie La Phalange, 1963.

"Haiti, 1804–2004: Literature, Culture, Art," special issue, *Research in African Literatures* 35, no. 2: (Summer 2004).

Haiti Democracy Project: "France Promises to Help Rebuild Haiti," Agence France Presse 15 April 2004. Haiti Democracy Project Web page item #2170, 18 April 2004, www.haitipolicy.org/content/2170.htm.

"Haiti et l'Afrique", special issue, *Présence Africaine* 169 (2005).

Hall, Stuart. "Creolization, Diaspora, and Hybridity." In *Créolité and Creolization*, edited by Okwui Enwezor et al. Ostfildern-Ruit: Hatje Cantz, 2003.

Hallward, Peter. "Option Zero in Haiti." *New Left Review* 27 (May–June 2004): 23–47.

Herrera Luque, Francisco. *Manuel Piar: Caudillo de dos colores*. Caracas: Editorial Pomaire, 1987.

Hobsbawm, Eric. *Nations and Nationalism since 1780*. Cambridge: Cambridge University Press, 1990.

Hoffmann, Léon-François. *Haitian Fiction Revisited*. Pueblo: Passeggiata Press, 1999.

———. "Introduction," *Toussaint Louverture*, by Alphonse de Lamartine. Exeter: University of Exeter Press, 1998.

———. *Littérature d'Haïti*. Histoire littéraire de la francophonie. Vanves: EDICEF, 1995.

———. *Le Nègre romantique: personnage littéraire et obsession collective*. Paris: Payot, 1973.

———. "Victor Hugo, les Noirs et l'esclavage." *Francofonia* (Bologna) 31 (1996): 47–90.

Howarth, W. D. *Sublime and Grotesque: A Study of French Romantic Drama*. London: Harrap, 1975.

Hunt, Alfred. *Haiti's Influence on Antebellum America: Slumbering Volcano in the Caribbean*. Baton Rouge: Louisiana State University Press, 1988.

Hurbon, Laënnec. *Culture et dictature: L'imaginaire sous contrôle*. Paris: L'Harmattan, 1979.

Hurley, Anthony. "Césaire's *Toussaint Louverture*: A Revolution in Question." In *Haïti et l'Afrique. Présence Africaine* 169 (2004): 199–209.

Instituto de Literatura y Lingüística (Academia de Ciencias de Cuba). *Diccionario de la literatura cubana*. Havana: Editorial Letras Cubanas, 1984. S.v. "Plácido," 1059–62.

James, C. L. R. *The Black Jacobins: Toussaint L'Ouverture and the San Domingo Revolution*. New York: Random House, 1938, 1963, 1989.

Jenkins, Brian. *Nationalism in France: Class and Nation since 1789*. Savage, MD: Barnes and Noble Press, 1990.

Jensen, Larry R. *Children of Colonial Despotism: Press, Politics, and Culture in Cuba, 1790–1840*. Gainesville: University Presses of Florida, 1988.

Jenson, Deborah. "From the Kidnapping(s) of the Louvertures to the Alleged Kidnapping of Aristide: Legacies of Slavery in the Post/Colonial World." *In* "The Haiti Issue: 1804 and Nineteenth-Century French Studies," special issue, *Yale French Studies* 107: 2005, 162–86.

———, ed. "The Haiti Issue: 1804 and Nineteenth-Century French Studies." Special issue, *Yale French Studies* 107 (July 2005).

Johnson, John J. *Simón Bolívar and Spanish American Independence: 1783–1830*. Princeton, N.J.: Van Nostrand, 1968.

Jonassaint, Jean. *Des romans de tradition haïtienne: sur un récit tragique*. Paris and Montreal: L'Harmattan and Cidihca, 2002.

Jones, Foster T. "Césaire's *Toussaint*: A Metahistorical Reading." *Studies in the Humanities* 11, no. 1 (June 1984): 44–49.

Knight, Franklin. *Slave Society in Cuba during the Nineteenth Century*. Madison: University of Wisconsin Press, 1970.

Kojève, Alexandre. *Introduction à la lecture de Hegel; leçons sur la phénoménologie de l'esprit*. Paris: Gallimard, 1947.

Kutzinski, Vera M. *Sugar's Secrets: Race and the Erotics of Cuban Nationalism*. Charlottesville: University Press of Virginia, 1993.

Laclau, Ernesto. "Identity and Hegemony: The Role of Universality in the Constitution of Political Logics." In *Contingency, Hegemony, Universality: Contemporary Dialogues on the Left*, by Judith Butler, Ernesto Laclau, and Slavoj Zizek. London: Verso, 2000.

Laclau, Ernesto, and Chantal Mouffe. *Hegemony and Socialist Strategy: Towards a Radical Democratic Politics*. Translated by Cammack Moore. London: Verso, 1985.

Lahens, Yanick. "L'apport de quatre romancières au rojman moderne haïtien." *Notre Librairie* 133 (January–April 1998): 26–36.

La Selve, Edgard. *Histoire de la littérature haïtienne depuis ses origines jusqu'à nos jours; suivie d'une Anthologie haïtienne.* Versailles: Imprimerie et stéréotypie Cerf et fils, 1875.

Law, Robin. "La cérémonie du Bois Caïman et le 'pacte de sang' dahoméen." In *L'insurrection des esclaves de Saint-Domingue (22–23 août 1791),* edited by Laënnec Hurbon. Paris: Karthala, 2000.

Lazarus, Neil. *Nationalism and Cultural Practice in the Colonial World.* Cambridge: Cambridge University Press, 1999.

Leeuwen, Boeli van. *Het teken van Jona.* Haarlem: In de Knipscheer, 1988.

Levine, Robert S. *Martin Delany, Frederick Douglass, and the Politics of Representative Identity.* Chapel Hill: University of North Carolina Press, 1997.

Loomba, Ania. *Colonialism/Postcolonialism.* London: Routledge, 1998.

Marquis, Christopher. "France Seeks UN Force in Haiti," *New York Times* 26 February 2004, Global Policy Forum, http://www.globalpolicy.org/security/issues/haiti/2004/0226france.htm.

Martínez Heredia, Fernando. "Nationalism, Races, and Classes in the Revolution of 1895 and the First Cuban Republic." Paper presented at "Open Secrets: Race, Law, and the Nation in the Cuban Republic 1902–1925," University of Michigan, Ann Arbor, November 15, 2001.

Marty, Anne. "Naturelles correspondances entre l'univers haïtien et le 'moi' universel chez Marie Chauvet." *Notre Librairie* 150 (April–June 2003).

Marugg, Tip. *De morgen loeit weer aan.* Amsterdam: De Bezige Bij, 1988.

Masur, Gerhard. *Simon Bolivar.* Albuquerque: University of New Mexico Press, 1948.

McClintock, Anne. *Imperial Leather: Race, Gender, and Sexuality in a Colonial Context.* New York: Routledge, 1995.

Medina, José Ramón. *Noventa años de literatura venezolana 1900–1999.* Caracas: Monte Avila, 1993.

Mendoza, Cristóbal L. *Prologos a los escritos del Libertador.* Caracas: Italgrafica, 1977.

Mercer, Kobena. "1968: Periodizing Postmodern Politics and Identity." In *Cultural Studies,* edited, with an introduction, by Lawrence Grossberg, Cary Nelson, and Paula A. Treichler. New York: Routledge, 1989.

Moreno Fraginals, Manuel. *El ingenio.* 3 vols. Havana: Editorial Ciencias Sociales, 1978.

Mossetto, Anna Paola. "Pour ne pas perdre son ombre: L'obsession de l'Histoire dans le théâtre haïtien." In *Théâtre et Histoire: Dramaturgies francophones extra-européennes,* edited by Anna Paola Mossetto. Torino and Paris: L'Harmattan Italia, 2003.

Munro, Martin, and Elizabeth Walcott-Hackshaw, eds. "Profondes et nombreuses: Haiti, History, Culture, 1804–2004." Special issue, *Small Axe* 18 (September 2005).

———. *Reinterpreting the Haitian Revolution and Its Cultural Aftershocks.* Kingston, Jamaica: University of the West Indies Press, 2006.

Muthu, Sankar. *Enlightenment against Empire*. Princeton: Princeton University Press, 2003.

Nelson, Dana D. *National Manhood: Capitalist Citizenship and the Imagined Fraternity of White Men*. Durham, NC: Duke University Press, 1998.

Nesbitt, Nick. "The Idea of 1804," *Yale French Studies* 107 (2005): 6–38.

———. "Troping Toussaint, Reading Revolution." In "Haiti, 1804–2004: Literature, Culture, Art," special issue, *Research in African Literatures* 35, no. 2 (Summer 2004): 18–33.

———. *Voicing Memory: History and Subjectivity in French Caribbean Literature*. Charlottesville and London: University of Virginia Press, 2003.

Nicholls, David. *From Dessalines to Duvalier: Race, Colour and National Independence in Haiti*. Cambridge: Cambridge University Press, 1979.

———. "Pompée Valentin Vastey: Royalist and Revolutionary." *Jahrbuch für Geschichte von Staat, Wirtsschaft und Gesellschaft Lateinamerikas* 28, no. 8 (1991): 107–23.

Nicolas, Mireille. "Mais bien sûr, M. Debray! Réflexions sur Haïti," 4 June 2004, Réseau information solidarité Amérique Latine, http://risal.collectifs.net/article.php3?id_article=992.

Nwankwo, Ifeoma Kiddoe. *Black Cosmopolitanism: Racial Consciousness and Transnational Identity in the Nineteenth-Century Americas*. Philadelphia: University of Pensylvania Press, 2005.

O'Brien, Conor Cruise. "Nationalism and the French Revolution." In *The Permanent Revolution: The French Revolution and Its Legacy, 1789–1989*, edited by Geoffrey Best. London: Fontana Press, 1988, 17–48.

Onyeoziri, Gloria Nne. "Le *Toussaint* d'Aimé Césaire: Réflexions sur le statut d'un texte." *L'Esprit Créateur* 32, no. 1 (1992): 87–96.

Pageaux, Daniel-Henri. *Images et Mythes d'Haïti*. Paris: L'Harmattan, 1984.

Paquette, Robert L. *Sugar Is Made with Blood: The Conspiracy of La Escalera and the Conflict between Empires over Slavery in Cuba*. Middletown, CT: Wesleyan University Press, 1988.

Pauléus-Sannon, Horace. *Histoire de Toussaint-Louverture*. 3 vols. Port-au-Prince: A. A. Héraux, 1920–33; 1932–38 (vol. 1, 1938).

Phaf-Rheinberger, Ineke, and Matthias Röhrig-Assunção. "History Is Bunk! Recovering the Meaning of Independence in Venezuela, Colombia, and Curaçao: A Cross-Cultural Image of Manuel Piar." In *A History of Literature in the Caribbean*, vol. 3, *Cross-Cultural Studies*, edited by A. James Arnold, 161–74. Amsterdam; Philadelphia: John Benjamins, 1997.

Philoctète, René. Interview. *Callaloo* 15, no. 3 (1992): 623–27.

Picquionne, Nathalie. "Lettre de Jean-François, Biassou, et Belair, juillet 1792." *Annales historiques de la Révolution française* 331 (January–March 1998): 132–39.

Pluchon, Pierre. *Toussaint Louverture: De l'esclavage au pouvoir*. Paris: Éditions de l'École, 1979.

————. *Toussaint Louverture: Un révolutionnaire noir d'Ancien Régime*. Paris: Fayard, 1989.

Plummer, Brenda Gayle. *Haiti and the United States: The Psychological Moment*. Athens and London: University of Georgia Press, 1992.

Pollard, Charles W. *New World Modernisms: T. S. Eliot, Derek Walcott, Kamau Brathwaite*. Charlottesville, London: University of Virginia Press, 2004.

Popkin, Jeremy. "Facing Racial Revolution: Captivity Narratives and Identity in the Saint-Domingue Insurrection." *Eighteenth-Century Studies* 36, no. 4 (2003): 511–33.

Quint, David. *Epic and Empire: Poetics and Generic Form from Virgil to Milton*. Princeton, NJ: Princeton University Press, 1993.

Reader, Keith. *Régis Debray: A Critical Introduction*. London: Pluto Press, 1995.

Reinhardt, Catherine. "French Caribbean Slaves Forge Their Own Ideal of Liberty in 1789." In *Slavery in the Caribbean Francophone World*, edited by Doris Kadish. Athens, GA: University of Georgia Press, 2000.

"La République haïtienne trahie par ses élites," *Le Figaro* 1 January 2004. Délégation de la Commission Européenne en Haïti: Revue de Presse Mensuelle du 1er décembre 2003 au 4 janvier, 2004, http://www.delhti.cec.eu.int/fr/presse/revue/decembre03.doc.

Rowell, Charles H. "Erma Saint-Gregoire," Interview. Translated by Mohamed B. Taleb-Kyar. *Callaloo* 15, no. 2 (Spring 1992): 462–67.

Said, Edward. *Culture and Imperialism*. New York: Knopf, 1993.

————. *Orientalism*. New York: Vintage, 1979.

Saint-John, Sir Spencer Buckingham. *Hayti or the Black Republic*. London: Smith, Elder, 1884.

Sala-Molins, Louis. *Le Code noir ou le calvaire de Canaan*. Presses universitaires de France, 1987.

————. *Les misères des lumières*. Paris: Laffont, 1992.

Scharfmann, Ronnie. "Theorizing Terror: The Discourse of Violence in Marie Chauvet's *Amour, Colère, Folie*." In *Postcolonial Subjects: Francophone Women Writers*, edited by Green et al. Minneapolis: University of Minnesota Press, 1996.

Schlereth, Thomas. *The Cosmopolitan Ideal in Enlightenment Thought: Its Form and Function in the Ideas of Franklin, Hume, and Voltaire 1694–1790*. Notre Dame: University of Notre Dame Press, 1976.

Schmidt, Hans. *The United States Occupation of Haiti, 1915–1934*. New Brunswick: Rutgers University Press, 1995.

Schoelcher, Victor. *Vie de Toussaint Louverture*. [1889] Edited by Jacques Adélaïde-Merlande. Paris: Karthala, 1982.

Scott, David. *Conscripts of Modernity: The Tragedy of Colonial Enlightenment*. Durham, NC: Duke University Press, 2004.

Scott, Julius. "The Common Wind: Afro-American Communication in the Era of the Haitian Revolution." PhD diss., Duke University, 1986.

Senghor, Léopold Sedar. "Lamartine, homme de pensée et d'action." *Centenaire de la mort d'Alphonse de Lamartine.* Actes du Congrès. Mâcon: Comité permanent d'Études Lamartiniennes, 1969.

Serrano, Lucienne J. "La dérive du plaisir dans *La danse sur le volcan* et *Amour, colère et folie* de Marie Vieux-Chauvet." *Francofonia* 25, no. 49 (2005): 95–113.

Shelton, Marie-Denise. "L'écriture de l'histoire." *Women in French Studies.* Special Issue (2005): 71–81.

Stimson, Frederick S. *Cuba's Romantic Poet: The Story of Plácido.* Chapel Hill: University of North Carolina Press, 1964.

Sundquist, Eric. *To Wake the Nations.* Cambridge, MA: Belknap of Harvard University Press, 1993.

Supplice, Daniel. *Dictionnaire biographique des personnalités politiques de la République d'Haïti (1804–2001).* [Belgium]: Imprimerie Lannoo, 2001.

Thomas, Nicolas. *Colonialism's Culture: Anthropology, Travel, and Government.* Princeton, NJ: Princeton University Press, 1994.

Tomich, Dale. *Through the Prism of Slavery: Labor, Capital, and World Economy.* Lanham, MD: Rowan and Littlefield, 2004.

Trouillot, Ertha Pascal, and Ernst Trouillot. *Encyclopédie biographique d'Haïti,* vol. 1. Montreal: Éditions Semis, 2001.

Trouillot, Michel-Rolph. *Haiti: State against Nation; Origins and Legacy of Duvalierism.* New York: Monthly Review Press, 1990.

———. *Silencing the Past: Power and the Production of History.* Boston: Beacon Press, 1995.

Vaval, Duracinée. *Histoire de la littérature haïtienne, ou l'âme noire.* Port-au-Prince: Imprimerie Aug A. Héraux, 1933.

Vergès, Françoise. *Monsters and Revolutionaries, Colonial Family Romance and Métissage.* Durham, NC: Duke University Press, 1999.

Verna, Paul. *Pétion y Bolívar: Cuarenta años de relaciones haitiano-venezolanas (1790–1830).* Caracas: Oficina Central de Información, 1969.

Viatte, Auguste. *Histoire littéraire de l'Amérique française des origines à 1950.* Paris and Québec: Presses universitaires de France and Presses universitaires de Laval, 1954.

Vinogradov, Anatolii K. *The Black Consul.* New York: Viking Press, 1935.

Walcott, Derek. *What the Twilight Says: Essays.* New York: Farrar, Strauss, and Giroux, 1998.

Wallace, Maurice. "'Are We Men?': Prince Hall, Martin Delany, and the Masculine Ideal in Black Freemasonry, 1775–1865." In *National Imaginaries, American Identities: The Cultural Work of American Iconography,* edited by Larry J. Reynolds and Gordon Hutner, 182–210. Princeton, NJ: Princeton University Press, 2000.

Wargny, Christophe. *Haïti n'existe pas: 1804–2004: deux cents ans de solitude.* Paris: Ed. Autrement, 2004.

Waxman, Percy. *Black Napoleon.* New York: Harcourt, Brace, 1931.

Webb, Barbara J. *Myth and History in Caribbean Fiction.* Amherst: University of Massachusetts Press, 1992.

White, Hayden. "The Historical Text as Literary Artifact." [1974] Rpt. in *Critical Theory since 1965,* edited by Hazard Adams and Leroy Searle. Tallahassee: Florida State University Press, 1986.

Williams, Linda. *Hard Core: Power, Pleasure, and the "Frenzy of the Visible."* Berkeley: University of California Press, 1999.

Young, Robert. *Postcolonialism: An Historical Introduction.* London: Blackwell, 2001.

———. *White Mythologies: Writing History and the West.* 2nd ed. London: Routledge, 2004.

# Contributors

A. JAMES ARNOLD, Professor of French at the University of Virginia, is a specialist of modern French and francophone Caribbean literature and author of *Modernism and Négritude: The Poetry and Poetics of Aimé Césaire* (1981), as well as books on Valéry and Sartre. He has edited *Monsters, Tricksters, and Sacred Cows: Animal Tales and American Identities* (1996), the three-volume literary history entitled *A History of Literature in the Caribbean* (1994–2001), and the special Caribbean issue of *Critique* entitled "Aux quatre vents de la Caraïbe." He is currently working on a set of digital editions in five languages of *The Buccaneers of America* (1678–86) by Alexandre-Olivier Exquemelin.

CHRIS BONGIE is Professor and Queen's National Scholar in the Department of English at Queen's University. He is the author of *Islands and Exiles: The Creole Identities of Post/Colonial Literature* (1998) and *Exotic Memories: Literature, Colonialism, and the Fin de Siècle* (1991) and editor of a translation and critical edition of Victor Hugo's 1826 novel about the Haitian Revolution, *Bug-Jargal* (2004), as well as being author of numerous articles on colonial, modernist, and postcolonial literature and culture. He recently published an edition of the first two French novels on the Haitian Revolution, Jean-Baptiste Picquenard's *Adonis, suivi de Zoflora et de documents inédits* (2006), and he is currently completing a book of essays entitled *Friends and Enemies: Francophone Post/Colonial Studies and the Memory of Hayti*.

PAUL BRESLIN is Professor of English at Northwestern University. He is author of *The Psycho-Political Muse: American Poetry since the Fifties* (1987), *You Are Here* (2000), and *Nobody's Nation: Reading Derek Walcott* (2001). His poems, essays, and reviews have appeared in such journals as *American Poetry Review, American Scholar, Callaloo, Modernism/Modernity, New Republic, New York Times Book Review, Ploughshares, Poetry,* and *Virginia Quarterly Review.* He has won six Illinois Arts Council prizes for literary essays and poems, and was twice winner of *Poetry* magazine's George Kent prize. In 2005 he co-edited a special Walcott issue of *Callaloo.* Currently, he is finishing up a second volume of poems and embarking on a study of narratives of the Haitian Revolution, inaugurated by the essay in this collection.

ADA FERRER is Associate Professor of history at New York University. She is the author of *Insurgent Cuba: Race, Nation, and Revolution, 1868–1898* (1999), winner of the 2000 Berkshire Book Prize, as well as numerous articles on race, slavery, nationalism, and revolution in the nineteenth-century Caribbean and Atlantic world. Her current research centers on the intellectual, political, and social impact of the Haitian Revolution (1791–1803) in Cuba and the Atlantic World.

DORIS L. GARRAWAY is Associate Professor of French at Northwestern University, and the author of *The Libertine Colony: Creolization in the Early French Caribbean* (2005). She has published articles on colonial and postcolonial francophone Caribbean literature and on French Enlightenment literature in journals such as *Callaloo, Eighteenth-Century Studies,* and *Studies in Voltaire and the Eighteenth Century.* In 2004 she organized the international symposium at Northwestern University entitled "The Haitian Revolution: History, Memory, Representation." Her current research focuses on the memory of the Haitian Revolution in Haitian literature.

E. ANTHONY HURLEY is Associate Professor of Africana studies and affiliate faculty with the French program in the Department of European Languages, Literatures, and Cultures at Stony Brook University (SUNY). He is the author of *Through a Black Veil: Readings in French Caribbean Poetry* (2000), and co-editor with Renée Larrier and Joseph McLaren of *Migrating Words and Worlds: Pan-Africanism Revisited* (1999). He has also written numerous articles and book chapters on French Caribbean literature, poetry, and postcolonial thought.

DEBORAH JENSON, Associate Professor of French at the University of Wisconsin–Madison, is the author of *Trauma and Its Representations: The Social Life of Mimesis in Post-Revolutionary France* (2001) and editor of a special issue of *Yale French Studies* entitled "The Haiti Issue: 1804 and Nineteenth-Century French Studies." She is the co-editor and co-translator, with Doris Kadish, of the forthcoming publication of Marceline Desbordes-Valmore's colonial novella *Sarah*. She recently has published articles in *Differences, The Columbia Encyclopedia of Twentieth-Century French Thought,* and the *Yale Journal of Criticism.* Her monograph *Beyond the Slave Narrative: Sex, Politics, and Manuscripts in the Haitian Revolution* is forthcoming.

JEAN JONASSAINT is Associate Professor of French at Syracuse University. He is the author of several books, including *Des romans de tradition haïtienne: Sur un récit tragique* (2002) and *Le pouvoir des mots, les maux du pouvoir. Des romanciers haïtiens de l'exil* (1986), as well as numerous articles on Haitian literature and literatures of migration. He has also edited several special journal issues on Haitian literature, francophone Canadian literature, and American literature.

VALERIE KAUSSEN is Assistant Professor of French and francophone literature at the University of Missouri. A specialist of Haitian literature, she is the author of several articles, including "Race, Nation and the Symbolics of Servitude in Haitian noirisme," in *The Masters and the Slaves: Plantation Ideology and Mestizaje in the Imaginary of the Americas* (2005) and "Slaves, Viejos, and the Internationale: Modernity and Global Contact in Jacques Roumain's *Gouverneurs de la rosée*," in *Research in African Literatures.* Her book *Migrant Revolutions: Haitian Literature in the Era of U.S. Imperialism and Globalization* is forthcoming.

IFEOMA C. K. NWANKWO is Associate Professor of English at Vanderbilt University. She is the author of *Black Cosmopolitanism: Racial Consciousness, and Transnational Identity in the Nineteenth-Century Americas* (2005), and a number of other comparative studies of U.S. African American, Caribbean, and Latin American literature and culture that have appeared in journals such as *American Literary History, The Langston Hughes Review, Radical History Review,* and *PALARA.* Her current projects explore inter-American and transatlantic encounters in the realms of identity, cultural memory, and language, and include a special journal issue on Afro-Latin Americans of West Indian descent and an edited collection (with Mamadou Diouf) on contemporary Afro-Atlantic expressive cultures.

# Index